Mastering Office 365 Administration

A complete and comprehensive guide to Office 365 Administration – manage users, domains, licenses, and much more

Thomas Carpe
Nikkia Carter
Alara Rogers

BIRMINGHAM - MUMBAI

Mastering Office 365 Administration

Commissioning Editor: Vijin Boricha
Acquisition Editor: Meeta Rajani
Content Development Editor: Sharon Raj
Technical Editor: Khushbu Sutar
Copy Editors: Safis Editing, Dipti Mankame
Project Coordinator: Virginia Dias
Proofreader: Safis Editing
Indexer: Pratik Shirodkar
Graphics: Tom Scaria
Production Coordinator: Aparna Bhagat

First published: May 2018

Production reference: 1160518

Published by Packt Publishing Ltd.
Livery Place
35 Livery Street
Birmingham
B3 2PB, UK.

ISBN 978-1-78728-863-8

www.packtpub.com

`mapt.io`

Mapt is an online digital library that gives you full access to over 5,000 books and videos, as well as industry leading tools to help you plan your personal development and advance your career. For more information, please visit our website.

Why subscribe?

- Spend less time learning and more time coding with practical eBooks and Videos from over 4,000 industry professionals

- Improve your learning with Skill Plans built especially for you

- Get a free eBook or video every month

- Mapt is fully searchable

- Copy and paste, print, and bookmark content

PacktPub.com

Did you know that Packt offers eBook versions of every book published, with PDF and ePub files available? You can upgrade to the eBook version at `www.PacktPub.com` and as a print book customer, you are entitled to a discount on the eBook copy. Get in touch with us at `service@packtpub.com` for more details.

At `www.PacktPub.com`, you can also read a collection of free technical articles, sign up for a range of free newsletters, and receive exclusive discounts and offers on Packt books and eBooks.

Contributors

About the authors

Thomas Carpe is a founder and managing principal of Liquid Mercury Solutions, a Baltimore-based Microsoft Gold partner specializing in Azure, Office 365, and SharePoint since 2009. He's been working with SharePoint since 2001, with Microsoft technology for over 20 years. He has several Microsoft certificates, including MCPD, MCSE, and MCITP. He is an acknowledged expert in SharePoint security, and he is the author of a large open source library and several software products built on SharePoint. He resides in Baltimore with his wife, children, housemates, and a menagerie of pets.

I'd like to thank my wife for supporting me through the difficult writing process while also fighting her own battle against cancer, my coworkers who covered for me, and our editor for being inhumanly patient. I'd also like to thank Eric Carpe and Kevin Gagnon for sharing the perspectives of those who haven't been working with Office 365 for many years already.

Nikkia Carter, director of collaboration and training for C3 Integrated Solutions, a Microsoft Gold & Silver partner in VA, has a bachelor's in computer science, a master's in IT project management, and is a CompTIA Certified Technical Trainer. She is a solutions developer, strategist, trainer, and tech speaker. She is a member of the Microsoft Voices for Innovation taskforce and of the International Association of Microsoft Channel Partners DC board. She also leads the SharePoint User Group DC.

I would like to thank Packt Publishing, especially Sharon Raj, for approaching me to write this book and for being patient when life got in the way! Thanks to Scott Brewster and Shadeed Eleazer for helping to review our work. Thanks to my coauthors for joining me on this endeavor!

Alara Rogers, not to be confused with Buck Rogers or Mr. Rogers, is often thought to be a brain in a tank, but this is not true; she is a space alien. Alara grew up in the land of IBM near Poughkeepsie, NY, and entered IT via database marketing and analytics. She has a bachelor's in psychobiology from the University of Pennsylvania. Nowadays, her main interests are business intelligence, process management, information architecture, and SharePoint as a platform for the rest. She writes science fiction in her spare time, and has been known to reply at length when someone is wrong on the internet.

I would like to thank Thomas Carpe for getting me this opportunity and Packt Publishing for saying yes. I would also like to thank Jane-Vett Rogers, my mother, who passed away in 2015. I wouldn't be a writer without her. And I want to thank Elinor Bowen, my first real boss, for getting me into IT in the first place.

About the reviewers

Markus Darda is the owner of DaComp GmbH (Switzerland). As a senior engineer and architect, he works for enterprise customers all over Europe designing and implementing Citrix and Microsoft environments.

He also has a lot of experience in migrating customers to Office 365 and Microsoft Azure. In the past, Markus has also reviewed the following books for Packt:

- *Hyper-V Network Virtualization Cookbook*
- *Citrix XenApp® 7.5 Desktop Virtualization Solutions*
- *Getting Started with Citrix XenApp® 7.6*

Citrix has named Markus as Subject Matter Expert (SME) on several products.

Shadeed Eleazer is a navy veteran and reputation management and social selling thought leader who is an architect of the official state websites of Maryland, Pennsylvania, and Wisconsin, powered by Microsoft SharePoint technologies. He is an Amazon best selling author. He specializes in on-premises to cloud migrations, enterprise social media, instructional systems design, and training. He is the founder of Managed Path Solutions, a Microsoft partner focused on the support of Microsoft technology platforms.

> *This book is dedicated to my Mom, Dad, and Grandparents, who instilled love and a great passion for learning. I especially thank my Grandmother, Lorraine Eleazer, who encouraged my early love for technology. Thank you to my family for their continued love and support.*

Packt is searching for authors like you

If you're interested in becoming an author for Packt, please visit authors.packtpub.com and apply today. We have worked with thousands of developers and tech professionals, just like you, to help them share their insight with the global tech community. You can make a general application, apply for a specific hot topic that we are recruiting an author for, or submit your own idea.

Table of Contents

Preface

Office 365 is one of Microsoft's most popular cloud offerings, a low-cost service that people subscribe to in order to access various Microsoft services and software. It is the replacement of Microsoft's Business Productivity Online Suite (BPOS), Microsoft's previous cloud offering. It is free or super-low-cost, depending on the subscription, for 501(c)3 nonprofits and accredited educational institutions.

Office 365 is securely accessible anywhere with a supported device and an internet connection, and is independently verified to comply with regulations such as FedRAMP, FISMA, HIPAA, ISO 27001, EU, and others, with over 900 controls that enable keeping compliant never-changing industry standards. Office 365 has a financially backed guarantee of 99.9% uptime.

As such, Office 365 is constantly being updated due to customer feedback and Microsoft's desire to offer evergreen and best-in-class services. Due to this, they are constantly updating and improving the service, as well as offering new services.

Who this book is for

This book is for those who are new to Office 365 administration, or may have worked with it for a while but are looking to verify their knowledge and take their skills to the next level. This book illustrates administration from the basics to more advanced topics.

What this book covers

Chapter 1, *The Office 365 Administration Portal*, introduces the reader to the Office 365 admin portal.

Chapter 2, *Using PowerShell to Connect to Office 365 Services*, enables you to connect PowerShell to various Office 365 services and perform tasks.

Chapter 3, *Administering Azure Active Directory*, helps you manage and administer various identities and groups.

Chapter 4, *Administering Exchange Online - Essentials*, covers the basics of administering Exchange Online—mailboxes and rules/message management.

Chapter 5, *Administering Exchange - Advanced Topics*, covers all the more advanced and/or obscure parts of Exchange Online administration.

Chapter 6, *Administering SharePoint Online*, introduces the reader to the SharePoint admin portal and other SharePoint administration techniques needed to manage SharePoint, including some PowerShell.

Chapter 7, *Office 365 Groups and Microsoft Teams Administration*, introduces the reader to administering Office 365 Groups and Microsoft Teams through the Office 365 admin portal and through PowerShell.

Chapter 8, *Understanding Security and Compliance*, shows how to secure Office 365 and enforce compliance, and help you manage security, create permissions, and enforce compliance.

Chapter 9, *Administering Skype for Business*, teaches the reader how to manage the instant messaging, voice, and video components of Skype for Business.

Chapter 10, *Administering Yammer*, introduces the reader to the Yammer admin portal. Some administration through PowerShell is also included.

Chapter 11, *Administering OneDrive for Business*, covers everything the reader needs to manage OneDrive for Business for their users.

Chapter 12, *Power BI Administration*, introduces the reader to the Power BI admin portal.

Chapter 13, *Administering PowerApps, Flow, Stream, and Forms*, introduces the reader to various new products available in Office 365, what they are useful for, and how to administer them.

Chapter 14, *Usage Reporting*, shows how to get support and monitor the service health of Office 365.

To get the most out of this book

The topics in this book assume that you have some knowledge of Office 365 and have used it as an end user. We assume that you know what the main components are in Office 365. We also assume that you are not already an advanced administrator of Office 365 who is looking for a book entirely comprising master's-level topics and techniques. Although, in some chapters, some techniques are of the master's level, most range from basic to advanced skills.

In order to perform the techniques in this book, we suggest setting up an Office 365 tenant that you can play around with before applying your newly acquired skills to your actual organizational tenant.

You can sign up for a free 30-day trial tenant at `https://products.office.com/en-us/business/compare-more-office-365-for-business-plans`. We highly recommend signing up for the E3 or E5 subscription and making yourself the global administrator (this happens automatically if you sign up with your info). You may also want to set up multiple users at different administration levels to test them out. You get 25 user licenses with every trial. You will also need PowerShell, SharePoint Online PowerShell, and Exchange PowerShell in order to execute the scripts.

Download the example code files

You can download the example code files for this book from your account at `www.packtpub.com`. If you purchased this book elsewhere, you can visit `www.packtpub.com/support` and register to have the files emailed directly to you.

You can download the code files by following these steps:

1. Log in or register at `www.packtpub.com`.
2. Select the **SUPPORT** tab.
3. Click on **Code Downloads & Errata**.
4. Enter the name of the book in the **Search** box and follow the onscreen instructions.

Once the file is downloaded, please make sure that you unzip or extract the folder using the latest version of:

- WinRAR/7-Zip for Windows
- Zipeg/iZip/UnRarX for Mac
- 7-Zip/PeaZip for Linux

The code bundle for the book is also hosted on GitHub at `https://github.com/PacktPublishing/Mastering-Office-365-Administration`. In case there's an update to the code, it will be updated on the existing GitHub repository.

We also have other code bundles from our rich catalog of books and videos available at `https://github.com/PacktPublishing/`. Check them out!

Download the color images

We also provide a PDF file that has color images of the screenshots/diagrams used in this book. You can download it from `https://www.packtpub.com/sites/default/files/downloads/MasteringOffice365Administration_ColorImages.pdf`.

Conventions used

There are a number of text conventions used throughout this book.

`CodeInText`: Indicates code words in text, database table names, folder names, filenames, file extensions, pathnames, dummy URLs, user input, and Twitter handles. Here is an example: "Now that you're connected, you can use commands such as `Get-Mailbox` and `Get-MailUser`."

Any command-line input or output is written as follows:

```
Connect-MsolService -Credential $Credentials
```

Bold: Indicates a new term, an important word, or words that you see onscreen. For example, words in menus or dialog boxes appear in the text like this. Here is an example: "You can click on the carat beside **Advanced settings for shareable links** to open up additional options."

 Warnings or important notes appear like this.

 Tips and tricks appear like this.

Get in touch

Feedback from our readers is always welcome.

General feedback: Email `feedback@packtpub.com` and mention the book title in the subject of your message. If you have questions about any aspect of this book, please email us at `questions@packtpub.com`.

Errata: Although we have taken every care to ensure the accuracy of our content, mistakes do happen. If you have found a mistake in this book, we would be grateful if you would report this to us. Please visit `www.packtpub.com/submit-errata`, selecting your book, clicking on the Errata Submission Form link, and entering the details.

Piracy: If you come across any illegal copies of our works in any form on the Internet, we would be grateful if you would provide us with the location address or website name. Please contact us at `copyright@packtpub.com` with a link to the material.

If you are interested in becoming an author: If there is a topic that you have expertise in and you are interested in either writing or contributing to a book, please visit `authors.packtpub.com`.

Reviews

Please leave a review. Once you have read and used this book, why not leave a review on the site that you purchased it from? Potential readers can then see and use your unbiased opinion to make purchase decisions, we at Packt can understand what you think about our products, and our authors can see your feedback on their book. Thank you!

For more information about Packt, please visit `packtpub.com`.

The Office 365 Administration Portal

1

While there's more than one way to perform most administrative functions in Office 365, the majority of administrators will find that most tasks can be performed conveniently and easily by using the Office 365 administration portal. In this chapter, we're going to go through the different parts of the main portal, and very briefly touch on the functions of the individual administration sites accessible from the portal, since most of those are covered in other parts of this book.

The following topics will be covered in this chapter:

- The dashboard
- The left sidebar's navigation
- Administrative portals for individual services

The dashboard

You can access the administration portal from any Office 365 site, including the main site at `https://portal.office.com`, by clicking on the apps icon in the top-left corner that looks like a tic-tac-toe board to get your list of apps, and then selecting **Admin**. But if you are going to be visiting the portal a lot, which is normal for anyone who has Office 365 administration as one of their general job duties, you might want to bookmark it directly. The direct link for it is `https://portal.office.com/adminportal`. However you choose to get there, the first thing you're going to see is the Office 365 administration dashboard.

Clicking on the apps icon opens your list of apps and allows you to access the portal by clicking on **Admin**:

The Office 365 administration dashboard

You cannot access everything that you can do in the Office 365 administration portal through the dashboard. On the left-hand side, there's a side navigation bar with expandable headings that grants access to the rest of the portal's functionality. There's also a heading at the bottom of the side navigation that shows all of the main administrative centers for Office 365. Those administrative centers will be covered in their own separate chapters.

Dashboard components

Dashboard components aren't necessarily identical between tenants. For instance, the one in the preceding example has a section for **Windows 10 Upgrade**, because this particular dashboard belongs to a tenant that has purchased a Windows 10 subscription product. My company's portal doesn't have the **Videos** section, but rather, a **Train yourself** section that shows links for training for admins and for end users.

We'll go over the components that you'd generally expect to find in most tenant dashboards.

DirSync Status

You'll only see this dashboard component if you're using **Active Directory (AD)** synchronization, either to an Azure Active Directory or on-premises. This dashboard component quickly tells you when the last directory sync was done, when the last password sync was done, and if either of them had any errors. Clicking on this component takes you to the same place you'd get to via the side navigation bar if you clicked **Health | Directory Sync Status**.

Users

You'll probably use **Users** more often than any other component. The **Users** dashboard component takes you to the same place as **Users | Active Users** on the side navigation bar. There are also direct links for adding, deleting, and editing users, and resetting passwords.

We'll go into more detail on the functions available in the **Active Users** area when we cover the side navigation bar, and even more in Chapter 3, *Administering Azure Active Directory*.

Billing

This component takes you directly to the **Subscriptions** link area under **Billing | Subscriptions**. It's important to note that the subscriptions you see here are the ones you've ordered directly from Microsoft. If you're purchasing Office 365 through a partner, you might not see anything here.

Some Office 365 customers purchase services through Microsoft, and others through the partnership **Cloud Solution Provider** (CSP) program. Some do both. If you buy any subscriptions from Microsoft, you'll see them under **Billing,** but any that you buy through a reseller will only appear in **Licenses**.

There are levels of administrator access that give you the ability to use the portal to maintain services, but not to interact with the financial end. If your level of administrator access doesn't give you billing access, you might not see this dashboard component.

Office software

It might seem strange to you that downloading Office software is an administrative component on the dashboard. Doesn't downloading your own software seem like something you do as a user, rather than as an administrator? The truth is, administrators are more likely to interact with the administration portal than they are with the Office 365 home page, where you'd normally find your software download link.

Clicking on the name of the component takes you to the *my software download* page, which you'd otherwise access via the Office 365 end user home page. It's not part of the administration portal at all at that point. But there are also links on the component for various administrative functions that have to do with Office software installation:

- **Install my software**: This is, confusingly, *not* the link that takes you to a place to install your own software. It's actually a link for setting up manual deployment of software for the users in your company. If there are any issues with internet speed (or worse, metering) at the physical offices where your users work, we highly recommend following the instructions here to perform a manual deployment, as it lets you get away with performing the download once, rather than once per user. That's outside of the scope of this book, but Microsoft provides instructions right on the **Manually deploy user software** popup.
- **Share the download link**: This opens an email in your default mail client, which has the link to the Office software download page in it.
- **Software download settings**: Here, you can exert some control over what software your users can install for themselves. At one point, the options included Office 2013 products, but they've been discontinued for most customers as of February 2017:
    - For PC, you can choose to block or allow the Office suite as a whole, the extra products that don't come with the Office suite (Project and Visio), SharePoint Designer, and standalone Skype for Business. You can also choose whether your users get upgrades to Office every month or every 6 months.
    - For macOS, you can block or allow Office itself, additional Office applications that need separate downloads, and Skype for Business.
- **Troubleshoot installation**: This opens a link on Microsoft's **Office 365 Admin Help**, covering how to deal with installations gone wrong.

Domains

This component takes you to the same place as **Setup** | **Domains** on the left-side navigation pane. The direct link options are **Add a domain**, **Delete a domain**, **Edit a domain**, and **Check health**, which checks on the DNS status of the domains you own.

It's a good idea, if you're not frequently looking at the advanced DNS options in your domain name provider, to occasionally check your DNS health. We've seen DNS entries that were placed when a domain was first migrated disappear from the clients' domain name provider, on occasion. This is particularly likely if your company has just migrated to a new provider or brought on a new website host, or has undergone other circumstances that could lead to changes to your domain. Office 365 is pretty robust, and in many cases, it will continue to work if domain name entries are wrong; but it won't necessarily work well.

More detailed information on how to configure DNS is covered in `Chapter 3`, *Administering Azure Active Directory*.

Support

The header of this component is not a link, and it won't do anything when you click on it. The options provided are **New service request** and **View service requests**, both of which can be accessed from the side navigation pane, under **Support**.

Windows 10 Upgrade

You'll see this component if your company has purchased any licenses for Windows 10 through the Windows 10 Enterprise E3/E5 subscription model. This is another component where the header itself doesn't go anywhere. The options within are **Install Upgrade**, **Share the download link**, **Create installation media**, and **Troubleshoot installation**. Except for **Share the download link**, which creates an email the same way the similar function did under **Office software**, all of these link to locations on Microsoft's websites and will take you out of the administration portal.

The functions of this component can't be accessed through the side navigation pane.

Videos

This component displays quick links to Microsoft training videos for various functions in the administration portal. If your company is a Microsoft partner or has purchased training services from Microsoft, you might see this as a component that invites you to train yourself or your end users; if that's the case, the material that's normally under **Videos** will be under **Train yourself**. For most tenants, however, what you'll see is the **Videos** component.

Message center

This is, sadly, more important than you might realize. Microsoft has, in recent years, been very assertive about shutting down software products, applications, and options that some businesses have come to rely on. The **Message center** is where announcements of new products *and* downgrades or retirements of older products will appear, and if you don't stay abreast of what Microsoft is doing, you might find yourself blindsided. The **Message center** is also accessible under **Health | Message center** in the side navigation pane.

Service health

When you click on this component, you'll be taken to the same place you could access from **Health | Service health**. It'll show you all of the Office 365 services and their health statuses, with incidents and advisories. The component will also allow you to jump directly to lists of incidents or advisories, with links that show how many services may be affected by either type of warning. Checking this on a regular basis is a good way to stay on top of issues with Office 365 *before* your users complain.

Setup guides

This component contains wizards, deployment advisors, and setup guides for various Office 365 products. Clicking directly on the header takes you to an overview page containing all of the wizards and guides. There's an option in the component and in the overview page called **Setup guidance**, which provides even more detailed guidance on setting up your Office 365 services, and there are direct links to the various setup guides and wizards that you can scroll through from directly within the component.

You'd expect that such extensive setup guidance would be accessible from the sidebar navigation, perhaps under **Setup**, but as of the time of writing, the dashboard component seems to be the only way to access this.

Active users

This shows a small version of the **Active users** graph from **Reports** | **Usage** (which is where you get to if you click on the header of this component), so you can get a sense of your company's Office 365 usage at a glance. The usage reports that you'll see upon clicking it show more detailed breakdowns of the various activities.

Dashboard summary

We've gone through the dashboard components that most administrators will see, but it's important to remember that these components change depending on what products your company has purchased, and Microsoft is also constantly changing its Office 365 offerings, expanding what's available, and occasionally pruning back older services. The dashboard I see today might not be one hundred percent identical to the dashboard you will see by the time this book reaches your hands, because this dashboard is one of the first places Microsoft will add new features to the administration portal, even before they're added to the sidebar navigation pane.

Now, let's turn our attention to the left sidebar. There's a lot of functionality in this navigation tree that can't be accessed any other way, and we'll go into a bit more detail on some of the functions we already touched on when they were also reachable from the dashboard.

The left sidebar navigation menu

Like many modern left sidebar navigation trees, this menu will collapse down to a narrow column of icons if you click the left-pointing carat on the right side of the bar, but the default on most browsers is for it to be full-sized. On mobile, you might find that it defaults to being minimized. (It's also small enough to be almost unreadable on a phone. I'd recommend that if you're going to be using mobile devices to access administrative functions more than occasionally, you should probably get the Office 365 admin app, available for iOS, Android, and Windows mobile. But a discussion of that app is outside the scope of this book.)

Users

The options under **Users** are **Active users**, **Contacts**, **Guest users**, and **Deleted users**.

Active users

There's a lot you can do in **Active users**, and you're going to be doing a lot of it. Interacting with your active users—adding new ones, disabling terminated ones, resetting passwords, and adding and removing licenses—is the bulk of the work that most Office 365 administrators do:

The Active users panel

The top bar for **Active users** gives you the options to add a user, change which users you're viewing, search users, export your list of users to CSV, and other functions, available under the **More** drop-down menu.

Again, the options you see here may vary, depending on what products you have (you won't see an option for **Directory synchronization** if you're not syncing Office 365 to Active Directory, for instance).

The most common activities are adding a user and resetting passwords (particularly if you don't sync to Active Directory), but a dynamic, quickly changing company may also have a lot of setting licenses to do. We'll go over those functions and how to work with the views of your users (a vital skill, if you're a large company with a lot of users) in some detail. Most of the other functions are fairly self-explanatory.

We'll go over much of this information again in Chapter 3, *Administering Azure Active Directory*, drilling down into PowerShell and some of its more obscure details.

Adding a user

To add a user, you'll enter the user's **First name** and **Last name**, and this will assemble the **Display name** by default. If you want the display name to be something different than the first and last names, change it after it populates by default; this won't affect the first or last names:

Add a new user

Most instances of Office 365 have more than one domain, but usually, one's the real domain, and one's `domain.onmicrosoft.com`, which hardly anyone uses. In most Office 365 tenants, the default domain has been set to whatever your company usually uses for public websites and the like. However, there might be circumstances where a user needs to be assigned to a different domain name. Enter the username, and use the drop-down menu to select the correct domain name if the default isn't the right one.

It's important to select a location if it hasn't prepopulated for you. You won't be able to add licensing until the location is set.

Whether you fill out the contact information or not is probably a matter of your company's policy. It won't affect a user's capabilities if you don't do it, but if you do, that information will be carried into Exchange and SharePoint, so it won't need to be reentered in the global address list or user profiles:

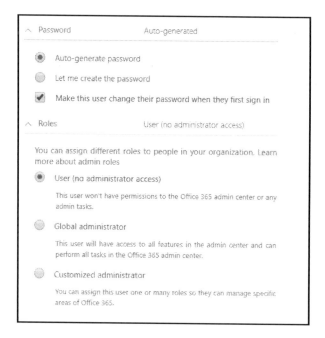

Password and role options

The options for setting the password include either autogenerating it and emailing it to the email you choose upon completion of the new user task, or creating it manually by yourself. For either option, you can force the user to change it when they sign-in, or allow them to continue to use it.

Most users will be assigned **User (no administrator access)**, and most IT staff who need administrative access will probably be assigned **Global administrator**, but in a large organization, you may well want to use the **Customized administrator** setting to fine-tune which rights you grant.

Finally, you will need to set the licenses. You'll see a series of toggle switches that represent all of the licenses your company has available:

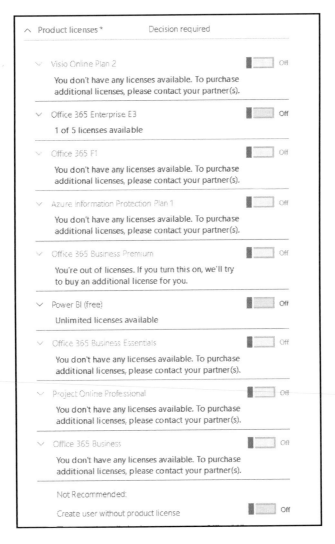

Assign licenses

The last toggle is **Create user without product license**. While Microsoft labels this as **Not recommended**, it might be a perfectly reasonable thing to do if you're not the one with the authority to purchase extra licenses; get the user created without a license, and they'll be able to get into the Office 365 portal and set their new password while you're waiting for the purchasing people to acquire the license. (This is also what you're likely to do if you need to create a service account.)

You must set one of the toggle switches, or it won't allow you to create the user. So, if there are no available licenses, use the one that creates the user without a license.

After you're done, you'll get a window telling you the user's password (if it was autogenerated) and offering to email that password to the default address (usually yours, if you're the primary Office 365 administrator.)

Using the user panel

You can reset passwords, set licenses and roles, disable or enable Office 365 sign-in, add new aliases and change which email address is primary, and perform many other functions, via the user panel.

To access the user panel, simply click on an active user, and it'll open to the right.

A lot of these functions are very similar to the equivalent that you'd perform for new users. For example, resetting a password is just like setting it for the first time for a new user:

Group memberships (5)	AdminAgents All Azure AD Users Azure Admins Developers More		Edit
Sign-in status	Sign-in allowed		Edit
Office installs	View and manage which devices this person has Office apps installed on.		Edit
Roles			Edit
Display name Office phone	@Alara Rogers (DA)		Edit

∧ ✉ Mail Settings

Mailbox permissions	There are no additional mailbox permissions set on this mailbox.		Edit
Email forwarding	None		Edit
Litigation hold	Off		Edit
Automatic replies	Off		Edit
Email apps	All email apps allowed		Edit
Show in global address list	Yes		Edit
More settings	Edit Exchange properties ◻		

∧ ☁ OneDrive Settings

Access	View and edit folders and files You will be granted permissions to manage this user's OneDrive		Access files
Quota	Storage used : 0 % of 1024 GB		
External sharing	Let people outside your organization access your site	On	Edit
Sign-out	Initiate a one-time event that will sign this person out of all Office 365 sessions across all devices. It can take up to 15 minutes for process to complete. This person will be able to immediately sign back in, unless you have also blocked their sign-in status.		Initiate
More settings	Edit Skype for Business properties Manage multi-factor authentication ◻		

The user panel

Assigning a license is just like assigning a license to a new user. But there are some functions that can be performed via the user panel that don't have an equivalent in the **Add a user** task:

- Group memberships aren't something that you can assign in **Add a user**, because the mailbox needs to be provisioned before groups can be assigned. By clicking **Edit** under **Group memberships** in the user panel, you can add the user to a group, see the groups they're already in, and delete them from groups they are members of.

- You can also change the sign-in settings. If you have an employee that's leaving the company at the end of the day, you can cut off their ability to sign in to Office 365 products without either deleting them or changing their password by simply setting their **Sign-in status** to **Sign-in blocked**. (There will be more on this topic in Chapter 3, *Administering Azure Active Directory*.) This is especially useful if they're synchronized with Active Directory and it's handled by a different department, so you don't have the rights to change their password or delete them. You should note, though, that because this disables sign-in, it won't affect a user who is already signed in until that sign in expires. So it's not the best tool to use for the person who's being frog-marched out the door by security right now and might still be signed in on their personal tablet.

- You can view the devices that a user has installed Office onto, and deactivate their installation. (Possibly a good idea to do to the home laptop of that employee in the previous example! However, you can only perform it on PC and macOS devices, not mobile ones, so you still can't get that tablet.) If an employee had a device stolen or destroyed, and they're at their five-device limit for Office installations, you can deactivate the lost device here, so that they can install it on their replacement device.

- If you click the expanding carat for **Mail Settings**, you can directly work with mailbox permissions, email forwarding, litigation hold, auto replies, what apps the user is allowed to use to access email with, and whether they're in the global address list, without having to go into Exchange. (We'll go into what these options mean in more detail in Chapter 3, *Administering Azure Active Directory* and Chapter 4, *Administering Exchange Online – Essentials*.) There's also a direct link to Exchange, which will take you straight into this user's Exchange properties.

- The expanding carat for **OneDrive Settings** gives you the option to get access to the user's OneDrive, which is very helpful if they're out of the office or have left the company, and there's important business information that they are storing in there. You can also turn external sharing to the user's OneDrive (meaning that the user can share with users outside of your company) on or off.

- You can kick off a one-time sign-out event that kicks the user out of every instance of Office 365 they're signed into. This is useful if you're changing their username, or in the case of that employee being frog-marched out the door in the example. Oddly, though this has nothing to do with OneDrive; it's stored under the **OneDrive Settings** carat.

- The direct links at the bottom let you edit the user's Skype for Business properties, or go directly to their multi-factor authentication settings.

Views

Views are covered in detail in `Chapter 3`, *Administering Azure Active Directory*, so we won't delve too deeply here.

There's a default view that shows all users. If you have a small company, that might be fine. As soon as you have a large number of users (or accounts, such as service accounts that were assigned email addresses, external contacts who were invited as guest users, former employees, special-purpose administrator accounts, and so on), the list can get unwieldy. You may want to use one of the other default views, or create one of your own. See `Chapter 3`, *Administering Azure Active Directory* for more information on how to do this.

Import multiple users

Finally, the last function of the **Active users** page that we'll discuss is the **Import multiple users** function. If you have a moderately large organization and you are *not* planning to synchronize with AD, you might want to import a large number of users at the same time:

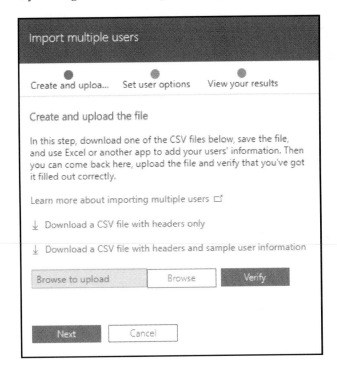

Import multiple users

You get to this feature by clicking the **More** drop-down menu at the top of **Active users**. Download a CSV file to use as a template (you can choose one with just the headers, or one with sample user data, to help you understand how to format your users), enter all of your users into it, upload with the **Browse** button, and then click **Verify** to make sure your formatting is correct. Click **Next** and follow the prompts. You'll be able to set a sign-in status and choose product licenses on the next page, and then send the results to yourself or someone else. (Note that the passwords handled this way will be in plain text, so you may want to require your users to change their passwords as soon as possible.)

Other functions of the **Active users** page are fairly self-explanatory, such as **Delete a user** or **Export**. Let's move on.

Contacts

Contacts are email addresses from outside of your organization that are recorded in Exchange so that users can find them in the global address list:

Contacts

It's easier to enter a contact than it is to enter a user—there are a lot fewer fields to fill out.

Display name and **Email** are the only required fields, although if you are going to use contacts heavily and need to be able to search for them with multiple criteria, you might want to fill in the other fields.

By default, contacts appear in the global address list, although you can exclude them with the **Hide from my organization address list** toggle. Contacts, as a concept, come from Microsoft Exchange, and are a means to include people from outside the company in distribution lists. They can also be included in Office 365 Groups, as of May 2017.

Guest users

Guest users, as a concept, are more closely related to SharePoint and OneDrive. A guest user has been granted access, via sharing, to a resource on SharePoint or OneDrive. They're only relevant if your organization allows external sharing.

A guest user will automatically be created if you create a sharing link for a specific email address within SharePoint or OneDrive. You can't create them here, but you can view and delete them.

Note that guest users don't have a presence in the global address list, and the same email address can't be both a contact and a guest user. If you have a need to give people who are frequently contacted by your users access to SharePoint and OneDrive while also having them as a global contact, and also having them on a list that automatically sends them and other people email, it might make more sense to use an Office 365 Group rather than a traditional distribution list, because members of those Groups can be both guest users and mail contacts at the same time.

Deleted users

Up to 30 days after you delete a user, they can be restored:

Deleted users

Use the **Deleted users** screen to see who has been deleted, export them if you need a CSV report, and restore them.

More vital information about the user recycle bin will be covered in Chapter 3, *Administering Azure Active Directory*.

Groups

While there's more functionality for working with groups in the Exchange Administration Center, many of the most common functions have been made available directly in the Office 365 administration portal, under **Groups**.

The two headings you'll find here are **Groups** (yes, really, it's the same word) and **Shared mailboxes**.

Groups

There are four types of groups within Office 365: distribution lists, security groups, mail-enabled security groups, and Office 365 lists. There are also shared mailboxes, but they have their own heading. We'll discuss the differences in Chapter 4, *Administering Exchange Online – Essentials*:

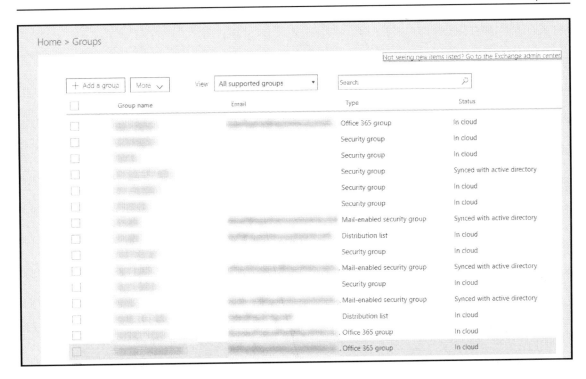

The Groups page

When you click on any group, a panel will open (usually to the right) displaying its properties, and you can edit many of the properties right there.

Distribution lists and mail-enabled security groups primarily live in Exchange, so their panels offer direct links to Exchange, to do further editing there, if desired.

Office 365 Groups and regular security groups are accessible via the Exchange administration site, but the Office 365 administration portal is equally competent at handling them, so Microsoft hasn't bothered including those links on their panels.

Within Office 365, you can edit:

- The name, description, ownership, and membership of a distribution list, and whether external senders are allowed.
- The name, description, ownership, and membership of a security group.

- The name, description, ownership, and membership of a mail-enabled security group, and whether external senders are allowed.
- The name, description, ownership, and membership of an Office 365 group, whether external senders are allowed, and whether senders should be automatically subscribed. It'll display your privacy settings—that is, is the group public or private—but you can't edit them after creating a group.

For a new group, there's a lot less functionality for creation than there is for editing, and particularly for the traditional types of groups; distribution, security, and mail-enabled security groups can't have owners or members defined during creation, and Office 365 Groups can only define the owner at creation, if you're using the administration portal.

Shared mailboxes

You can edit a lot of the properties of a shared mailbox by using the shared mailbox panel when you click on one of the shared mailboxes on this page:

The Shared mailboxes page

Using this panel, you can edit the name, email, email aliases, forwarding, auto-replies, litigation hold status, membership, and other settings, such as whether sent items get copied to the mailbox, whether the mailbox is in the global address list, and so on. You can also delete the mailbox, go directly to Exchange administration to work with the mailbox, or read about how to use **Shared mailboxes** in Outlook:

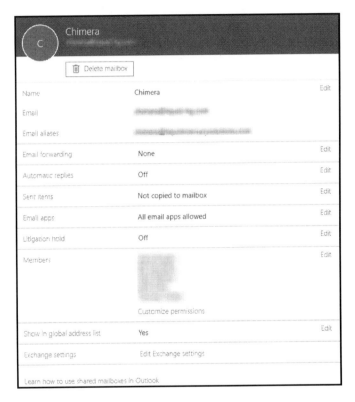

The shared mailbox panel

Again, there's a lot less functionality for actually creating mailboxes. You can set the name and the email address, and that's all. For all other properties, you'll need to wait for it to be created, and then edit it.

Resources

The next heading on the side navigation bar is **Resources**. The three subheadings are **Rooms & equipment**, **Sites**, and **Public website**.

Rooms and equipment

In Exchange, you can assign a room or a piece of equipment (for example, a projector) to a meeting by giving it an email address:

Rooms and equipment

To enter a room or equipment, you click **Add** and choose which one—**Room** or **Equipment**. You then fill out the name and the email address you're assigning to it (it would also be a good idea to fill in the capacity, location, and phone number).

Rooms can be abstract entities; my company, for instance, has no physical conference rooms, but we assign conferencing vendors, such as GoToMeeting and WebEx, as rooms.

The panel for editing a room allows you to edit the same things you set when you created the room, but it also allows you to set whether repeated meetings are allowed, whether automatic processing (inviting a room to a meeting automatically reserving the room without requiring human intervention) is allowed, and who's a delegate for the room (the person who receives the room's email; also, the person who can choose to reject a booking for the room). There's also a direct link to the settings in Exchange.

Sites

The **Sites** page displays all SharePoint site collections in the tenant (excluding individual OneDrive sites), and shows what type of sharing is allowed (that is, no external sharing, new and existing external users, or anonymous guest links allowed). You can edit the type of sharing here.

If you choose **Add a site**, you jump to the SharePoint management portal, to the page for creating a new site collection. That's outside the scope of this chapter, but is covered in `Chapter 6`, *Administering SharePoint Online*.

Public website

This entry seems to be purely vestigial. Office 365 hasn't allowed new public websites to be created in several years, and as of this writing, Microsoft is planning to eliminate all the existing ones at the end of March 2018. Don't be surprised if, by the time you are able to buy this book, this entry has disappeared entirely.

Billing

In many organizations, the people who handle the billing aren't the site administrators; responsibilities are often divided between finance and IT departments. If that's your position, you'll probably only ever need to touch the subheadings **Subscriptions** and **Licenses**; and possibly, not even **Subscriptions**. Sometimes, though, particularly in small organizations, the person who manages Office 365 also manages the spending on it, so we'll cover the various parts.

Subscriptions

This page is more to provide information than to be a place with things that you can edit or act on. It'll show your active product subscriptions (and when you click on one, it'll tell you how many licenses you have for it), expired subscriptions, disabled subscriptions, and deprovisioned subscriptions:

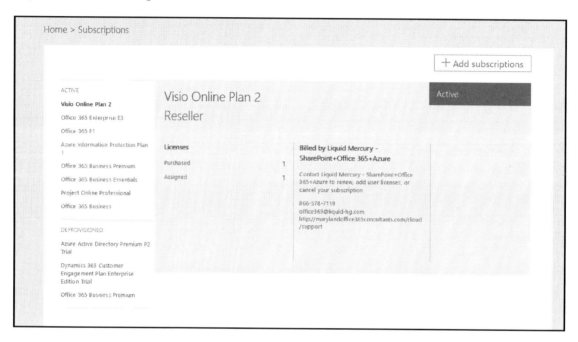

The Subscriptions page

Expired subscriptions will have run out 30 days ago (or less), and all of the data in them is still accessible; disabled subscriptions will have run out between 31 and 90 days ago, and the data in them can be accessed by an administrator, but not by the user. Deprovisioned subscriptions have had their data deleted. Often, a free trial your company might have used at one point will show up as a deprovisioned subscription.

You can add a subscription here. Clicking on **Add subscriptions** takes you to the **Purchase services** page.

Bills

If your company purchases directly from Microsoft, you'll see the invoices for your services on this page. You can use the drop-down menu to access **This month**, **Last month**, the **Past 3 months**, **Past 6 months**, **Past year**, and **Specify date range** quickly. If you want more detailed breakdowns or to view individual invoices prior to the last month, click on **View details**. You can also view the invoices as PDFs:

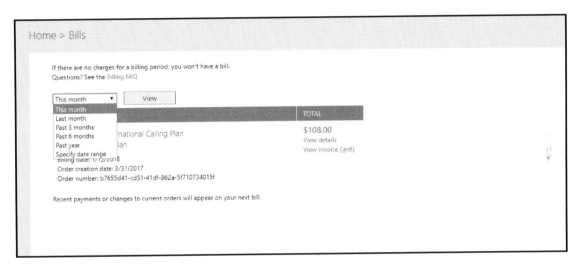

Bills page

If you purchase your Office 365 from a Microsoft partner through the CSP program, another reseller, or through a specialty program (for example, there is special handling for nonprofits, as well as annual purchases through MS Open), you will not see anything here. The **Bills** page only shows Microsoft invoices.

Licenses

If you purchase your licenses directly from Microsoft, your **Licenses** page will show your products, the number of valid licenses you have for each product, the number of expired licenses (this includes disabled licenses, but not necessarily deprovisioned ones), and the number of licenses assigned, with a prompt to assign licenses if you have unassigned ones, or unassign licenses if you don't have enough. There will also be a link for each product, to allow you to buy more:

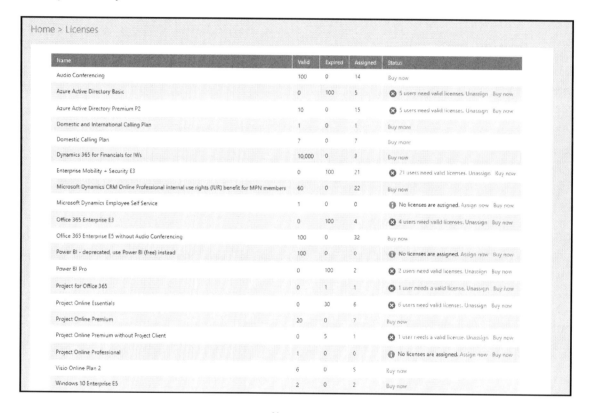

Home > Licenses

Name	Valid	Expired	Assigned	Status
Audio Conferencing	100	0	14	Buy now
Azure Active Directory Basic	0	100	5	❌ 5 users need valid licenses. Unassign Buy now
Azure Active Directory Premium P2	10	0	15	❌ 5 users need valid licenses. Unassign Buy now
Domestic and International Calling Plan	1	0	1	Buy more
Domestic Calling Plan	7	0	7	Buy more
Dynamics 365 for Financials for IWs	10,000	0	3	Buy now
Enterprise Mobility + Security E3	0	100	21	❌ 21 users need valid licenses. Unassign Buy now
Microsoft Dynamics CRM Online Professional internal use rights (IUR) benefit for MPN members	60	0	22	Buy now
Microsoft Dynamics Employee Self Service	1	0	0	ℹ️ No licenses are assigned. Assign now Buy now
Office 365 Enterprise E3	0	100	4	❌ 4 users need valid licenses. Unassign Buy now
Office 365 Enterprise E5 without Audio Conferencing	100	0	32	Buy now
Power BI - deprecated, use Power BI (free) instead	100	0	0	ℹ️ No licenses are assigned. Assign now Buy now
Power BI Pro	0	100	2	❌ 2 users need valid licenses. Unassign Buy now
Project for Office 365	0	1	1	❌ 1 user needs a valid license. Unassign Buy now
Project Online Essentials	0	30	6	❌ 6 users need valid licenses. Unassign Buy now
Project Online Premium	20	0	7	Buy now
Project Online Premium without Project Client	0	5	1	❌ 1 user needs a valid license. Unassign Buy now
Project Online Professional	1	0	0	ℹ️ No licenses are assigned. Assign now Buy now
Visio Online Plan 2	6	0	5	Buy now
Windows 10 Enterprise E5	2	0	2	Buy now

Licenses page

If you purchase through a CSP partner or another distribution program, you won't see the prompts to assign, unassign, or buy now. Your distributor or Microsoft partner handles that; you should contact them for more licenses. Instead, you may see a link directing you to contact information for your Microsoft partner.

Purchase services

Even if you generally purchase your licenses through a CSP partner or reseller, Microsoft will still offer you the chance to buy products directly from them on this site.

Believe us when we say that this creates no end of opportunities for confusion.

Avoid doing this. If your company's buying through a distributor or CSP, you are probably getting a better deal than what Microsoft offers directly. They've actually rigged the incentives so that distributors can offer a better deal than they do, because they'd rather that partners and distributors do the selling; Microsoft isn't famous for its keen interest in support and customer service for large numbers of individual consumers and small business users:

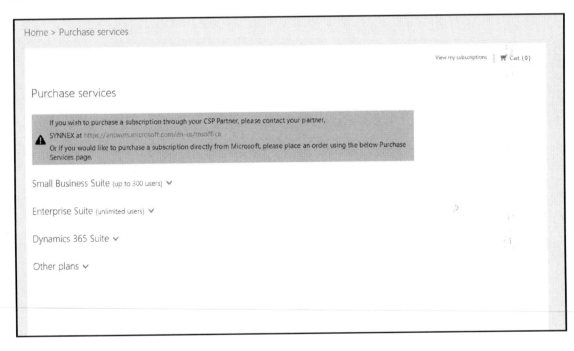

Purchase services page

Of course, if you are purchasing directly from Microsoft, there's no reason not to use this site to purchase products, as long as whoever authorizes spending in your company has given you the OK.

Each carat by a suite listing (such as **Small Business Suite**, **Enterprise Suite**, **Dynamics 365 Suite**, and **Other plans**) expands so that you can see the full listing of all the products for sale in that category. Most products require an annual commitment if you're buying from Microsoft, so be sure you've got funding secured for a full year.

Billing notifications

Regardless of whether your tenant shows invoices to view (meaning that you purchase some services directly from Microsoft) or not, you'll have a list on this page of everyone that's authorized to receive billing statements. Whether the billing statements will be directly attached to the emails or not is a switch you can toggle **On** and **Off**:

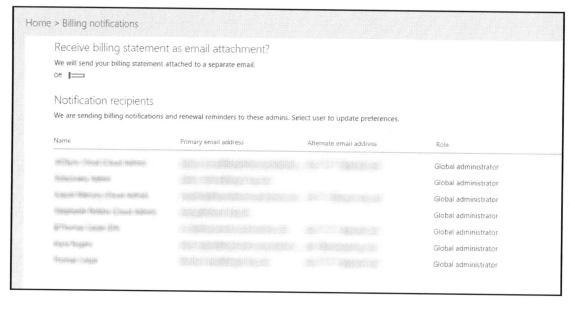

Billing notifications page

You cannot directly add to this list; it's a list of all global and billing administrators, and any custom administrator that contains billing administration rights. However, by clicking on a user in this list, you can change what administration rights they have, which can effectively delete them from the list if you downgrade their rights.

Support

There are two styles of **Support** screen that you might see, depending on if Microsoft has rolled out their newer Support UI to your company or not. In one, clicking on **New service request** or **View service requests** takes you to a separate page; in the other, you get a right-side pop-out panel, like all of the other pop-out panels you've encountered thus far. We'll touch on both, since how long it will take Microsoft to decommission the older version fully is not easily predictable.

Customer lockbox request

The **Customer Lockbox** feature comes with an Office 365 E5 plan automatically, and can be purchased as an add-on to any Enterprise plan. If your company has no such plans, you can safely skip this section. (However, this is one among many reasons that we recommend that every Office 365 customer purchase at least one E3 plan.)

When Microsoft support engineers answer service requests, they sometimes need to access your company's data. Without the **Customer Lockbox** feature, they will access what they need as they need it, and will relinquish access after they're done; but you, the customer, will have no control of or knowledge of their access. With the lockbox feature, you receive an email telling you there's a customer lockbox request, and you log in to the page to approve or deny the request.

The **Customer Lockbox** feature, if your tenant has a license that gives you access to it, can be turned on and off in **Security & privacy**, under **Settings**. More on that will follow.

Settings

The **Settings** page covers a variety of different functions that apply to your organization and don't fit particularly well in any of the other subsections.

The Services & add-ins page

The **Services & add-ins** page will show you a long, *long* list of various services and add-ins that an Office 365 administrator can activate or administer from this page. It's outside the scope of this chapter to go over them all; some will be covered in more detail in Chapter 13, *Administering PowerApps, Flow, Stream, and Forms*:

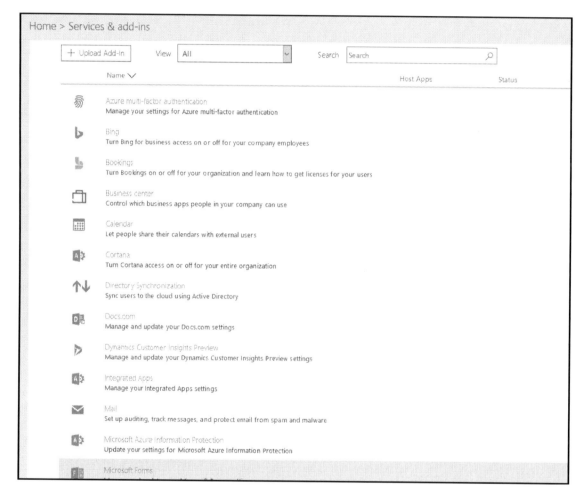

Services & add-ins

In the top-left corner, there's a button for uploading an add-in, which could be something purchased from a third party or created by developers in your company. The add-ins that you can deploy here are Office web add-ins that you can globally deploy for all users of Word, Excel, Outlook, and/or PowerPoint, in your company.

The Security & privacy settings

This is the page you use to set your Office 365 **Password policy** (options include the days before passwords expire and the number of days before a user is notified of imminent password expiration), the **Sharing** settings (whether your users can add guest users—with this setting off, users cannot share with external users from OneDrive or SharePoint), and self-service password reset:

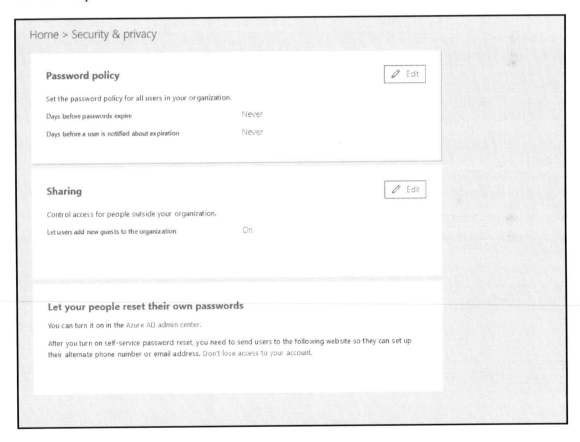

Home > Security & privacy

Password policy   Edit

Set the password policy for all users in your organization.

Days before passwords expire   Never

Days before a user is notified about expiration   Never

Sharing   Edit

Control access for people outside your organization.

Let users add new guests to the organization   On

Let your people reset their own passwords

You can turn it on in the Azure AD admin center.

After you turn on self-service password reset, you need to send users to the following website so they can set up their alternate phone number or email address. Don't lose access to your account.

The Security & privacy settings

If your company has the **Customer Lockbox** feature, this is also where you can turn it on or off.

DirSync errors

The **DirSync errors** report shows all objects that are experiencing a conflict in DirSync. In our experience, many of these errors are false alarms, or at least not particularly serious. However, keep in mind that all high-level admins will get emails alerting them to their (continued) existence. These issues are caused when properties that are supposed to be unique—for example, the `UserPrincipalName`—are assigned to more than one record. A common cause of this would be the existence of a mail contact within a distribution group with the same email as a guest user. Clicking on the object in error will give you more details on how to resolve the error.

Organization profile

Here is where you keep information about your company, including the email address of the technical contact, up to date. In small companies, it's often the case that the CEO or owner of the company assigned themselves as the technical contact when the Office 365 tenant was created, and later, they ended up flooded with error messages that clogged their inbox and should have been going to IT, anyway. You can fix that issue here:

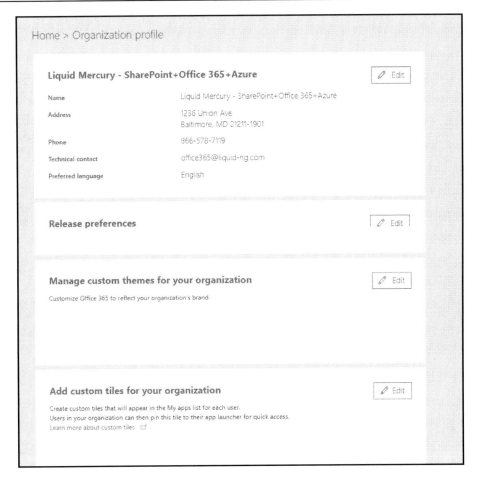

The Organization profile page

There are other settings that affect your organization here. You can decide what the release schedule for your company will be: Will you get the new Microsoft releases of Office 365 updates as soon as they come out? Will you get them when Microsoft pushes them out to everyone? Or, will you choose a few users to bravely go where no user has gone before, so that they can break what no one has broken before, and advise everyone else accordingly?

There are settings here for managing custom themes, custom tiles, and custom help desk information, as well, and you can find out what continent your data centers are on.

Partner relationships

If you purchase Office 365 from Microsoft and you don't have any Microsoft partners that you're working with, this page will be blank. Distributors, CSPs, partners of record, and other Microsoft partners that you may have granted delegated administration privileges to, will be listed here:

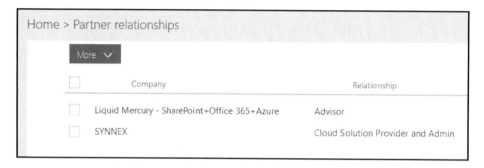

The Partner relationships page

You can look up your Microsoft partner's phone number and email address. If, for some reason, you need to move on, you can remove them from delegated administration access.

Setup

There are actually many more setup-related pages available than Microsoft makes available in the **Setup** heading of the sidebar navigation. It might be that Microsoft will eventually make those available in the sidebar, as well; as of right now, you can access the others through the dashboard component setup guides, discussed at the beginning of this chapter. The ones that you can access through the sidebar as of this writing are **Products**, **Domains**, and **Data migration**.

Products

The **Products** page is actually very similar to the **Licenses** page, but much more user-friendly and attractive. It displays the products your company is subscribed to, with icons showing what applications those products entitle you to. (Sometimes, the same application has multiple licensed products that can apply to it; for example, **Audio Conferencing** and **Domestic Calling Plan** both apply to Skype for Business. And many products offer multiple applications within; any Office plan that includes software will include Word, Excel, PowerPoint, and Outlook, for example.):

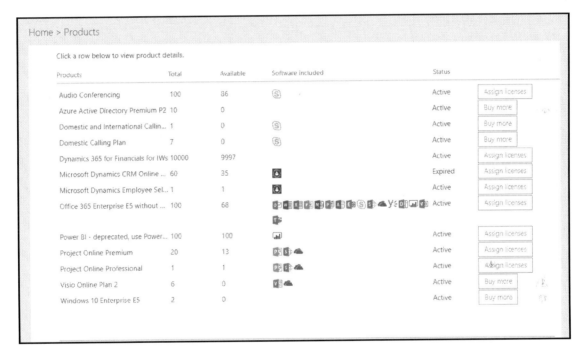

The Products page

As with the **Licenses** page, it'll show you how many licenses you have, how many are free to be used, and what their status is, and will give you the opportunity to assign licenses if some are free, or buy more if none are. Disabled and deprovisioned products won't show in this view. Note that **Buy more** just takes you to the **Subscriptions** page and **Assign licenses** takes you to **Active users**.

Domains

For most companies, you're only likely to engage with the initial setup of domains once or twice, and if you're coming on board to administer an existing Office 365 site that's already been set up with the company domain, you might never need to touch this page.

Because having a domain is very important to how your users are provisioned, we'll cover setting up a domain in detail in `Chapter 3`, *Administering Azure Active Directory*.

Data migration

The **Data migration** page shows various common email providers that you might be migrating data from, as well as giving you a convenient link for uploading a PST file.

There are also many guides of various types for onboarding onto and migrating to various Office 365 services, such as SharePoint, Teams, OneDrive, and so on, and detailed instructions for migrating from Gmail.

If this is your very first experience with Office 365, quite probably, you'll want to skip the extra helping of antacids and get the assistance of a Microsoft partner to help you make the switch. Microsoft partners will bring the experience of many different migrations for many types of organizations, and will have the tools and processes needed to make your transition to Office 365 a smooth one.

Reports

The reports that are available here are **Usage** and, under the heading **Security & compliance**, **Rules** and **DLP** (**DLP** stands for **data loss prevention**) reports. The more detailed security and compliance reports, such as protection and auditing, have moved to other areas, and we'll cover them in later chapters.

Usage

The **Usage** reports show an overview of the usage of some of the most important online components of Office 365 (such as Exchange, OneDrive, SharePoint, and so on) for **7 days**, **30 days**, **90 days**, or **180 days**, followed by detailed bar charts of various types of activities within those components (for example, the charts for Exchange track messages sent, received, and read, separately):

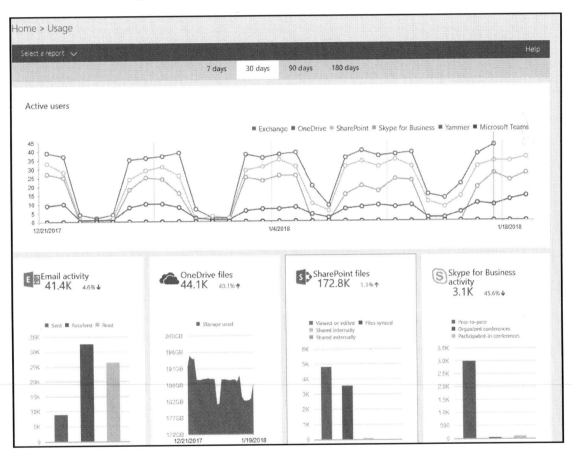

Usage reports page

These are the effective ways to track user adoption and see if there are any issues that need addressing. (If there's very little content on your company's main SharePoint team site, and yet usage and the number of files are unusually high, there may be a site collection that someone else created and is using that isn't being tracked by your centralized governance, for instance.)

The Security & compliance option

The protection reports that were at one point under this heading have moved to the **Security & Compliance** center, and will be discussed in Chapter 8, *Understanding Security and Compliance*. The auditing reports have moved to the Exchange administration center, and will be discussed in Chapter 4, *Administering Exchange Online – Essentials*. What's left are reports on **Rules** and the **DLP** policies:

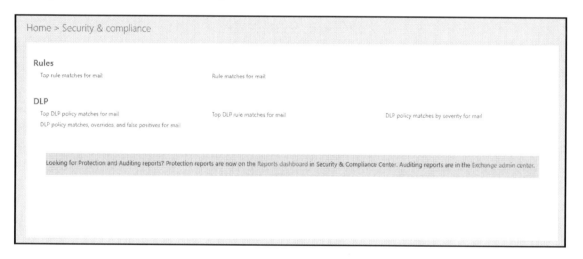

The Security & compliance page

Rules are created in Exchange, and the **DLP** policies are created in the **Security & Compliance** center, so they will be discussed in more detail in the future chapters mentioned in the preceding paragraph. The reports are on the number of rule and DLP policy matches that have passed through your Office 365 systems within 7, 14, or 30 days, or a custom date range.

Health

The **Health** component is somewhat unusual, in that all of its subheadings are components of the dashboard, as well, so we have already covered the entire section in the preceding material.

Administrative portals for individual services

Under all of the components within the administration portal, there are a number of additional portals for administering specific services, under the expandable heading **Admin centers**:

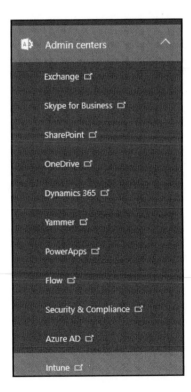

Admin centers

It's outside the scope of this chapter to go into any detail regarding those administrative centers; most are covered within their own chapters. (Note that this screenshot comes from a tenant which also has **Dynamics 365** and **Intune**; neither of those are within the scope of this book, as neither are technically a part of Office 365. Intune is part of Windows Azure, and Dynamics 365 is its own separate product. Azure AD, despite the name, is part of Office 365, as well as Azure.)

Summary

In this chapter, we went over all of the components of the Office 365 administration portal, demonstrating what you can do with these components, and, in many cases, why you would want to use them. We drilled down into the detailed functionality of the most commonly used components. We also briefly touched on the various other administration centers that one can access via this portal, and listed the chapters in which you can expect to find more detailed information about those specific portals.

One thing that we have *not* done is discuss performing administrative tasks with PowerShell. Many of the functions that can be performed on this portal can also be done in PowerShell. A detailed description of how to use PowerShell to administer every possible Office 365 function is outside the scope of this book, but the next chapter will explain how to connect to Office 365 using PowerShell, and will give a general overview of the functionality that PowerShell covers.

2

Using PowerShell to Connect to Office 365 Services

PowerShell is an incredible tool that can make your work in Office 365 much more efficient by allowing you to automate repetitive tasks and skip past the often slow loading pages of the Office 365 administration portal.

Before you can start using PowerShell, however, you'll need to be familiar with the various modules, and how to connect to each one. Later, we'll show you how you can use PowerShell to administer various Office 365 services.

In this chapter, we'll explore:

- Required software you'll need to download
- Connecting to your Office 365 tenant
- Connecting with predefined credentials
- Connecting to Exchange Online
- Connecting to SharePoint Online
- Connecting to Skype for Business
- Connecting to other services
- Connecting to customer tenants using delegated access
- Connecting to multiple services in a single session
- Important security considerations

Software prerequisites

Depending on which services you want to manage, there are several software components you need to manage Office 365 using PowerShell. Fortunately, these are free to the public and available for download on Microsoft's website.

Core components

To work with Office 365, you'll need to download the Azure AD management shell and potentially also the **Microsoft Online Services Sign-in Assistant (MOSSIA)**—formerly live ID. From time to time, Microsoft makes these available through the Office 365 administration portal, but the specific page you need to go to has changed several times over the past few years. Direct links are provided as follows for your convenience:

- **MOSSIA for IT professionals RTW**:
  `https://go.microsoft.com/fwlink/p/?LinkId=286152`
- **Azure AD (Office 365) for PowerShell v1.1.166.0**:
  `https://go.microsoft.com/fwlink/p/?linkid=236297`

The Sign-in Assistant download labeled for IT professionals will allow you to use either the 32- or 64-bit version if you wish; it was intended for those who intend to deploy Office applications from a local network file share. Note that MOSSIA is installed along with the Office 365 desktop, so strictly speaking it isn't required. There are certain aspects of the PowerShell commands that sometimes work better with this version, so it's recommended for this purpose.

The newest version of Azure AD for PowerShell (currently v1.1.166.0) includes advanced authentication (Adallom) support, device registration commands, and more. At the time of writing, it is not available through the admin portal.

Supporting modules

Azure AD PowerShell tools provide you with the basics you need for your Office 365/Azure AD subscription, but you'll need other tools to reach the assorted services associated with your Office 365 account. These include:

- **Exchange Online PowerShell module**: More in `Chapter 4`, *Administering Exchange Online – Essentials*, and `Chapter 5`, *Administering Exchange - Advanced Topics* (no download required)
- **SharePoint Online Management Shell**: More in `Chapter 6`, *Administering SharePoint Online* (`https://www.microsoft.com/en-us/download/details.aspx?id=35588`)
- **Skype for Business Online, Windows PowerShell module**: More in `Chapter 9`, *Administering Skype for Business* (`https://www.microsoft.com/en-us/download/details.aspx?id=39366`)

Each of these should be installed beforehand to ensure that you can complete the examples shown in this chapter.

Other useful downloads

Some other useful tools and related modules are also available, including the latest version of PowerShell that is part of WMF v5.1. There are also great tools for working with SharePoint Online. The examples in this book do not cover these; you may want to download and explore them on your own:

- **Windows Management Framework 5.1**: `https://www.microsoft.com/en-us/download/details.aspx?id=54616`
- **Azure Resource Manager PowerShell module**: Not covered in this book (`https://www.powershellgallery.com/packages/AzureRM`)
- **Azure Information Protection module**: Not covered in this book (`https://www.microsoft.com/en-us/download/details.aspx?id=53018`)

There are also a handful of other useful tools for Office 365 available at `http://connect.microsoft.com/site1164/Downloads`.

Connecting to your Office 365 tenant

You may already be familiar with how Microsoft uses the term **tenant**. For those who are new to Office 365, understand that a tenant refers to a set of Office 365 services that are isolated to a single customer. In layman's terms, this a is **subscription**. However, a tenant can have multiple subscriptions associated with it, for the various plans in Office 365 or Windows Azure. In fact, a single customer may choose to have more than one tenant, such as a development tenant and a production tenant.

Assuming you are the global administrator for your tenant, PowerShell will connect you to the correct tenant based on the provided username and password. This is possible because DNS suffixes used in usernames must be unique to a single tenant; they can't be used for more than one tenant at a time.

Let's connect to our tenant. We start this process by launching the Azure Active Directory module for PowerShell.

Type the following command and hit *Enter*:

```
# Import-Module AzureAD ## This isn't needed if you open Azure AD PowerShell
from the Start Menu using the installed shortcut.

Connect-MsolService
```

You will see a dialog box like this one, where you can enter your username and password:

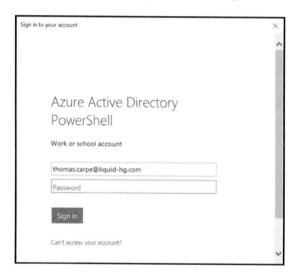

If the dialog box you see looks more like a standard Windows credentials box (like the kind you would see if you ran the `Get-Credential` command), this means you're using an older version of the PowerShell module that doesn't support advanced multi-factor authentication (Adallom):

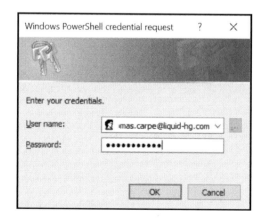

It may still work, but in some cases, you won't be able to authenticate successfully this way. In such a case, it's best to go download the current version of the PowerShell module which does support advanced authentication.

If the connection is successful, it will not produce any output. That's normal. A failure would generally be displayed in red text, like any other PowerShell error message:

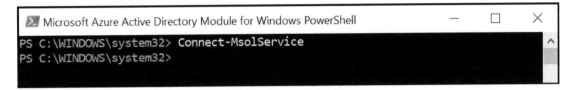

Now that you're connected, you can use other PowerShell commands for Office 365 such as `Get-MsolUser` or `Get-MsolDomain`.

Using predefined credentials to connect

There are times when it will be convenient to store the username and password you want to use to connect, such as when running an unattended automated script.

You can use the `-Credential` parameter to pass credentials into the `Connect-MsolService` command. This parameter takes an object of type `PSCredential`. This can be done easily with the `Get-Credential` command. However, as you've seen previously, this command requires input from the user. To create a `PSCredential` object without user interaction, you will need to have a username and a password stored in a `SecureString` object.

You can easily create a secure password as follows:

```
$SecurePassword = Read-Host -Prompt "Enter password" -AsSecureString
```

However, this example also requires user input. To create a secure password from a plain text string, you can do the following:

```
$PlainPassword = "P@ssw0rd"
$SecurePassword = $PlainPassword | ConvertTo-SecureString -AsPlainText
-Force
```

Please note that the preceding example isn't a recommended best practice for security reasons. In a real-life case, you'd want to read the password from a secured key in the registry or maybe use the Windows Credential Manager. These can both be accessed from PowerShell, but examples of how to do this are beyond the scope of this book. We encourage you to develop your skills with PowerShell further and search for examples on the internet that will greatly improve the security of your automated scripts.

With our `SecureString` in place, we can now create our `PSCredential` object:

```
$UserName = "username@domain.onmicrosoft.com"
$Credentials = New-Object System.Management.Automation.PSCredential `
-ArgumentList $UserName, $SecurePassword
```

Now that we have our credentials, let's connect to Office 365:

```
Connect-MsolService -Credential $Credentials
```

In the example that follows, you can see how this all comes together. I used `Read-Host` to enter my password so that it wouldn't appear on screen, but I could just as easily have used a string:

You can see that connecting to Office 365 with stored credentials isn't too much more complicated than connecting interactively. Connecting this way opens the door for automation that can run unattended, which creates a whole new world of possibilities for managing Office 365.

Connecting to Exchange Online

Connecting to Exchange Online involves creating a remote PowerShell session. This session is created using a special URL that points to your tenant. When you import the session, it downloads all the commands that the remote Exchange server understands.

You do not need to connect to Office 365 using `Connect-MsolService` before connecting to Exchange Online. Note that if you run the following scripts without setting `$Credentials` first, it will prompt you for authentication before connecting:

```powershell
$TenantName = "my365tenant"
$exchUri = "https://ps.outlook.com/PowerShell-LiveID"
if (-not [string]::IsNullOrEmpty($TenantName)) {
   if (-not $TenantName.EndsWith('onmicrosoft.com')) {
      $TenantName = "$TenantName.onmicrosoft.com"
   }
   $exchUri = "$($exchUri)?DelegatedOrg=$($TenantName)"
}
Write-Host -ForegroundColor Cyan "Connect to Exchange Online"
Write-Host "Uri: $exchUri "
$global:ExoSession = New-PSSession -ConfigurationName Microsoft.Exchange
-ConnectionUri $exchUri -Credential $Credentials -Authentication Basic
-AllowRedirection -Verbose <#:$VerbosePreference #>

Import-PSSession $global:ExoSession -DisableNameChecking -Verbose
#:$VerbosePreference | Out-Null
```

In the preceding code example, you can see that several pieces have been commented out. This is to make the code produce output that will help you understand how it works. You could incorporate the code into a PowerShell function, and re-enable these parts to hide the output except for when you need it for debugging purposes and so on.

Here's the entire command sequence in action:

To get a full list of available commands you can run `Get-Command` and feed it the temporary name of the module as shown in the following command:

```
Get-Command -Module tmp_4m3pgtnt.aa0
```

The list is quite long, so it won't be shown here. The `Import-PSSession` command creates a module object, so you can also modify the previous example to grab this object's `Name` property directly, rather than using copy and paste.

Now that you're connected, you can use commands such as `Get-Mailbox` and `Get-MailUser`. We'll cover these in detail during `Chapter 4`, *Administering Exchange Online – Essentials*.

Connecting to SharePoint Online

SharePoint is a beast unto itself; it could easily warrant us writing an entire book. In this chapter, we'll stay focused on the ways you can connect to SharePoint Online from PowerShell.

First, let's take a quick look at numerous ways you can interact with SharePoint:

- SharePoint Online Management Shell
- SharePoint REST API
- Client-side object model
- Legacy SharePoint web services and FrontPage Server Extensions
- SharePoint PnP PowerShell modules and others

SharePoint Online Management Shell

SharePoint Online Management Shell is the PowerShell module that Microsoft provides which gives you access to high-level administrative functions. If you're accustomed to working in SharePoint on-premises, this is basically the subset of the function from central administration that is permitted in Office 365.

This module allows you to perform those administrative tasks that are above the level of a site collection administrator, such as creating a new site collection. Anything at a lower level will require another approach.

But before you can add a site collection or change the sharing permission, you'll need to connect. Here's how to accomplish that:

```
Import-Module Microsoft.Online.SharePoint.PowerShell
$TenantName = "my365tenant"
$sharePointUri = "https://$TenantName-admin.sharepoint.com"
# Use these if connecting using delegated admin privs
## $DelegateName = "$TenantName.onmicrosoft.com"
## $sharePointUri = "$sharePointUri?DelegatedOrg=$DelegateName"
Write-Host -ForegroundColor Cyan "Connecting to SharePoint Online"
Write-Host $sharePointUri
Connect-SPOService -Verbose <#:$VerbosePreference #> -Url $sharePointUri
-Credential $Credentials
```

Much like our previous examples, if you haven't specified a value for $Credentials, you'll be prompted to enter a username and password. However, unlike other modules for Office 365, the SharePoint Management Shell does not use remote PowerShell sessions.

Here's the output from the commands shown previously:

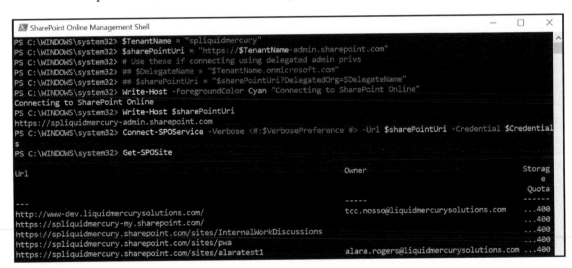

Once you're connected, you're free to use any of the commands from the SharePoint module. If you're not sure what they are, you can use Get-Command like so to show a list of available commands:

```
Get-Command -Module Microsoft.Online.SharePoint.PowerShell
```

Client-side object model

In your travels, you may come across PowerShell examples that leverage **client-side object model (CSOM)** to complete tasks in SharePoint Online. CSOM has the benefit of providing granular access to the SharePoint API. It has the shortcoming of requiring the programmer to understand not only the complexity of SharePoint's server-side API but also the nuances of asynchronous communication models used primarily for writing web services.

Nevertheless, there will be many times when CSOM is your only option for automating tasks in SharePoint Online. It's important to understand the basic pattern to connect to a SharePoint site and perform actions using this powerful framework.

You can leverage CSOM by copying the required DLLs of the SharePoint client libraries, using NuGet package manager, or by downloading them directly. Here, we'll use the download, but using NuGet with Visual Studio is the recommended way to keep things current. Download CSOM for SharePoint Online from `https://www.microsoft.com/en-us/download/details.aspx?id=42038`.

Here's how to connect to a SharePoint web service using `SPContext`.

First, we need to import the types defined in the CSOM assemblies so we can use them in PowerShell. Note that your DLLs may be stored in a different location depending on how you got them:

```
$DllPath = "c:\Program Files\Common Files\microsoft shared\Web Server
Extensions\15\ISAPI"
# Change $DllPath to wherever you are keeping your assemblies
Add-Type -Path "$DllPath\Microsoft.SharePoint.Client.dll"
Add-Type -Path "$DllPath\Microsoft.SharePoint.Client.Runtime.dll"
# You might need additional references if you need publishing, search, user
profiles, etc.
# Add-Type -Path "$DllPath\Microsoft.SharePoint.Client.Taxonomy.dll"
```

Now, let's set a few variables. To connect to SharePoint, we need the URL for a SharePoint web service and a username/password to connect with:

```
# Get variables needed to connect to SharePoint website
$Credentials = Get-Credential
$TenantName = "my365tenant"
# Change $TenantName to your Office 365 tenant
# For sub-sites you'll want to modify $WebUrl too
$WebUrl = "https://$TenantName.sharepoint.com"
```

It's important to understand that CSOM doesn't connect to all of SharePoint at once. Connections are given some content, which is a combination of credentials and a URL that points to a single SharePoint web. This *web* may be the root of a site collection (sometimes called a site) or it may be a subweb. If you want to connect to a different SharePoint subweb, you'll most likely need a separate `ClientContext`.

Here's the code to create the context object:

```
# Convert Credentials to SPO Credentials
$SpoCredentials = New-Object
Microsoft.SharePoint.Client.SharePointOnlineCredentials($Credentials.UserNa
me,$Credentials.Password)
$Context = New-Object Microsoft.SharePoint.Client.ClientContext($WebUrl)
$Context.Credentials = $SpoCredentials
$Web = $Context.Web
```

Now that we're (theoretically) connected, we can get the web title and display it. Before proceeding, we check that `$Context` has a valid value, indicating the connection was successful:

```
If (!$Context.ServerObjectIsNull.Value)  {
    # How to read a client object's properties in CSOM
    $Context.Load($Web)
    $Context.ExecuteQuery()
    $Title = $Web.Title

    Write-Host -ForegroundColor Green "Connected to SharePoint Online"
    Write-Host "Web url: '$WebUrl'"
    Write-Host "Title: '$Title'"
    # Now you can write your own code to do CSOM calls against the web
context
}
```

In CSOM, you must first load an object, its properties, or a query. You may do this more than once for different objects or properties. Next, you run that query using the `ExecuteQuery` function. This pattern reflects the disconnected and asynchronous nature of CSOM, but it does add a great deal of complexity compared to traditional SharePoint's server-side API and PowerShell commands.

Failure to load objects or properties will result in properties with empty values or errors, such as: `The collection has not been initialized. It has not been requested or the request has not been executed. It may need to be explicitly requested.`

Here's our script in action:

This is a very rudimentary example. To read properties from CSOM and call commands on the server efficiently, you're likely to need a great deal of additional code. See the *Other tools and frameworks* section for some tips on how to accelerate your efforts.

SharePoint REST API

Because REST services are much simpler than other frameworks for communicating with web applications, they have gained a great deal of traction over the past half-decade or so. This is no exception in SharePoint, and the SharePoint REST API which began with SharePoint 2010 has increased its capabilities greatly over time.

While REST services may be more familiar and useful to C# or JavaScript programmers, it is not impossible to connect to them from PowerShell. Here, we'll show you a simple example of how this can be done.

For brevity, the code here builds on the previous CSOM example. You'll need to ensure that `$SpoCredential` and `$WebUrl` have valid values.

We start by forming a REST URL. These follow a standard convention, starting with the website URL followed by `/_api` and a REST query. In our example, we'll use `web/lists` as our query to return information about the lists and libraries in our SharePoint site:

```
$RestUrl = "$WebUrl/_api/web/lists"
$Accept = "application/json;odata=verbose"
$ContentType = "application/json;odata=verbose"
[Microsoft.PowerShell.Commands.WebRequestMethod]$Method =
[Microsoft.PowerShell.Commands.WebRequestMethod]::Get
```

Next, we create the web request and assign its properties, including the method GET.

Note the commented sections which apply to other types of REST calls such as POST, PUT, and MERGE. When you're ready to try more sophisticated REST operations like these, there are plenty of great examples online:

```
$request = [System.Net.WebRequest]::Create($RestUrl)
$request.Credentials = $SpoCredentials
$request.Headers.Add("X-FORMS_BASED_AUTH_ACCEPTED", "f")
$request.ContentType = $ContentType
$request.ContentLength = 0
$request.Accept = $Accept
$request.Method = $Method
<# Skip these for now; this is a simple example
$request.Headers.Add("X-RequestDigest", $RequestDigest)
$request.Headers.Add("If-Match", $ETag)
$request.Headers.Add("X-HTTP-Method", $XHTTPMethod)
# This is for methods such as POST where we need to send some data
If ($Metadata -or $Body) {
  If ($Metadata) {
    $Body = [byte[]][char[]]$Metadata
  }
  $request.ContentLength = $Body.Length
  $stream = $request.GetRequestStream()
  $stream.Write($Body, 0, $Body.Length)
}
#>
```

Now that we've assembled our request, we can execute it and get the response back from the SharePoint server. We have to do a lot of packing and unpacking, since these objects implement IDisposable. Again, sections we don't need for this example are commented, but have been left in place to help you understand the more complex response processing:

```
# Process REST Response
$response = $request.GetResponse()
Try {
  If (!$BinaryStringResponseBody) { # Always false in our example
    $streamReader = New-Object System.IO.StreamReader
    $response.GetResponseStream()
    Try {
      $data = $streamReader.ReadToEnd()
      $results = $data | ConvertFrom-Json
      # output to the console
      $results.d
    } Finally {
      $streamReader.Dispose()
    }
  } <# Else { # $BinaryStringResponseBody
    $dataStream = New-Object System.IO.MemoryStream
    Try {
      # Steam-CopyTo isn't implemented in this example
      Stream-CopyTo -Source $response.GetResponseStream()
      -Destination $dataStream
      # output to the console
      $dataStream.ToArray()
    } Finally {
      $dataStream.Dispose()
    }
  } #>
} Finally {
  $response.Dispose()
}
```

In the preceding command, $data holds the raw response from the server and $results is the converted JSON object.

Readers familiar with REST and PowerShell outside of SharePoint may wonder why we do not use Invoke-WebRequest to make this call. While this should be possible, the call will fail to convert $SpoCredentials; using $Credentials alone will result in a 403 error.

Here's our complete REST request and the response output:

```
SharePoint Online Management Shell                                      —    □    ×
PS C:\WINDOWS\system32> $RestUrl = "$WebUrl/_api/web/lists"
PS C:\WINDOWS\system32> $Accept = "application/json;odata=verbose"
PS C:\WINDOWS\system32> $ContentType = "application/json;odata=verbose"
PS C:\WINDOWS\system32> [Microsoft.PowerShell.Commands.WebRequestMethod]$Method = [Microsoft.PowerShell.Commands.WebRequ
estMethod]::Get
PS C:\WINDOWS\system32> $request = [System.Net.WebRequest]::Create($RestUrl)
PS C:\WINDOWS\system32> $request.Credentials = $SpoCredentials
PS C:\WINDOWS\system32> $request.Headers.Add("X-FORMS_BASED_AUTH_ACCEPTED", "f")
PS C:\WINDOWS\system32> $request.ContentType = $ContentType
PS C:\WINDOWS\system32> $request.ContentLength = 0
PS C:\WINDOWS\system32> $request.Accept = $Accept
PS C:\WINDOWS\system32> $request.Method = $Method
PS C:\WINDOWS\system32> $response = $request.GetResponse()
PS C:\WINDOWS\system32> Try {
>> $streamReader = New-Object System.IO.StreamReader $response.GetResponseStream()
>> Try {
>> $data = $streamReader.ReadToEnd()
>> $results = $data | ConvertFrom-Json
>> # output to the console
>>          $results.d
>> } Finally {
>> $streamReader.Dispose()
>> }
>> } Finally {
>>          $response.Dispose()
>> }

results
-------
{@{__metadata=; FirstUniqueAncestorSecurableObject=; RoleAssignments=; Activities=; ContentTypes=; CreatablesInfo=; ...
```

Let's extend this example to display the title for each SharePoint list from the `$results.d` variable. At first, if you dig into this collection, it may not be so obvious how to get this information. The data we want is contained in `$results.d.results`. Retrieving it in PowerShell is extremely easy; it can be done with just one line of code:

```
$results.d.results | Select Title
```

Likewise, you can read other well-known list properties, such as description.

The preceding example uses a simple GET request to read data. It can't handle POST requests, nor does it interpret the results correctly if the response is a binary stream. REST calls can get fairly complex—sometimes even more so than CSOM calls.

Despite the simplistic nature of the previous code, it demonstrates that REST can be used to obtain quite a lot of data from SharePoint using just a few lines of code. And, unlike CSOM, no special DLLs were required to make this work. It can be quite a useful tool to add to your SharePoint utility belt.

Legacy SharePoint web services, WebDAV, and FrontPage Server Extensions

While legacy web services are beyond the scope of this book, they are worth mentioning because there are still rare cases in which connecting to these services is the only available option to perform certain tasks in SharePoint. Many of these services have existed since Windows SharePoint Server 2.0 (circa 2003), SharePoint Portal Server (2001), or even earlier.

From time to time, you may come across a venerable blog post that uses these frameworks to connect to SharePoint. Readers of this book should not be expected to understand how these archaic frameworks can be leveraged or how they came about, but it is important to know that they exist. Key to understanding this is the fact that not everything that worked for older versions of SharePoint (especially in an on-premises environment) can be expected to work today in SharePoint Online.

Other tools and frameworks

As time passed and frustrations grew due to having to work with CSOM and other low-level SharePoint APIs, solutions began to emerge seeking to simplify interactivity between SharePoint and PowerShell. Some are free and some come with a price; every one offers the promise of increased capabilities with reduced complexity.

While it would be impossible to cover every available framework and their available commands in any detail, it's important to understand these resources exist. Eventually, when you hit the limits of what can be done using the tools described previously—or perhaps sooner—you'll want to explore what these tools can do for you:

- **Sharegate**: While this product got its start as a tool for migrating files into SharePoint, over the years it has gained many functions for reporting and management. Practically everything Sharegate can do in the UI can be done in PowerShell too. Its price is US $1,500 to US $3,000 per year (http://sharegate.com).
- **CloudPower**: For sophisticated SharePoint automation and management needs, the authors of Kraken created CloudPower, a set of PowerShell scripts that interact with SharePoint. CloudPower is a commercial product with both free and paid editions, ranging from US $250 to US $1,250 per year (http://liquidmercurysolutions.com/apps/cloudpower).

If the idea of paying for supported commands to interact with SharePoint doesn't appeal to you, or is simply beyond your reach, you could try some of these open-source offerings:

- **SharePoint PnP**: This is a set of tools published by Microsoft's Patterns and Practices team. It includes a library of code for accessing the SharePoint APIs, including PowerShell commands. It is a very powerful set of tools, but perhaps it is not always the most user-friendly or fault-tolerant option, since it was written by developers for developers and is available for free as an open-source project (`https://www.powershellgallery.com/packages/SharePointPnPPowerShellOnline`).
- **Kraken SharePoint client**: First developed for SharePoint 2010, Kraken is a set of tools available for streamlining access to SharePoint and SharePoint Online. Kraken is an open-source library; as such it can be accessed from C# or PowerShell or similar (`https://github.com/LiquidHg/kraken/tree/master/Kraken.SharePoint.Client`).
- **Gary Lapointe's PowerShell modules**: This is an older set of PowerShell commands that has been around for a while. It was one of the first toolkits published, so it may be out of date in some cases (`https://github.com/glapointe?tab=repositories`).

Certainly, there are many more SharePoint tools out there that would be of use to admins using PowerShell. It's a big—and constantly changing—universe! We encourage you to continue your search online and check back often for new offerings.

Connecting to Skype for Business

Like Exchange Online, Skype for Business has its own module that uses remote PowerShell sessions. Similarly, you will be prompted if you don't provide a value for $Credentials. You might also need to specify the UserPrincipalName that corresponds to the credentials you provide—although it's not 100% clear exactly why this is necessary.

Connecting is fairly straightforward, as the example here shows:

```
Write-Host -ForegroundColor Cyan "Connect to Skype for Business Online"
$global:S4bSession = New-CsOnlineSession -Verbose <# :$VerbosePreference #>
-Credential $Credentials
Import-PSSession $global:S4bSession -Verbose <# :$VerbosePreference | Out-
Null #>
```

With Skype for Business, things get a bit complicated if you're trying to connect to a site through delegated admin access. This involves providing values for the –OverrideAdminDomain parameter (but not –OverrideDiscoveryUri or –OverridePowerShellUri). We'll cover this in detail in just a bit.

Here's the resulting output:

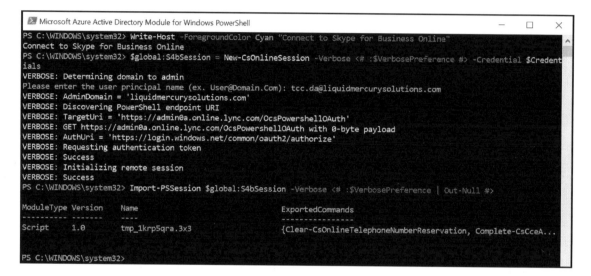

Connecting to other services

We'll cover Office 365 Security & Compliance in Chapter 8, *Understanding Security and Compliance* and connecting to PowerShell will be among the topics described there. For now, it is sufficient to understand that these tools use the remote PowerShell session techniques, so working with them is essentially the same as connecting Exchange Online and Skype for Business. There is one caveat to keep in mind: Security & Compliance requires special roles in Azure AD, so it will not work through delegated administration the way other components do.

There are other services such as Windows Azure Resource Management and Azure Information Protection, each of which has their own special technique to connect and manage. To cover each one here would be impractical. Fortunately, there is a great deal of information online that can help you get started using PowerShell with these services.

Connecting to customer tenants using delegated access

If you're an IT professional providing services to Office 365 customers, connecting to Office 365 tenants for your clients can be a bit more complicated than the examples shown previously.

Most commands in the Azure AD PowerShell module will allow you to specify a `-TenantId` parameter. This is a GUID associated with each of your customer's tenants. But where does this value come from? You can use the `Get-MsolPartnerContract` to display a list of tenant IDs for the clients you have delegated access to:

```
Get-MsolPartnerContract -All
```

Unfortunately, this ID by itself is not very useful. You'll have to combine it somehow with other commands to get something you can identify as a specific client.

For example, the following command will pipe all your customer tenants into a `Foreach-Object` loop and output the domains associated with each:

```
Get-MsolPartnerContract -All | %{ Get-MsolDomain -TenantId $_.TenantId }
```

There is also a global variable which changes the way the Office 365 PowerShell commands behave. When you set this value, all commands will work against the specified tenant, even if no `-TenantId` parameter is explicitly provided:

```
$global:MsolTenantId
```

Just as working with customer tenants has idiosyncrasies in the Office 365 PowerShell module, connecting to each of the supporting services also gets a bit more complicated if you need to do so through delegated access.

Exchange Online delegated

Connecting to Exchange Online through delegated access is a matter of tweaking the connection URL for the remote session. This is done using the `?DelegatedOrg=` query string parameter, which accepts the fully qualified tenant DNS name (for example, `my365tenant.onmicrosoft.com`). Our example in the previous section already takes this into account and modifies the URL accordingly.

Skype for Business delegated

Delegated access in Skype for Business is pretty clear. Provide the full tenant domain name to the `New-CsOnlineSession` command in the `-OverrideAdminDomain` parameter, and that's all you need to do. There are other options for messing with the connection URLs. In most cases, you shouldn't need to alter these at all.

SharePoint Online delegated

You may have noticed, in our SPOMS example, a couple of lines of commented code. These are to provide an additional query string parameter to the connection URL, specifically `?DelegatedOrg=`, which is similar to connecting via Exchange Online. Likewise, this parameter accepts a tenant name (usually in the form `*.onmicrosoft.com`) that will allow you to connect to the client administration site using delegated access.

Unfortunately, there's no way to connect directly to SharePoint sites using delegated access. Instead, you share the site with your external account and then, after confirming you can connect from the website, you'll need to get the full name of the SharePoint user for the external account.

Although this user may look like `someone_gmail.com#EXT#@my365tenant.onmicrosoft.com` in Azure AD, it typically looks something like `i:0#.f|membership|someone@gmail.com` in SharePoint Online. How will you confirm this obscure value? Well, that's where CSOM or one of the other tools described previously will come in very handy.

Once you know your sign-in credentials, and how to communicate them in SharePoint's weird esoteric language, you should be able to connect via CSOM or REST with your external (delegated) account just as you would with a native account in the customer's tenant.

You can also just create a global administrator account in the customer's domain and use that. It would probably be far easier.

Connecting to multiple services in a single session

If you have been paying close attention through the various subcomponents of Office 365, you may have observed that there is absolutely nothing that prevents us from connecting to all these services at the same time. This is useful, for example, if you need to make a change to mailboxes in Exchange Online based on information found in the Office 365 user's account, or if you want to add items to a SharePoint list based on the contents of a user's Outlook calendar. The possibilities are limitless.

Take exceptional care in circumstances where you need to connect to different services using different credentials, such as when copying data between two Office 365 tenants. Similarly, when you close one session and open another, you may need special code to handle the contingency of overriding commands that already exist due to a temporary PowerShell module created by a remote session. This is typically handled using the – NoClobber parameter, but you should be absolutely certain that you're connected to the session that you want to interact with.

Important security tips

Recently, there have been several newsworthy attacks against Office 365 accounts. Accounts that have access to administrative functions in Office 365 make particularly attractive targets. It's only a matter of time before such attacks result in a serious data breach. Don't be the person that lets their company experience this embarrassing and costly mistake.

You can protect yourself (and your customers) by making sure that you follow these security tips:

- Ensure your global administrator rights aren't associated with the account you use for everyday access to email and other Office 365 services
- Enable Office 365 multi-factor authentication for privileged accounts
- Avoid saving your administrator credentials
- Always open the Office 365 administration portal using an in-private/incognito browser session
- Consider using privileged identity management or Customer Lockbox, which are both Office 365 services available to help you control access to accounts with high-level permissions

We'll talk about these security strategies and cover more tips in Chapter 8, *Understanding Security and Compliance*.

Summary

In this chapter, we learned how to connect to your Office 365 tenant interactively and with predefined credentials. We demonstrated how to set the tenant ID for connecting to customer tenants with delegated access. We also showed you how to use remote PowerShell sessions for Exchange Online, SharePoint Online, Skype for Business, and other services, and how to connect to more than one service in a single session. We also discussed important security considerations that affect how you use PowerShell to manage Office 365.

In the next chapter, we will cover the administration and management of Office 365 user identities and groups.

Administering Azure Active Directory

3

Azure Active Directory serves as the backend storage for identities, groups, permissions, and licenses in Office 365. In the previous chapter, we covered how to connect to all the Office 365 services including Azure **Active Directory** (**AD**). In this chapter, we'll start putting those skills to work, learning tasks such as:

- Choosing the best way to manage users for a given situation
- Provisioning new accounts and assigning licenses to users
- Resetting user passwords and changing other user settings
- Offboarding users and freeing up licenses without losing data
- Adding and configuring DNS domains
- Managing Office 365 licenses
- Managing administrative roles (permissions)
- Connecting Azure AD to Windows AD

Many of these topics were covered in `Chapter 1`, *The Office 365 Administration Portal*. Here, at the risk of repeating ourselves, we're taking a slightly different perspective, focusing on how administrators manage users throughout the life cycle of the organization. Aspects of this that touch on the admin portal will be reviewed, and we'll explore alternative ways to perform the same tasks with which you may already be familiar.

Interacting with Azure AD

As is customary in most Microsoft products, there is more than one way to manage Azure AD users and groups. Most of the time, you'll probably use the Office 365 portal to perform simple and routine tasks. If you've activated your Windows Azure subscriptions, you also have access to the same users and groups through the Azure portal. For complex functions and automation, the Azure AD PowerShell modules described in this can be used. Because PowerShell is such a useful tool, we'll show you many examples of how to work with it.

Office 365 portal

The first and most familiar way you'll find for interacting with users in Office 365 is in the Office 365 portal itself. For basic and simple one-off tasks, you will probably find it faster to use the website rather than any other method. However, keeping track of the distinctive features will require frequent use and attention, since Microsoft is constantly improving and changing the way the portal works. Case in point—Microsoft changed this tile display some time back, removing the familiar but larger metro tiles. The look and feel of the interface will often change as part of the user experience:

Admin portal icon

You can find the **Admin** portal in your **Apps**, or you can bookmark this link to create a shortcut that goes directly to it: `https://portal.office.com/adminportal/home#/` `homepage`.

Once in the Office 365 portal, navigate to Azure AD by clicking **Users** or **Groups** directly under **Home** in the left-hand navigation, as shown:

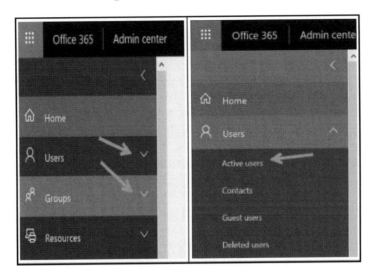

Navigating to admin portal users and groups

 You can also link directly to each by using these URLs:

- https://portal.office.com/adminportal/home#/users
- https://portal.office.com/adminportal/home#/groups

The relevant subnavigation sections and their purposes are:

- **Users**:
    - **Active users**: Shows all accounts that are active in the system, even those where login is denied.
    - **Contacts**: Contacts can be used in certain cases to send emails to people outside the organization. They are stored in the Exchange online admin portal.
    - **Guest users**: These are external users who have been invited into your tenant using a Microsoft account or similar mechanism.
    - **Deleted users**: These are accounts in the end user recycle bin. More on this later.

- **Groups**:
    - **Groups**: Primary view to create and manage Office 365 Groups, distribution lists, mail-enabled security groups, and regular security groups.
    - **Shared mailboxes**: While, strictly speaking, **Shared mailboxes** is not a group, this area was created to simplify administration and offer the chance to create an Office 365 Group or distribution list instead. Shared mailboxes themselves are traditionally managed in the Exchange Online admin center.

We'll talk about each one in detail as we explore common activities you'll perform with users and groups throughout the rest of the chapter.

Azure portal

Azure portal provides many similar abilities to the Office 365 portal, but as you can see here, the user interface is quite different. Most Office 365 administrators will probably be more comfortable working primarily within the Office 365 portal, and using Azure portal only when it is needed:

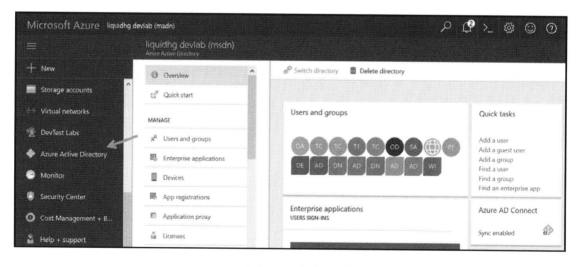

Managing Azure AD in the Azure portal

Here's the URL to go directly to the Azure AD blade: `https://portal.azure.com/#blade/ Microsoft_AAD_IAM/ActiveDirectoryMenuBlade/`.

Azure AD PowerShell module

Of course, we've learned previously how easy it is to connect to Azure AD and other 365 services using PowerShell. PowerShell also has other benefits.

For example, Microsoft might change the user interface for Office 365 and Azure portals, as they've done before quite often, and sometimes radically. By comparison, PowerShell commands stay mostly consistent over time.

Also, scripts can be used to create repeatable and self-documenting processes. These can travel with us as we work within different Office 365 customer environments.

Finally, in some cases, PowerShell simply makes it possible to do things that aren't exposed through the portal websites at all.

These are just a few reasons to take advantage of this opportunity to learn the PowerShell commands, even where it may seem easier to simply log in to the portal and click a button.

Managing Office 365 users

Most of the work you'll do with Office 365 users will be in the **Users | Active users** section. There are other sections under **Users: Contacts, Deleted users**, and **Guest users**. But we'll skip those for now. They will be covered later, in other sections.

Here's what the **Active users** page looks like:

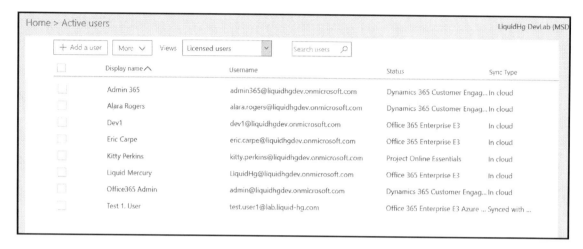

Active Users

Across the top of the page, we have the **Add a user** button, the **More** button, a drop-down that lets you choose from one of several out-of-the-box or custom views, and the user search box:

- The **Add a user** button is the primary way to onboard users. We'll talk about that process in more detail in just a bit.
- The **More** button lets you import bulk users. This is also where you would go to configure two-factor authentication or directory synchronization (**Active Directory Federation Services** (**AD FS**) or AD Connect). It also lets you reset passwords and delete users, both of which you can do from the user details page. There's a handy refresh feature too, in case you're working in PowerShell and the portal at the same time.
- The **Views** drop-down will let you choose if you want to see all users, global admins, unlicensed users, guest users, or some other type of user criteria you define yourself. It's interesting to note that **Deleted users** is not one of the views available here.
- The user search box will let you find a user based on part of their name.
- The **Export** button lets you copy the currently selected view to a downloadable CSV file that you can open in Excel. This can also be done with PowerShell, giving you access to more user information than is shown on the screen.

Each user in the list shows a checkbox (for selecting one or more items), **Display name**, **Username**, **Status**, and **Sync Type**. Most of these have purposes that are self-evident.

The **Status** column will display for you if the user is unlicensed or, if they have licenses assigned, which products have licenses. For most Office 365 customers, this will be easy to read and the user will have only a single license such as **Office 365 Business Premium**. However, if you make heavy use of licenses for many product SKUs, then the usefulness of this field will be limited. In such cases, you'll want to refer to the section on managing licenses with PowerShell to allow you to read this information at a glance.

The **Sync Type** column will be useful only to those customers who are leveraging AD Connect to integrate Office 365 with Windows **Active Directory Domain Services (AD DS)**. There are only two options, **In Cloud** and **Synced with Active Directory**. Cloud-only accounts and AD-synced accounts can live side by side in the same tenant. Since AD-synced accounts have many settings that may not be changed in the portal, this can be extremely helpful for knowing which type of account is in use.

Finding existing users

From **Active Users**, you can search for, sort, and filter the users to display those you need.

Sorting the results is accomplished by clicking the heading of the column you want to sort by. Clicking the heading will produce a chevron next to its title, with the direction indicating ascending (points up) or descending (points down). In our experience, it's not possible to have a primary and secondary sort. However, this could be accomplished with either Excel or PowerShell.

Filtering the user list can be done using the **Views** drop-down. Here's a list of all the default views:

- **All users**: The entire directory
- **Licensed users**: Users with at least one Office 365 product SKU
- **Guest users**: Users from outside your organization
- **Sign-in allowed**: Login is enabled
- **Sign-in blocked**: Login is disabled
- **Unlicensed users**: Users with no license
- **Users with errors**: These would typically be sync errors
- **Billing admins**: Users with security role for billing administrators
- **Global admins**: Users with security role for global administrators
- **Password admins**: Users with security role for password changes/resets
- **Service admins**: Users with a security role for one or more Office 365 services, such as Exchange or SharePoint

- **User management admins**: Users with a security role for adding, changing, or deleting users
- **Add a custom view**: Create your own custom criteria

As mentioned, the user search box allows you to find a user quickly based on all or part of their name, username, or email address. Note that it will find users only in the currently selected view.

Creating and managing custom views

Custom views of users can be a handy way to make searching for a user who fits certain criteria a bit easier. (PowerShell also serves as a handy tool in this way.) There are lots of reasons you may want to do this. Feel free to use your imagination!

For example, let's create a view that shows us only users who have been synced from the local AD. To create a view, click the **Views** drop-down and scroll to the bottom, then click **Add custom view**:

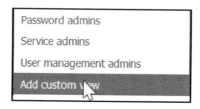

Custom user views drop-down

This will bring up the **Custom view** dialog. We'll need to specify a few options on this screen:

- **Name your view**: Synced with AD
- **Other conditions**: **Synchronized users only**

When you're done, click the **Add** button to save your changes. Your views will appear below the out-of-the-box **Views** but above the **Views** based on admin roles.

Here's another useful view:

- **Name your view**: Mailboxes in danger
- **Other conditions**: **Unlicensed users with Exchange mailboxes or archives**

Unfortunately, the means of editing or deleting a view isn't particularly obvious. There's not any specific page you navigate to in order to manage user views. Instead, select a view from the drop-down at the top of the **Active users** page, then a button will appear to the right of the drop-down to allow you to make changes to it:

Edit custom user view button

The language on the button has changed over time. Microsoft documentation refers to it as the **Edit this filter** button. In the preceding screenshot, it's shown as **Edit this view**, though you must hover over it to see the full text.

To delete a view, first edit it, then scroll down to the bottom of the **Custom view** dialog and click **Delete**.

You can only edit or delete the views that you create. To make this interface even more annoying than it already is, whether the **Edit this view** button is visible or not is the only way to differentiate between an out-of-the-box view and a custom view, so if you create a lot of views like we did, you may lose track of which ones are yours and which came with Office 365.

Those interested in automating tenant setup for multiple Office 365 customers will be disappointed to learn that there's no evidence that any of the user view management capabilities appear to be exposed through PowerShell in any way at all. If you dreamed of rolling out a couple of handy custom views to be used across 100 tenants, good documentation of your process and a helpful intern will be your friends.

It's a good thing you most likely won't need to do a lot of frequent tasks within **Custom views**.

Getting users information with PowerShell

The simplest way to get user information from Office 365 is to get all users with the **Get-MsolUser** command, like this:

```
Get-MsolUser -All
```

This will bring back a collection of every user in your tenant, which may take a while if you have a lot of users. Here's an example of the output:

```
UserPrincipalName
DisplayName
-----------------                                                ------
-----
thomas.carpe_liquid-hg.com#EXT#@liquidhgdev.onmicrosoft.com      Thomas
Carpe
incrediblemeh_gmail.com#EXT#@liquidhgdev.onmicrosoft.com         Eric
Carpe (MS Account)
eric.carpe@lab.liquid-hg.com                                     Eric
Carpe
beowulf@lab.liquid-hg.com
@AppPool Beowulf
alara.rogers@lab.liquid-hg.com                                   Alara
Rogers
bender@liquidhgdev.onmicrosoft.com                               Bender
B. Rodriguez
tcarpe_colossusconsulting.com#EXT#@liquidhgdev.onmicrosoft.com   Thomas
Carpe (MS Account)
prof.fry@liquidhgdev.onmicrosoft.com
Professor Fry
phillip.fry@liquidhgdev.onmicrosoft.com
Phillip J. Fry
thomas.carpe@lab.liquid-hg.com                                   Thomas
Carpe
adsync.user@liquidhgdev.onmicrosoft.com                          @Role
Azure AD Sync
leela@liquidhgdev.onmicrosoft.com
Turanga Leela
Sync_CAVECORE_6a0b46f7d409@liquidhgdev.onmicrosoft.com           On-
Premises Directory Synchronization Service A...
```

This is a pretty good example of a typical Office 365 tenant that's been in use for a while. Because this is a development site, it has some real users (Thomas, Alara, and Eric), some test accounts (the cast of *Futurama*), some guest accounts (Microsoft accounts used by customers, staff, or contractors with names redacted for privacy), and some service accounts used by systems like AD Connect or servers that send email notifications using Office 365. You can see clearly, even from the UPN of each user, that guest accounts look very different.

Suppose we wanted to see all the properties about a specific user? A slight variation of the same command, plus a list formatter, will do the trick:

```
PS C:\WINDOWS\system32> Get-MsolUser -UserPrincipalName
thomas.carpe@lab.liquid-hg.com | fl
ExtensionData                        :
System.Runtime.Serialization.ExtensionDataObject
AlternateEmailAddresses              : {}
AlternateMobilePhones                : {}
AlternativeSecurityIds               : {}
BlockCredential                      : False
City                                 : Baltimore
CloudExchangeRecipientDisplayType    :
Country                              : United States
Department                           : Product Development
DirSyncProvisioningErrors            : {}
DisplayName                          : Thomas Carpe
Errors                               :
Fax                                  :
FirstName                            : Thomas
ImmutableId                          : 14CFJxGVhUSHxyFL3OhOmg==
IndirectLicenseErrors                : {}
IsBlackberryUser                     : False
IsLicensed                           : False
LastDirSyncTime                      : 9/29/2016 12:19:43 AM
LastName                             : Carpe
LastPasswordChangeTimestamp          : 9/12/2016 6:18:09 PM
LicenseReconciliationNeeded          : False
Licenses                             : {}
LiveId                               : 100300009A2ABB77
MSExchRecipientTypeDetails           :
MobilePhone                          :
ObjectId                             : 7df78b6a-1626-4c49-
b99e-380c1b2bf272
Office                               :
OverallProvisioningStatus            : None
PasswordNeverExpires                 : True
PasswordResetNotRequiredDuringActivate : True
PhoneNumber                          : 410-633-5959
PortalSettings                       :
PostalCode                           : 21211
PreferredDataLocation                :
PreferredLanguage                    :
ProxyAddresses                       :
{SMTP:thomas.carpe@liquidmercurysolutions.com}
ReleaseTrack                         :
ServiceInformation                   : {}
SignInName                           : thomas.carpe@lab.liquid-hg.com
```

```
SoftDeletionTimestamp                        :
State                                        : MD
StreetAddress                                :
StrongAuthenticationMethods                  : {}
StrongAuthenticationPhoneAppDetails          : {}
StrongAuthenticationProofupTime              :
StrongAuthenticationRequirements             : {}
StrongAuthenticationUserDetails              :
StrongPasswordRequired                       : True
StsRefreshTokensValidFrom                    : 9/12/2016 6:18:09 PM
Title                                        : Muppet Master of Mayhem
UsageLocation                                :
UserLandingPageIdentifierForO365Shell        :
UserPrincipalName                            : thomas.carpe@lab.liquid-hg.com
UserThemeIdentifierForO365Shell              :
UserType                                     : Member
ValidationStatus                             : Healthy
WhenCreated                                  : 8/22/2016 9:53:58 PM
```

So, from this information, we can see many things about this user, including when they last synced and that their job includes managing a great deal of felt.

Let's say you want to dump user information to a file? You can do this like so:

```
Get-MsolUser -All | Export-Csv -Path C:\TEMP\Office365Users.csv
```

There are a lot of interesting things that can't be displayed readily using `Get-MsolUser` command, such as what Office 365 plans the user is entitled to, or to what groups they've been assigned. If you want that kind of extended information, you'll need different commands to get it. Those will be covered in detail later on.

There's still more power in `Get-MsolUsers` command, though.

Want to see who's in the user recycle bin? That's easy enough:

```
PS C:\WINDOWS\system32> Get-MsolUser -ReturnDeletedUsers

UserPrincipalName                       DisplayName  isLicensed
-----------------                       -----------  ----------
bela.lugosi@liquidhgdev.onmicrosoft.com Bela Lugosi  True
```

Here we see the king of the vampires, resting quietly in his tomb. We'll hear more about this Nosferatu later when we talk about deleting and resurrecting users from the recycle bin. (See what we did there?)

There are lots of useful parameters for `Get-MsolUser` command, including `EnabledFilter`, `LicenseReconciliationNeededOnly`, and `UnlicensedUsersOnly`, just to name a few. For everything else, you can pipe the output to `Select-Object` and create your own criteria to filter the results based on whatever custom query you desire.

Once you have a set of objects returned by `Get-MsolUser`, you can use the UPN or object ID to pass those to commands such as `Set-MsolUser`, `Delete-MsolUser`, and more. Give it a try; we think you'll see that it's fairly straightforward and easy to get the hang of.

Onboarding users

Whether you're migrating into Office 365 or you've been using it for a while, one of the most common administrative tasks you're likely to perform will be setting up new accounts.

Now that we know more about what's available for existing users, let's create some.

How you do this will vary substantially based on whether you leverage AD FS or AD Connect, but we'll assume for now that you'll be creating your accounts exclusively as **In Cloud**.

Adding a single User

Adding a user in Office 365 is a straightforward process. Let's walk through the steps starting at **Home** | **Active users** | **Add a user**.

In the **Add a user** dialog that opens, at a minimum you'll need to enter first/last name, display name, and login name. You may also choose the user's domain, which will be the default for your tenant. As shown here, helpful tips will appear to the right on each field that you click:

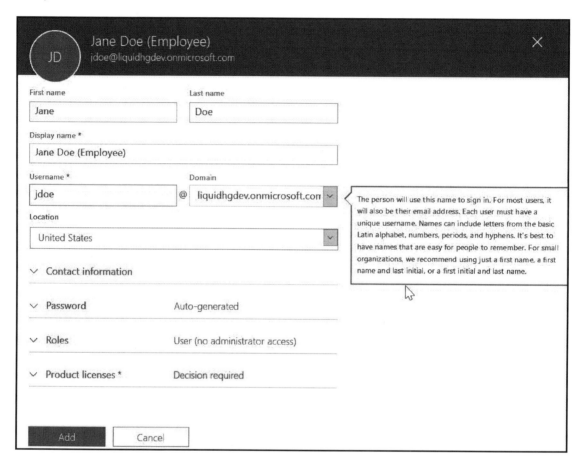

Add user dialog

As you can see, contact info is optional as well as the default options for password generation, but you will need to specify a license for the user (or otherwise indicate that you want to create one without a license). Let's take a moment to explore each section further:

- The **Contact information** section lets you enter basic details about the user, who they work for, and how to reach them. Often, we don't yet know all these details when creating new accounts. That's okay; everything in this section is optional.
- The **Password** section is a bit more interesting and useful. We can auto-generate a password or specify our own, and we can require the user to set their own password when they next log in or make our choice permanent. We tried to use a very complex passphrase: `I wonder what this button does`. Yet Office 365 gave us a warning that this password is weak. That's because it is too long for the maximum password length allowed in Office 365, which is 16 characters. *Through 20 years of effort, we've successfully trained everyone to use passwords that are hard for humans to remember, but easy for computers to guess.* (Randall Munroe, `https://xkcd.com/936/`). Unfortunately, in most cases, you don't have a choice; you must create traditional passwords that meet Office 365's complexity requirements. (See more about bypassing this requirement in the *Using PowerShell to add users* section.)
- Next up, the **Roles** section is where you specify any administrator privileges. We've talked about administrator roles elsewhere throughout this book, so we won't go into too much detail here.

If you do specify any roles, you'll need to provide an alternate email address, which much belong to a domain that is not configured in this Office 365 tenant. This email address will receive a substantial number of only-sometimes-important notifications about billing, expiring licenses, and so on, and only some of them will also be sent to the user's primary email in Office 365. So, you should choose this with care; you may also want to add forwarding rules to the external address to pass such emails back into the account you usually use.

Once upon a time, Microsoft partners could also use this section to determine if a global admin was permitted to access customer tenants or only the partner's tenant. However, such options seem to have disappeared.

- Last but not least, we have the **Product licenses** section, wherein a choice must be provided. If you truly wish to create a user without a license, you can flip the switch for **Create user without product license**. In most cases, you'll want to assign an Office 365 plan. Doing this will cause the license to expand and show you individual subcomponents of the license. (We've collapsed it here to make the screenshot size more reasonable.) This can be important in cases where two licenses carry the same sub-components; in our experience, the UI can sometimes be buggy. You may need to unselect some duplicate subcomponents such as **SharePoint Online (Plan 1)** to get the licenses to provision successfully.

And that's about all there is to creating a new user, except for the confirmation screen or dealing with any errors that might arise. You'll have an opportunity to send the password (to the user or yourself) in an email, edit this user's details, or jump immediately to creating another user:

Adding user confirmation

Adding bulk users

While we covered adding users previously in Chapter 1, *The Office 365 Administration Portal* chapter, we did not go into detail about adding many users at once.

Office 365 provides a utility that allows you to do this via the website. Many veteran Office 365 admins will eschew this option, because it does not provide the flexibility that can be achieved using PowerShell scripts. We'll cover it briefly here, so that its capabilities and limitations are familiar to you.

Choosing **Home** | **Active users** | **More** | **Import multiple users** will take you to the following dialog:

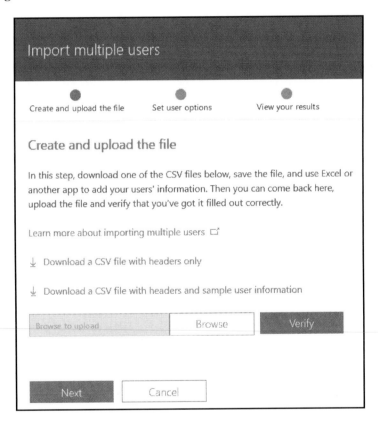

Creating bulk users

As you can see, you can download an empty template or one with sample data. We recommend the sample data, since it will give you a fair idea of the expected values to be provided for each column.

The spreadsheet you create or edit should have the following column headings in the first row:

- User Name*
- First Name*
- Last Name*
- Display Name*
- Job Title
- Department
- Office Number
- Office Phone
- Mobile Phone
- Fax
- Address
- City
- State or Province
- ZIP or Postal Code
- Country or Region

Only those columns marked with an asterisk (*) are required. The `User Name` column should be the UPN (login name), and must end in a valid domain for the Office 365 tenant. Users provisioned in this way are all created with the same choice of Office 365 license, so you can see why savvy administrators prefer PowerShell. You can also choose to disable login for all the new users:

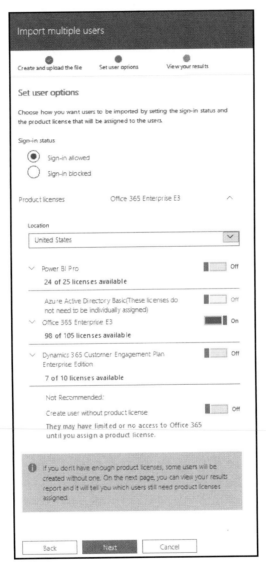

Setting bulk user options

Once users are created, you'll be given the chance to download a file that contains all their temporary auto-generated passwords, which you can also choose to send via email (though this is not considered to be very secure). Note that limited password configuration and notification options are other reasons that push experienced admins to use PowerShell instead:

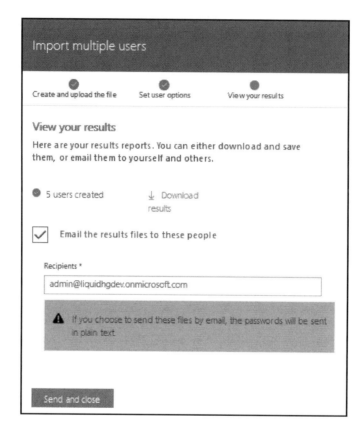

Creating bulk user results

Now you've seen all there is to creating bulk users using the Office 365 Admin portal. Let's take a look at how this kind of activity can be automated using the much more sophisticated PowerShell commands.

Using PowerShell to add users

Adding users with PowerShell is a fairly straightforward process that uses the New-MsolUser command. However, there are a lot of parameters to keep track of.

Here are the basics that you'll likely use every time you create a new account:

- −DisplayName: Display name; might appear differently than first and last name.
- −FirstName: User's given name.
- −LastName: User's family name/surname.
- −UserPrincipalName: The user's login name such as user@tenantname.onmicrosoft.com.
- −UsageLocation: Two-digit country code, such as US or UK—important because it is required for certain services such as Exchange Online and Skype for Business.
- −LicenseAssignment: An array of valid SKU part numbers (license codes) that will be assigned to the user, for example @("tenant_id:AAD_BASIC", "tenant_id:ENTERPRISEPACK", " tenant_id:PROJECTESSENTIALS"," tenant_id:EMS", and "tenant_id:DYN365_ENTERPRISE_PLAN1"); you can get a list of valid strings using the Get−MsolSubscription command—just remember to prefix them with the tenant name and a colon.
- −Password: An optional password, temporary or permanent depending on other options that you specify; if you do not specify −Password, a random one will be generated for the user.

Here's a very simple example:

```
PS C:\WINDOWS\system32> New-MsolUser -FirstName John -LastName Deer -
DisplayName "John Deer (Contractor)" -UserPrincipalName
jdeer@liquidhgdev.onmicrosoft.com -UsageLocation "US" -LicenseAssignment
"liquidhgdev:ENTERPRISEPACK" -Verbose


Password UserPrincipalName                 DisplayName
isLicensed
-------- ------------------                 -----------             ---------
-
Zot42*** jdeer@liquidhgdev.onmicrosoft.com John Deer (Contractor) True
```

Note that in the preceding example, the generated password is returned in the command's output. (We've redacted the output for security reasons, but it is normally perfectly readable.) This is very important, since we did not specify a password. It will be the only time the user password is provided. Unlike the Office 365 admin portal, you will need to use this to notify the user manually—or through whatever scripting method you may devise.

If you want to keep accurate records for organizational structure and contact information, the following parameters, which are mostly self-explanatory, will also be useful:

- `-Office`: Office location
- `-Department`: Department within the company the user works within
- `-Title`: User's job title
- `-MobilePhone`: User's mobile phone number
- `-PhoneNumber`: Business or home phone number—whichever makes more sense in your organization
- `-Fax`: Fax number (for those who are still using these)
- `-StreetAddress`: User's street address
- `-City`: Locality (city, town, village, and so on)
- `-State`: State or province
- `-PostalCode`: Zip or postal code
- `-Country`: Address country code

The following parameters will help you when creating accounts that have unusual security requirements:

- `-BlockCredential`: If true, the user can't login; we couldn't think of a good use case for this other than perhaps having a new hire and not wanting to activate the account on the day you create it.
- `-ForceChangePassword`: If true, the provided password is temporary, and the user must change it when they next log in.
- `-PasswordNeverExpires`: If true, password expiration will not be enforced. We highly recommend that you do not do this for ordinary users; it should only be used for service accounts and other such situations where changing passwords might break system functionality.
- `-StrongPasswordRequired`: If true, the password must be 8-16 characters, must not contain the username, and must contain at least one lowercase letter, uppercase letter, and nonalphanumeric character; additionally, it must not contain any spaces, tabs, or line breaks.
- `-AlternateEmailAddresses`: An external email address (not on any configured domain in Office 365) that can be used for account recovery; this is required for users who will be given administrative roles in Office 365.
- `-AlternateMobilePhones`: A mobile phone that can be used for account verification; this is required for users who will be given administrative roles in Office 365.

In multinational organizations, the following parameters can be helpful in designating geographic or language preferences that are different than the default for the tenant:

- `-PreferredDataLocation`: In late 2017, Microsoft introduced Multi-Geo, a paid service that allows a single tenant to be spread across different geographic areas worldwide; while details are sparse, you may specify regions such as NAM for North America, EUR for Europe, AUS for Australia, Asia-Pacific Canada, India, Japan, South Korea, the United Kingdom, and France. Note that additional tenant configuration is required for this setting to work as intended.
- `-PreferredLanguage`: Though PowerShell documents do not specify, this parameter accepts a language/culture code such as en-US (American English), en-UK (English in the UK), es-ES (Spanish as spoken in Spain), or fr-CA (French Canadian).

And finally, here are a few advanced options:

- `-LicenseOptions`: When you need to assign only individual parts of a license, you can use this array of objects to do so; note that generating a collection of license options is significantly more complex than merely passing a collection of SKU part numbers
- `-ImmutableId`: For those using AD Connect, this is the immutable ID of the user's federated identity in the AD; it should not be specified for **In Cloud** accounts
- `-TenantId`: Used by Microsoft partners when managing multiple customer tenants

That's about all there is to creating new users in Office 365. A quick search online will provide plenty of examples that will let you create users based on data in a CSV file and many other useful scripts.

- **Use PowerShell to create bulk users for Office 365**: `https://blogs.technet.microsoft.com/heyscriptingguy/2014/08/04/use-powershell-to-create-bulk-users-for-office-365/`
- **Culture and language codes**: `https://msdn.microsoft.com/en-us/library/ee825488(v=cs.20).aspx`
- **Multi-Geo**: `https://techcommunity.microsoft.com/t5/Security-Privacy-and-Compliance/Introducing-Multi-Geo-in-Office-365/ba-p/107016`.

Working with user settings

Once you find the user(s) you want to manage, you can perform many common tasks such as resetting their password, disabling or enabling their login, assigning licenses, and more.

Some actions are possible to perform on bulk users, but it will depend on the specific action and the status of each user you've selected in some cases. Some functions won't work in bulk, or can create problems if you choose users with contradictory statuses. For example, adding licenses in bulk can be problematic if the selected users have different licenses at the start.

In many ways, setting user options via the admin portal is very similar to specifying these options when you create a new user.

Simply clicking on a user's name will cause the portal to open the dialog for changing their properties. Many of the settings we'll discuss are accessed simply by choosing one of the various **Edit** buttons shown here:

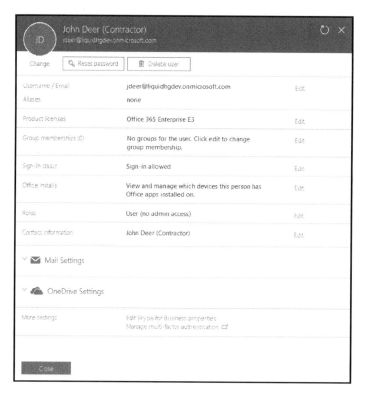

User settings

Unbeknownst to most admins, you can also select multiple users—even after the single-user dialog is open. This is accomplished by clicking the checkbox to the left of the user's name:

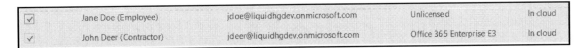

| | Jane Doe (Employee) | jdoe@liquidhgdev.onmicrosoft.com | Unlicensed | In cloud |
| | John Deer (Contractor) | jdeer@liquidhgdev.onmicrosoft.com | Office 365 Enterprise E3 | In cloud |

Select multiple users

Doing so will open the bulk user actions dialog, as shown here:

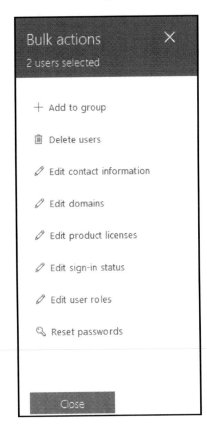

Multiple user properties dialog

Uploading a photo

This is often overlooked, but it could be smart to upload a photo to each member of your team. Perhaps as you're creating an employee's ID badge, you could also upload that picture into Office 365. This is a wise idea from both interpersonal and security standpoints. It will ensure that people spread out across the organization can recognize each other as people, and it could also make it more difficult for hackers to infiltrate your company with human engineering attacks:

Changing a user image

To add an image to a user, look for the **Change** link immediately under the circle with the person's initials in the upper left-hand corner.

For some reason that we can't really fathom, setting a user's photo in PowerShell is done through a remote session to Exchange Online, like so:

```
Set-UserPhoto -Identity $Identity -PictureData
([System.IO.File]::ReadAllBytes($FilePath)) -Confirm:$false
```

Does this mean users without mailboxes don't have photos in Office 365? This question has been left as an exercise for the reader.

 For more information visit: https://blogs.technet.microsoft.com/ cloudtrek365/2014/12/31/uploading-high-resolution-photos-using-powershell-for-office-365/.

Changing a user's login name or email address

Clicking the **Edit** link to the right of a user's login name will open a dialog that allows you to change their username, add email aliases, and replace the username with any existing alias. To change the login name, simply create a new alias and then use the **Set as primary** button to replace the user's login name with the newly created email alias:

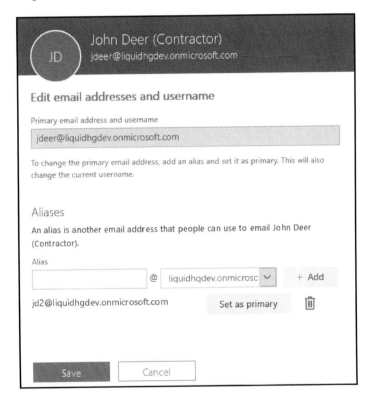

Changing a username and aliases

While there's no bulk option to change user login names, there is a bulk option to change their login domain, which can be useful in cases where you added users with the `*.onmicrosoft.com` domain and need to change them over to a company domain later.

Note the following warnings, which are provided when you change users' login domains. They also apply equally if you change a user's login name:

- If they have Exchange, and their email addresses are the same as their usernames, the email addresses will also be changed
- If this user has Skype for Business, they'll need to reschedule any Skype for Business meetings they organized and tell external contacts to update the contact information for them
- This user will also need to update their username in any apps they use, such as Outlook, OneDrive, and any mobile apps

That last one is possibly the most important one:

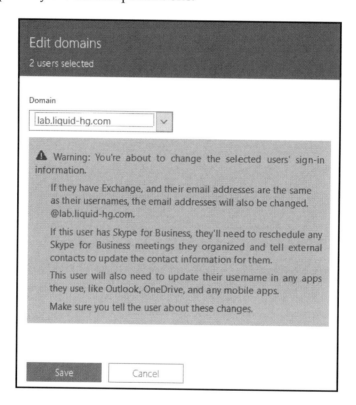

Bulk setting login domain

To change a user's login name, use the special `Set-MsolUserPrincipalName` command, as follows:

```
Get-MsolUser -UserPrincipalName jdeer@liquidhgdev.onmicrosoft.com | Set-MsolUserPrincipalName -NewUserPrincipalName jd@lab.liquidhg.com
```

The preceding command uses `Get-MsolUser` to retrieve the desired user, and then it pipes the output to `Set-MsolUserPrincipalName`, whereupon the `-NewUserPrincipalName` parameter will make changes to the login name.

For information about how to add or remove email address aliases in PowerShell, please see `Chapter 4`, *Administering Exchange Online – Essentials*.

Updating contact information

Editing contact information for users is self-evident, and can be done using the **Edit** button to the right of the **Contact information** section or using the **Edit contact information** link in the bulk user menu. Note that the bulk user option will replace all existing contact information, including blanks, so use with care. PowerShell would be a better option if you need to preserve existing information.

To set contact info in PowerShell, first use **Get-MsolUser**. Pipe the output from this command to **Set-MsolUser** and specify any of the parameters for contact information such as:

- `-Office`
- `-Department`
- `-Title`
- `-MobilePhone`
- `-PhoneNumber`
- `-Fax`
- `-StreetAddress`
- `-City`
- `-State`
- `-PostalCode`
- `-Country`

Here's a very simplified example:

```
$user = Get-MsolUser -UserPrincipalName jdeer@liquidhgdev.onmicrosoft.com
 $user | Set-MsolUser -Title "Muppet Master" -Department "Sesame Street" -
Office "CTW"
```

In many cases, if you want to leave a value unchanged, you could pass the output from
`Get-MsolUser` along or simply not specify the parameter at all. For example, you could
write a complex script to update user contact data from a spreadsheet, but only if there isn't
already data in Office 365.

Enabling or disabling login

You can activate or deactivate a user's ability to log in using the admin portal. Use the **Edit**
link to the right of **Sign-in status** to accomplish this task. There's also a bulk option to
enable and disable user login. Look for **Edit sign-in status** in the bulk user menu.

To disable a user sign-in with PowerShell, use the following:

```
Get-MsolUser -UserPrincipalName jdeer@liquidhgdev.onmicrosoft.com | Set-
MsolUser -BlockCredential $true
```

Resetting passwords

Resetting a user's password is incredibly easy. Find the **Reset password** button at the top of
the single user options dialog, just below their name and to the right of their initials/image.
In the bulk user menu, it's near the bottom of the list. In either case, once clicked, the
options will look exactly as they were when you created a new account:

Resetting passwords for single/multiple user(s)

To reset a user's password to a random temporary password in PowerShell, use the following:

```
Set-MsolUserPassword -UserPrincipalName "jdeer@liquidhgdev.onmicrosoft.com"
-ForceChangePassword
```

Note that you'll have to somehow tell the user what password to use. To set it manually, use the following:

```
Set-MsolUserPassword -UserPrincipalName "jdeer@liquidhgdev.onmicrosoft.com"
-NewPassword "pa$$word123"
```

Adjusting the user's licenses

For a single user, the **Product licenses** section will display a brief summary of their assigned plans. This is useful mainly in cases where the user has only a few licenses assigned, since the list will be truncated after it reaches four or five items. Clicking the edit link to the right of this section will bring up a dialog that is very much like the one used when creating a new user. You can unassign licenses currently allocated to the user, or assign new ones. While you can often do both in a single step, there are cases where the license assignments will have dependencies or other requirements that will force you to perform the reassignment in multiple steps. For these cases, PowerShell is often a better option:

Editing licenses for single/multiple user(s)

The bulk options for editing licenses are somewhat limited. You can add to the user's existing licenses, or you may choose to replace the existing licenses entirely. Replacing licenses will offer you the ability to remove all licenses for the selected group of users. Unfortunately, there's no option available to remove a given license from all selected users. This can make certain license changes difficult to do in bulk, such as if you need to unassign any E3 license and assign an E5. In such cases, PowerShell is probably your best option short of making changes one user at a time.

To make license changes in PowerShell, unfortunately, there's no `-LicenseAssignment` parameter for the `Set-MsolUser` command. Instead, we make use of the `Set-MsolUserLicense` command. In this command, `-AddLicenses` and `-RemoveLicenses` can both accept arrays of strings that correspond to SKU part numbers, as we described for creating users.

The simplest way to add an E3 license is like so:

```
Set-MsolUserLicense -UserPrincipalName "jdeer@liquidhgdev.onmicrosoft.com"
-AddLicenses "tenant_id:ENTERPRISEPACK"
```

Likewise, to remove it:

```
Set-MsolUserLicense -UserPrincipalName "jdeer@liquidhgdev.onmicrosoft.com"
-RemoveLicenses "tenant_id:ENTERPRISEPACK"
```

There are a myriad other ways to accomplish the same task in PowerShell. For now, we'll leave those to your imagination and curiosity.

Assigning groups

Office 365 Groups have a lot of new features for communication and collaboration. These were covered previously in Chapter 1, *The Office 365 Administration Portal* and in greater detail later in Chapter 7, *Office 365 Groups and Microsoft Teams Administration*. Likewise, many aspects of group management relate specifically to the types of groups used for email, and we go into more detail about those in Chapter 4, *Administering Exchange Online – Essentials*. In this section, we'll step through those areas just enough to get you familiar with them, focusing on how to create a group and add members, primarily as a mechanism for managing security.

It's easy to add or remove a user to/from groups within the individual user edit options. You could also change membership from the group option itself, which we'll cover elsewhere:

Editing group membership for single/multiple user(s)

While there's no option to manage group membership in bulk, you can add multiple users to a group with the **Add to group** link in the bulk user menu. This dialog will let you search for a group and add many people to it in a single step:

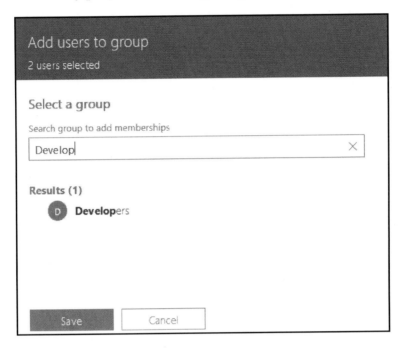

Adding users to a group

Managing group membership in PowerShell will be covered in Chapter 7, *Office 365 Groups and Microsoft Teams Administration*.

Managing admin roles

Managing admin roles is handled comparably to managing groups. Once you've entered the dialog for single or bulk users, the experience will look much the same as it did when assigning roles for a new user, with choices for User (no administrator access), Global Administrator, and Custom Administrator. The last of these will allow you to limit admin roles, though not as much as PowerShell would allow:

Roles	User (no admin access)		Edit	🖉 Edit user roles

Editing admin roles for single/multiple user(s)

Adding a user to an administrative role can be done in PowerShell, like so:

```
$user = Get-MsolUser -UserPrincipalName jdeer@liquidhgdev.onmicrosoft.com
  Add-MsolRoleMember -RoleMemberEmailAddress $user.UserPrincipalName -
RoleName "Global Administrator"
```

Likewise, removing an admin role can be accomplished with the `Remove-MsolRoleMember` command in a similar fashion.

Email-centric user and group features

For convenience, the Office 365 admin portal allows you to manage users' email addresses, as well as shared mailboxes, distribution groups, and contacts without needing to open the Exchange admin center. These features were covered in detail during Chapter 1, *The Office 365 Administration Portal*, so please refer to it for more information on these topics.

Offboarding users

There are a few things that are important to know before terminating a user's account and removing their license.

Deleting a user in the portal

Deleting a user or many users are both mostly self-explanatory:

Deleting single/multiple user(s)

Microsoft warns:

> *"When you delete users, their data is deleted and their licenses can be assigned to other users. You can restore deleted users and their data for up to 30 days after you delete them."*

That's quite true, unless the users are removed from the end user recycle bin for some reason. The most common reason for this is an administrator error, followed closely by unintended consequences of automated actions performed by AD Connect.

To delete a user in PowerShell, simply use the `Remove-MsolUser` command, like so:

```
Remove-MsolUser -UserPrincipalName "someuser@tenant_id.onmicrosoft.com"
```

The user recycle bin

It's important to understand what happens behind the scenes when a user is deleted from Azure AD. Failure to properly control this process can result in the permanent loss of a user's mailbox or other important data.

First, when a user is deleted, the account does not disappear. It is moved to the user recycle bin. These users can be restored to active status at any time.

If no other action is taken, deleted accounts will remain in the recycle bin for up to 30 days. However, it is possible for you to permanently delete them. It is also possible that the account may be permanently deleted if a new account with the same username is created. (Those using AD Connect should pay special attention to this second possibility, since AD Connect may recreate an account if it's found in the local directory after being deleted in the cloud.)

Here's a quick tip on what not to do:

```
Get-MsolUser -All | Remove-MsolUser -Force
 Get-MsolUser -ReturnDeletedUsers | Remove-MsolUser -RemoveFromRecycleBin
```

Why this is a bad idea is (at least) a three-part answer. Please post your answers in essay form to the Office 365 user voice forum or using an Office 365 support ticket.

If you choose to test the preceding command, do not do this on your production tenant; use a free trial account to see what will happen. It will not be pretty. Spoiler alert: if you do this, or anything like it, chances are very good that Microsoft will not be able to help you recover mailboxes or other user data. If you're very fortunate, you might have a Microsoft partner with delegated access who can help you regain access to your tenant after all its users have been deleted.

Best practice: There is almost never a justifiable reason to empty the end user recycle bin. If you must get rid of a user in the recycle bin, do so one user at a time and with great care.

Alternative strategies to deleting a user

Because deleting a user potentially means deleting their mail and documents, system administrators should strongly consider other approaches. Based on our experience, here are some of the most frequently used best practices.

Disabling user login

Experienced admins know that it's almost always a mistake to delete a user immediately. Deletion triggers an assortment of consequences, some of which can't be reversed easily—or at all.

Instead, the immediate responsible action to take is to disable the user's ability to sign in. If you have concerns that someone may accidentally unlock the account, you can optionally change the password as well for an added layer of protection.

Later, you can perform other activities like those described in this section to ensure the user's mail and files are preserved after their departure. Once you've gone through your company's data preservation process, you may safely remove the user's licenses and delete the Office 365 account.

For many reasons, this advice applies equally to Windows AD accounts as well as Office 365 users. In the case where a user needs to rejoin the organization at some future date, creating an identical login name with a unique SID leads to problems in many systems that rely on AD. Some organizations even require that no account should ever be deleted. Perhaps instead, to help keep things well-organized, you might move the user's account into a specific OU for inactive accounts.

Specific steps on how to disable access are described in detail in the *Working with user settings* section.

Converting to a shared mailbox

One of the simplest ways to keep a user's mail after their Office 365 account is no longer being used is to convert the user to a shared mailbox. There are limits as to how many such mailboxes you can create, but this will provide a window in which the data can be transferred to another user's mailbox folders, downloaded as a PST, or backed up in some other fashion. Smaller companies may never hit the limit at all, or may simply decide after a while that preserving the mail is no longer important.

One positive aspect of this approach is that you can take advantage of shared mailboxes even in smaller companies that aren't leveraging enterprise plans in Office 365. Thus, if you have all Business and Business Premium type licenses, you won't need to acquire any E3 license that would be needed to use in-place hold.

Note that this approach does not apply to files stored in OneDrive for Business, so if you need to preserve these, you should look at other methods for doing so. These may include a third-party backup service, conventional backups of the local files, or moving the files to a records center or other SharePoint site.

To convert a mailbox, use the Exchange admin center. Browse to mailboxes under **recipients**, select a user, and click **Convert** link under **Convert to Shared Mailbox**. Follow the instructions to complete the process. Once done, you can safely unassign the user's Exchange Online license without fear that the mailbox could be deleted:

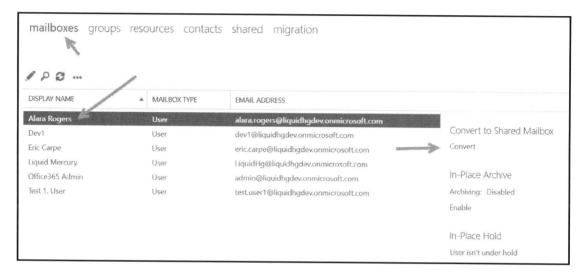

Converting user mailbox to shared mailbox

Downloading the mailbox to a PST

If you have delegated permission to access a user's mailbox, you can move or copy its content to a PST using Outlook's native archiving feature. We don't generally recommend this approach, because it is labor intensive, consumes a lot of bandwidth, and ties up a workstation for long periods of time. That being said, many Office 365 customers have gone this route either due to budget constraints or simply because admins are more familiar with this method than with other options.

It's important to point out that backing up Outlook is not going to preserve files in OneDrive for Business. Other steps would be required to protect those assets.

Switching to archive license

Many people assume that Exchange Online Archiving is the license you would use for backing up the data of an employee who has left the company. However, that's not the case at all.

Instead, Microsoft offers the Exchange Online Archiving license as an add-on option for the on-premises Exchange server to keep old mail on a long-term basis without this counting as the user's mailbox quota. A typical example would be to archive all mail that is more than 2 years old. While this method of preserving historical mail may be appropriate in hybrid environments, it is not a suitable option for Office 365 customers who are entirely in the cloud. In such cases, mailbox retention (in-place hold), third-party backup solutions, or **data loss prevention (DLP)** policies are the preferred way to preserve mailbox data.

However, it may interest Office 365 administrators to know that archive mailboxes is an option that is available to all licensed Outlook users, whether the license is for Office 365 or a traditional product such as Outlook 2013 or 2016. In fact, archiving is included in all Exchange Online plans, and a special license is not needed to use it (though it must be activated to have any effect).

 Learn more about Archiving at: `Archive Mailboxes in Exchange Online`
`https://technet.microsoft.com/en-us/library/dn922147(v=exchg.150).aspx.`

Acquiring a third-party backup solution

One way to be sure that your user's information is preserved after their account is deleted is to use a backup solution. Such solutions are readily available, and can back up mail and files for as little as $5 per user per month. Better yet, they are typically administered through a handy web interface, not PowerShell.

The best thing about having a backup solution is that it will typically cover more types of data than other approaches. Specifically, in addition to Exchange Online, these solutions typically also back up data in OneDrive for Business and SharePoint. If there is a downside to choosing this option, it would be that you may need to keep paying for the user's license for as long as you need the backup copy of the data. Be sure to check with your vendor for details before deciding on a particular backup solution.

Using mailbox retention (in-place hold)

Another method for preserving emails that scales more effectively than the shared mailbox hack is to use a retention policy (sometimes called litigation hold). Enabling mailbox retention prevents the mail from being deleted even if the mailbox itself is no longer available.

It is important to keep in mind that to use mailbox retention as a strategy, the administrator must have at least an E3 license, though our tests have shown that it can be enabled for users who have lower end accounts such as Business Premium. (You must also be in the legal hold, or more typically a discovery management, administrative role.) Thus, if you're connecting through a Microsoft partner account supporting the end customer, you cannot use your delegated access permissions to perform these activities. This may lead to additional costs for the end customer to create administer accounts for you to use.

To enable in-place hold on a mailbox, connect to the Exchange Online remote session in PowerShell, as we described in Chapter 2, *Using PowerShell to Connect to Office 365 Services*. Once you're connected, use commands like these to set the hold:

```
Get-Mailbox -Identity user@myemaildomain.com | Set-Mailbox -
LitigationHoldEnabled $true
```

If PowerShell isn't your thing, fortunately you can also enable in-place hold from the Exchange admin center. Browse the user's mailbox under **recipients**, click to highlight it, and look for the hold option along the right-hand menu, as shown:

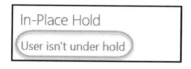

Hold status

You may notice that there's no link shown to let us change this setting. Don't worry, you can edit the mailbox and find the option under the **mailbox features** section. Scroll down until you're just above **Mail Flow** and you should see the link to enable in-place hold there. Note it may be called the **Litigation hold Dashboard**:

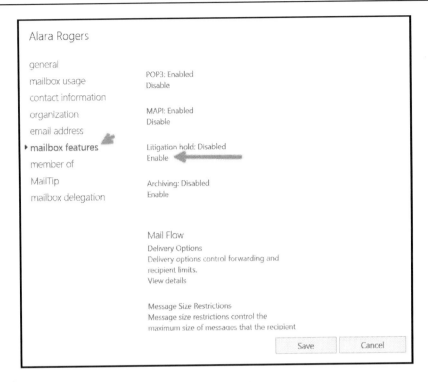

Enable hold in Exchange admin center

Does that seem a bit cumbersome to you? We agree. Recently, Microsoft also made this option available directly under user management in the Office 365 admin portal. Select a user, and you'll find it under **Mail Settings**, like so:

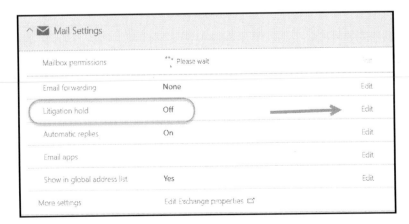

Enable hold in admin portal users

Learn more about in-place/litigation hold at:

```
In-Place Hold -
https://technet.microsoft.com/en-us/library/ff637980(v=exchg.160
).aspx.
```

DLP

DLP is a system that allows you to create sophisticated policies to prevent the loss of information in your organization. At its simplest, DLP can be configured to prevent accidental or purposeful deletion of emails or files that match certain business rules. For example, we may create a policy that places a hold on any email containing `Top Secret` in the subject or body.

DLP is a sophisticated feature of Office 365, and it could easily fill its own book. If you're interested in implementing this kind of functionality, it's probably best to seek the help of a Microsoft partner who specializes in DLP and cloud security in general. Such partners will have access to industry-specific and ready-made templates, which will greatly accelerate your efforts.

Data loss prevention in Exchange 2016:

```
https://technet.microsoft.com/en-us/library/jj150527(v=exchg.160
).aspx.
```

Safeguarding

Just as a layered defense makes the best approach to security, the same is true for safeguarding your employee's data when someone leave the business. Backup and retention systems can fail, and well-intentioned administrators can make mistakes. The more safeguards you have in place, and the more you do as a matter of routine, the less likely you'll suffer a perfect storm resulting in the permanent loss of files or other critical information.

Advanced topics

DNS domains, managing external guest users, and integrating with on-premises user directories are topics that are somewhat more esoteric than the ones we've already covered, and not every organization will have a need for them but for organizations that do need them, they can be very important. We'll cover these subjects in this section.

DNS domains

While DNS domains aren't exactly like users and groups, they haven't been covered elsewhere. Without a custom DNS domain, all your users will end in `@tenantname.onmicrosoft.com`. Since domains have a direct impact on the user names you can provision, we'll review here what it takes to add a domain to Office 365 and configure it so that you can use it as the suffix for login names and email addresses.

An important caveat: domain names in Office 365 are first come, first served and must be unique across the entirety of all Office 365 tenants worldwide. Therefore, if you added a domain to an old trial account or some other department in your company is also working within Office 365 and added the domain to their tenant, it will not be possible for you to add the domain until that conflict is resolved. We have witnessed this when someone who tried Office 365 before they left the company and their information was lost; it also happens when customers move from big Office 365 aggregators like GoDaddy or Comcast to a partner who will give them more control over their tenant. In cases like these, you will need help from Microsoft, a partner, and/or the other vendor to restore enough access to the old tenant to remove the domain.

Adding and configuring a DNS domain

You can access domain configuration options from the administration portal from **Setup | Domains**.

For system administrators familiar with managing DNS, the options available to you in Office 365 will seem extremely straightforward. For everyone else, they'll seem like arcane language from the phylactery of a long dead necromancer.

By default, the only domain configured for your Office 365 tenant will have a name like `tenant_id.onmicrosoft.com`. Chances are that you'll actually want to use your real domain name, something like `mycompany.com`, to receive emails and things like that. To do so, you'll have to provide proof to Microsoft that you own the domain name you want to connect with your tenant.

But why, you say, can't Microsoft just tell that I own that domain for `mycompany.com` and not make me jump through flaming hoops and fight velociraptors to make it work in Office 365? The answer here is quite simple. Microsoft is not the all-knowing, all-seeing eye of Sauron they would like everyone to believe that they are.

In fact, your domain name was most likely registered with some other company who specializes in that sort of thing, such as Network Solutions, Register.com, relative newcomer GoDaddy, Namecheap, or easyDNS—our personal favorite. There are literally thousands of ICANN-certified registrars to choose from.

If you have a domain registered with GoDaddy or one of a handful of other registrars with whom Microsoft has developed a deep partnership, your configuration in Office 365 could be quite easy. For these select few, Microsoft will provide a wizard that you can walk through: provide your credentials and they will do the rest for you. They've even been kind enough to make sure you can establish ownership of your domain without breaking your current email service. Isn't that nice?

For everyone else, we get to do things the hard way. There are three stages to DNS configuration in Office 365. For the sake of illustration, let's call them authorization, integration, and cutover.

Authorization stage

In the initial stage, you simply need to verify for Microsoft's purposes that you aren't adding a domain that is owned by somebody else. While technically there's more than one way to do this, we always recommend that you do it with a TXT record. The alternative method of using an MX record is only suitable for companies who are starting fresh and do not need to worry about misdelivered emails to an existing service provider.

So, you start the process by entering your domain into Office 365. They give you a TXT record with a specific code that you need to add to your DNS host. Once that's done, they verify the code, and voilà! The domain is now usable as a suffix for Office 365 users.

Integration stage

At this stage, ownership of your domain has been established, but other settings that make Office 365 services work haven't yet been configured. Microsoft will provide you with instructions on what records to create, but here's an example summary just in case:

Cat.	Type	Host name	Points to address/value
	MX*/**	[yourdomain.com]	lab-liquidhg-com02e.mail.protection.outlook.com
	TXT**	[yourdomain.com]	v=spf1 include:spf.protection.outlook.com -all
	CNAME**	autodiscover.[yourdomain.com]	autodiscover.outlook.com
	CNAME	sip.[yourdomain.com]	sipdir.online.lync.com
	CNAME	lyncdiscover.[yourdomain.com]	webdir.online.lync.com
	CNAME	enterpriseregistration.[yourdomain.com]	enterpriseregistration.windows.net
	CNAME	enterpriseenrollment.[yourdomain.com]	enterpriseenrollment.manage.microsoft.com

Cat.	Type	Port	Wgt.	Priority	Name	Target
	SRV	443	1	100	[yourdomain.com]	sipdir.online.lync.com
	SRV	5061	1	100	[yourdomain.com]	sipfed.online.lync.com

Typical Office 365 DNS configuration

Note the previous table assumes that email is the only mission critical, noninterruptible service in your enterprise. If Lync/Skype for Business is in use on-premises for your organization, you'll likely need special handling that isn't covered here.

In most if not all cases, the **time to live** (TTL), will be 1 hour.

* This MX record will vary substantially from tenant to tenant, and while other settings may be uniform, it must be checked on each domain configuration.

** MX, TXT spf, and CNAME auto-discover records can have a profound impact on the operability and functionality of existing Exchange and Outlook systems. The timing of any changes to these records should be carefully considered, and appropriate changes to the AD should be timed accordingly. Contact your Microsoft partner for guidance.

Cutover Stage

This is the stage in which MX, TXT spf, and CNAME auto-discover records cited previously may finally be changed so that new emails will be delivered into Office 365. There are different strategies for performing cutover, including cutover-first-and-migrate-later, cutover-after-migration, and hybrid configuration with Exchange on-premises. If you are unclear about these options, you should discuss your options with a qualified Microsoft partner.

Configuring DNS with PowerShell

While technically speaking, the commands exist to automate creation of DNS, these are not very practical.

That's because every organization most likely has chosen its own preferred DNS registrar. Even if the Office 365 side of the process is fully automated, the registrar and DNS host changes will likely be different every time you perform this task. Creating scripts is not likely to pay a large dividend on the time taken to do so, especially considering that most Office 365 admins will add at most a few domains and never need to do so again.

Most likely, we're assuming Microsoft created these commands for its own purposes, perhaps to facilitate their partnership with GoDaddy or other DNS providers. If you work for a direct reseller who has its own DNS hosts (or is cultivating relationships with registrars), then perhaps this topic will be of interest to you.

Managing external guest users

Guest users are people from outside your organization. Anyone with either an Office 365 account in a different tenant or a Microsoft account can be a guest user. Good examples would include customers, vendors, independent contractors, and users from connected tenants. Technically speaking, while guest users do have accounts in your Azure AD, they're treated quite differently than normal users.

As you can see, there's no interface in Office 365 for creating guest users. Your choices are to head on over to the Azure AD portal, or create a guest invite through sharing in either OneDrive for Business or SharePoint:

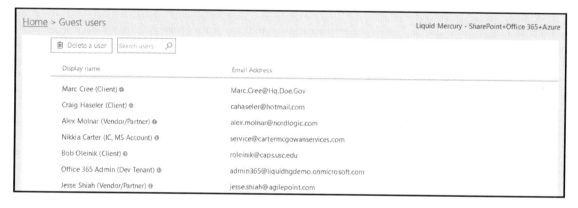

Guest users

However, Microsoft did make it easy to find and delete guest users. That's good, because cleaning up guest access in Office 365 has been a big security challenge for a long time.

Integrating with your on-premises user directory

Many organizations already have AD or something similar operating on their on-premises network, and it can be frustrating to have to maintain the same user in two different places. Microsoft offers several options for integrating Azure AD with these on-premises systems.

Available integration options

Here are the available integration options as of writing this book.

Windows Essentials Experience

Windows Essentials is a lightweight integration between Office 365 and Windows AD. It was originally envisioned as a solution for organizations of 50 people or less, and it first became available in Windows 2012 R2 as a replacement for Small Business Server. However, customer demand soon caused Microsoft to open this up to users of later editions of Windows Server, and it can now be added as a server role in Standard, Enterprise, and Data Center editions.

AD Connect (also known as AD Sync or Directory Sync)

Though this technology has been rebranded many times, the concept is essentially the same as it was several years ago. You install a lightweight version of a **Forefront Identity Manager (FIM)** server on one of your domain computers. This service runs every few hours, reading both Windows AD and Azure AD to synchronize changes between the two.

Due to its complexity, and its history of needing significant maintenance, we do not generally recommend AD Connect to organizations of less than 50 people. However, it is important to point out that AD Connect has significantly improved since its previous versions, AD Sync and DirSync. Ultimately, you will need to decide based on how you want to perform user management tasks, your security needs, and other considerations.

AD FS

AD FS is a next-generation claims-based authentication system that uses SAML. When you enable AD FS federation in your office 365 tenant, all responsibility for the login process will shift from Office 365 to your organization. Thus, Microsoft expects your systems to be fault-tolerant and highly available.

Mixed systems

If you choose any of these options, you do not have to choose to do things entirely one way for everyone in your organization. Which mix of authentication technologies is best for you is a complex choice, and you have many options.

For example, you may decide to use AD Connect for only users in a specific AD domain or OU, while using Essentials Experience for others. You may decide to integrate user accounts, while managing shared mailboxes and distribution groups entirely as In Cloud accounts. You may also configure AD FS and SSO for one DNS domain while leaving available a set of backup user accounts that do not rely on AD FS.

Alternative options

Finally, it's also possible to use some other SAML-based authentication system instead of Office 365 or AD FS. Though there aren't very many options on the market today, it would be impractical to go over every option currently available, and such information is likely to go out of date quickly. Things to consider will be those if you're looking at AD FS. Since authentication is key to accessing and using Office 365, you should also think about whether Microsoft and/or other vendors offering such solutions provide a clear roadmap for configuration and ongoing support.

How AD integration affects the new user creation process

As we mentioned before, leveraging tools such as AD Connect or AD FS will change the way you migrate into Office 365 and how you will bring new employees into the organization. Going into great detail would be well beyond the scope of this chapter, but here's an overview of what you can expect.

When you use Essentials Experience, you can choose to create your Office 365 accounts separately, or you can trigger their creation when you create an AD user. If you need to, you can associate an existing account in Office 365 with an account in AD. Passwords are synced from AD to Office 365 provided that the user doesn't change their password in Office 365 manually. This scenario is ideal in many cases, because it does not require special tools such as ADSI Edit to configure a user's email addresses. It also allows you to perform most of your user management in Office 365, and only use AD where you truly need it.

If you go the route of using AD Connect, AD will be *the system of record* and most information about users and groups will originate there. Also, any changes you may need to make will most likely need to be made in the local AD, not Office 365. (There are some newer features such as attribute write-back, but in our experience the portal will lock down most user fields to prevent them from being changed.)

Perhaps just as significant, users who are removed from AD will disappear from Office 365. They may be deleted by the system without any administrator confirmation, including their mailbox. Keep this in mind, and be sure to test your processes so that you know what will happen.

With AD FS or SAML federation, since you'll still need to have Office 365 accounts matching those in your AD, part of using AD FS will involve configuring AD Connect as well. Therefore, everything that applies to how AD Connect affects onboarding and offboarding processes for your users will also apply to AD FS.

AD and your DNS domains

Supposing you decide to go the route of using AD Connect, there will be a few things you must keep in mind.

AD Connect expects your local AD domain to have a valid DNS name that will work on the internet. This is fine if your AD forest was configured with .com, .net, or some other valid name. There was a model for naming internal domains from 2000 to about 2012, where the internal domain would end in .local (for example, mycompany.local) or some similar top-level domain that had no meaning on the internet. If your organization has such a naming scheme, you will have to complete several additional steps to ensure it can work with Office 365.

Adding a UPN suffix to your domain

If your AD domain doesn't match the DNS domain you want to use in Office 365, or if you have multiple DNS domains you want to use for login names, you'll need to add additional domain suffixes to AD.

Doing so is quite easy. In your domain controller, go to **Active Directory Domains and Trusts**, right-click the very top node as shown, and choose **Properties**. From there, add the suffixes you want to support:

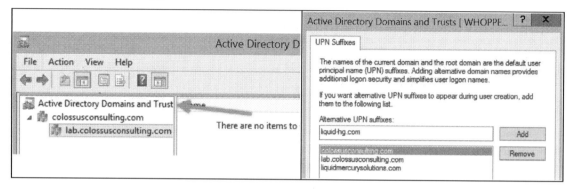

AD additional UPN suffixes

Changing the UPN for each Windows user

Once you have UPN suffixes configured to support the logins that you'll use in Office 365, you'll need to go into the **Properties** for each user, and ensure their UPN uses the correct domain suffix.

To do this, go to **Active Directory Users and Computers**, find the user and open properties. The domain suffix is under the **Account** tab:

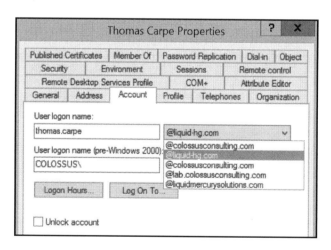

AD user UPN suffix

Of course, this can be quite onerous if you have a lot of users, so you may want to use PowerShell to do this. Now, we'd be happy to show you, but our editors think this book is already too long, so please head over to Microsoft's *Hey, Scripting Guy!* blog and have a read of how to do it at (configure UPN suffixes with PowerShell):
`https://blogs.technet.microsoft.com/heyscriptingguy/2013/08/13/add-user-princip`
`al-names-in-active-directory-via-powershell/`.

Summary

In this chapter, we've explored the lifecycle of an Office 365 user from when they're hired until after they exit the organization. You should now be capable of performing any such tasks that are required of you, including account provisioning, changing security, disabling accounts, and cleaning up guest access. You should also better understand different approaches for retaining user data, what's involved in configuring DNS domains, and how that can affect services such as email delivery, as well as the effect that integration with on-premises directory services will have on how these processes work.

4
Administering Exchange Online Essentials

There are many different roads that you may have traveled in order to get to the point where you are now, administering Exchange Online for your organization:

- Some will be experienced Exchange 2013 or 2016 administrators who are used to this interface, as it's very similar to the EAC for on-premise products. For you, we apologize; most of what you'll see in this chapter will be old hat for you, but we'll do our best to call out any differences you need to be aware of.
- Some will be experienced Exchange 2007 or Exchange 2010 administrators who've never used on-premise 2013 or 2016. There have been a lot of changes, but there will still be a good bit here that you're already familiar with.
- Some will have never administered any form of Exchange. This chapter is written to ensure that you know everything you need to do your job successfully.

Administering Exchange Online can be done in multiple ways. Many functions of Exchange Online can be handled through the Administration Portal, which we covered in Chapter 1, *The Office 365 Administration Portal*. Those same functions, and most of those that remain, can be performed in the Exchange Admin Center. Finally, there are some tasks that can only be performed with PowerShell (and some that are much more efficient to perform that way).

For administrators of on-premise Exchange, who might be used to managing Exchange by remoting into the server itself, you can't do that anymore, but the EAC for Exchange Online is very similar to the interface you're used to for Exchange 2013 and/or 2016. If you're used to using PowerShell, much of your experience will carry over.

Exchange Online administration is a large enough topic to warrant an entire book of its own. In order to give you the best and most detailed information about how to handle the most important tasks in Exchange, we've had to focus on a few of the most commonly used tabs, and only lightly touch on the others. We'll include links where you can get more information, and refer you to other chapters in this book where appropriate.

As we cover PowerShell commands for administering Exchange, we'll assume that you've already read Chapter 2, *Using PowerShell to Connect to Office 365 Services*, so we will not be covering how to connect to Exchange Online via PowerShell in order to administer it.

Exchange is a large and complex topic, and many of its more advanced features aren't going to be used by most organizations, or won't be used very often. For that reason, we've divided the Exchange administration chapter into two: the essentials and the advanced topics.

Topics included in the chapter are:

- The dashboard
- Recipients
- Permissions
- Compliance management
- Organization
- Protection
- Advanced threats
- Mail flow

The dashboard

In order to access the Exchange Admin Portal, you'll most likely need to go to the Office 365 Administration Portal and enter via Exchange in the Admin Centers. (This was covered in `Chapter 1`, *The Office 365 Administration Portal*.) It is possible to connect directly via `https://outlook.office365.com/ecp/` as well. Don't leave off the `ecp` at the end; that's what distinguishes the Exchange admin Portal from your Outlook web mail:

Exchange admin center

dashboard	Welcome	
recipients		
permissions	**recipients**	**permissions**
compliance management	mailboxes	admin roles
	groups	user roles
organization	resources	Outlook Web App policies
	contacts	
protection	shared	
	migration	
mail flow		
mobile	**compliance management**	**organization**
	in-place eDiscovery & hold	sharing
public folders	auditing	add-ins
	data loss prevention	
unified messaging	retention policies	
	retention tags	
hybrid	journal rules	
	protection	**mail flow**
	malware filter	rules
	connection filter	message trace

Exchange admin dashboard

Once you're in, you'll be presented with a dashboard that shows direct links for every main page on the portal, organized under headings, and a side navigation that takes you to a page for that heading.

We've selected the heading **Recipients** on the left navigation. Within **Recipients**, there are six tabs: **Mailboxes**, **Groups**, **Resources**, **Contacts**, **Shared**, and **Migration**. If we'd selected **Mailboxes** directly from the dashboard screen, we'd come to the same place. The other headings and dashboard direct links work the same way:

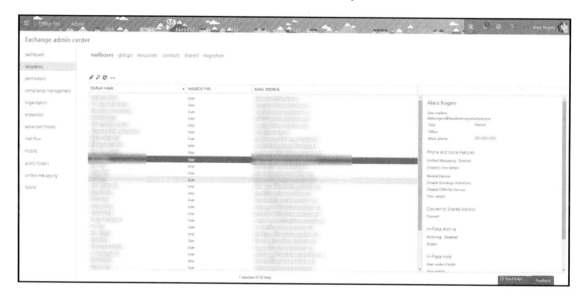

Mailboxes, under Recipients

Recipients

Recipients is the most important part of Exchange, and you will probably spend much of your time in exchange online working with the functions here. However, these areas also have a great deal of overlap with the Administration Portal (covered in Chapter 1, *The Office 365 Administration Portal*), as Microsoft have made it simpler to administer the functions of Recipients from the main portal that most administrators will access.

Mailboxes

Mailboxes are the heart of Exchange, the main purpose behind the whole thing. In a moderately large company with a normal amount of turnover, you'll probably spend more time administering mailboxes than any other part of Exchange, unless there are legal reasons why you need to spend a great deal of time on compliance and regulatory features.

Let's take a closer look at the functions of the Mailbox page.

When you select a user in the Mailbox window, a user mailbox panel opens to the right with a summary of the user's information and quick links to perform some functions without having to directly edit the user or go to any of the more specialized pages.

The functions you can perform here include:

- Enable or disable **unified messaging**
- Enable or disable the user's ability to connect a mobile device to Exchange via ActiveSync, allowing them to use mail apps on their phone or tablet
- Enable or disable the user's ability to connect to **Outlook Web Access (OWA)** via their mobile device
- Convert the user to a shared mailbox (we'll cover why you'd want to do that in the section on *Shared mailboxes*)
- Set or release in-place archiving
- View the in-place holds set for this user (this functionality is being deprecated and replaced with **Content search** in the **Security & Compliance** center, so for more details read the `Chapter 8`, *Understanding Security and Compliance*
- Allow the user to use OWA at all (disabling this will prevent the user from accessing Outlook on the web from a PC, macOS, or mobile device)

Most of the time, what you want to do won't be covered by these options, so you'll have to edit the user. At the top left of the mailbox pane, there are four icons: **Edit**, **Search**, **Refresh**, and **More**.

Note that there's no *add* or *delete* functionality here. The **Mailboxes** tab shows users, and users must be added or deleted via the Office 365 administration portal. Generally, after adding a user there and assigning a license that includes a mailbox, you might need to wait up to 15 minutes before the user appears here in Exchange (though it is usually less time than that.) You must assign the user a license that includes a mailbox for them to appear in Exchange.

With a user selected, you can click the pencil icon, which represents edit.

To perform most of these functions in Exchange Online Management Shell, you'll be making use of the command `Set-Mailbox`, which has many, many parameters—too many to go over directly here. We'll cover some of these parameters as we go.

Editing the user mailbox

The **Edit User Mailbox** dialogue opens in a new window. There are nine separate tabs in this dialogue, but usually you won't need to use all of them. On the first one, you can edit the **First name**, **Display name**, and **Alias**, but you can only edit the email address via the administration portal (or PowerShell):

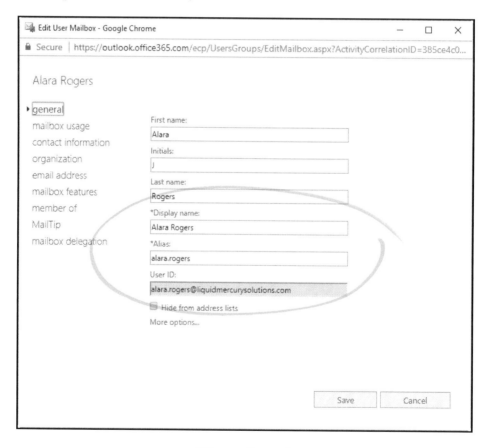

Editing user mailbox: general

There are two ways to edit the email address in PowerShell, but one is generally considered better than the other:

```
Set-Mailbox "Alara Rogers" -EmailAddress alarasnewemail@alarajrogers.com
```

This uses the `Set-Mailbox` command and the display name in the place of the `-Identity` parameter (which is implied; you can make it explicit by prefixing the identity with the `-Identity`) and the `-EmailAddress` parameter to set the new default email address. The problem with this one is that it overwrites the old one, so potentially all records of the original address may be gone:

```
Set-Mailbox "Alara Rogers" -WindowsEmailAddress
alarasnewemail@alarajrogers.com
```

The `-WindowsEmailAddress` parameter is generally preferred because it appends the new email address to the record and then sets it as the default; it doesn't delete anything. Only use the first if you are sure there will be no negative consequences when removing the original email address entirely from the record.

We won't cover all of the tabs in detail; some have significant overlap with user editing functions in the administration portal.

The mailbox usage tab

The **mailbox usage** tab shows the last login and how much of the mailbox quota has been used, but you can't use it to adjust the mailbox quota for the user in this tab, or in fact anywhere in the Exchange admin center. If you do want to edit the mailbox quota, you'll have to use PowerShell.

After connecting to the Exchange Management Shell, you can use this command to adjust the quotas at which the user receives a warning, at which the user can no longer send mail, and at which the user can no longer receive mail:

```
Set-Mailbox -Identity "Alara Rogers" -IssueWarningQuota 94.5gb -
ProhibitSendQuota 94.75gb -ProhibitSendReceiveQuota 95gb -
UseDatabaseQuotaDefaults $false
```

The `Identity` parameter can be set to the user's display name or username, and can be made explicit or implicit (as in the previous example). Note that you have to use the parameter `-UseDatabaseQuotaDefaults $false` so that it won't default to the standard for your tenant.

To confirm that the change was made, you can use this **mailbox usage** tab after refreshing.

The **contact information** tab collects the same information discussed in `Chapter 1`, *The Office 365 Administration Portal* and is self-explanatory.

Organization allows you to specify organizational details, such as the user's manager and subordinates, their department, and if you didn't enter it previously, their title and company name.

The email address tab

All of the valid email aliases for a user appear here and can be edited. When you edit, you have the opportunity to set a different address as the default. If you do, the different address will have **SMTP** type in capital and bold letters; this indicates the default address. The **SIP** address (usually, but not always—the same as the **SMTP** address) is the one used by Skype for Business and the **SPO** address (generally an obscure-looking GUID) is used by SharePoint Online:

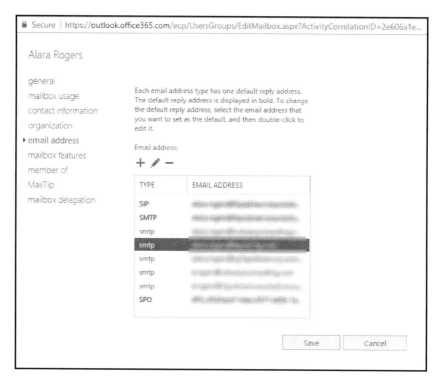

Editing mailbox: email address

We already mentioned how to use PowerShell to append a new email address, but what if you want to use PowerShell to set multiple email addresses? Look at the following:

```
Set-Mailbox "Alara Rogers" -EmailAddresses
"SMTP:alarasnewemail@alarajrogers.com","alara@alarajrogers.com"
```

By using the `SMTP` prefix, you can establish which of the email addresses should be primary. Since you're using the `-EmailAddresses` parameter, you must add all the email addresses you're using (including any you already had; remember that `-EmailAddresses` overwrites whatever email addresses were already there.)

The mailbox features tab

The small window for editing a user mailbox can't show all of the mailbox features at once; you'll need to scroll. In this screenshot, all of them have been appended to the same screenshot for ease of display:

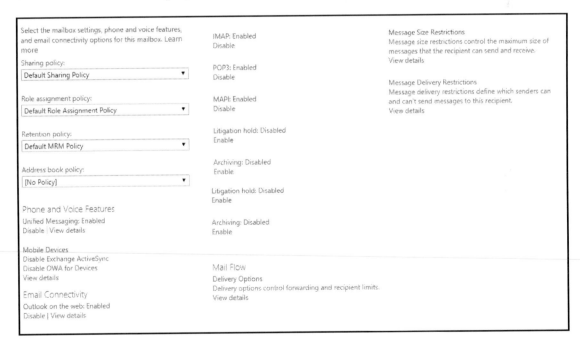

The mailbox features tab

Here's where many of the real details are. You can set the following on this screen:

- **Sharing policy**: This controls the sharing of calendars and contacts with users outside the organization, and will default to whatever your organization's standard policy is, but you can create additional policies and apply them to specific users. The sales team, for instance, might have the need to be able to share calendar information with prospects and strategic partners in proposal creation, more so than the IT department or facilities management.

- **Role assignment policy**: This controls the rights of administrators based on their roles in your organization. You can set multiple **role-based access control (RBAC)** roles and assign them to different administrators to keep tight control over who can do what.

- **Retention policy**: This policy covers deletion and archiving. As with the others, it'll default to whatever the standard for your organization is, but you can set other policies and specify them for individual users.

- **Address book policy**: Having multiple address book policies allows you to separate your users into groups so you can provide customized views of your organization's address book.

- **Phone and Voice Features**: Unified Messaging combines voicemail and email into a single mailbox for ease of access and control.

- **Mobile Devices**: These are the same options mentioned in the user mailbox panel—enable or disable ActiveSync and OWA for mobile devices. The default is for these services to be enabled.

- **Email Connectivity**: In addition to enabling or disabling OWA, you can also enable or disable access via **IMAP**, **POP3**, or **MAPI**.

- **Litigation hold**: A litigation hold preserves all mailbox content, preventing deletion and applying version control to changes. These are most commonly performed when a court ruling requires that the contents of a mailbox be preserved, but there can be other reasons for applying one as well.

- **Archiving**: Enabling archiving for a mailbox allows a user to move messages 2 years and older into an archive that's still kept online, but which doesn't count against the user's mailbox quota.

- **Mail Flow | Delivery Options**: These settings control forwarding (allowing the user's email to be forwarded to a single recipient) and recipient limit (maximum number of email addresses on To, CC, and BCC lines). You cannot change the recipient limit (which defaults to 500) in Exchange Online; this setting exists for information only. (It's the same setting in on-premise Exchange, and administrators of Exchange 2013 or 2016 on-premise *can* change it there.)
- **Mail Flow | Message Size Restrictions**: You can set a maximum, in kilobytes, for the size of a message that can be received or sent by this mailbox. The maximum can be set anywhere between 0 and 153,600 KB, but the default is generally somewhere around 36,000 KB.
- **Mail Flow | Message Delivery Restrictions**: These settings restrict who can and can't send messages to the user. One setting allows you to block everyone but users on a specific whitelist, or else accept everyone by default (with an option to require that users be authenticated); the other allows you to reject messages from blacklisted users, or else from no one. Be careful with this setting—some restrictions that seem like common sense anti-spam and phishing protection to IT might block important and legitimate mail, so make sure you discuss plans with the affected users or their management before making changes to the defaults.

Many of these settings can be adjusted with the PowerShell `Set-Mailbox` command. The sheer number of parameters available for this command makes the details out of the scope of this book, but take a look at `https://technet.microsoft.com/en-us/library/bb123981(v=exchg.160).aspx` for detailed information on the parameters you can set. (Should Microsoft move things around again so that this link breaks, you can always use your favorite search engine and request `Set-Mailbox` PowerShell parameters to find where they've moved it to.)

`Member Of` simply lists the distribution groups the user is a member of, without editing capability. `MailTip` lets you set a custom mail tip (a message that appears when the sender adds this user as a recipient—information such as `This mailbox is not monitored` for an auto-reply mailbox, for example).

The mailbox delegation tab

The **mailbox delegation** tab covers three options: **Send As**, **Send on Behalf**, and **Full Access**:

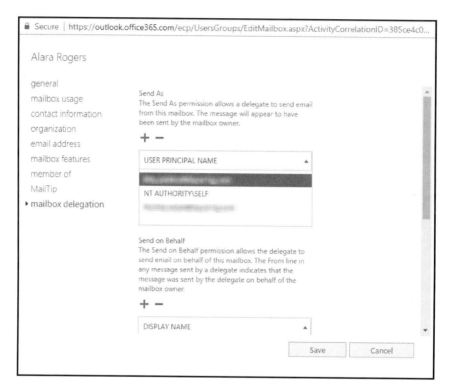

The mailbox delegation tab

Other members of your organization can be added to all three dialogues:

- **Send As**: This option allows the user who is being added as a delegate for this mailbox to send mail that looks like it comes from this mailbox.
- **Send on Behalf**: This option lets the delegate send mail that's marked as *on behalf of* from this mailbox.
- **Full Access**: This is actually not full access at all. The delegate can open the mailbox and can perform many of the functions that the owner can, but it doesn't include the **Send As** or **Send on Behalf** functions, so it's not really full access. A better description would be full *read* access.

Creating a user mailbox

You can't create a user mailbox in Exchange Online; to do that with the web browser, you'd need to do it in the Office administration portal. But you can do it with PowerShell with the `New-Mailbox` cmdlet:

```
$password = Read-Host "Enter password" -AsSecureString

New-Mailbox -Alias alara -Name alara.rogers -FirstName Alara -LastName
Rogers -DisplayName "Alara Rogers" -MicrosoftOnlineServicesID
alara.rogers@liquidmercurysolutions.com -Password $password -
ResetPasswordOnNextLogon $true
```

This creates a mailbox for the user, but you'll need to assign a license in the administration center, or the mailbox will be disabled after the grace period.

For more parameters for `New-Mailbox`, read `https://technet.`
`microsoft.com/en-us/library/aa997663(v=exchg.160).aspx`, but be careful: many of the parameters listed there only work in the on-premise version of Exchange.

Groups

There are multiple types of groups in Exchange Online. The types include distribution lists, dynamic distribution lists, security groups, and Office 365 groups. If you've already read `Chapter 1`, *The Office 365 Administration Portal*, you might be wondering where the mail-enabled security groups went. The fact is, this is Exchange Online; everything here is mail enabled. *Security group* in Exchange Online is automatically a mail-enabled security group. You won't see the security groups that aren't mail enabled:

- **Distribution list**: Also called a **distribution group**. A distribution list is an email address that serves as an alias for a list of other email addresses. It isn't a mailbox on its own; the mail that goes to it ends up directly in the inboxes of the members.
- **Dynamic distribution list**: This is a distribution list created by rules. A normal distribution list has members assigned to it manually; a dynamic distribution list adds members based on rules running on various attributes. For instance, if you've been setting **Department** in the **Organization** tab of every mailbox user, you could create dynamic distribution lists based on membership in a specific department. They're useful for lists where the membership changes frequently, such as lists of **all users in the company** or **all users in a department**.

- **Security group**: Security groups are Active Directory groups. If you're seeing one in Exchange Online, it's a mail-enabled security group, meaning that it's an Active Directory group that has an email address assigned to it. Like a distribution list, the security group won't function like a separate mailbox; the mail will go separately to each individual. Unlike a distribution list, the Exchange Online admin can't edit the membership of a security group without also having access to Active Directory.
- **Office 365 Group**: An Office 365 Group is unique to Microsoft's online services, and is not available in on-premise versions. It functions somewhat like a shared mailbox in that the emails don't go directly to the inbox of the user, but a separate mailbox (in Outlook, it's generally under the heading **Groups**, directly under the user's primary mailbox).

The main value of an Office 365 Group is that it integrates with multiple Office 365 products: Outlook, Planner, SharePoint, Yammer, and Teams, to name some of them.

On the **Groups** page, you can see your groups, edit a group, and create a new group.

Creating and editing groups

Creating and editing groups is much like editing user mailboxes. The concepts of ownership and membership are new, though, and they'll appear multiple times throughout different types of non-user mailbox types you can create.

Creating a distribution Group

On the **new distribution group** creation page, you set the **Display name**, **Email address**, **Owners**, and members:

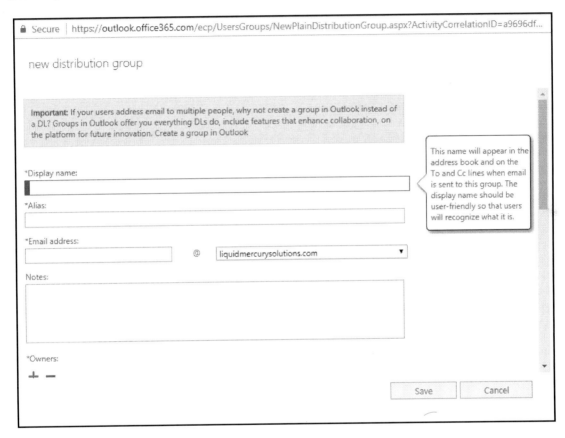

Creating a distribution list

You cannot set delivery management (who is allowed to send to the group) on creation, and it defaults to **senders within organization only**. For many lists, where you want to be able to receive email from the general public, you'll want to change that as soon as the group is created and you can edit it. You also cannot set message approval, group delegation, or mail tips, though you can add a note that will remind you or other administrators what the group is for.

To create a distribution group or security group with PowerShell, use the cmdlet `New-DistributionGroup`:

```
New-DistributionGroup -Name Sales "Sales" -Type "Security"
```

`-Type` is optional; if you don't add it, it will default to `Distribution`. You can use the parameter `-Members` to add members at the point of creation (comma delimited, and without quotes separating the usernames), or `Add-DistributionGroupMember` to add members to an already created group.

Read `https://technet.microsoft.com/en-us/library/aa998856(v=exchg.160).aspx` for more details on how to use this command.

Editing a distribution group

Add an owner to the group by clicking the plus sign while on the **ownership** tab; remove one by highlighting the name and clicking the minus sign. There can be multiple owners of a group. Owners have rights that are specified in **membership approval** and **delivery management**, and to a lesser extent **message approval**. Obviously, if there is only one owner you cannot remove them.

The **membership** tab is very similar. By default, the owner is a member. Members receive the emails from a distribution list or security group. In an Office 365 Group, members have access to the shared group mailbox:

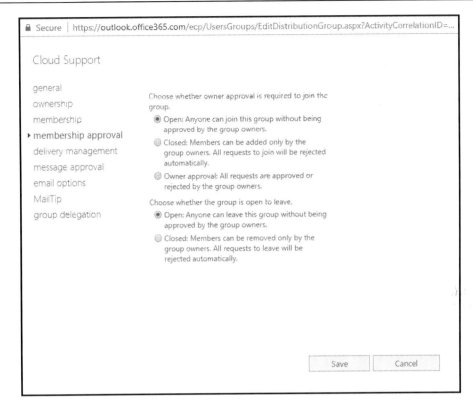

The membership approval tab

The options for **membership approval** control who can join the group and how they can leave.

The **delivery management** tab controls who can send messages to a group. The basic options are **senders inside the organization** and **senders inside and outside of the organization**. The default when you create a group will be **senders inside** only; if you intend a distribution list to be able to receive mail from the outside, you'll have to edit it to change this setting, because it can't be set at creation.

You can also restrict senders to only a specific user or users by adding them to the list. Don't add any users to this list unless you want those users to be the only ones who can send; as soon as one user has been added, the list becomes a restriction and only those who are on it can send to the group.

The **message approval** tab allows messages to go through moderation before being approved. Once you turn it on, messages will go to users who have been added to the list of group moderators first, to be approved or denied; if you haven't added anyone to the list of moderators, the messages will go to the group owners.

To edit a distribution group or security group with PowerShell, use the cmdlet `Set-DistributionGroup`:

```
Set-DistributionGroup -Identity "Support" -DisplayName "Cloud Support"
```

 This is just one example; for more details on the parameters you can use, read `https://technet.microsoft.com/en-us/library/bb124955(v=exchg.160).aspx`.

Creating a dynamic distribution list

You can't actually set an **Owner** for a **new dynamic distribution group**; membership is set by rules you create, not an owner's choices:

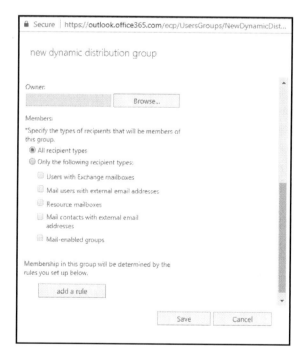

Creating a dynamic distribution group

To create one in PowerShell, use the `New-DynamicDistributionGroup` cmdlet:

```
New-DynamicDistributionGroup -Name "Operations" -IncludedRecipients
"MailboxUsers,MailContacts" -ConditionalDepartment "HR","Facilities",
"Finance"
```

There are other ways to specify the membership of your dynamic distribution group with the cmdlet as well; read `https://technet.microsoft.com/en-us/library/bb125127(v=exchg.160).aspx` for more details.

Editing a dynamic distribution group

The edit screen for a dynamic distribution group allows similar options to a regular distribution group, without options for ownership or membership, and with settings for rules.

Set the parameters of a dynamic distribution group using PowerShell with the cmdlet `Set-DynamicDistributionGroup`:

```
Set-DynamicDistributionGroup -Identity NewYorkUsers -IncludedRecipients
MailboxUsers -ConditionalStateOrProvince "NY"
```

 Read more about this cmdlet at `https://technet.microsoft.com/en-us/library/bb123796(v=exchg.160).aspx`.

Creating or editing a security group

A mail-enabled security group is an entity that exists within Active Directory as well as within Exchange Online. You can add AD groups to ownership and membership if you are in AD, but you can't do that in the Exchange Online admin portal unless the AD group in question is also a mail-enabled security group, because Exchange can only see groups if they have email. You can add any email-enabled account to a mail-enabled security group.

Security groups have the advantage that they can be assigned a set of consistent rights. A mail-enabled security group can receive mail the way a distribution list does, and can have SharePoint rights assigned the way any AD security group can. There are other uses for mail-enabled security groups as well, but unless you are syncing to an on-premise Active Directory and have file shares on a network, the most important use is usually integration between SharePoint and Exchange.

Creating a security group is exactly the same as creating a distribution list, but it will create an entity in your Active Directory and you'll be able to add AD Groups to it there, if you have admin rights to AD. In Exchange Online you can only add other mail-enabled entities, such as users, groups, resources, shared mailboxes, and other mail-enabled security groups, but you can't add a security group that isn't mail enabled through Exchange.

AD rights will have to be added in AD. You can't do that here.

You edit a mail-enabled security group in Exchange Online exactly the same way you'd manage a distribution list. The screens are all the same. The only difference is that you may see other AD security groups as owners or members, and because they might not have email addresses themselves you might not be able to edit them. The place to edit these would be Active Directory.

Creating an Office 365 Group

The Office 365 Groups are Microsoft's new innovation, and they're pushing for them hard. Right now, if you try to create a distribution group, it'll try to push you toward creating an Office 365 Group (referring to it as creating a group in Outlook; an Office 365 Group and a Group in Outlook are the same thing, as an Office 365 Group can be created by a user, using Outlook as the interface). Create and edit them in much the same way as you do other groups; the options aren't identical, but they're close.

The owner defaults to the account you're logged in as, but you can change it by browsing to a different user.

For all groups, removing them is as simple as clicking on the group name in the main **Groups** window and then clicking the trash can icon to delete.

You can create an Office 365 Group with the cmdlet `New-UnifiedGroup`:

```
New-UnifiedGroup -DisplayName "Finance Department" -Alias finance
```

For more parameters for this cmdlet, visit `https://technet.microsoft.com/library/mt219359(v=exchg.160).aspx`.

Editing an Office 365 Group

Office 365 Group editing is similar to editing a distribution list, although Microsoft has done some work to rearrange the tabs and make it a bit easier to access everything you need to:

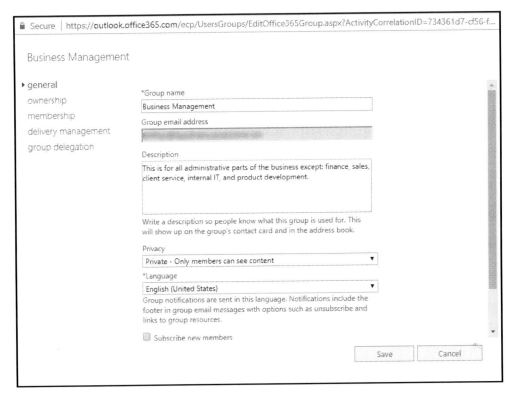

Editing an Office 365 Group

You can edit an Office 365 Group with the PowerShell cmdlet `Set-UnifiedGroup`:

```
Set-UnifiedGroup -Identity "Business Management" -PrimarySmtpAddress
bizmgmt@yourcompany.com -RequireSenderAuthenticationEnabled $false
```

For more information, take a look at `https://technet.microsoft.com/library/mt238274(v=exchg.160).aspx`.

Resources

Resources include rooms and equipment. A room has a capacity; booking a room by inviting it to a meeting limits the number of users that can also be invited to the meeting by the **Capacity** setting for the room. Equipment is understood to be one per customer, first come first serve, so as soon as one person has booked equipment for a time period no one else can. Adding equipment to a meeting does not restrict the number of people who can be invited to the meeting:

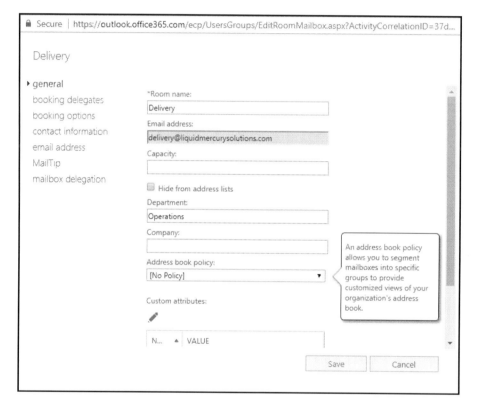

Editing resource (room): general

When we edit a resource, we can set its **Room name**, **Email address**, **Capacity** if it's a room, and information that can be used to filter views containing it, such as **Department**, **Company**, and **Address book policy**. (We went over address book policy in the section on user mailboxes.)

The other two major considerations for a resource, which are different from user mailboxes and groups, are **booking delegates** and **booking options**:

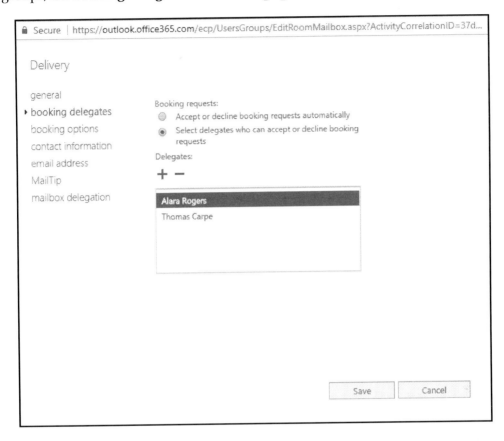

Edit resource (room): booking delegates

The **booking delegates** tab are like moderators for rooms; they can accept or deny booking requests. You don't have to have them; the first set of options is the choice of whether to accept or decline requests automatically, or to assign booking delegates and review them personally. If you do assign booking delegates, be aware that all requests for this resource will funnel through the delegates, so make sure there are enough assigned for the load you expect:

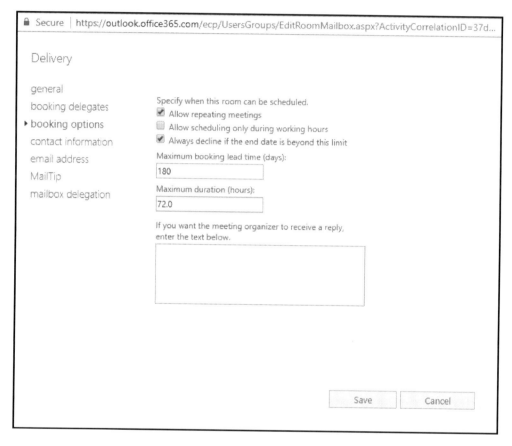

Edit resource (room): booking options

The **booking options** tab for a room include repeating meetings, restricting the schedule to working hours only, declining if the end date is beyond a certain limit (which is specified as the maximum booking lead time, expressed in days), setting the maximum duration of a meeting, and entering text for an automated reply to the meeting organizer.

There are different options for equipment.

Creating a resource

Most of the options available for room editing are not available at room creation. You can set the **Room name**, **Email address**, **Location**, **Phone**, and **Capacity**. Any other settings you want to specify must be set in the edit screens after creation:

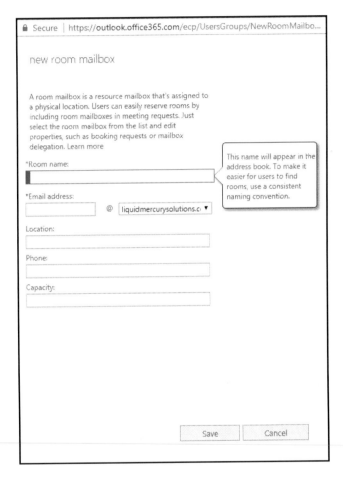

Creating resource (room)

Creating an equipment resource is even simpler. You create the name and email address, and that's all. Location, phone number, and capacity don't make any sense when applied to equipment, which might be a device that can be moved (a projector, for instance), which doesn't have a phone, and which has no capacity—it's assigned to a meeting and that's the end of it.

To create a resource via PowerShell, you use the `New-Mailbox` cmdlet (or convert an existing mailbox to a resource with our old friend `Set-Mailbox`):

```
New-Mailbox -Name Florida -OrganizationalUnit "Conference Rooms" -
DisplayName "Florida Conference Room" -UserPrincipalName
floridaroom@yourcompany.com -Room
```

Contacts

A mail contact is an email address outside your organization that you want to be able to add to distribution lists and include in your global address book:

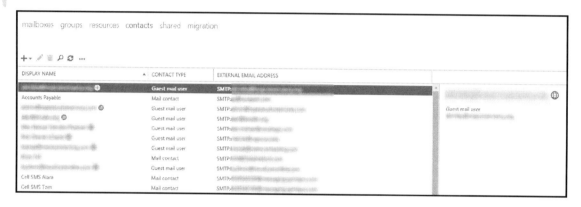

The contacts page

We discussed the difference between mail contact and guest users in Chapter 1, *The Office 365 Administration Portal*. A guest mail user is a guest user whose email is recorded in Exchange as if they were a mail contact. You cannot create or edit a guest mail user in Exchange; they appear here more for information than anything else. If you need to edit them, use the Azure AD portal.

You can create a mail contact or a mail user here. A mail contact is essentially an entry for an external contact; it doesn't require a license because the contact doesn't have any rights within any of your Office 365 products. All the contact item does is add the primary email address, phone number, and fax number for the contact to the global address book for your organization, making it available to any Office 365 product that can consume it.

A mail user has been granted some rights within your Office 365 and/or Active Directory environments. Guest mail users are created when one of your users sends a sharing invitation to someone outside your organization; mail users are created here, when the administrator wants to maintain more control over the process:

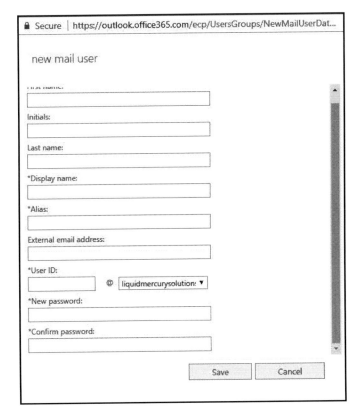

Creating a new mail user

A mail user has an external email address, which is their email address within their own organization, and a user ID, which usually takes the form of an email address and is within your organization. Because mail users will authenticate to your tenant, you provide them with a user ID and password. If you need them to have access to any licensed products, such as rights within SharePoint, you'd add a license in the administration portal, as discussed in Chapter 1, *The Office 365 Administration Portal*.

To create a mail user with PowerShell, use the cmdlet `New-MailUser`:

```
$password = Read-Host "Enter password" -AsSecureString
New-MailUser -Name "Alara Rogers" -ExternalEmailAddress
alara@alarajrogers.com -MicrosoftOnlineServicesID alara@alarajrogers.com -
Password $password
```

To create a mail contact, use the cmdlet `New-MailContact`:

```
New-MailContact -Name "Alara Rogers" -ExternalEmailAddress
"alara@alarajrogers.com"
```

Note that for the mail user, you need to set a password, but you don't need to do that for a mail contact.

Shared mailboxes

A shared mailbox is a good solution when you need a single repository for mail coming in to a particular address:

Shared mailboxes

With a distribution list, copies of an email sent to the list are sent out to each of the members of the list, and those copies operate independently. If one person should hit **Reply** without **Reply all**, other members of the distribution list won't be CC'd or have any way to know that one member responded.

A shared mailbox functions in many regards just like your user mailbox; mail comes to it and stays there, in its own mailbox. Someone with rights to the shared mailbox can reply to a message that's in the mailbox, using the identity of the mailbox, and everyone else with those rights will see that that particular email has been replied to. In addition, shared mailboxes can be converted to user mailboxes, and vice versa, which makes them a useful means of retaining the mail from a terminated employee.

What a shared mailbox is *not* is a username within Office 365. You cannot log in to Office 365 with a shared mailbox's credentials. They do not have passwords and they do not (usually) have licenses assigned:

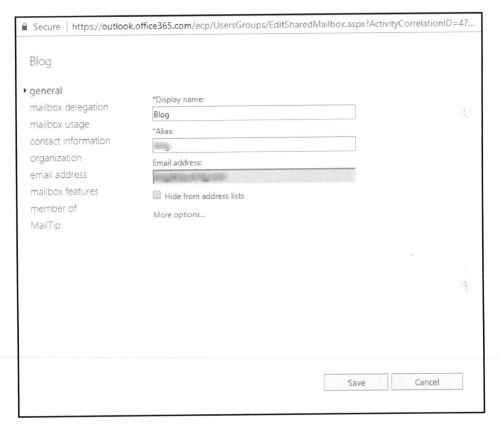

Editing a shared mailbox

The shared mailbox looks almost the same in editing as the user mailbox; the only significant difference is the placement of **mailbox delegation** and the fact that **mailbox delegation** doesn't include **Send on Behalf** as an option. All email sent from the shared mailbox is sent as the shared mailbox, not on behalf of it:

Creating a shared mailbox

The creation of the shared mailbox, however, is more similar to the creation of a group, in that adding users is important enough to appear on the creation screen. There are no owners of a shared mailbox, only members. By default, members that are added are added to both **Full Access** and **Send As**. If you want to remove one set of rights or the other, you'll have to edit the group.

The PowerShell for creating a shared mailbox is actually the same as for creating any kind of mailbox. It's the `New-Mailbox` command we covered in **recipients | mailboxes**. Use the `-Shared` parameter to create it as a shared mailbox.

The migration tab

Mail migration is a complicated topic that could itself support a small chapter. We'll cover it in `Chapter 5`, *Administering Exchange – Advanced Topics*.

The permissions tab

We'll cover permissions in `Chapter 5`, *Administering Exchange – Advanced Topics*.

The compliance management tab

Much of what's in **compliance management** has been moved to, or is closely related to, items that are in the **Security & Compliance** admin center, so much of this will be covered in more detail in `Chapter 8`, *Understanding Security and Compliance*. Given that, we'll reserve this tab for `Chapter 5`, *Administering Exchange – Advanced Topics*.

The organization tab

The **organization** section includes sharing rules and add-in governance, both of them specific to Exchange. They're fairly straightforward and rarely used, so we will cover them in `Chapter 5`, *Administering Exchange – Advanced Topics*.

The protection tab

Office 365 does a lot of the work of screening spam and phishing attacks for you, especially if you have a license for one of the higher-end security products that Microsoft offers. But for those who want to take their organization's defense into their own hands, particularly for larger companies or companies with a high profile, the functions of the **protection** section can be some of the most important in Exchange. We'll cover this section in Chapter 5, *Administering Exchange – Advanced Topics*.

Advanced threats

Many of you might not have this section available to you at all. Advanced Threat Protection is offered by Microsoft only on tenants where at least one of your accounts has an Enterprise-grade license, so if all you've got is Business Premium and front-line accounts, you won't see this section at all. An E5 license will come with Advanced Threat Protection; the service can be added ad hoc to an E1 or E3 plan for an additional fee, but can't be added to the plans with *Business* in the name, or the front-line workers' plans.

At the moment, the service and the interfaces used to access it are in rapid flux as Microsoft rolls out these protections for SharePoint, OneDrive, and Teams to different tenants. For that reason, and because not all Office 365 tenants have the service, we'll cover it in Chapter 5, *Administering Exchange – Advanced Topics*.

The mail flow tab

The **mail flow** tab is one of the other important areas of Exchange Online; it allows the administrator to shape where mail goes, who it goes (or does not go) to, and to trace it when there are problems.

The rules tab

Most of us are familiar with rules in Microsoft Outlook, such as `forward all mail coming from invoices@myvendor.com to accountspayable@mydomain.com unless the subject message contains 'Re'` or other such algorithms. Many of us keep our mailbox uncluttered (or try to, anyway) and organize mail using such rules.

You can establish rules here on the server as well, but the functionality is somewhat more limited than the rules that users can create for themselves. There are things you can do here that are technically rules, but so commonly performed by administrators that they've actually been given their own entry in a drop-down menu, such as **Apply disclaimers...** or **Generate an incident report when sensitive information is detected...**:

Create a new rule...

Apply rights protection to messages...

Apply disclaimers...

Bypass spam filtering...

Filter messages by size...

Generate an incident report when sensitive information is detected...

Modify messages...

Restrict managers and their direct reports...

Restrict messages by sender or recipient...

Send messages to a moderator...

Send messages and save a copy for review...

Rule creation

Creating a rule

We can edit existing rules with the pen icon, or click on the plus sign to get a drop-down menu of actions we can take, the first of which is **Create a new rule...**. While the other things we can do are also technically rules, they are rules with most of the options pre-programmed, so think of them as rules from templates. **Create a new rule...** is the option that gives us the flexibility to create any sort of rule that Exchange Online will allow:

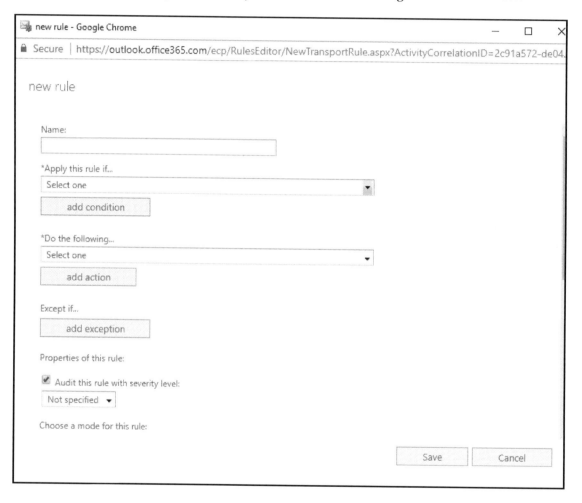

New rule

There are many possible conditions for rules (though, again, not as many as a user has access to for rules in their own mailbox). Rules must be joined by *and* operators; if you need an *or* operator, you'll have to put what belonged behind the *or* operator in a different rule, and you won't have *not* operators at all (although you will have a section for exceptions).

Rule conditions

The top level rule conditions are:

- Sender is/has
- Recipient is/has
- The subject or body is/has
- Any attachment is/has
- Any recipient is/has
- The message is/has
- The sender and the recipient are/have
- The message properties are/have
- A message header is/has

For each of these, there are a group of conditions. They're different for each top-level condition; sender includes **is a member of this group**, **is external/internal**, **address includes any of these words**, **domain is**, and so forth, while the subject or body's conditions include any of these words, **matches these text patterns**, and so on.

Set your conditions. Remember that because there are only and operators, every condition you set will be applied in this rule. So if you say *sender is in my domain* and *subject or body text includes the word* peanut butter, the rule will only apply when the sender is in your organization's domain *and* the words peanut butter appear in the subject or body of the email.

Rule actions

When the rule's conditions have been met, an action is taken:

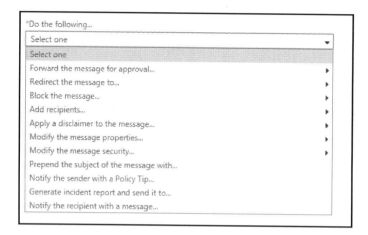

Rule actions

You can take multiple actions as well. Again, they are joined by and operators.

There are exception conditions you can put into place after defining the actions. These negate the rule. So if your rule is looking for the words `peanut butter` in the subject, and will forward to `peanutbutterdirector@yourcompany.com`, but an exception looks for the word `jelly`, then the rule won't apply to an email titled `Peanut butter jelly time!`

In order to enter exception conditions, you'll have to click **More options...** at the bottom of the window. Note that exceptions, unlike rule conditions and rule actions, are joined with `or` statements. So if you have an exception for `jelly` and an exception for `celery`, either the presence of `jelly` or the presence of `celery` in the subject line will negate `peanut butter` and ensure that the rule action isn't taken.

Other rule settings

You can choose to audit the rule with a severity of **Low**, **Medium**, **High**, **Not specified**, or do not audit the rule. Auditing the rule ensures that the rule will appear in reports and message traces; setting the rule to not audit means you will never see any evidence in exchange logs or reports as to whether the rule worked or not, which obviously has strong implications for troubleshooting.

The severity allows you to control whether or not this particular rule shows up in a particular report, as severity is an option you can filter on in reports. The severity **Not specified** shows up as **Low** in reports.

You can enforce the rule, test it with policy tips (a box that appears in the email composition window to warn a user that they appear to be violating the rule), or test it without policy tips. Policy tips are only available for organizations that have data loss prevention licensed (an E3 or E5 license is required).

If you click **More options...** at the bottom of the new rule window, you'll get the following options:

- Activate the rule on a given date
- Deactivate the rule on a given date
- Stop processing more rules after this one
- Defer the message (that is, don't deliver it) if the rule processing doesn't complete
- Match the sender address in the header, the envelope, or the header and envelope

You can also add comments explaining what the rule does. It's a good idea to do that, especially if the rule is complex.

Rules from template

There's a long list of other rules available in the drop-down list; those are special purpose rules from a pre-established template.

In addition to creating a new rule (either from scratch or from template), you can edit a rule, copy a rule, use the up and down arrows to move rules around in the priority list, and click on a drop-down menu to see a report on the use of the rules over various time periods, tracked by received or sent and also by whether the rule severity was **High**, **Medium**, or **Low**.

The message trace tab

A user is complaining that they never got a very important email. Did it end up in their junk mail and they never noticed? Did your spam rules keep it from reaching them? Or perhaps the vendor who was supposed to send it misspelled their email address. To find this out, you'd use **message trace**:

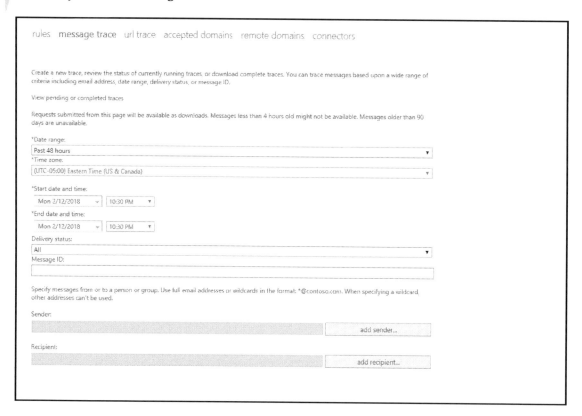

Message trace

You can set a time period for your trace—24 hours, 48 hours (the default), 7 days, or a custom amount. If you choose one of the default time periods, or a custom period of 7 days or less, you don't actually need to pick any other settings.

Your **Time zone** will default to the one set for your tenant, but you can change it if you like. If you picked a custom date range, you can choose a **Start date and time** and an **End date and time**.

Choose the **Delivery status** of the messages you want to look at. You can pick from a number of options, including **All, Delivered, Failed, Quarantined, Expanded**, or others.

You can add the message ID if there's a specific message you're looking for.

You can pick one or multiple email addresses for the sender and/or recipient fields, or a wildcard such as `*@yourdomain.com`. If you use a wild card, you can't use any other email addresses.

Click the button **Include message events and routing details with report** if you need that data.

Choose the **Direction—Inbound, Outbound**, or **All**.

Enter the **Original client IP address** that the email you're looking for originates from or was sent to.

Finally, name your report and put in an email for notification when the report is done.

If your report is for a time period greater than 7 days, you need to specify a message ID, a sender, or a recipient. You can only get the report live (meaning, moments after you click and send directly to your browser) if your time period is 7 days or less. For longer periods of time, it'll go churn in the background and eventually produce a CSV file for you. To see the progress, and download your report, click the link **View pending and completed traces**.

URL trace

These reports are very similar to the ones for message trace, but only users with ATP can access them. You can search based on a URL or a *workload*, which means whether it's mail, an Office client, or some other product. You can also search by message recipient, but not the sender.

Aside from those differences, it's essentially similar enough to **message trace** that we won't cover it in detail here.

The accepted domains tab

The **accepted domains** tab regulates which domains your users can send email from. An authoritative domain is one that is attached to your Office 365 tenant; mail sent from an authoritative domain has to belong to one of your users. If there are no matching usernames, the email will be rejected.

Internal relay is the choice you'll need if some of your users' email addresses aren't known to Office 365, such as if you have a hybrid configuration where some of your users are wholly on-premise.

You can also set a specific domain to be the default, and set a domain to accept all subdomains.

The remote domains tab

The **remote domains** tab alter the properties of mail sent to specific domains outside the company (or, potentially, *all* domains outside the company), to limit the flow of what types of emails can be sent:

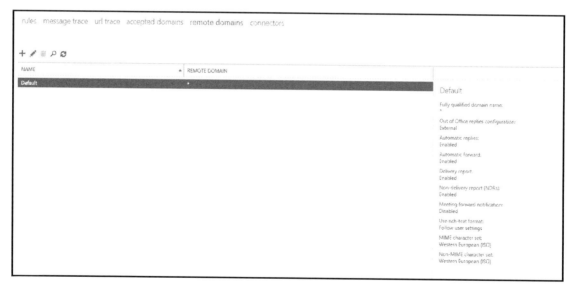

Remote domains

The default remote domain provided with Office 365 is *, applying to all domains but your own. You can edit this domain and also create new remote domain rules:

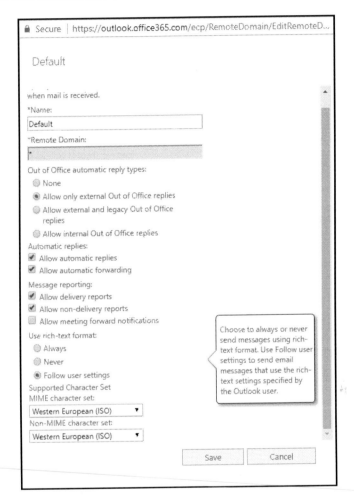

Edit the default remote domains

Settings you can provide for remote domains include:

- What out-of-office reply types are allowed? None, external only, or internal as well?
- Are automatic replies allowed? What about automatic forwarding?
- Are delivery reports allowed? What about non-delivery reports? What about meeting forward notifications?

- Rich text: use it always? Never? Or as specified by the user?
- Which character set is allowed for MIME and for plain text messages. (This setting won't overwrite whatever was specified in the message.)

The connectors tab

Not every organization will need to create a connector. Microsoft has some guidelines for when connectors will need to be made:

- You have Exchange Online only for the email protection services; your actual email is hosted on-premise.
- You have some mailboxes in Exchange Online and some on-premise. You might be better served by a hybrid deployment than a connector, but there are circumstances where a connector could be helpful.
- You need to be able to send email from multifunction devices (printers, scanners, fax machines) or applications.
- You want to implement tight security for email exchanged with a partner organization.

If any of these apply to you, connectors might be the right solution. If not, you can probably skip this section:

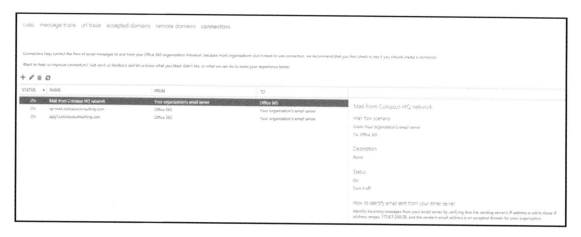

Connectors

If you think you need a connector, go ahead and click the plus sign. You'll be asked to fill out what type of mail server you're connecting from, and what kind you're connecting to. The options for *from* are **Office 365**, **Your organization's email server**, **Partner organization**, and **Internet**. Options for *to* are generally the same but vary depending on what you chose for *from*; if you're connecting from anything other than Office 365, the only *to* option you get is Office 365.

The wizard will further advise you—if you pick a scenario that doesn't need a connector, it won't let you make one. It'll let you know if a connector is optional in a scenario; if it's mandatory, it'll let you know what else might need to be configured.

Whichever option you choose, the wizard will walk you through it. Since connectors aren't usually needed—and when they are it's usually because an on-premise server exists—the details are outside the scope of this book.

The mobile tab

The **Mobile** tab regulates what your users can do with their Exchange connectivity on mobile phones and similar devices. It covers the access that mobile devices have to Exchange, and the policies that will be applied to mobile devices as they access mailboxes. For most users, the default rules are sufficient, so for space considerations, we'll cover these in Chapter 5, *Administering Exchange - Advanced Topics*.

The public folders, unified messaging, and hybrid tabs

These are topics that are outside the scope of this book, but here's a brief description of each:

- Public folders are no longer supported by Outlook 2016. If your company does not already have public folders, we don't recommend that you start using them.
- Unified messaging connects Exchange Online with on-premise communication solutions such as Skype for Business Server or VOIP. Since it's primarily concerned with integrating with on-premise solutions of one type or another, it's not within the scope of this book.

- A hybrid deployment is when your organization's on-premise Exchange server is integrated with Exchange Online, such that some mailboxes are hosted in the cloud and some are on premises. Since this is heavily concerned with on-premise Exchange, it's outside the scope of this book.

Summary

In this chapter, we covered the most important and commonly used features and functions of Exchange Online. As you can see, Exchange Online is a complex enough topic that it could support a book all on its own, but we've at least touched on each of the topics, and drilled down into details of the most important ones.

The most important functions within Exchange Online are **recipients** and **mail flow**. These are also two of the most complex topics, with many subtopics. Every company that uses Exchange Online should have someone on the staff who has a good understanding of how to use these features.

Almost everything that can be done in the Exchange Online's browser interface can also be done in the Exchange Management Shell inside PowerShell, and many tasks can only be performed that way. An administrator who's going to be making heavy use of Exchange would be well served by practicing their PowerShell skills. Good use of scripting can make tasks that would be arduous and lengthy much shorter and simpler.

In the next chapter, we'll cover the advanced Exchange topics we weren't able to address here.

5
Administering Exchange Advanced Topics

In the last chapter, we covered the most common uses of Exchange Online. There are, however, a number of more advanced topics that we lacked space for in a single chapter. Most of these topics won't be needed often by most tenants, and many tenants will not need them at all, but for the sake of the few who will, we've dedicated a chapter to the advanced Exchange Online sections.

Services that Microsoft has already stopped supporting and services that require tying your Exchange Online tenant to an on-premises server are outside the scope of this book and won't be covered, but we'll walk you through everything else. The topics that we'll cover here are:

- Mail migration
- Permissions
- Compliance management
- Organization
- Protection
- Advanced threats
- Mobile

Mail migration

Mail migration is a complicated topic that could support a small chapter by itself. There are four different types of migration into Exchange Online, as well as migration out of it.

A full discussion of migration is outside the scope of this book, because for the most part, by definition, it deals with areas outside of Office 365. We'll briefly touch on the types of migrations, and some of their prerequisites:

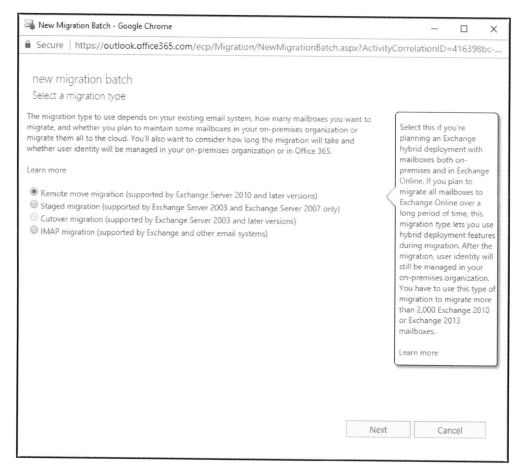

Migration to Exchange Online

Remote move migration

A **remote move migration** moves mail from an on-premises Exchange Server (2010 or higher) to Exchange Online. It can also be used in a hybrid deployment, to move mail between the on-premises Exchange and Exchange Online, in either direction. You'll need to enable the MRS Proxy on the on-premises Exchange Server.

Mailboxes moved in this way are specified in migration batches. You will use a CSV file to identify the specific mailboxes to be moved.

Staged migration

Staged migration is only available to organizations planning to use AD Sync to connect their existing Active Directory to Office 365. It can be used for Exchange 2003 or 2007. You'll need a CSV file of the mailboxes you're moving, as with remote move migration; the wizards in this section will provide you with a template to make one. If you have more than 2,000 mailboxes, this is the migration strategy to use.

If you have Exchange Server 2003 or 2007, but you are not using AD Sync, you'll need to use a cutover migration—unless you have over 2,000 licenses. If that's the case, your situation may be complex enough that you should consult a Microsoft partner for the best way to go forward.

Cutover migration

A **cutover migration** is used when there are fewer than 2,000 mailboxes or AD Sync isn't running, and the Exchange Server version is 2003 or 2007. Cutover migrations move all of your mailboxes at the same time. It isn't necessary to use a CSV file to specify which mailboxes to move; they're all going to move.

IMAP migration

IMAP migration is used when the server you're moving from isn't Exchange at all. You'll need to provide the IMAP settings for the source point and a CSV file of the mailboxes to be moved.

For all migrations, the process is: select the type of migration you want and click **Next**; upload a CSV file if it's required; and choose whether to automatically start or manually start the migration. If you've chosen a manual start, you can come back to it later and start it from the dashboard.

Using the dashboard, you can monitor the progress of your migration and get reports on completed migrations.

Migration from Exchange Online

You can choose to migrate out of Office 365, as well, if you're already set up for a hybrid configuration. Select **Migrate from Exchange** instead of **Migrate to Exchange** when creating your migration batch:

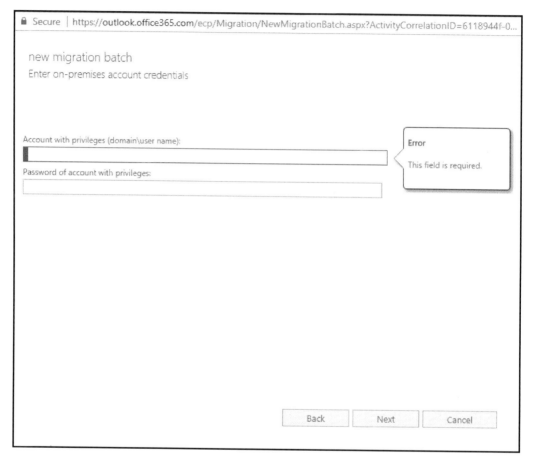

Migration from Exchange Online

You can use a CSV file to specify which users to move, or you can select them by clicking the plus sign, which will show you a pane of all users that you can select from.

More details

Since the full details of how to perform the migration process are outside the scope of this chapter, you should consult Microsoft's documentation for more information. As of this writing, the URL `https://support.microsoft.com/en-us/help/2798131/how-to-migrate-mailbox-data-by-using-the-exchange-admin-center-in-offi` gives a good overview, with jumping-off points to drill down on specific migration pathways.

Permissions

Because there are so many different functions that can be performed within Exchange, Exchange uses the concept of admin roles and admin role groups to ensure that administrators have only the specific permissions they need.

Admin roles

An **admin role** is a permission set, usually specific to a feature, granting rights to administer that feature only:

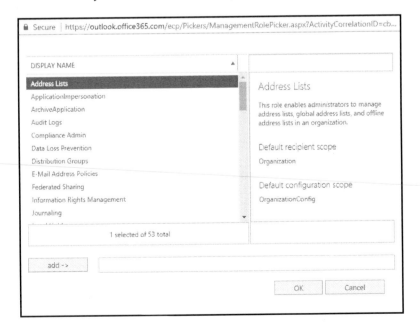

Admin roles

For example, the admin role **Address Lists**, as shown in the screenshot, grants the administrator within that role the right to manage address lists, including global and offline address lists. The role **Data Loss Prevention** lets the admin manage DLP settings.

An admin role group is a collection of admin roles. Administrators are assigned to admin role groups, rather than having specific admin roles assigned to them:

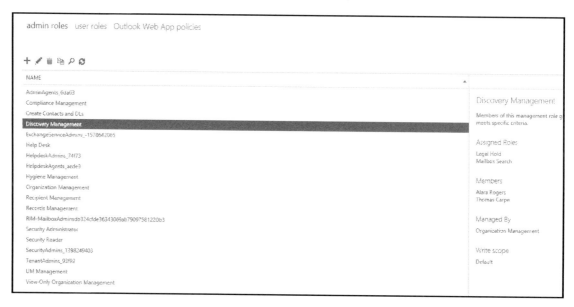

Admin role groups

For example, the admin role group **Discovery Management** contains the admin roles **Legal Hold**, which allows an administrator to configure data retention policies in the context of the **Legal Hold** feature, and **Mailbox Search**, which allows the administrator to search mailboxes within the organization:

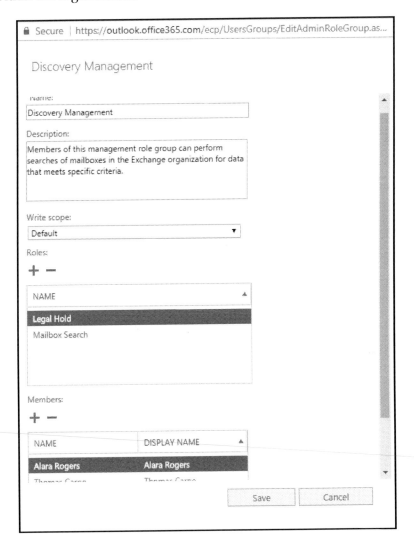

Edit an admin role group

To edit an admin role group, select it, and click on the pen icon. You can add or remove roles from the admin role group, and add or remove members.

The write scope will usually be **Default**, if you haven't added any additional management scopes. Management scopes are a means of limiting the rights you're granting an administrator to a specific defined area or filtered set of criteria, such as a specific OU or a defined list of recipients. You can create a management scope via PowerShell; there's no option to create one within the browser interface.

For example, the following code snippet creates a management scope that only applies to records within the Executives OU of the domain yourdomain.com:

```
New-ManagementScope -Name "Executive Mailboxes" -RecipientRoot
"yourdomain.com/Executives" -RecipientRestrictionFilter {RecipientType -eq
"UserMailbox"}
```

For more details on this cmdlet, you can go to https://docs.microsoft.com/en-us/powershell/module/exchange/role-based-access-control/new-managementscope?view=exchange-ps, where, as of this writing, there's further documentation. Note that Microsoft moves things around, so if you find the link is broken, don't despair; just use your search engine.

Creating a new admin role group uses exactly the same interface as editing one that already exists. Add the name (and a description, if desired), set the scope, add the admin roles, and add usernames to the group.

User roles

Exchange also has user roles, which determine what rights users have to their own mailboxes and make changes such as creating new shared mailboxes or distribution lists:

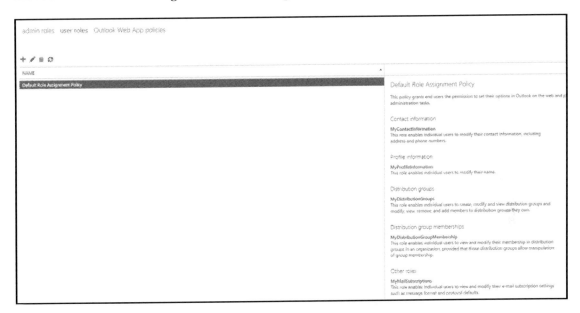

User roles

The default role assignment policy grants users rights to do a number of things, such as edit their own contact information and profile information, create distribution groups and modify the ones they've created, and view and edit things like their voicemail settings, their basic options, their retention policies, their custom and marketplace apps, and so on. The only right that exists which is not provided by the **Default Role Assignment Policy** is My Mailbox Delegation, which allows users to assign the Send on Behalf rights to delegates to their own mailbox:

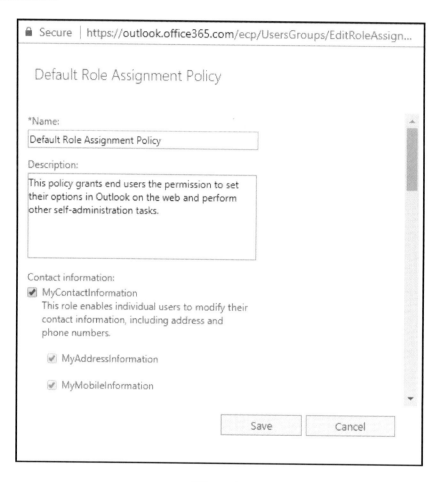

Edit a user role

You can edit the default user role or create a new one. If you create a new one, you can add a user to it by going to **Mailboxes**, then **Mailbox Features**, and changing the drop-down **Role assignment policy**. (See the previous chapter on editing mailboxes.)

Outlook Web Access policies

OWA policies control how users can interact with Outlook in a web browser:

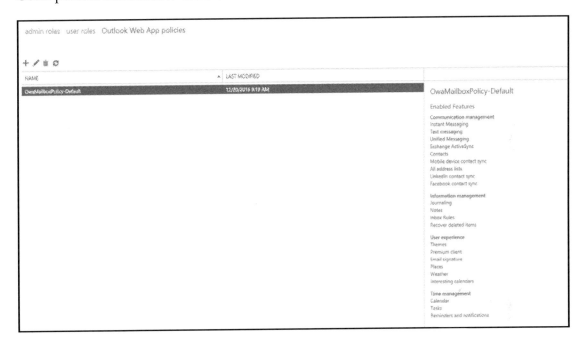

OWA default policy

There will be a default policy applied to your users, where almost all of the options that can be applied to the OWA will be, giving them an experience that's very similar to what they get from Outlook. Options include things such as **Contacts** (use Contacts in OWA), **Inbox Rules** (the user can create rules in OWA), **Time Management** (calendars and reminders work in OWA), and so forth. The two options that are turned off by default are **Places** (shows location suggestions for meetings) and **Local Events** (shows events happening in the area).

If you create a different policy, you can assign it to a user via Mailboxes, but the path is somewhat obscure. Edit the user mailbox and go to **Mailbox Features**. Scroll down to **Email Connectivity**, as shown in the section on editing user mailboxes, and click on **View details** under **Outlook on the web**. It will show you the existing OWA policy for that mailbox. Click **browse**, and you'll have the opportunity to choose a different policy.

If you're planning on doing this in bulk, it will likely be better to use PowerShell. The PowerShell command for changing the mailbox policy on a mailbox is as follows:

```
Set-CASMailbox –Identity {username} –OwaMailboxPolicy:PolicyName
```

In the preceding, the username is in an email format (for example, `user@domain.com`) rather than the display name.

> There are many, many options for the `Set-CASMailbox` command. Currently, Microsoft's documentation is located at `https://docs.microsoft.com/en-us/powershell/module/exchange/client-access/set-casmailbox?view=exchange-ps` covers this cmdlet in more detail.

Compliance management

Much of what's in compliance management has been moved to, or is closely related to, items that are in the Security & Compliance admin center, so much of this will be covered in more detail in a later chapter (`Chapter 8`, *Understanding Security and Compliance*). Given that, we won't go into a tremendous amount of detail here.

In-place eDiscovery and Hold

The **in-place eDiscovery and Hold** feature is scheduled to be moved entirely to **Content search** in **Security & Compliance** later in 2018 or early 2019, and the same functionality is available there now, so we won't cover this one.

Auditing

While **auditing** can also be done in the **Security & Compliance** admin center, it's done differently in Exchange, and the dissimilarities are enough to make it worth addressing here:

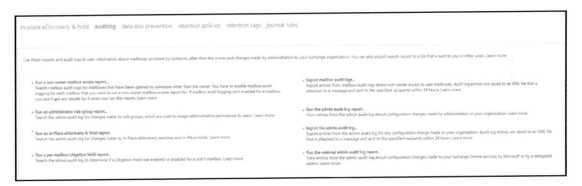

Auditing

On the **auditing** page, there are several links to specific reports, which are pre-built with the appropriate keywords to find the items specified by the report description. Reports include an **administrator role group report**, an **admin audit log report** that tracks changes made by administrators, an **In-Place eDiscovery and Hold report**, a **per-mailbox Litigation Hold report**, and so on.

One of the major differences between auditing in Exchange and in the Security & Compliance admin center is that Exchange audits are limited to matters relating to Exchange: mailboxes and Exchange settings. The Security & Compliance audits can address multiple parts of Office 365, including file and folder audits, SharePoint audits, and so on. See the chapter on Security & Compliance for more details:

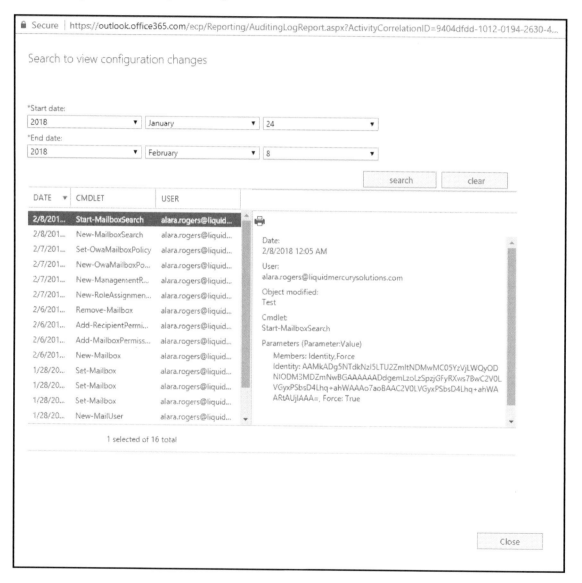

Request an admin audit log

For any report you run, you'll be asked to enter a date range. Many reports also include other parameters, such as mailboxes or admin role groups, but this example, an admin audit log, does not.

This report shows every change made to Exchange by an administrator within the date range I selected (by default, it is about 3 weeks). The nice thing here is that it also shows you the PowerShell cmdlet used, even if you used the web browser interface! So, if you made a change with the browser interface, found it tedious, and would like to automate further changes with scripting, you can generally look up what command corresponds to the change you made.

Data loss prevention

Data loss prevention is a premium product in Office 365, and is only available with E3 and E5 licenses.

As with auditing, data loss prevention policies can be created either here or in the **Security & Compliance** center; if created in that center, they can be applied to SharePoint and OneDrive as well as Exchange, whereas policies created here can only be applied to Exchange:

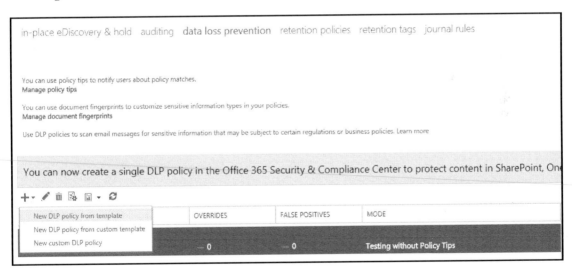

Data Loss Prevention policy creation

There are three types of policy that you can create: from a template, from a custom template, and custom.

A DLP policy created from a template involves choosing a template from a long list. Many countries' laws are reflected in these templates, which cover financial data, medical information, identity keys, and others. The DLP policy will look for data in emails that matches the template, and flag it:

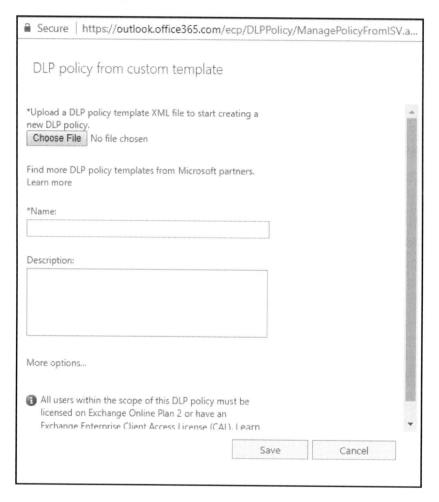

Create a DLP policy from a custom template

If you have an XML file delineating a type of data to look for, you can upload that XML here as a template and use it to create a DLP policy. Some third-party vendors can sell you a custom XML template, as well:

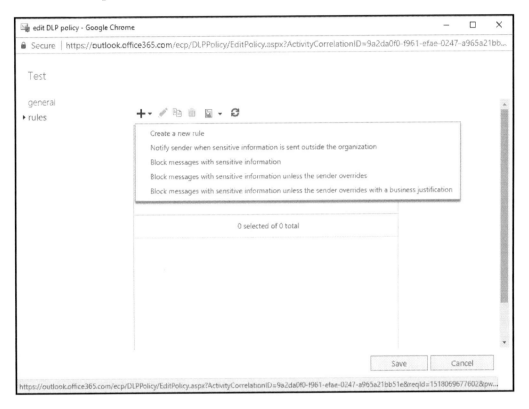

Create a custom DLP policy

Creating a custom DLP policy (as opposed to creating one from a custom template) only allows you to establish the name, the description, whether the policy is enabled or not, and how it should be enforced (enforce it, test it with policy tips, or test it without). You will have to edit the custom DLP policy once it's been created to actually set the rules for what it's looking for.

For more information on this topic and methods to create more inclusive DLP policies that apply across all of your organization's data, see Chapter 8, *Understanding Security and Compliance*.

Retention policies and retention tags

A retention tag is a rule that defines a retention period and an action. A retention period is specified as a number of days, or never, if you intend to allow items to be retained indefinitely. **Actions** include **delete and allow recovery**, **permanently delete**, and **archive**. The location of the archive is the user's archive mailbox; if they don't have one, nothing will happen here:

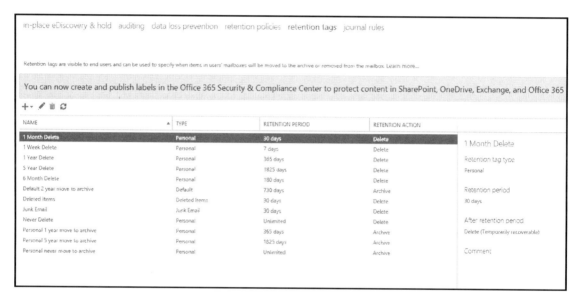

Retention tags

Retention tags can be **Default** (automatically applied to an entire mailbox), **Personal** (applied by users to specific files and folders), or automatically applied to a default folder:

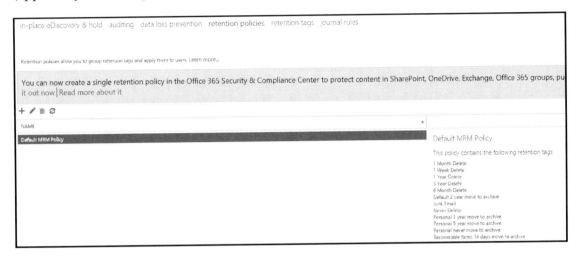

Retention policies

A **retention policy** is a collection of retention tags. These represent all of the available tags that an item assigned to a particular policy can use.

You have a default out-of-the-box retention policy that contains all of the available out-of-the-box tags. You can add new tags on the retention tags page, and then assign them to the default policy, or you can create a new policy in **retention policies** to add them to.

Mailboxes in Exchange can be assigned retention policies via **Mailbox Features**, as discussed previously. To add retention policies to anything other than a mailbox, you should use the Security & Compliance version of the feature.

Journal rules

Journaling is a feature required by some financial and governmental institutions, and other places that require a high degree of accountability and oversight. A journal rule will forward all email coming in that meets certain criteria to a specific email address that you assign, which must be a mail contact outside of your organization. If email to that address is undeliverable, the email will go to the address you specify for undeliverable mail:

Journaling rules

To set up a journal, you need to set up the following things first:

- A mailing address for the journal
- A mail contact or mail user, based on the mailing address for the journal
- A new email account in your organization, or an old account repurposed, to serve as the repository for undeliverable journal mail

There's no point in starting to create a journaling rule without having these things in place already; the process won't let you continue if you don't have them all:

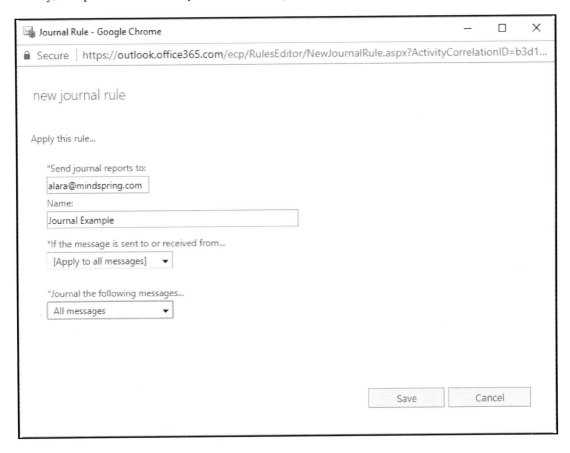

Create a journaling rule

When you create a journal rule, assign **Send journal reports to** to the external email address you have set aside for this. You cannot use an Office 365 account. (Not even one from a different tenant. Microsoft explicitly forbids using an Office 365 account as a repository for journaled mail.) Keep in mind that a typical journaling rule results in very, very high traffic.

You can choose to filter by who the sender or recipient is, or apply the rule to all messages. You can also choose whether to journal internal messages (within your organization), external (to or from the outside of your organization), or both.

The PowerShell to create a journaling rule is as follows:

```
New-JournalRule -Name "Rule Name" -Recipient
optional.name@yourorganization.com -JournalEmailAddress "Mail Contact Name"
-Scope Global -Enabled $True
```

The parameter `-Recipient` establishes a filter by sender or recipient, and will journal all mail sent to or from the specified account. It's optional. `-Scope` is also optional, and controls whether the journaled mail is internal, external, or global (meaning all). Leaving off an optional parameter sets the default to all.

Organization

This section is a bit of a catch-all; these are settings that apply to your entire organization, and don't easily fit in anywhere else.

Sharing

Sharing settings control the sharing of Exchange information (specifically, calendar information such as free/busy, and more detailed information about appointments) with people in other domains:

Sharing settings

You can create a relationship between your organization and another one that will apply to either all of your users, or a specific security group:

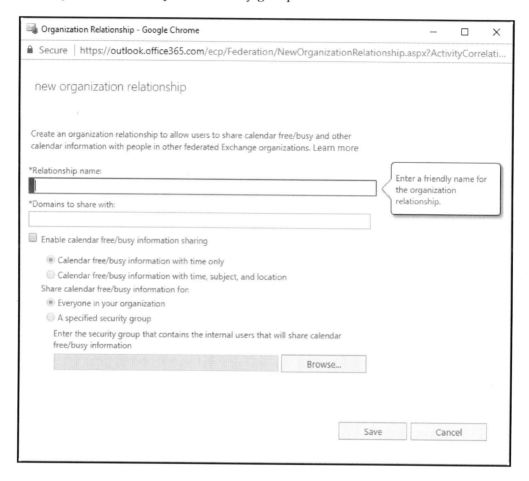

New organization relationship

You can enable the sharing of free/busy information with the time only, or with the subject and location, as well. Limit sharing to a specific security group, or apply it to everyone in your organization.

You can also turn on individual sharing, where individuals have the right to choose to share free/busy information with external organizations as they wish:

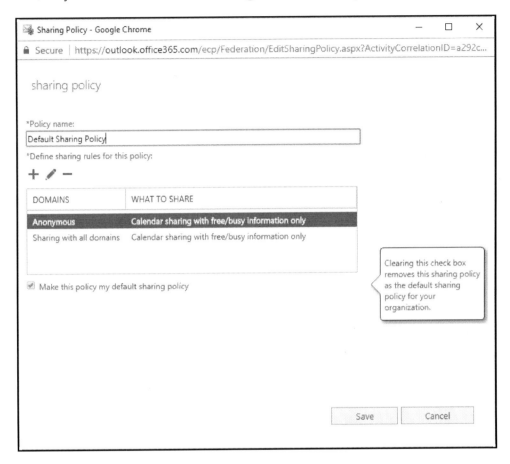

Default sharing policy

You have a default sharing policy with Office 365, with the options **Anonymous** and **Sharing with all domains**, allowing individuals to share with whomever they'd like—but the only things they can share are free/busy information. You can edit the default policy or create a new sharing policy:

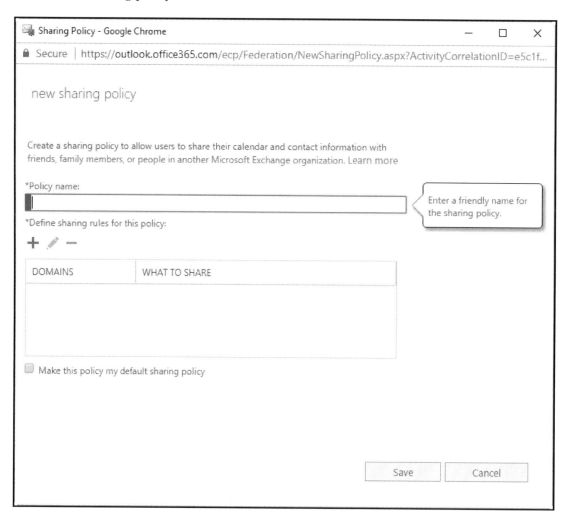

New sharing policy

You can assign new rules to a new sharing policy, or add them to the default policy:

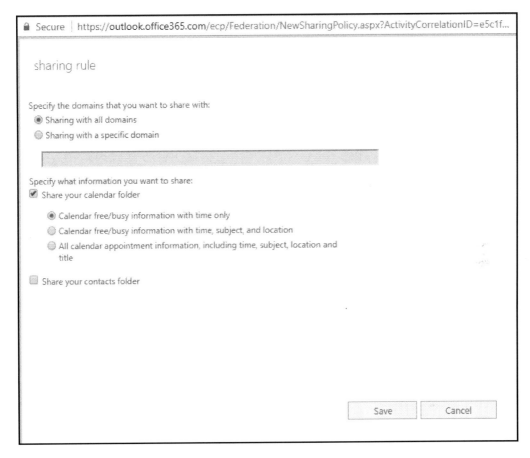

New sharing rule

You can specify sharing with all domains, or a named domain that you choose. You can also allow calendar folders to be shared with free/busy only, free/busy with time, subject, and location, or full appointment information. You can also allow the sharing of a contacts folder.

If you want to create an anonymous sharing policy, add the word **Anonymous** to the **specific domain** box.

A sharing policy is a collection of rules that a user can choose to apply, if they are authorized for that sharing policy. Users can be assigned to only one sharing policy at a time. That is set at the user mailbox level, under **Mailbox features**, as mentioned in the preceding section on mailboxes.

Add-ins

On the add-ins page, you can see what Exchange add-ins are available for your organization, add new ones, and allow users to access them; you can also choose whether all users have the add-in enabled, whether it's enabled by default but they can turn it off, or whether it's disabled by default but they can turn it on.

Protection

For a mid-sized to large enterprise, the functions of the Protection section are some of the most important in Exchange. They can be valuable for smaller companies, as well—particularly, companies that have drawn the attention of malicious actors on the internet, for whatever reason.

Malware filter

Aside from specifying attachments to filter, the malware filter policy mostly pertains to who gets notified if a message is not delivered due to malware being detected:

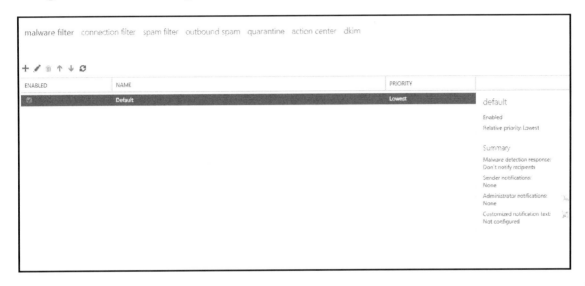

Malware filters

Your Office 365 tenant comes with a default malware filter. This filter does not notify users if their messages have been quarantined, does not filter attachments of any extension, does not notify internal or external senders or administrators if a message goes undelivered due to malware, and does not have any rules regarding who the policy applies to.

You can edit the default malware filter (in which case, you'll use the **settings** tab on the left-hand side, after you've clicked the pen icon to edit, because the **general** tab that you see first only has the ability to edit the name and description), or create a new malware filter:

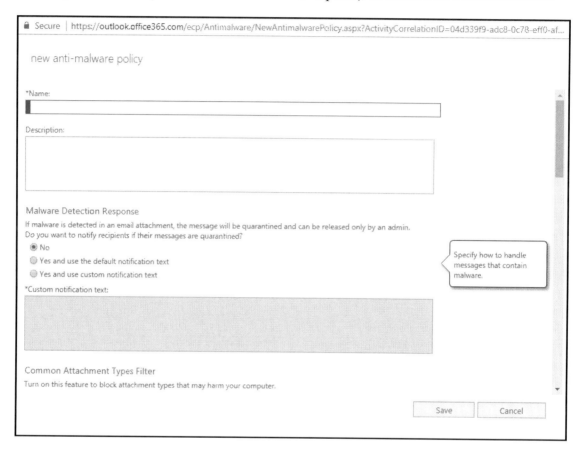

New malware filter

The settings include:

- Notify recipients if their messages were quarantined, using either the default notification text or a custom notification text; or, don't notify them.
- Filter certain attachments, using either the default list that's provided or editing and customizing the list; or, do not filter attachments.

- Notify senders if their messages were not delivered—either internal senders, external senders, or both.
- Notify administrators if messages were undelivered—either from internal senders, external senders, or both; you must specify the email address(es) of the administrators.
- Create customized text for sender and administrator notifications—for internal senders, external senders, or both.
- Add rules to control who this policy applies to, based on the identity of the recipient.

Connection filter

There is only one connection filter; you can edit it, but not create a new one. **Connection filters** are used to whitelist or blacklist IPs from sending to recipients in your organization:

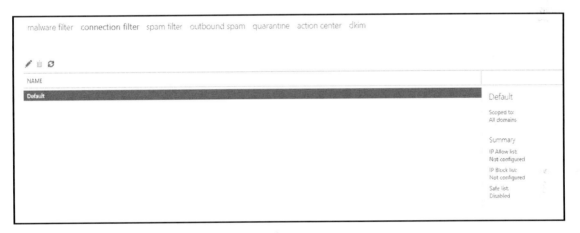

Connection filter

Note that the header for this edit box may say **edit spam filter policy**, not **edit connection filter policy**, but don't be confused. We'll cover the spam filter policy next. The edit box is quite different looking; trust us:

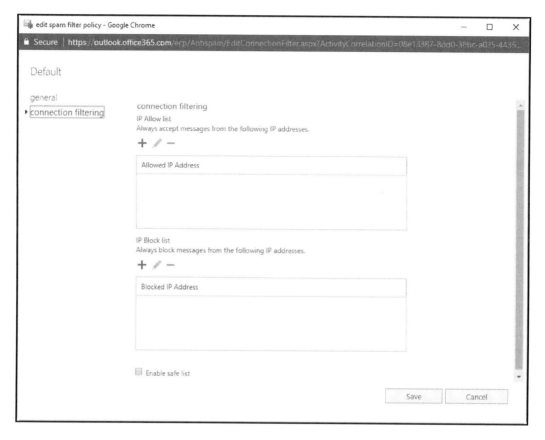

New connection filter

The **general** tab only has the name and description, so use **connection filtering** to change the settings. The connection filter allows you to enter IP addresses for senders that will automatically be accepted (as not being spam), and/or IP addresses for senders that will be blocked. It also allows you to enable the safe list: Microsoft subscribes to a third-party list of trusted senders, and will bypass spam filtering on email coming from those IP addresses if you enable this function.

Spam filter

The **spam filter** is rather more complicated than the connection filter:

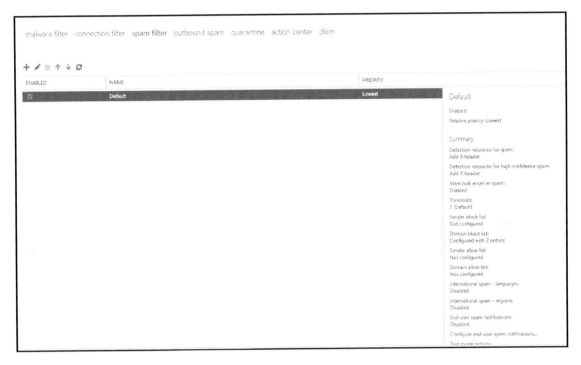

Spam filters

Again, you get a default spam filter with Office 365. As with the malware filter, you can create a new one, or edit the default that you already have.

The default options include:

- Move both ordinary spam and high confidence spam to the `Junk Email` folder.
- Mark bulk email as spam, with a threshold of **7** (**1** allows the most bulk email to be flagged as spam, and **9** allows the most email through).
- The quarantine time period is 15 days.
- No block list defined (a block list is similar to the IP block list in connection filters, but uses specific senders or domains, not IPs).

- No allow list defined (same as with block lists, except performing the opposite action).
- No languages or countries are filtered.
- None of the optional toggles that increase the likelihood of finding spam are turned on.

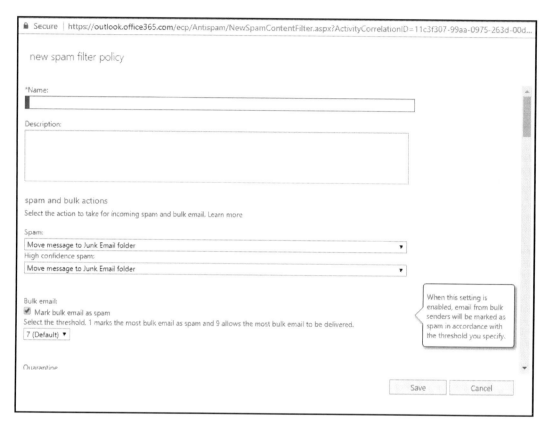

New spam filters

When you create a new spam filter, the options that you can set are as follows:

- **On finding probable spam (marked simply as spam)**: Spam is considered mail that has a score of 5 or 6 (on a scale of -1 to 9; but for some reason, Microsoft doesn't actually use the values of 2, 3, or 4, and allows the user to configure settings for 7 or 8). You can set this value to **Move messages to Junk Email folder**, **Delete message**, **Quarantine message** (and then configure the length of the quarantine in days), **Redirect message to email address** (which you then configure), **Prepend subject line with text** (you then enter the text), or **Add X-header** (and then configure that). The default X-header is, **This message appears to be spam**.

- **On finding high confidence spam (marked as high confidence spam)**: High confidence spam is considered mail that has a score of 7, 8, or 9. The service doesn't give anything the score of 7 or 8, but you can do that yourself with custom transport rules, if you want. This is mail that is almost certainly spam. You have the same options for this type of spam as you do for the type listed above.

- **Bulk email**: Identify the confidence level for bulk email that gets it treated as spam. 1 identifies mail loosely, so it marks the most email as bulk email. **9** identifies mail tightly, so it marks the least email as bulk email. The default setting is **7**. You can choose whether or not identified bulk email is considered to be spam.

- **Block list**: Here, you can set a specific sender, a specific domain, or a specific top-level domain (such as `*.biz` or `*.info`) to be blocked. This is distinct from the connection filter blocking, which works on IP addresses.

- **Allow list**: Here, you can whitelist email from a specific sender, a specific domain, or a specific top-level domain, so that it will come through even if the algorithms identify it as spam.

- **International spam**: Identify email that is written in a specific language, or from a specific country, as spam.

- **Advanced options**: Increase the spam score when the following are present:
  - Image links to remote sites
  - Numeric IP addresses in the URL
  - URL redirecting to a different port
  - URL is a `.biz` or `.info` website

- **Advanced options**: Mark messages as spam if they include the following:
  - Message is empty, has no subject line, and contains no attachment.
  - The HTML contains JavaScript or VBScript (used for running scripts).

- The HTML contains Frame or IFrame tags (used for formatting text and graphics).
- There are object tags in the HTML (used to allow plugins and applications to run in the HTML window).
- There are embed tags in the HTML (allows various data types, such as sound and video, to be included in the email).
- There are form tags in the HTML (used to create web forms; these are often used in phishing attacks and email advertisements).
- There are web bugs in the HTML (tracks whether the message has been read).
- Use Microsoft's sensitive word list.
- SPF record has failed (SPF failure is common in phishing messages).
- Conditional Sender ID filtering has failed (checks for identify spoofing).
- NDR backscatter is positive (messages match the non-delivery report bounce characteristics; it is not necessary to use this if your organization is using Exchange Online Protection).

All of the advanced options have off, on, and test modes. The options for the test mode are as follows:

- None
- Add the default X-header text
- Send a bcc message to an address that you configure

You can also configure rules to determine who the spam policy applies to, based on the identity of the recipient.

There's a setting that isn't present in the **new** or **edit** screen for a spam policy; you must set it on the main screen. When you've clicked on a spam policy to highlight it, in the information about that policy on the right-hand side, there will be a link to **Configure end-user spam notifications**. With this, you can enable the policy's users to receive a notification of all of the email they got that was marked as spam, every X number of days, where you set X.

Outbound spam

The **outbound spam** filter is much simpler. Like the connection filter, there's only one; you can edit it, but you cannot add new ones:

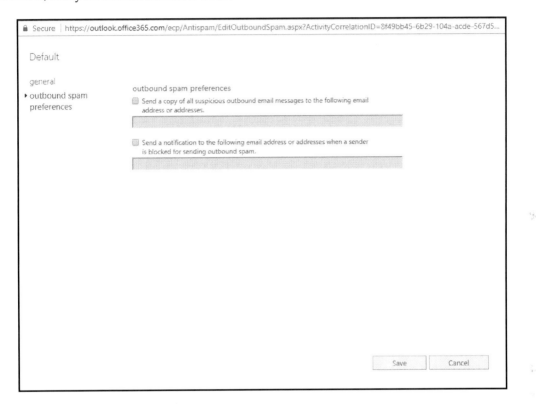

Outbound spam filter

The settings are as follows:

- Send a copy of the outbound email addresses that are found to be suspicious to a specific email address (or addresses) that you provide.
- Send a notification to a specific email address or addresses when a sender is blocked for sending outbound spam.

Quarantine

If you don't have quarantine configured in your spam filter or malware filter, obviously, there won't be any information here.

If a message that one of your users was supposed to receive never arrived, you can check here to see if it ended up in quarantine by mistake:

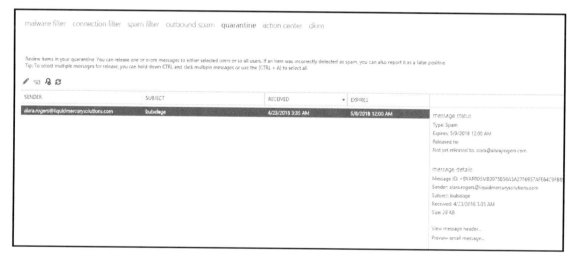

Quarantine

Clicking on the message allows you to choose to release it and report it as a false positive, or release it and unblock the sender. If you decide not to take any action, the message will automatically delete out of quarantine, usually in 7-15 days, depending on the reason it was quarantined:

message status

Type: Spam

Expires: 5/7/2018 8:00 PM

Released to:

Not yet released to: alara@alarajrogers.com

Release to...

Release selected message(s) and report as false positive...

Release selected message and allow sender...

message details

Message ID:
<BYAPR05MB3975B56A5A27F6957AFE64C9FB890@BYAPR05MB3975.namprd05.prod.outlook.com>

Sender: alara.rogers@liquidmercurysolutions.com

Received: 4/22/2018 11:35 PM

Subject: bubelage

Close

Quarantine details

Note that the quarantine in Exchange Online, as of this writing, appears to be partially breaking down; in tenants with Exchange Advanced Threat Protection, which comes with an E5 plan and can be purchased separately with E1 and E3 plans, we were unable to see any quarantined messages in the quarantine section at all. The messages showed up in the **Security & Compliance** center without any trouble. And, in an account without Advanced Threat Protection, we could only see messages quarantined for malware in Security & Compliance; there was no way to view them in quarantine in Exchange Online, though we could still see ones quarantined for spam. So, Microsoft may be in the process of shutting down the quarantine viewing capability in Exchange entirely.

Action center

If a user has been blocked because Microsoft's algorithms have determined that they are sending spam, you can unblock them here, but not indefinitely. There's a limit to the number of times an administrator can do this for a specific user; after a certain point, you will get an error, and will have to contact support.

You can also use the `Get-BlockedSenderAddress` and `Remove-BlockedSenderAddress` cmdlets in PowerShell to bring back information about a given blocked sender address:

```
Get-BlockedSenderAddress –SenderAddress smtpaddress@domain.com
```

And, you can use them to remove the address from blocked senders:

```
Remove-BlockedSenderAddress –SenderAddress smtpaddress@domain.com
```

DKIM

DomainKeys Identified Mail (DKIM) is an authentication process that verifies identities within your domain so that senders and recipients can be protected from phishing attacks and other identity spoofing:

DKIM

All of the domains that you have access to through your tenant will be listed here. You cannot edit or add domains here, but on the right-hand side, when you've highlighted a domain, you'll be given a link to enable DKIM.

If you try to enable DKIM before entering required **CNAME** records, you'll get an error message. Go to DNS and enter two **CNAME** records of the following format:

```
Hostname: selector1._domainkey.yourdomain.com

Target/address/value: selector1-yourdomain-
com._domainkey.yourtenantname.onmicrosoft.com
```

Replace `yourdomain.com` with your actual domain name and suffix, and replace `yourtenantname` with whatever the name of your Office 365 tenant is. Usually, but not always, this is the part of your domain before the suffix.

The second CNAME is just like the first, but with the number 2 instead of the number 1:

```
Hostname: selector2._domainkey.yourdomain.com

Target/address/value: selector2-yourdomain-
com._domainkey.yourtenantname.onmicrosoft.com
```

After this, you can click **Enable**, and DKIM will activate:

Sign messages for this domain with DKIM signatures: Enabled

Disable

Rotates the public and private DKIM keys by creating new keys and using the alternate DKIM selector:

Rotate

Status:
Signing DKIM signatures for this domain.

Last checked on:
2/11/2018 9:41 PM

DKIM enabled

This provides a stronger level of protection for identities within your organization than SPF records, protecting your users from having their identities spoofed.

Advanced threats

Many of you might not have this section available to you at all. Advanced Threat Protection is only offered by Microsoft on tenants where at least one of the accounts has an enterprise-grade license, so if all you have are Business Premium and front-line accounts, you won't see this section. An E5 license will come with Advanced Threat Protection; the service can be added ad hoc to an E1 or E3 plan for an additional fee, but can't be added to plans with Business in the name or front-line workers' plans.

Some of the services offered here apply to your entire organization; protections placed on SharePoint, OneDrive, and Teams will work for any member of your organization, whether they personally have ATP or not. However, email account protections apply only if the user account has ATP activated.

Reports for Advanced Threat Protection appear in the **Security & Compliance** center, so we'll refer to the Chapter 8, *Understanding Security and Compliance* for a discussion of those:

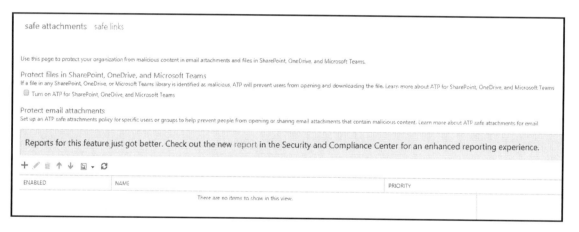

Advanced Threat Protection

Safe attachments

Recently, Microsoft extended the Safe Attachments policies to SharePoint, OneDrive, and Microsoft Teams. You can activate the policy for all of those products by clicking the box labeled **Turn on ATP protection for SharePoint, OneDrive, and Microsoft Teams**.

For policies that pertain to email accounts, you must first create a policy. There isn't one by default, the way there is in other areas:

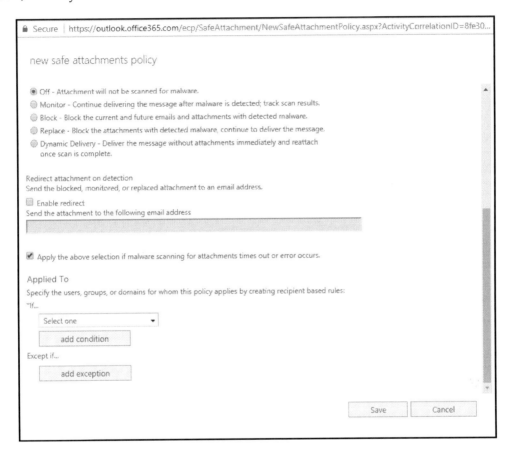

New safe attachments policy

Choose the actions to take if the system identifies unknown malware in an attachment:

- **Off**: The attachments aren't scanned for malware at all.
- **Monitor**: The message will be delivered after malware is detected. Track the scan results.
- **Block**: Block current and future emails and attachments with detected malware.

- **Replace**: Block the attachments with detected malware, but deliver the message.
- **Dynamic Delivery**: Deliver without attachments immediately, and reattach after the scan is over. This option is only available for email accounts hosted in the cloud; if the user's email box is located on-premises, you can't choose this.

Choosing monitor, replace, or block actions might delay email delivery by a good bit, so consider the options carefully.

You can choose to have blocked, monitored, or replaced attachments sent to a specific email address by clicking **Enable redirect** under **Redirect attachment on detection**, and then setting the email address.

You can also choose to have whatever you chose previously applied to timeouts on malware scanning. Finally, you can set rules to choose which users to apply the policy to, based on the recipient's identity.

Regardless of the rules set, the policies can only be applied to users who have the Advanced Threat Protection license.

Safe links

The **safe links** policy scans links present in email and documents in Office products such as Word, Excel, or PowerPoint (and, on Windows machines only, Visio). It blocks users from being able to click through to malicious websites, spoofed websites, and websites that you, as the administrator, have added to a block list.

The way it works is by rewriting URLs on the fly, so that Microsoft can inspect them for malicious content. If there is no such content, the user is smoothly redirected to the original location. If there is potentially suspicious content, the user is redirected to a warning message. Unless you turn on the option that says that they can't do this, users who've reached the warning message page can still go to the site they're being warned about. You can whitelist URLs and domains so that the user can always directly click through to them, and you can block URLs and domains so that even if Microsoft finds no malicious content, the user still gets the warning:

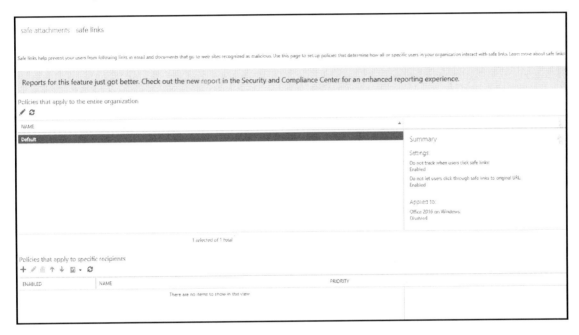

Safe links

Organization policy

For policies that apply to the entire organization, there's only one policy; you can't create a new one, but you can edit it:

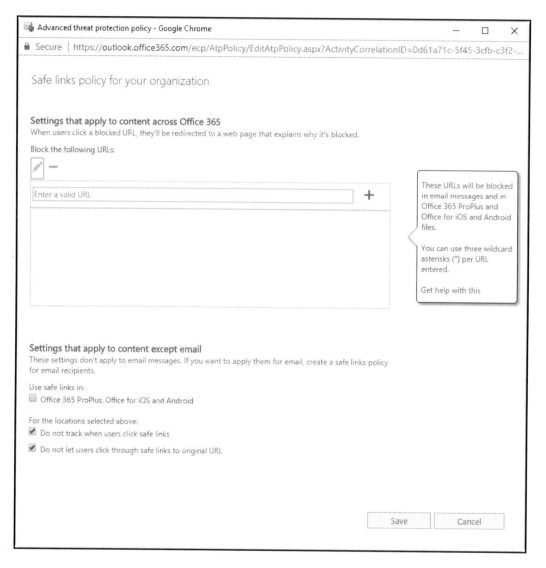

Edit the organization's safe links policy

You can set URLs to block, which will be applied to email, as well. You can also activate safe links in Office 365 desktop/laptop and mobile applications. Determine whether or not you will track when users click safe links, and decide whether users can click through safe links to the original URL.

Specific recipient policy

Specific recipient policies are applied to recipients by rules, but don't forget that they won't apply to any recipient who doesn't have a license for ATP. You don't have one by default, so you'll have to create one to take advantage of the feature:

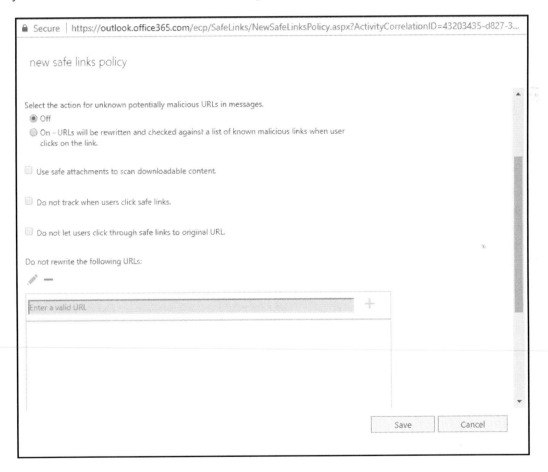

Recipient-based safe links policy

To create a safe links policy, after clicking the plus sign and adding the name and description, you can set the following options:

- Rewrite URLs and have potentially malicious URLs in messages checked against a list of malicious links when the user clicks on them, or keep the feature off.
- If the feature is on:
    - Use safe attachments to scan downloadable content.
    - Don't track it when users click safe links.
    - Don't let users click through the safe link to the original URL.
- Add domains and URLs to your whitelist, the **do not rewrite** list (you can use wildcards, such as `*.packt.com`, or full URLs).
- Set rules to define the recipients that this particular policy applies to.

Mobile

Mobile is the last tab in Exchange that we'll be covering in this chapter. This section regulates what your users can do with their Exchange connectivity on mobile phones and devices.

Mobile device access

In this section, we control the access that mobile devices have to Exchange:

Mobile device access

The first thing that you can set on this page is the **Exchange ActiveSync** policies. Click on the **edit** box to the far right and the following screen appears:

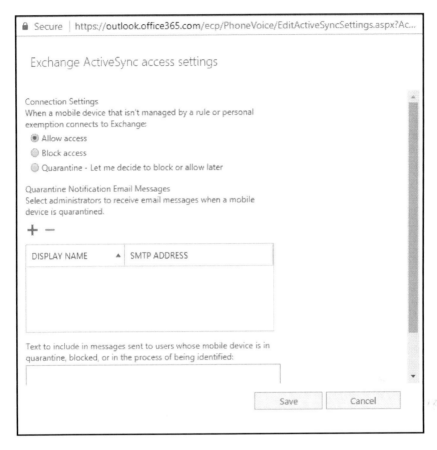

Exchange ActiveSync access settings

Set mobile devices that aren't managed by rules or personal exemptions to be allowed access to Exchange, be denied from accessing Exchange, or be quarantined, for the admin to make the decision later. For quarantines, you need to set the admins who will get email notifications that there's a device in quarantine, and you should provide text for the message to be sent to the users of blocked or quarantined devices.

Directly under that is the quarantine area, where you can review any quarantined devices and choose to allow or block them.

Finally, there are device access rules that you can create. None are provided by default. Choose a device family (based on the applications that access Exchange) and/or a specific model (based on the actual devices that connect to Exchange in your tenant), and set them to be allowed, blocked, or quarantined:

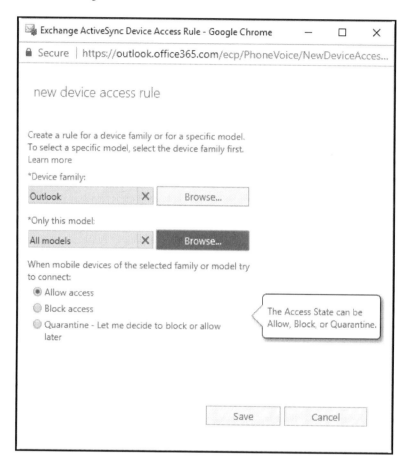

Device access rule

Mobile device mailbox policies

The last tab we will cover manages mobile device mailbox policies. These rules apply to how mobile devices access mailboxes:

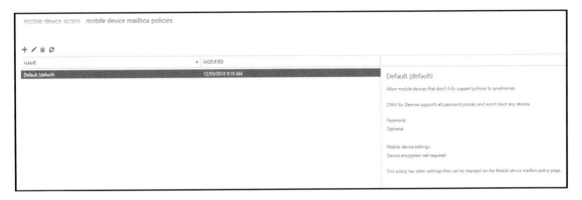

Mobile device mailbox policies

There's a default rule set for you. You can edit the default, or create a new one:

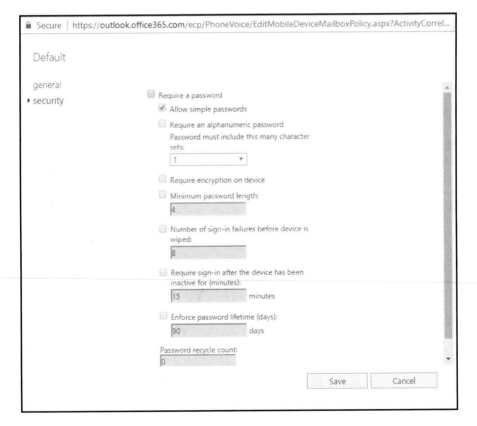

Edit the mobile device mailbox policy

The first setting asks whether mobile devices that don't fully support all of these policies should be allowed to synchronize at all. In your default policy, the answer given to this is **yes**. The rest of the settings pertain to device passwords: Is a password required? Is a simple password allowed, or do you need an alphanumeric one? How complex should it be? How many idle minutes are permitted before the user must log back into their device with their password? And so forth.

The truth is, very few of the security policies that you can establish for mobile devices can be set here. The rest can be set with PowerShell.

 A full description of all settings that can be configured with PowerShell is outside the scope of this book, but as of this writing, Microsoft has an article with all of the details on how to do it at `https://technet.microsoft.com/en-us/library/bb123783(v=exchg.160).aspx`.

Note that when you have multiple mobile device mailbox policies, you can set them per individual user through **Recipients | Mailboxes | Mailbox Features**, using the dropdown for **Mobile Devices** to select the policy you want.

Summary

In this chapter, we covered the topics that most administrators are less likely to use within Exchange Online: mail migration, permissions, compliance management, organization, protection, advanced threats, and mobile.

Next, we'll deal with a part of Office 365 that's even more complex than Exchange: SharePoint.

6
Administering SharePoint Online

SharePoint is a big part of Office 365. As one of the four pillars of Office 365, it is an exceptional tool for the **small- and medium-sized business (SMB)** space. It is also great for nonprofits. It is exceptional because it's so flexible. So many things can be built on one platform. It is one of the most popular tools for intranet, portals, online forms, dashboards, document management, project management, and workflow for the government and enterprise space. They have been using it for years and if you are in, or ever have worked in, one of these areas, you have more than likely used SharePoint even if you didn't know what it was.

In this chapter, we will be looking at administering SharePoint Online in two ways:

- SharePoint admin center
- SharePoint

This topic is super vast, so we are going to go over the most important things you should know about as well as a general overview. We are going to explore the following:

- General overview of SharePoint
- Administering through the SharePoint admin center
- Administering via PowerShell
- Administering via SharePoint Online
- Some words of wisdom

General overview of SharePoint

SharePoint is a Microsoft product based on web technology that enables organizations to create sites, portals, and intranets. On this platform, you can use the **out-of-the-box** **(OOTB)** parts and modify those parts as well as apps available through the SharePoint Store; you have the ability to make custom parts using code.

There are quite a few options available OOTB. There are lists and libraries such as:

- Lists:
    - Tasks
    - Contacts
    - Custom list
    - Links
    - Announcements
    - Calendar
    - Issue tracking
    - Survey
    - Promoted links
    - Discussion board
- Libraries:
    - Document library
    - Picture library
    - Form library
    - Wiki page library
    - Asset library

These lists and libraries come with columns and views out of the box. For example, a tasks list comes with a column for the task name, priority, assigned person, status, description, and so on. You can modify the columns and/or make your own columns. You can pick from columns, such as those shown in the following screenshot:

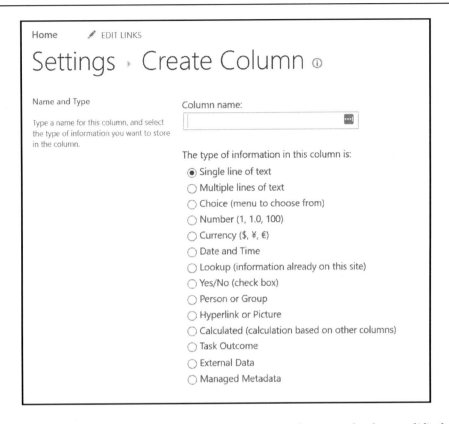

Like columns, lists and libraries come with certain views that can also be modified, and new ones can be created. OOTB, the tasks list comes with views that show all tasks, active tasks, tasks assigned by a person, your own tasks, and so on. All lists and libraries come with one or many spreadsheets like views but some, such as the calendar list, have a view that has a completely different look, like a calendar:

Also available to you are OOTB sites and you have the ability to modify the OOTB sites as well as create your own. These sites come with certain lists and libraries and a home page. Some of the available OOTB sites are:

- Team
- Project
- Collaboration
- Document center
- Records center
- Enterprise search
- Publishing

You can also create new collaboration sites, but creating them is not done in the place where you would create the other sites. You would go to the SharePoint home page and click on **+new site**. You need to be aware that although you see an option for team site, you also need to note that a team site is not the only thing created. An Office 365 group is also created. This may be overkill, so use this option to create a team site only if you really need to. We will discuss Office 365 Groups in `Chapter 7`, *Office 365 Groups and Microsoft Teams Administration*.

If you decide you need to use code in the SharePoint Online environment, you can no longer deploy to the farm. Office 365 is a multi-tenancy environment and SharePoint Online is part of it. Because of this, Microsoft will not allow for code to be deployed at the farm level, just in case your code causes other features to break. You can write code on the client side using JavaScript and jQuery, write more custom apps using C# and the app model, modify some things by writing PowerShell code, and make changes to the master page and page layouts using HTML, CSS, and JavaScript.

Modifying the master and layout pages is still not a best practice. It is actually worse to do so here because Microsoft is constantly pushing out changes to the Office 365 environment which can cause such customizations to break often. We highly suggest using jQuery to change the look, and the design manager. It is also best to keep your designs simple. If that is not possible, we highly suggest a third-party application such as LiveTiles.

Administering via the SharePoint admin center

Now we are going to get into some details. Let's look at administering by way of the SharePoint admin center in Office 365. Again, we are going to look at the parts that you most need to know.

Getting to the SharePoint admin center

In order to get the SharePoint admin center, you must be one of the following:

- Office 365 global administrator
- SharePoint administrator (not to be confused with a SharePoint site collection administrator)
- Microsoft Partner with delegated administrator rights

The first person that sets or sets up the Office 365 tenant for your organization is set as the global admin. This global admin can create other admins such as SharePoint admins or even other global admins.

Admins are created in the **Users** section of the Office 365 admin center. People can also be assigned as an admin later. See Chapter 2, *Using PowerShell to Connect to Office 365 Services* for instructions.

Once you are in the Office 365 admin center, the link to the SharePoint admin center can be found in the left navigation. You can also get there if you know the SharePoint URL for your tenant. You can then add -admin before .sharepoint.com. For example, http://<tenantname>-admin.sharepoint.com.

Managing the site collections

When you first arrive in this admin center, the first thing you see and have the ability to manage is the site collections. At a glance, you can see how many site collections your organization has set up so far:

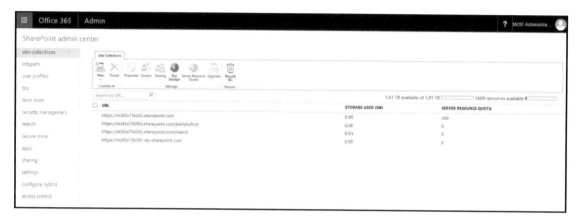

 If your tenant also has licenses for projects then you will see an extra button for project as well as a URL pertaining to that service.

You can also see how much space and server resources you have used versus how much you have left.

Creating new site collections

To create a new site collection, click on the **New** button and choose **Private Site Collection**.

 If your tenant has licenses for projects, you will also see an option for creating a new project site collection. If your tenant was created before 31 January 2017, you may also have the option of creating a new public site collection. Do not use this option. Microsoft is phasing out the use of this type of site collection. If you want/need a public facing site, we suggest using another medium, such as WordPress or Wix. You can get 50% off your first year of a Wix or GoDaddy website by initiating it through your Office 365 admin center under **Resources | Public Website**.

After clicking the **Private Site Collection** option, you get a pop-up form to fill out:

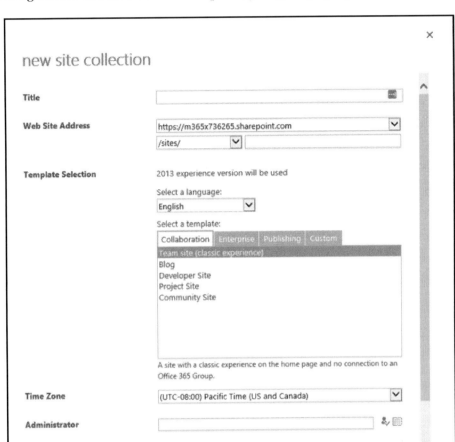

Following are the contents of the form:

- **Title**: Give your new site collection a name. This name should be fairly descriptive. Don't worry about spaces.
- **Web Site Address**: If you have multiple domains, you may be able to have the option to choose a different domain (`<tenantname>.sharepoint.com`) for the first dropdown; however, most organization will only have one. For the second dropdown, you can choose between **/sites/** and **/teams/**. Most use **/sites/**.

In the textbox, put a custom name. It should resemble your title but should not be long and not contain spaces or special characters. Spaces and special characters are translated into strings of characters (one space is %20). For example, if you name your site `Bill's Private Site Collection`, you may make the path ending `/billprivatesc` or better yet `/bpsc`.

The reason for a short path ending is to try to conserve space in the URL. Remember, a URL path in SharePoint is limited to 255 characters, so the shorter the better!

- **Template Selection**: Choose the base type of your site collection.

If you choose any template other than **Team Site (classic experience)**, your templates option for creating subsites will be limited.

- **Time Zone**: Select the time zone in which your organization is based. The staff can select their personal time zone if needed.
- **Administrator**: This will be the main site collection administrator. You can add additional site collection admins in the site collection's **Site Settings** later.
- **Storage Quota**: If your Office 365 tenant was set up recently, your storage may already be set to be automatically managed in the **Settings** section of the SharePoint admin center and this field may be missing. If you want to manage this quota manually, set the setting under **Settings** and the field will appear.
- **Server Resource Quota**: This is the number of resources for the server to use. It defaults to blank (zero) but a higher number will be needed if you are using apps from the SharePoint Store, or a solution that is custom made or from places like CodePlex. If you are using any such add-on solution, we recommend setting this to `300`.

Scroll down to get to the **OK** button.

Deleting site collections

To delete a site collection, choose it by clicking the checkbox next to the site collection you want to delete. The **Delete** button will no longer be grayed out. Click on the **Delete** button to send the site collection to the **Recycle Bin**. The site collection will live in the **Recycle Bin** for 30 days. After that, Microsoft may be able to recover it, but don't count on it:

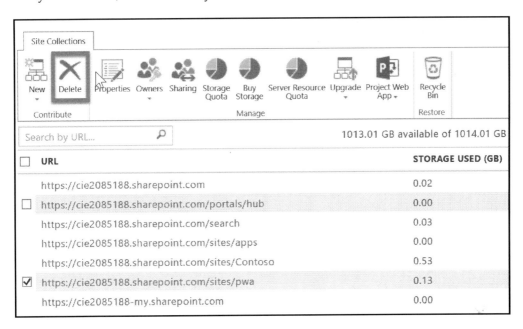

The infopath option

InfoPath is still one of the best ways to create forms that are browser based in SharePoint. You can use InfoPath to create polished and professional looking browser-based forms that can be used for simple data collection but can also perform more complex functions such as reporting, managing dashboard, workflow, and so on.

Depending on how new your tenant is, you may need to turn their use on in this admin center so that these forms can be published to SharePoint and used via the browser. You will need to turn on their use in order to see the InfoPath button on the **LIST** ribbon:

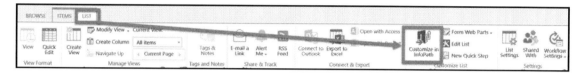

You will also need to turn on their use in order to see the ribbon of SharePoint Designer when modifying a list:

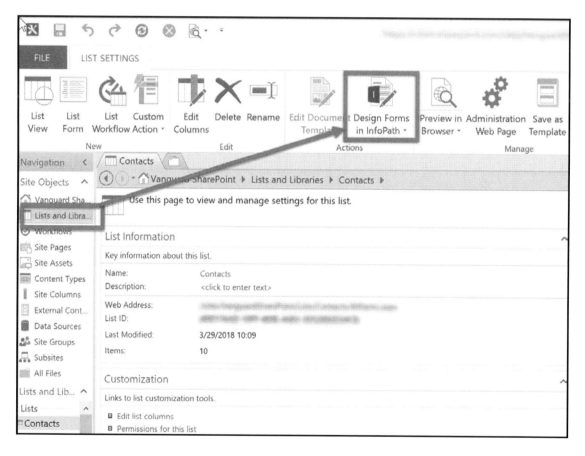

You may have heard that InfoPath is on the chopping block. While that is true, Microsoft has extended the date for deprecation twice. Why? Because InfoPath is prevalent in the enterprise and government spaces. Rest assured that InfoPath will live until a viable and fully capable solution comes about that is as good or better than InfoPath and has a fairly easy migration path, as well as being at the same price point. InfoPath is *free* as InfoPath designer and InfoPath filler came with Office Professional Plus and the filler came with Office Professional. Our money is on Microsoft's PowerApps and Flow but only time will tell.

When enabling the settings, you may see a popup. Microsoft announced in 2015 that they plan to retire InfoPath forms but keep moving the date back. Microsoft is trying to discourage the use of these forms but they can still be used. As of the writing of this book, the date for InfoPath end of support is April 2023 for SharePoint 2013 and 2016 on-premises and until further notice for SharePoint Online. Since government and much of enterprise is moving or has moved to Office 365, we are pretty sure you can use InfoPath for a while to come. This blog will give you details on InfoPath deprecation: `https://blogs.office.com/en-us/2014/01/31/update-on-infopath-and-sharepoint-forms/`.

 Due to Microsoft's intentions, they have not made a new InfoPath since version 2013. If you have Office Professional Plus 2013, you will have InfoPath 2013; however, as soon as your Office is upgraded to 2016, you will lose InfoPath and have to download it separately. You can download it from `https://support.microsoft.com/en-us/help/3114946/may-3--2016--update-for-infopath-2013-kb3114946`.

From the Office 365 home page, click on **Other Installs**.

On the next page, click on **Tools & add-ins** then on **Download and install** under the **InfoPath 2013** header:

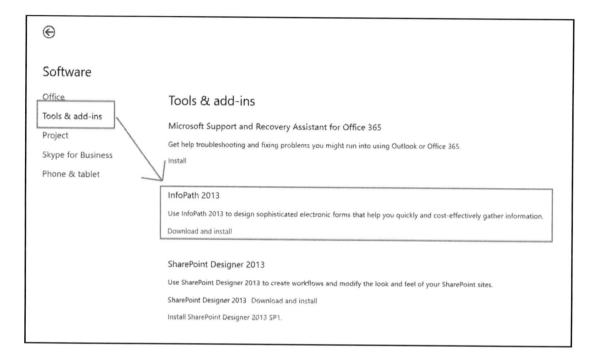

The user profiles option

There may be times where you have an external user who has issues accessing the system and may need to be kicked out then invited back in. This is a very real case where you may need to ensure that they are fully removed from the system and that is where this section will come into play. You would perform the following tasks:

1. In your SharePoint environment, remove that user from the SharePoint permissions groups or items that they received access to. Make sure all instances are deleted.

2. Come to this section in the SharePoint admin center, go to **Manage User Profiles**, then search for the user and delete the user. Make sure all instances are deleted.

You may need to search for the external user in a few different ways (first name then last name, last name then first name, and so on).

3. Go to the Office 365 admin center and delete them from **Users** | **Active users** and delete the external user:

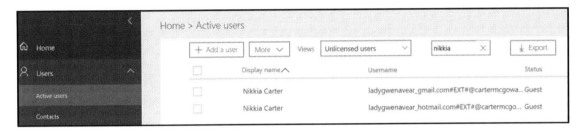

4. Send the external user a new invite from SharePoint.
5. Ask the external user to clear the browser cache and cookies before accepting the invite.
6. Have the external user then accept the invite and bookmark the site for later use.

> An external user may cause an issue requiring these steps if they click on the link in the invite again after initial acceptance. Notify them that they should bookmark the site after accepting and *not* click the link in the invite again.

If the setting in the **sharing** section is set to make sure external users accept using the same email the invite was sent to, make sure you notify that person. You can learn more in the *Sharing* section of this chapter.

Unless you are the administrator for the external user's Office 365 and they are using an Office 365 account to sign in to your SharePoint Online environment, you will *not* be able to manage their password. Make sure that person is aware of this so that they, hopefully, don't come to you later expecting your help.

The sharing option

In SharePoint, there is the ability to share with external people.

 External people are people who do not have an Office 365 license in your organization's tenant.

This can allow for your users to work better with teams consisting of vendors, partners, customers, and so on. This can also lead to a nightmare if not properly controlled. Fortunately, these controls are becoming more granular and Microsoft is hearing the cries from IT. The **sharing** settings in the admin center is one of the newer additions to the set of controls you have available. The following screenshot illustrates what controls are available. Let's walk through them:

The Sharing outside your organization setting

This setting allows you to control how your users can share with external people. While not letting sharing occur with people outside of your organization would be safer, it is not practical in most cases, especially not in today's work environment. Because of this, you can allow your users to share with boundaries.

 If you allow for anonymous access links, we recommend having them expire after a certain time period, which you can set.

Also, you may want to consider changing your **Files** setting (whether or not external users can **view** or **view and edit**) and your **Folders** setting (whether or not external users can **view** or **view, edit, and upload**).

The Who can share outside your organization setting

We recommend this setting if it is feasible in your organization. It allows for greater security in which only a few people will be responsible, as opposed to just allowing everyone to share externally. Of course, you should make sure those people understand their responsibilities and are trained and governed accordingly.

 In order to use this setting, you must first have some security groups. They are created in the Office 365 admin center under **Groups**. You can have either a **Security group** or a **Mail-enabled security group**. We recommend the latter with an email attached to that group, which will allow your other users to email requests directly or via a request system with a workflow. Once you create the group, you may have to wait up to 60 minutes before it becomes available.

The following screenshot shows the options for the **Groups**:

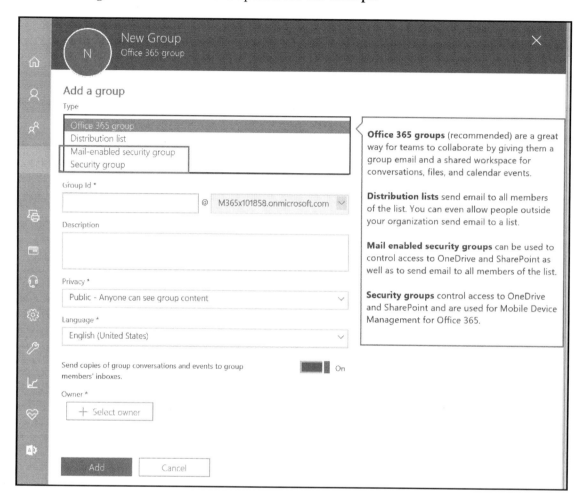

The Default link type setting

This setting sets the link type that is being offered by default to your users when they try to share a link. We recommend starting with the most restrictive: the **Direct - only people who have permission** option. This will help to minimize mistakenly making a link that is more than what's needed.

This doesn't prevent users from switching to a different link type.

The Default link permission setting

This setting sets the link's permission, either **View** or **Edit**, which is being offered by default to the external users. We recommend starting with the most restrictive: the **View** option. This will help to minimize mistakenly sending out a link that is more than what's needed.

The Additional settings option

The first setting gives you the ability to limit sharing with external users via their domain (that is, `abccompany.com`). You can allow or block external sharing from these domains. This can be particularly useful if you only have a certain set of other organizations that you work with and if that list doesn't change often. If the list changes frequently, this setting can become a nuisance:

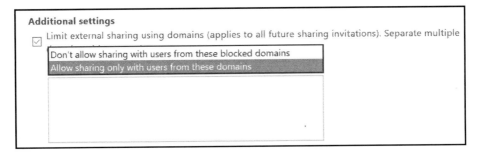

If you add a domain to be blocked, none of your users will be able to share with anyone from that domain.

We recommend setting the next two settings for increased security:

☑ Prevent external users from sharing files, folders, and sites that they don't own

☑ External users must accept sharing invitations using the same account that the invitations were sent to

Note: We automatically selected this setting because you're limiting external sharing using domains.

When users share via anonymous access links, people who receive the link don't need to sign in to access the shared content. Therefore these additional settings don't apply to anonymous access links.

This set of settings does *not* apply to anonymous links.

 The last setting is auto-set for you if you decide to allow or block external sharing with certain domains. We highly recommend checking this setting whether you use the allow/block per domain option or not. This will prevent users from forgetting which email they accepted and will prevent them from accepting with a personal account.

The Notifications settings

These settings are on by default and we recommend turning these settings on if they are not on in your tenant. These notifications for your users in their OneDrive for Business can help them to keep a better handle on the files and folders they share with external users.

The settings option

This is another set of settings that you need to work with when you first set up your tenant and that you will come back to while you are the admin. This set of settings has been here since the beginning but has and will continue to change over time. Let's explore the settings here. This set of settings is pretty extensive, but we will look at all of them.

The Show or Hide Options setting

Change can be overwhelming and sometimes it is necessary to ease your users in by giving them a few options. The **Show or Hide Options** setting can be used to hide the OneDrive for Business and SharePoint tiles so that it doesn't appear on your user's app launcher, also known as *the waffle*. In order to turn off tiles in the waffle, you need to turn off your user's license.

You can do so in the Office 365 admin center (see the following screenshot) or by using PowerShell:

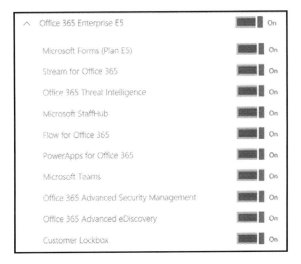

The Site Collection Storage Management setting

We recommend using automatic storage management unless you really need to manage the storage personally.

The OneDrive for Business experience setting

We recommend that you use the new experience. The engine behind OneDrive for Business used to be `groove.exe`. The `groove.exe` engine had a few problems, to say the least. This engine was replaced by the `onedrive.exe` engine which is the backbone for the commercial version of OneDrive. The `onedrive.exe` engine is less problematic. The new experience uses the `onedrive.exe` engine. You may still need to ensure that your users are using the new OneDrive for Business app. If your users have Windows 10, then they already have the new app. If not, they may need to download it from here:

- **Windows:** `https://support.office.com/en-us/article/Get-started-with-the-new-OneDrive-sync-client-in-Windows-615391c4-2bd3-4aae-a42a-858262e42a49m`
- **macOS:** `https://support.office.com/en-us/article/Get-started-with-the-new-OneDrive-sync-client-on-Mac-OS-X-d11b9f29-00bb-4172-be39-997da46f913f`

The SharePoint Lists and Libraries experience setting

Microsoft is starting to modernize the SharePoint platform by adding new modern experiences for pages as well as lists and libraries. If your users already have experience with SharePoint either online or on-premises, you may want to have the lists and libraries use the classic experience:

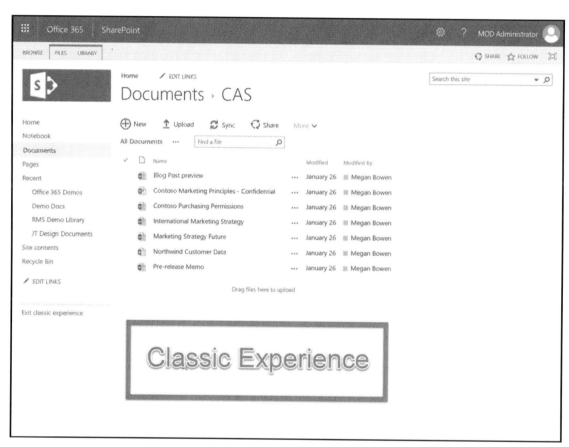

If your users are new to SharePoint, then you may want to use the modern experience:

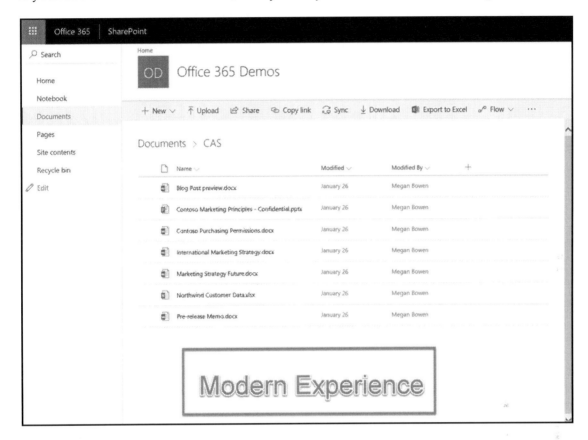

Another option is to set the experience to modern in the SharePoint admin center, then change the experience on a case by case basis by changing the settings for the experience under the **Library Settings** or **List Settings** | **Advanced Settings** (at the bottom of the page):

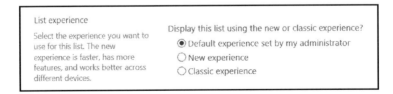

Individual users can also toggle between the experiences using the link on the left navigation when in the list or library.

There are differences between the two experiences that you should be aware of. Since there are no tabs or ribbons in the modern experience, the list or library settings are under the gear icon. Also, in the modern experience, certain types of view shading won't be visible and you can open a list form in InfoPath.

In the classic experience, you can't get to modern features such as Flow, PowerApps, copy to, move to, and so on. Another thing to note is that **Site contents** is also affected by the option:

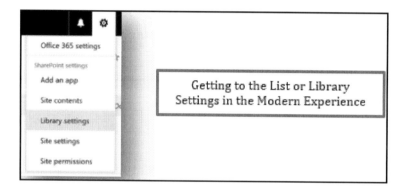

Here is a screenshot of the new, modern look:

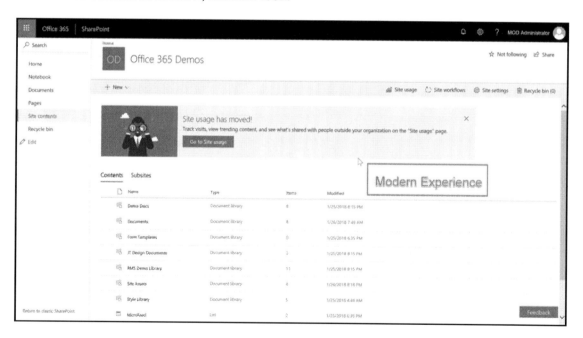

Here is a screenshot of the older, classic look:

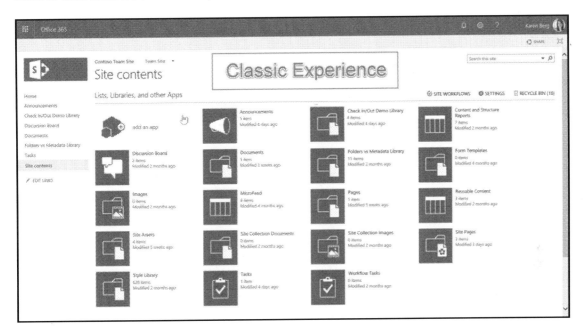

The Admin Center experience setting

The SharePoint admin center has a lot of controls and options, albeit not as many as on-premises SharePoint's central administration. If you find this daunting, you can simplify the options down to the essentials. By default, the setting is on **Use Advanced**:

This setting does not affect any other admin center.

The Office Graph setting

Office Graph is a Microsoft technology that connects everyone in your organization's tenant via relationships between your staff and the objects, such as files, that are related to them. Not allowing use of the Office Graph will remove access to things like Delve and other associated capabilities, such as allowing your developers to write code using Office Graph.

The Enterprise Social Collaboration setting

This type of collaboration is one of the newer ways to work with others. The collaboration platform is similar to others such as Facebook, but it is used for work. Yammer was one of the first platforms for this type of collaboration. Microsoft bought Yammer and integrated it into the Office 365 platform. Newsfeed is a smaller platform that has been offered in Office 365 from the beginning. This setting gives you the option of using a larger platform or a smaller one.

 Yammer is still not currently covered under the Office 365 Trust Center.

The Streaming Video Service setting

Currently, there are two video streaming services in Office 365, the Office 365 Video and Microsoft Stream. The Office 365 Video center was the first to appear in Office 365. It is a place, similar to YouTube, where your organization can post videos and put those videos in channels. This Video space does not count against the 1 TB of space you get in SharePoint and you can use the video web part to display any of the videos in SharePoint. This Video center is only available for those with an Office 365 tenant.

Microsoft Stream is Microsoft's newest platform for video and is similar to the Office 365 Video center. The technology behind this center is more advanced, allowing for capabilities such as automatic facial recognition and transcription of video, and it is available for those with an Office 365 tenant as well as those without.

Currently, both of these centers are separate services and are available in Office 365 tenants, but Microsoft plans to transition the Office 365 Video center into Microsoft Stream. For more details, see `https://stream.microsoft.com/en-us/documentation/stream-migrate-from-o365/`.

This setting controls whether these services will be available in your tenant. When turned off, the tiles will also be removed from the app launcher.

The Site Pages setting

In versions of SharePoint that didn't offer a modern experience, SharePoint users with full control and above could only create web part pages and Wiki pages. With the advent of the modern experience came the ability to use the authoring canvas. With this setting, you can give those users the ability to create site pages using the authoring canvas, otherwise known as modern pages:

The Global Experience Version Settings setting

When Office 365 first became available, the version of SharePoint was 2010. Shortly after the 2013 version of SharePoint became available, it became available in Office 365 and this setting became available. This setting allowed the SharePoint admin to create SharePoint 2010 and/or 2013 version site collections. This setting is currently grayed out so that only the SharePoint 2013 version can be created (and all 2010 versions have since been rolled over to the 2013 version). It is unclear if this setting will become active again or if it will just disappear. Time will tell.

The Information Rights Management (IRM) setting

The **Information Rights Management (IRM)** setting is a way to manage what your users can do with files from SharePoint. With IRM, they could be prevented from printing, copying text, and from uploading documents to the library that aren't protected by IRM. Although IRM works at the list or library level, this setting must be turned on in the SharePoint admin center in order to use it at that level.

The Site Creation setting

This setting allows or prevents use of the **+ Create site** button on the SharePoint home page. By clicking that button, users who can create sites will have the ability to create a **Communication site** or **Team site**. Communication sites created this way will be a separate site collection and will be visible in the **site collections** section of the SharePoint admin center:

This setting also allows for you to set if you want those users to be able to create the team site, communication site, and/or a classic site. The last three other options set whether the site collection created will have **/sites/** or **/teams/** as part of the URL (as in `mycompany.sharepoint.com/sites/newsitecollection`), whether a secondary contact will need to be listed when the site is created, and can also give those users the ability to create sites based on a custom site template (using the form at this URL). The link to the form/site template can be absolute or relative:

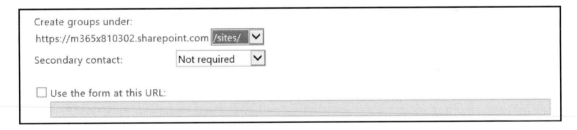

Creating a team site via the **+ Create site** button does not create a traditional SharePoint team site, as you may think. It actually creates an Office 365 group which also creates a special SharePoint team site. If you want to create a traditional SharePoint team site, do not use this option.

Also, team sites created this way will be separate site collections but they will *not* be visible in the **site collections** section of the SharePoint admin center. Since Office 365 Groups were created based on the Exchange distribution lists, they will be visible in the **Groups** section of the Office 365 admin center.

The Subsite Creation setting

When an Office 365 group is created, a corresponding SharePoint site is created. This setting can be used to allow or prevent the creation of subsites under the Office 365 group's corresponding SharePoint site.

The Custom Script setting

When you first set up your tenant, we would highly recommend allowing for custom scripts. If you do not have custom script allowed, you may encounter weird issues that don't seem to be related to this setting at all, such as problems with created project sites. It can take up to 24 hours before this setting becomes active. Trust us, make sure this is enabled.

The Preview Features setting

You can allow your users to see and try any of the features that become available as a preview. Because these features are a preview and not general availability, they may not meet the service level requirements and may not be supported if you need tech support.

Learn more here: `https://support.office.com/en-us/article/Enable-or-disable-preview-features-in-SharePoint-88c69842-7eba-4372-953f-e4cff5818b88?ui=en-USrs=en-USad=US`.

This is an all or nothing setting, unlike the setting in Office 365 admin center that allows you to set a certain subset of people to be able to see and use preview features. Use with caution.

The Connected Services setting

The only service that you have the ability to block is the ability to create SharePoint 2013 workflow currently.

 This *does not* prevent the creation of SharePoint 2010 workflows, which can still be created in the SharePoint 2013 version.

The Access apps setting

We highly recommend turning **Access apps** off or preventing new ones if some are already being used in your SharePoint environment. Microsoft has announced that **Access apps** are being discontinued and that they will be completely shut down as a service by April 2018. If you do have some currently, we recommend migrating to a different solution as soon as possible.

 Microsoft's announcement of discontinuing the use of **Access apps** in SharePoint Online was abrupt, albeit not wholly unexpected. Access was meant to be a low-cost way for individuals and small organizations to create databases, but due to the current availability of low-cost SharePoint Online and the free version of SQL Server, it is not surprising that access is being phased out. If you are using access, we also highly recommend migrating those solutions as well.

The Mobile Push Notifications – OneDrive for Business setting

We recommend allowing push notification to your users especially if they are using the OneDrive for Business mobile app. If they are not, suggest that they get it, unless you have some policy against it, of course.

The Mobile Push Notifications – SharePoint setting

We recommend allowing push notification to your users especially if they are using the SharePoint mobile app. If they are not, suggest that they get it, unless you have some policy against it, of course.

The Comment on Site Pages setting

This setting allows or prevents users with Contribute permission, at the least, to access your site's pages to leave comments:

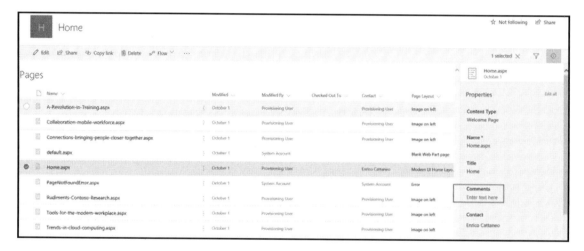

The access control option

Most organizations allow their users' mobile devices to access the organizational system. This can help your users work better when they are remote or mobile. This is something we believe should be encouraged, but we also believe and highly recommend that you, as the admin, and your organization should secure your data. In this section of the SharePoint admin center, you can set some of the settings needed. This is a fairly new section; expect it to evolve over time:

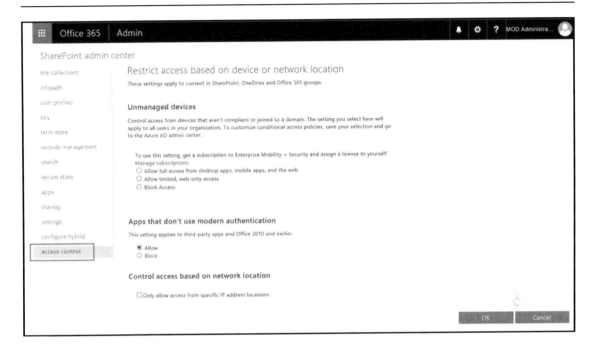

Administering via PowerShell

If you are good at coding and/or scripting, you may want to give PowerShell a try. It can make some of your tasks easier and quicker. In order to use PowerShell in the SharePoint Online environment, you will need to download SharePoint Online Management Shell. You can download it from here: `https://www.microsoft.com/en-us/download/details.aspx?id=35588`.

 Make sure you download the bit version, 64- or 32-bit, that matches the Office bit version on the computer you are downloading it to. Most people have 32-bit Office, whether they have a 64-bit machine or a 32-bit one.

Once downloaded, search for it on your computer, then click on it and the console will open:

```
SharePoint Online Management Shell                                       —    □    ×
Cannot load PSReadline module.  Console is running without PSReadline.
PS C:\windows\system32>
```

You may notice that PSReadline is not loaded. We recommend that you load it. Go to GitHub here to do so: `https://github.com/lzybkr/PSReadLine`. You may also need to allow for scripting in order to execute the script. See this PowerShell documentation for more details: `https://docs.microsoft.com/en-us/powershell/module/Microsoft.PowerShell.Security/Set-ExecutionPolicy?view=powershell-5.1`.

In order to connect to your SharePoint Online environment, you will need to run the following script (make sure you replace the text inside the quotes with `$adminUPN`, and `$orgName` with your details and your organization details):

```
$adminUPN="<the full email address of a SharePoint administrator account,
example: jdoe@contosotoycompany.onmicrosoft.com>"

$orgName="<name of your Office 365 organization, example:
contosotoycompany>"

$userCredential = Get-Credential -UserName $adminUPN -Message "Type the
password."

Connect-SPOService -Url https://$orgName-admin.sharepoint.com -Credential
$userCredential
```

Here is a listing of some of the commands you may want to get acquainted with: `https://technet.microsoft.com/en-us/library/fp161364.aspx`.

To learn more about how to use each of these commands more thoroughly, do a Bing search to get the syntax. We know what you may be thinking: *Bing, really*? Yes, Bing is actually better at searching for Microsoft stuff. Go figure!

For ease of use, you may want to put all of the needed lines of code shown previously into a file using Notepad, WordPad, Notepad++, or your favorite editor, then save the file as `<filename>.ps1`. Once saved, change the directory to that location in the console (that is, `cd C:\myscript.ps1`) and then run it by typing `.\<filename>.ps1` (that is, `.\myscript.ps1`).

Administering SharePoint Online via SharePoint

In order to administer SharePoint, it is also very important that you know how to administer the user permissions to ensure users have access to what they need access to and can't access what they should be accessing. Permissions can be a difficult concept to grasp and, just to make things more interesting, permissions in your SharePoint will evolve over time. It is imperative that you and your fellow admins have a good understanding of permissions and the best practices to prevent this from becoming a nightmare to manage.

Permission levels and groups

Permission levels are collections of permissions that allow users to perform a set of related tasks (that is, the read permission level includes the ability to view items, open items, and download items, but not upload them back, view pages, and view versions). Each of the permissions can be included in more than one permission level.

It is best practice to assign individual users to groups, then assign appropriate permissions to groups depending on where the group is being used and what level of access they should have there. A group is a set of users that are defined at the site collection level.

You must consider a user's group membership carefully because a user's permissions determines what that user will have access to. Always assign the least amount of permissions a user can use to do their job and try not to have a user assigned to an element with two different permissions. The higher permission will trump the lower.

Here is a list of permission levels, straight from SharePoint:

To get to this, you will need to be a site collection admin. Go to the gear, then **Site Settings**, and make sure you are at the top of the site collection. You will know you are at the top because you will see a lot of options under **Site Collection Administration**. Click **Site permissions** under the **Users and Permissions** section.

 If you see **Go to top level site settings** under **Site Collection Administration**, click the link and it will take you to the top.

On the **PERMISSIONS** ribbon, in the **Manage** section, click on **Permission Levels**:

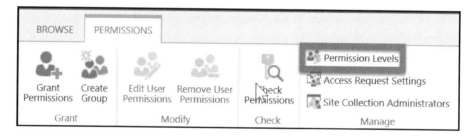

Roles and responsibilities

Here are the default roles and a description of what they can do:

- **SharePoint administrators**:
  - Full control permission over the SharePoint admin center.

- The SharePoint admin has control over everything in that admin center. They can do everything previously explained in this chapter. This admin may not have the ability to access all site collections by default *but* they have the power to add themselves as the site collection admin at any time and they can add others to any site collection as well.

- **Site collection administrators (SCAs)**:
    - Full control permission level for the entire site collection(s).
    - SCAs can access content in all sites and elements in the site collection(s) they are assigned to. They can add users to the site collection they are assigned to and all subsites and elements within the site collection; they can also perform administrative and auditing tasks relevant to their assigned site collection(s). Their power is all or nothing, meaning they are either an SCA for the site collection(s) or they are not. If they are, SCAs *cannot* be kept out of anything in the site collection(s).

- **Owners**:
    - By default, members of the owners group have the full control permission level in the site they are assigned to.
    - They can add users and perform any administrative tasks relevant to their site and any site below, except where inheritance was broken *and* their access removed or demoted.

 A user who creates a site under a top-level site automatically becomes a site owner for that site.

- **Members**:
    - By default, members of the members group have the contribute permission level.
    - At the site level, they can only add, edit, and delete items in existing lists and document libraries, as well as work with web parts, but they can't make new site elements.

- **Visitors**:
    - By default, members of the visitors group have the read permission level.
    - They can only view pages, list items, and documents. They can also download files but can't upload them back.

In the case of the admins and owners, most especially the SharePoint admin, it is best practice to have more than one.

When adding, modifying, and deleting user permissions, you can add users in two ways:

- To groups
- Individually

 Giving permissions to users in this manner is not best practice and we do not recommend doing this, but understand that there is an exception to every rule. Choose this option very carefully.

Some words of wisdom

There is so much more that we can dig into here, but alas, if we did, this book would be horribly long! We will leave you here with a few words of wisdom from hard-learned lessons, so take heed:

- Remember **Keep It Simple SharePoint (K.I.S.S.)** admin. When managing permissions, we highly recommend keeping your permission structure as simple and as flat as possible.
- Notate and update. Notate (*and keep updated)* your permissions structure somewhere, preferably in a SharePoint admin or developer site or list, with permission such that only the other admins and/or developers can access and update it. Creating this type of site would be great for other things, such as keeping versions of your InfoPath form, code, design documents, and other stuff that will help you (and those that follow you and work with you) in the know. You can save your permissions structure as a spreadsheet, but using a SharePoint list would be even better.
- Permissions everywhere is *not* good. Although you can put permissions on everything in SharePoint from the site collections all the way down to individual items and files, don't! Just because you can doesn't mean you should. That will create a serious nightmare down the road. Use with caution.

- Owners, members, and visitors are so early 2000s. Currently, groups named with traditional owners, members, and visitors are no longer best practice as they make you think owners equals full control, members equals contribute, and visitors equals read when that may not be (and more than likely is not) the case. Instead, use role-based names, for example, finance team or leadership. We realize this is a really generic example but if you think about those finance people, you can probably already think of the places they should have access to and at what level. In the case of leadership, it gives those leaders a warm and fuzzy feeling, while you, as the admin, can give them access that is safe for their skill level.

- Learn in layers. Start from the end user perspective, then from a power user perspective, so that you understand things from a user perspective.

- Stay in the know. Technology changes are rapid and speeding up. Try to read and learn as much as you can. Learn to roll with the punches or be knocked out by them.

- Understand the business side. Know the processes and the reasons why things are done. This makes you more valuable and you will be able to suggest changes that make sense for your organization.

- Understand your users and why people are doing what they are doing. Try to develop things that will make their lives easier.

- Don't forget about governance, user training, and user adoption. These are the keys to making sure everyone knows the rules. Some think if you build it they will come, but they may not if they don't understand it or like it at first. And if they do come, they will make a supreme mess, and quickly, if not governed properly and shown how to do things. Explain why SharePoint will help them and why they should do it a certain way. Your leadership should drive the use of SharePoint from the top, but it should also be driven from the bottom.

In the SharePoint community, there are lots of gurus who have been there and done that. Here are a few names; there are many more where these came from. Feel free to give them or us a shout:

- Marc Andersen
- Susan Hanley
- Todd Klindt
- Jeremy Thake
- Andrew Connell
- Laura Rogers
- Fabian Williams

- Erica Toelle
- Matthew J. Bailey
- Benjamin Naulin
- Naomi Moneypenny
- Christian Buckley
- Gina Montgomery
- Swetha Sankaran
- And don't forget us, Nikkia Carter, Alara Rogers, and Thomas Carpe

You can learn a lot from these people and you should look them, and us, up. Keep in mind that even those of us who have been around the block a few times could learn something new, especially since SharePoint is so vast and constantly evolving. If you learn something new, even if it is a new twist on something *old*, share! Blog on your own blog, as a guest in a community, or on another techie's blog. Do a write-up in the tech community or speak at a SharePoint user group. Here is a list of a few communities and events you should check out for starters (most are free):

- `https://collab365.community/`
- Collab365 Global Conference
- SharePoint Fest
- SharePoint Saturday (`http://www.spsevents.org/`)
- Microsoft Ignite
- `https://www.meetup.com/` (search for SharePoint user groups in your area)

Don't be shy. We would love to have you join us!

Summary

In this chapter, we looked at the SharePoint admin center and the settings that you should be most aware of. Due to the vastness of SharePoint administration and the options available to you, we gave you an overview and focused on the areas that most SharePoint admins focus on.

In the next chapter, we will dive in by looking at the administering of Office 365 Groups and Microsoft Teams.

7
Office 365 Groups and Microsoft Teams Administration

Office 365 Groups was introduced by Microsoft in 2014; in 2016, Microsoft made Microsoft Teams available. Both have attracted user attention and are now being used more and more.

In this chapter, we will be looking at how to administer Office 365 Groups and Microsoft Teams. We are going to explore the following topics:

- An overview of Microsoft Teams and Office 365 Groups
- Things to keep in mind
- Administering Office 365 Groups via Office 365
- Administering Microsoft Teams via Office 365
- Administering via PowerShell

An overview of Microsoft Teams and Office 365 Groups

Office 365 Groups and Microsoft Teams are both collaborative spaces, like **SharePoint Online (SPO)**, but they are not highly configurable. You can add some connectors and apps to both applications but that is the extent of their configurability. This can be an advantage if you want to quickly set up a place to manage projects but don't want to devote, or don't have, the time to set up a full SharePoint site. When either Office 365 Groups or Microsoft Teams is set up, a SharePoint site is also set up automatically for a little bit of extra magic.

Teams and Groups seem to be very similar on the surface but Microsoft actually took a different approach with each when their respective technologies were developed.

Inside Office 365 Groups

Office 365 Groups is based on Exchange technology—the email distribution list, to be exact. When one is created, a distribution list is created as well as a place for **Files**, a **Calendar**, a Planner, and a OneNote **Notebook**. Since Groups is based on the distribution list, members can email a group using the distribution or by posting to the **Conversations** board, as shown in the following screenshot:

With Office 365 Groups, you can also add on **Connectors**, such as to Twitter and MailChimp, in order to expand the groups' capabilities. Office 365 Groups can be public (seen even by those with no permission to access them) or private, and members can also be managed by Office 365 admins and group owners. Members can be internal or external to an organization.

Microsoft Teams

Microsoft Teams is a collaboration platform with which Skype for Business is scheduled to be integrated. When a team is created, a **Conversations** board is too, as well as a place for **Files**, **Planner**, and a **Wiki**, as shown in the following screenshot:

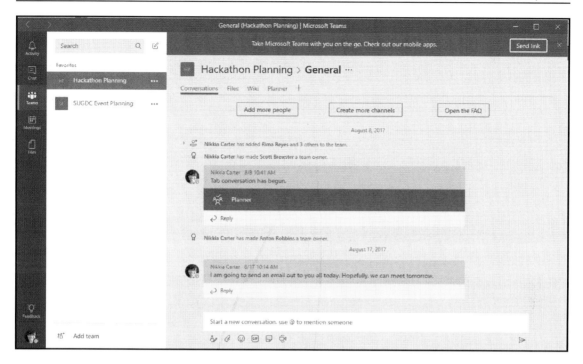

Additional apps can be added to Microsoft Teams, such as a **OneNote** notebook, a **Calendar**, and Hootsuite. Since it is based on Skype for Business, and not on the distribution list as Office 365 Groups is, members cannot email the group using the distribution; however, conversations that take place on the board can turn into video conferences or an online meeting, where users can add things such as GIFs and emoticons. Since Teams is also meant for internal team members that need constant contact with each other, it also has an app that most people choose to leave open all day. Teams can be public (seen even by those with no permission to access them) or private, and members can be managed by Office 365 admins and team owners. Members in a team can only be internal but when a team is created, as is a group and a SharePoint site, so external members can be added later.

Things to keep in mind

There are a few things you should keep in mind when dealing with Office 365 Groups and Microsoft Teams:

- When you create a group, a SharePoint site collection is created behind the scenes; when you create a team, both a group and a SharePoint site collection are created.
- You cannot see the generated site collections through the old SharePoint admin center, only through the new SharePoint admin center (which is still not generally available as of March 2018).
- The SharePoint site collections and groups may also be visible on your SharePoint home page.
- The generated site collection is a partially stripped-down team site. Some site collection features, such as apps, and pages, such as the library templates gallery, are not available; although some may be accessible with URL manipulation, you will not have access to complete actions, such as adding a library template to the library templates gallery.
- Since site collections are created separately, searching across site collections doesn't work in the same way as searching normally. You will have to create custom search scopes or search from the SharePoint home page.
- When you create a channel in a team, a corresponding folder is created in `Files` in the group and in the main document library of the SharePoint site collection.
- Files flow between the connected site collections, groups, and teams but conversations and emails do not.
- Conversations in Office 365 Groups are connected to a distribution list in Exchange, and conversations in Teams are connected to a message board backed by Skype for Business.
- More customization options, such as content types or workflows, need to be created in the SharePoint site collection and will only work there (this is one of the reasons for the creation of the SharePoint site collection behind the scenes).
- You can add up to 2,500 members to Office 365 Groups.
- Office 365 Groups can be used for permission groups across site collections but those groups will not visible via **People and Groups**, as with others.
- Groups can also be seen in the **Office 365 Admin Center** under **Groups**; however, you can't get into the groups from there.
- SharePoint, Microsoft Teams, and Office 365 Groups all have apps available in the Windows, Apple, and Google Play stores.

Administering Office 365 Groups via Office 365 Groups settings

To get to the part of the admin center where the Office 365 Groups controls are, go to **Office 365 Admin Center | Settings | Services & add-ins**. Scroll down the page and click on **Office 365 Groups**, as shown in the following screenshot:

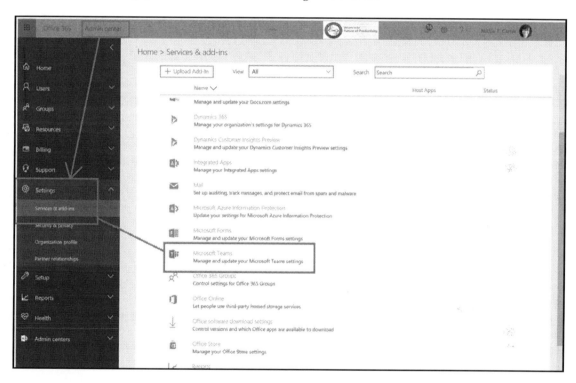

You must be a global admin to manage these settings.

Once you click on the **Office 365 Groups** service, you will see the options available for external users, as shown in the following screenshot:

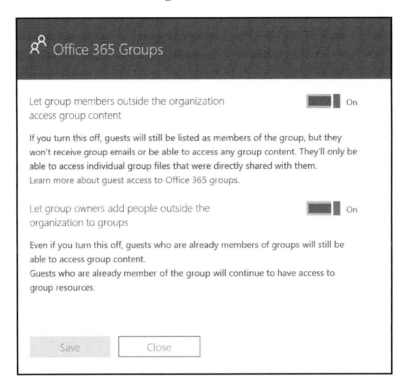

If you turn on **Let group members outside the organization access group content**, external people can be added to your **Office 365 Groups**. If this setting is turned on by itself, it means that anyone in your organization can add external users as guests to a group. If you want to limit this ability to only group owners, you need to enable the second setting.

 External users may be given access to the SharePoint sites created when a group is created, unless external users are removed in the SharePoint admin center.

This setting may be on by default.

Make sure you click the **Save** button when making any changes.

If you turn on **Let group owners add people outside the organization to groups**, only group owners and global admin members will be able to add external users as guests to groups.

 If you turn this setting on after guests have been added, those guests will retain the same access. You will have to remove them and add them again if you want this setting to apply.

Make sure you click the **Save** button when making any changes.

Creating a new Office 365 group

To get to the part of the admin center where the Office 365 Groups controls are, go to **Office 365 Admin Center** | **Groups** | **Groups**, as shown in the following screenshot:

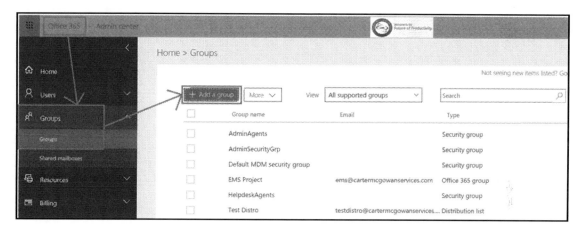

Click on the **+Add a group** button and fill out the form as follows:

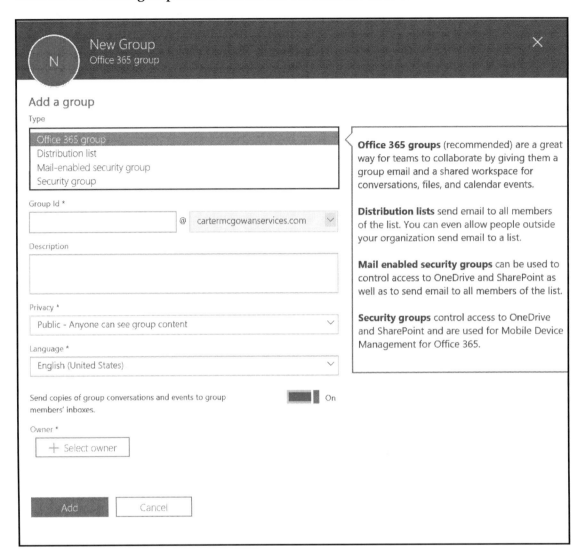

By default, Office 365 Group is the type of group that is created without clicking the drop-down list and choosing the **Office 365 group** option. If you want a distribution list or a different kind of **Security group**, you need to make sure you click on the drop-down menu.

Let's walk through what's needed in the form; the fields are as follows:

- **Group Id**: This is the email address for the group. You can choose a domain based on those available from your tenants.
- **Description**: This is a description of your group.
- **Privacy**: With this, you can choose whether a group is public, where all can see it and its content, or private, where only members can see it and its content.

 This setting cannot be changed once set, so consider your options very carefully.

- **Language**: This sets the language of the group.

 In practice, we noticed that the language of the welcome email is also affected by this change.

The option to **Send copies of group conversations and events to group members' inboxes** is set to on by default. If you leave this on, all members will receive notifications of calendar events and emails or conversations; they will have the option to turn notifications off. If you turn this setting off, no members will receive notification of calendar events and emails or conversations. This can also be changed by individual members.

Administering Teams via Office 365 admin center

To get to the part of the admin center where the Office 365 Groups controls are, go to **Office 365 Admin center** | **Settings** | **Services & add-ins**. Scroll down the page and click on **Microsoft Teams,** as shown in the following screenshot:

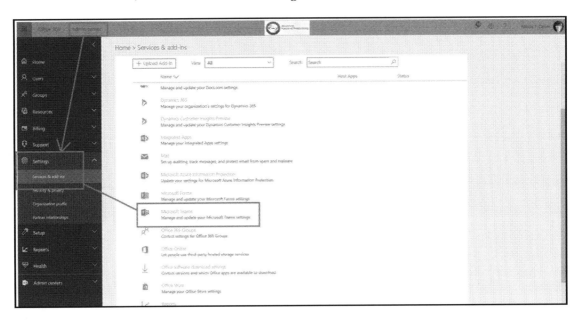

 You must be a global admin to manage these settings.

Once you click on **Microsoft Teams**, you will get a side panel with settings:

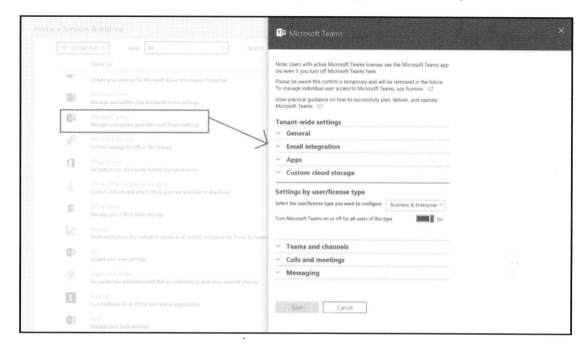

Make sure you are aware of the notations at the top of the panel, as shown in the following screenshot:

Note: Users with active Microsoft Teams licenses see the Microsoft Teams app tile even if you turn off Microsoft Teams here.

Please be aware this control is temporary and will be removed in the future. To manage individual user access to Microsoft Teams, use licenses.

View practical guidance on how to successfully plan, deliver, and operate Microsoft Teams.

Let's go through the **Tenant-wide settings** first, shown as follows:

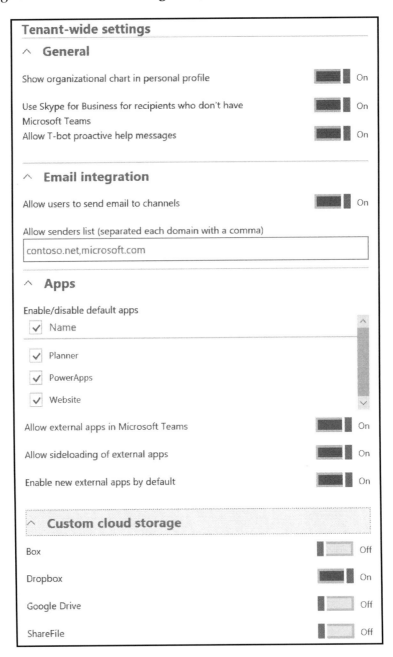

- **General**: Here, you can turn on the organizational chart in each person's personal profile, allow users who don't have Microsoft Teams but receive an invitation to join using Skype for Business, and allow the T-bot to give users helpful messages.
- **Email integration**: This newer option is very helpful; it allows certain users to send emails to a team's channels.
- **Apps**: In your team, you and your users have access to some default apps. You can turn access for certain apps either on or off. You can also set whether you want to allow access for external apps and side-loading external apps.
- **Custom cloud storage**: This gives your users the ability to use other cloud storage apps in Teams.
- **Setting by user/license type**: Here, you have two options: **Business and Enterprise** and **Guest**. You can choose whether users of each group have access to Teams or not:

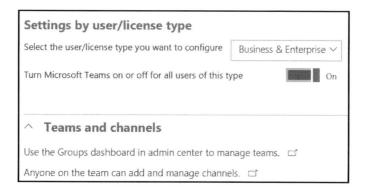

- **Teams and channels**: Both of these options launch different windows:
    - **Use the Groups dashboard in admin center to manage teams**: This option opens Groups in the Office 365 admin center where you can manage the group that is created when a team is created. Remember, when a team is created, so are groups and a SharePoint site.
    - **Anyone on the team can add and manage channels**: Currently, this option opens a docs.microsoft.com article on all of the team's options.

- **Calls and meetings**: These options allow you to set settings for calls and meetings via Teams:

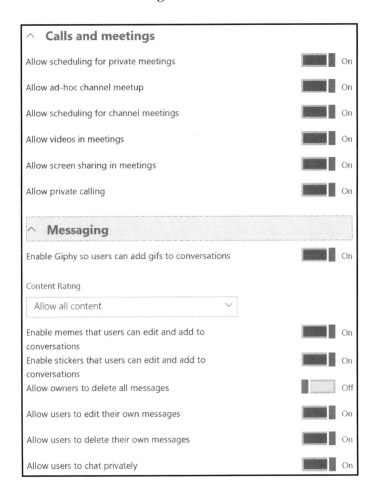

You can't create teams in the Office 365 admin center **Groups** section. You can only manage aspects of the team, such as the members, via the group.

Meetings can involve up to 80 people and private chats can include up to 20. These figures include the person who set the meetings up.

- **Messaging**: This set of options allows you to set settings for messaging via Teams.

> Remember to click the **Save** button once you have set all of your options.

Administering via PowerShell

There are PowerShell commands that you can use for both Office 365 Groups and Microsoft Teams. Let's look at the available commands for both.

Administering via PowerShell administration for Office 365 Groups

You can use PowerShell commands to manage your Groups. Here is a list of those available so far:

- Get-UnifiedGroup
- New-UnifiedGroup
- Remove-UnifiedGroup
- Set-UnifiedGroup
- Add-UnifiedGroupLinks
- Get-UnifiedGroupLinks
- Remove-UnifiedGroupLinks

To run these cmdlets, you will need to connect to Exchange Online and you have to be an Office 365 administrator. You will need to run them on Windows 10, 8.1, or 7 SP 1 or Server 2008 R2, 2012, 2012 R2, or 2016. You will also need to run Windows PowerShell or Windows PowerShell **Integrated Scripting Environment** (**ISE**) as an administrator. If you have Windows 8.1 or Windows 10, these are already installed. Note that the first time you run the cmdlets, you will need to run the following:

```
Set-ExecutionPolicy RemoteSigned
```

If you don't, you will see the following error:
Files cannot be loaded because running scripts is disabled on this system. Provide a valid certificate with which to sign the files if required.

You will need to run the following commands. The first three need to be run before you run any of the cmdlets. The last needs to be run after you have finished running all the cmdlets you plan to run, shown as follows:

```
$UserCredential = Get-Credential
```

You will be prompted for your credentials. Again, you will need Office 365 administrator credentials as follows:

```
$Session = New-PSSession -ConfigurationName Microsoft.Exchange
-ConnectionUri https://outlook.office365.com/powershell-liveid/
-Credential $UserCredential -Authentication Basic -AllowRedirection
```

If you are using Office 365 run by 21Vianet, you will need to replace `-ConnectionURI` with the URL `https://partner.outlook.cn/PowerShell`. If you are using Office 365 in Germany, you will need to replace `-ConnectionURI` with `https://outlook.office.de/powershell-liveid/`:

```
Import-PSSession $Session
```

Start your remote session with the following cmdlet:

```
Remove-PSSession $Session
```

When you have finished running your cmdlets, the preceding command will close the session.

Now that we have looked at the prerequisites, you can look at cmdlets in more detail in this Microsoft TechNet article: `https://technet.microsoft.com/en-us/library/dn641234(v=exchg.160).aspx`. We recommend taking a look at the Office 365 Group cmdlets section of the article.

The following is a script that I put together after reading a few articles online and conferring with Microsoft.

To run the script, use the following command in the PowerShell window:

```
.\<filename>.ps1 [-Office365Username admin@xxxxxx.onmicrosoft.com] [-
Office365Password Password123]
```

The username and password are optional but if you do not add them to the command, you will be prompted for them. Remember you need the same credentials as an Office 365 administrator.

The following is the first half of the script:

```
#Accept input parameters
Param(
   [Parameter(Position=0, Mandatory=$false, ValueFromPipeline=$true)]
   [string] $Office365Username,
   [Parameter(Position=1, Mandatory=$false, ValueFromPipeline=$true)]
   [string] $Office365Password
)
#Constant Variables
$OutputFile = "C:\scripts\DistributionGroupMembers.csv"  #The CSV Output file that is created,
change for your purposes
$arrDLMembers = @{}
#Remove all existing Powershell sessions
Get-PSSession | Remove-PSSession
#Did they provide creds?  If not, ask them for it.
if (([string]::IsNullOrEmpty($Office365Username) -eq $false) -and
([string]::IsNullOrEmpty($Office365Password) -eq $false))
{
   $SecureOffice365Password = ConvertTo-SecureString -AsPlainText $Office365Password -Force
   #Build credentials object
   $Office365Credentials  = New-Object System.Management.Automation.PSCredential
$Office365Username, $SecureOffice365Password
}
else
{
   #Build credentials object
   $Office365Credentials  = Get-Credential
}
#Create remote Powershell session
$Session = New-PSSession -ConfigurationName Microsoft.Exchange -ConnectionUri
https://ps.outlook.com/powershell -Credential $Office365credentials -Authentication Basic -
AllowRedirection
#Import the session
```

The second half of the script is as follows:

```
Import-PSSession $Session -AllowClobber | Out-Null
#Prepare Output file with headers

Out-File -FilePath $OutputFile -InputObject "Distribution Group DisplayName,Distribution Group
Email,Member DisplayName, Member Email, Member Type" -Encoding UTF8
#Get all Distribution Groups from Office 365
$objDistributionGroups = Get-DistributionGroup -ResultSize Unlimited
#Iterate through all groups, one at a time
Foreach ($objDistributionGroup in $objDistributionGroups)
{
   write-host "Processing $($objDistributionGroup.DisplayName)..."
   #Get members of this group
   $objDGMembers = Get-DistributionGroupMember -Identity
$($objDistributionGroup.PrimarySmtpAddress)
   write-host "Found $($objDGMembers.Count) members..."
   #Iterate through each member
   Foreach ($objMember in $objDGMembers)
   {
      export-csv 'C:\scripts\list.csv' -InputObject
"$($objDistributionGroup.DisplayName),$($objDistributionGroup.PrimarySMTPAddress),$($objMem
ber.DisplayName),$($objMember.PrimarySMTPAddress),$($objMember.RecipientType)" -Encoding
UTF8 -append
      write-host
"`t$($objDistributionGroup.DisplayName),$($objDistributionGroup.PrimarySMTPAddress),$($objMe
mber.DisplayName),$($objMember.PrimarySMTPAddress),$($objMember.RecipientType)"
   }
}
#Clean up session
Get-PSSession | Remove-PSSession
```

PowerShell administration for Microsoft Teams

You can use PowerShell commands to manage your teams. The following is a list of some of the available commands:

- `Add-TeamUser`
- `Get-Team`

- Get-TeamChannel
- Get-TeamFunSettings
- Get-TeamGuestSettings
- Get-TeamMemberSettings
- Get-TeamMessagingSettings
- Get-TeamHelp
- Get-TeamUser
- New-TeamChannel
- New-Team

 More details on these cmdlets can be found in a Microsoft TechNet article at https://blogs.technet.microsoft.com/skypehybridguy/2017/11/07/microsoft-teams-powershell-support/.

A lot of the cmdlets we've looked at are currently in beta. Remember that you will need to run Windows PowerShell as an administrator.

You will need to run Install-Module MicrosoftTeams if you haven't already installed this module. When you are prompted to install and import the NuGet provider, enter Y. Note that you may be prompted for an untrusted repository. You will want to enter A for Yes to all. Once the module is installed, you can then run the Connect-MicrosoftTeams cmdlet to connect to Teams. Once prompted for your credentials and signed in, you will be given the names for Account, Environment, Tenant (GUID), TenantId (GUID), and TenantDomain. Once connected, you can run your cmdlets.

 More details on all of these cmdlets can also be found at https://docs.microsoft.com/en-us/powershell/module/teams/?view=teams-ps. There is also a GitHub repository available at https://github.com/microsoftdocs/office-docs-powershell.

Summary

In this chapter, we looked at Office 365 Groups and Microsoft Teams. We went through a brief overview of both programs and then delved into how to administer each.

In the next chapter, we will take a look at Security & Compliance center.

8
Understanding Security and Compliance

There's no doubt that online security is more important today than it's ever been before. One can hardly avoid the almost daily stories about new vulnerabilities, information leaks, and data theft or extortion. Once upon a time, security concerns were one of the major objections to moving company data to the cloud. However, incidents at companies such as Equifax, Facebook, and Twitter continue to prove that a large IT infrastructure and in-house security team are no guarantee against modern threats. Although Microsoft is certainly not immune, it is reasonable to acknowledge that when it comes to data security, they can apply more resources, manpower, and experience than typical small-to-midsized organizations and many larger ones.

Office 365 has many features that extend this protection. Although these used to be scattered across the entire platform, Microsoft has done much work recently to bring them together under the central Office 365 Security & Compliance umbrella.

In this chapter, we'll describe the following security-related topics:

- Purposes of Security & Compliance
- Alerts
- Permissions
- Classifications
- Data loss prevention
- Threat management
- Search and investigation
- Reports
- Service assurance
- Security score card
- Using PowerShell with Security & Compliance

It would be impossible to review every available screen and click in Security & Compliance in just one chapter; one could easily imagine an entire book on cloud security. Instead, we'll do our best to review the essential concepts you need to know as a system administrator that will help you work with IT security professionals to realize what's possible and get the most out of what's included in Office 365.

This chapter is also much less abstract and more one-on-one than some of our others. That's because, removed from context and real-life consequences, the topic of security can become quite dry and even dull. If we truly want to help improve our cybersecurity efforts, then it's best not to put the audience to sleep. Wherever possible, we'll be using real-world examples to illustrate key concepts.

As experts who've been involved in internet security in one way or another for over 20 years now, we've collected a lot of stories over the years. These anecdotes can be both informative and entertaining, but it would be difficult to credibly share these experiences without somehow also disclosing their origin, often to the great embarrassment of nearly everyone involved. In all cases, while the information we will share is true, the names have been changed to protect the innocent and, sometimes, the guilty. The names are fake—and sometimes even silly—but the stories are quite real.

Security & Compliance overview

In the early days, security features were spread out across the many products in the Office 365 family. Some were in Exchange, whereas others were in SharePoint. Microsoft created the Security & Compliance center to establish a centralized location where administrators can work with these individual features and have a comprehensive view of cloud security.

When Security & Compliance was first launched, there wasn't much meat on its bones. A lot has changed since then; if you checked it out a while ago, please give it another look. Over the past couple of years, Security & Compliance in Office 365 has undergone rapid expansion and change. It wouldn't be surprising to find features that are not covered in this chapter, or to find that things aren't exactly as we describe here. We'll do our best to describe things as they are today, with an eye toward how they might change in the future.

To access Security & Compliance, you must either have the global administrator role or the security administrator role. Without one of these roles, the Security & Compliance tiles/links won't even appear. However, this alone won't be enough to access all its features. (See the *Permissions* section later for more details.)

You'll find it in your Office 365 apps, alongside other applications, such as Word, Excel, and the admin portal. More than likely, it will be quite far down the list. You can also find it under **Admin centers** in the left-hand navigation of the Office 365 admin portal, in case, you wanted to click twice instead of just once:

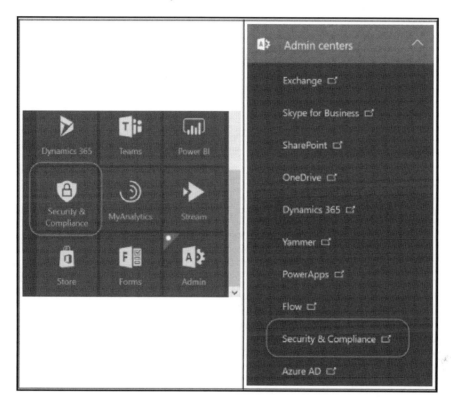

Security & Compliance navigation

Save time and visit Security & Compliance directly at `https://protection.office.com`.

Either of these will take you to the **Security & Compliance** home page, which serves as a jumping off point for many unique features and tools. Different subsections are shown along the left-hand navigation using familiar icons, similarly to the admin portal. Page content is displayed as tiles, which may change from time to time and can be customized to your preferences:

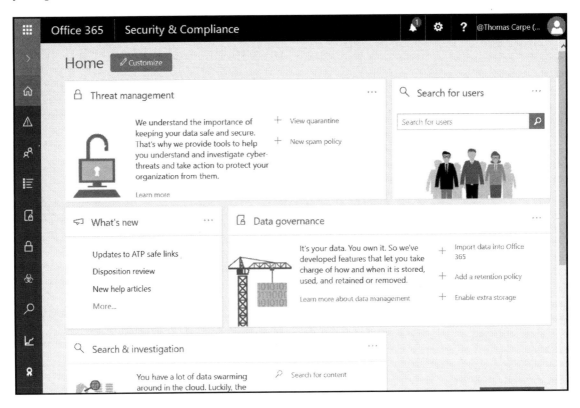

Security & Compliance dashboard

You might be tempted to just jump into the various tools in **Security & Compliance**, roll up your sleeves, and get messy. Your enthusiasm is laudable, but most likely followed by throwing up your hands and shouting, "It doesn't work!" Most likely, the problem is just that you haven't yet been given permissions to access Security & Compliance features yet. For this reason, we'll talk about **Permissions** first, even though it won't appear in this order on the site itself.

Permissions

Permissions to Security & Compliance are handled through **role-based access control (RBAC)**. If you're used to having your way around Office 365 because you're the global administrator, you may find this very annoying. Exchange admins will be familiar with RBAC because it plays a large role in mailbox permissions, especially if you've ever needed to migrate from an on-premises Exchange server to Office 365. Likewise, those who have experimented with eDiscovery, identity and access protection, or privileged identity management will find the roles for Security & Compliance are largely the same.

There are eight key roles used in Security & Compliance. Of course, Microsoft provides detailed descriptions of these. We'll sum them up more concisely, proceeding in the order that (arbitrarily) made the most sense to us:

- **Default roles**:
    - **Organization Management**: This automatically includes global administrators. It can control Security & Compliance center permissions and also manages settings for device management, DLP, reports, and preservation. This is the role you most likely have on day zero, and it is not the same as *full control*.
- **Privileged security roles**:
    - **Security Administrator**: You can think of this role as the security *root*; in many ways, it can be more powerful than global administrator. This includes Microsoft Support and your Microsoft Partner with delegated administration privileges. This role is everything that a **Security Reader** role has, plus administrative permission for AIP, identity and access protection, PIM, Office 365 service health, and Security & Compliance.
    - **Security Reader**: This includes Microsoft Support and your Microsoft Partner with delegated administration privileges. It has read permissions to AIP, identity and access protection, PIM, Office 365 service health, and Security & Compliance.
- **eDiscovery roles**:
    - **eDiscovery Manager**: This is not quite as powerful as an eDiscovery admin. This can perform searches and place holds, create and edit eDiscovery cases, add or remove case members, and create and edit Content Searches associated with a case.

- **Reviewer**: This is the most restrictive eDiscovery role. This can view the list on the cases page in the Security & Compliance center. This can't create, open, or edit an eDiscovery case. This allows viewing case data in advanced eDiscovery.

- **Special/Limited roles**:
  - **Compliance Administrator**: This allows you to change settings for device management, DLP, reports, and preservation. Think of this role like **Organization Management** without the ability to edit Security & Compliance permissions.
  - **Service Assurance User**: This can access the **Service assurance** section in **Security & Compliance** to get guidance, reports, and third-party audits.
  - **Supervisory Reviewer**: This can create and edit policies defining what communications are subject to review in an organization.

Note that there are also some places where you may need to assign roles outside of Security & Compliance center to make features in this section work properly. Specifically, these are rights that must be assigned in the **Exchange admin center (EAC)** or Azure AD Management portal (for IAP/PIM). For example, to search the audit log or to view all reports, an **Organization Management** user must be assigned permissions in EAC.

In our experience, the web interface for role-based permissions can be somewhat unreliable. For example, we tried to add a global administrator account to some of the RBAC security roles, only to find that the account didn't even show up in the list at all. You may have better results using PowerShell to manage roles, as described in Chapter 3, *Administering Azure Active Directory*.

 Read more about Security & Compliance permissions at https://support.office.com/en-us/article/Permissions-in-the-Office-365-Security-Compliance-Center-d10608af-7934-490a-818e-e68f17d0e9c1.

Service assurance

Although this section is listed as the very last option in navigation, it's probably the second most important section in **Security & Compliance**, next to **Permissions**. As an administrator, you're unlikely to come here often unless you have specific compliance requirements to report on. If you do, you'll want to drop in here first before exploring other Security & Compliance features.

The **Service assurance** section includes information that Microsoft has brought together to explain how they preserve security, privacy, and compliance in Office 365 and other services on the Microsoft cloud (for example, Azure). This section is largely to help you find relevant documentation. However, there are a few chores you'll want to get out of the way when you initially configure your tenant.

 Read more about setting up Security & Compliance for the first time at `https://support.office.com/en-us/article/service-assurance-in-the-office-365-security-compliance-center-47e8b964-4b09-44f7-a2d7-b8a06e8e389c?ui=en-USrs=en-USad=US`.

Configuring Security & Compliance settings

To begin, you should go to the **Settings** page and configure the basic information needed to describe the company security needs. This includes selecting a region and industry:

Region and industry settings

The Microsoft Cloud Service Assurance Portal contains Microsoft's confidential information. By accessing or using this web site, you agree not to disclose such information without Microsoft's prior written consent.

Select one or more regions and industries that are applicable to your organization, and we'll make sure to provide you with the service assurance resources that matter most to you.

Region: North America ▾   Industry: Consumer, Education, ... (8) ▾   Save

Security & Compliance settings

The settings on this page will both allow you to choose more than one option, so if your organization is distributed across the globe or serves customers in more than one vertical, you should check all the options that apply.

Assigning permissions to non-IT staff

This section provides a wealth of information that will be useful to security planners, consultants, and business owners who need to comply with a variety of different regulations or map the functionality in Office 365 to their security plans, checklists, or audit questionnaires.

Most organizations that require a security plan will require a separation of duties between IT and security/risk management staff. As the dashboard explains, the members of your information security team, including auditors, will not have access to this information unless you give them permissions as a **Service Assurance User**. So, at a minimum, you'll need to assign this role to someone from management, such as the designated security officer and/or auditors.

Security assurance information

The three sections of **Compliance reports**, **Trust documents**, and **Audited controls** are purely informative. They will be used by your Security and Risk Management team to demonstrate that Office 365 meets compliance requirements whenever the organization's IT systems are placed under review, whether internally, via self-reporting questionnaire, or as part of an independent audit.

Having properly set the permissions and settings will ensure that the correct people have access to this information and that their view is filtered to only those documents on the site that apply to their specific role and needs.

Nevertheless, it is very important to point out that these documents contain general statements about Office 365. They do not describe your company's internal processes or how you've configured the Office 365 services to meet those requirements.

For example, Office 365 contains features that can help meet NIST requirements. Among these, NIST demands that privileged users must log in with accounts that ensure people are accountable for the actions they take. Therefore, users with administrative access must use accounts that represent people (for example, `thomas.carpe` not using shared or service accounts such as *administrator* or *root*).

While audit log reports and alerts will help you monitor such accounts to ensure they are not being used except in emergencies, there's nothing inherent in the Office 365 configuration or specified in any of the documents in Security & Compliance center that specifically ensures that you have set things up this way.

You'll need to create some alerts yourself, track the mappings between the configurations you've set and official requirements, document these in a security plan or checklist, and occasionally check in to ensure that the things you've put in place remain enforced over time.

Pay close attention to the **Customer Responsibilities Matrix** documents that are listed under the **Trust documents** section, as these will identify what the system does automatically and what requires you to set it up correctly. The documents are long. Going through them with a fine-toothed comb can take quite a while. A Microsoft Partner who specializes in cloud security will have expertise and resources that can help you accomplish these tasks with less effort than it would take to roll your own.

Alerts

The **Alerts** section is where you go to view and configure notifications that will be sent out to administrators to help ensure they're aware of various activities that can impact security.

A specific example of an alert is when an administrative user exercises their administrative privileges for Exchange, the system will notify everyone that their access level has been temporarily elevated.

Alerts dashboard

The **Dashboard** gives you at-a-glance information about recent alerts, details for recent alerts, and jumping off links to view, create, and edit alert settings:

Alert trends from the Alerts Dashboard

View alerts

If you follow the **View all alerts** link in the dashboard, as shown earlier, it will take you to the **View alerts** page. This will show you the same data that was available in the dashboard title—just more of it. On this page, you also have the ability to export or filter the data. **Filters** exist for **Status**, **Policy**, **Contributing user**, **Time strange**, **Severity**, and **Category**.

Checking the box next to an alert will show you its detailed screen, from which you can decide how you want to respond to it. If you check more than one, you can respond in bulk, but the details of the alerts will not be shown:

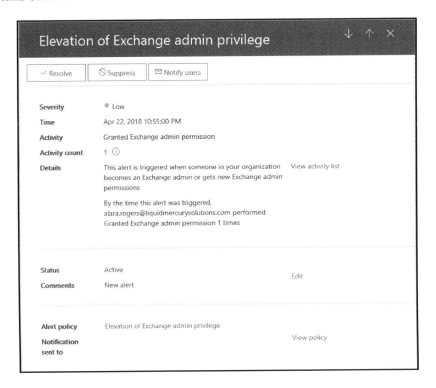

Alert details dialog

You can decide how you want to respond to an alert. Choices are to **Resolve**, **Suppress** (for 1 to 365 days), or **Notify users**.

Obviously, you will want to be very conservative about suppressing alerts for any reason, even if they are low risk. Just because something looks like a false alarm today does not mean that it always will be.

You should **Resolve** any issues that you know are not a threat. As a best practice, it is always recommended to leave a specific comment that explains the reason that the alert did not represent an actual threat, such as **This was legitimate work needed to onboard new employees hired that day**. Such comments will benefit you greatly if or when your actions come under review after a real security incident.

Notify others if you suspect they may be a problem or if they require more investigation. Depending on your security policies and the specific situation, keep in mind that you may or may not want to notify everyone on the team.

Alert policies

Out of the box, Office 365 includes 10 alert policies, but you can always add more to suit your needs. Existing alerts can also be searched, sorted, and filtered for manageability.

Here's a summary of the default alerts, by severity:

- **High**:
    - **Mails have been delayed**: This is triggered when Office 365 is unable to deliver mail to a connected mail server, such as Exchange or a partnered SMTP server, for an extended period.
    - **Malware campaign detected after delivery**: This is triggered when a malware campaign has been detected and intercepted after delivery to a user's inbox. You should respond to ensure that the user did not open the mail or suffer any ill effects from it.
    - **Malware campaign detected in SharePoint and OneDrive**: This is triggered when malware has been detected in a SharePoint document library or OneDrive for Business folder.
    - **Unusual increase in email reported as phish**: This is triggered when the number of phishing emails (as reported by users) rises sharply. This can indicate an aggressive attack, potentially against your organization specifically, and administrators should alert users about the phishing attack and its characteristics.
    - **Unusual external user file activity**: This is triggered when the volume of file activity by external users grows in an unusual way, which can indicate that a guest user has been given access to more than they should have and is bulk-downloading data.

- **Medium**:
  - **Unusual volume of external file sharing**: This is triggered by large increase in files being shared to an outside user, which while there are legitimate cases, may also indicate attempted data exfiltration
  - **Unusual volume of file deletion**: This is triggered by mass delete, which can be legitimate, but could also indicate vandalism or a disgruntled employee who is abusing their access

- **Low**:
  - **The creation of forwarding/redirect rule**: This is triggered if a user sets their inbox to forward emails
  - **The elevation of Exchange Admin privilege**: This is triggered when a new administrator is added, or in certain cases when an administrator who has EAC permissions exercises them
  - **Malware campaign detected and blocked**: This is triggered when an unusually high volume of malware was intercepted successfully before arriving in users' mailboxes

In case you decide that the existing alert policies aren't enough, the choices you have are quite extensive. Virtually anything that you can research via the audit log reports can likewise trigger a notification—even read access to a specific file in SharePoint!

Classifications

Simply put, **Labels** are categories applied to documents or emails for the purposes of determining how they will be handled. This can mean that they will be retained, or it could mean they will be deleted after a certain time has passed. Classification refers to the combination of a document label and a set of policies associated with that label.

Labels

By default, Office 365 has no labels created. Therefore, you will need to create your own or hire a firm specializing in document and information security to help you do this.

Here are some examples:

- **Company internal**: Documents that may not be shared outside the organization.

- **Client confidential**: Documents with proprietary information controlled by a **nondisclosure agreement** (**NDA**) with a customer. To limit liability, these typically need to be deleted once they are no longer needed.
- **Controlled Unclassified Information** (**CUI**): Sometimes also named **Sensitive but Unclassified** (**SBU**).
- **Employee file**: Document must be retained for HR compliance reasons. Typically, they are kept for 7 years, then deleted to limit potential liability.
- **Sharing approved**: Management has reviewed the contents of the document and determined that sharing it outside the organization is acceptable. In some cases, these may be redacted versions of controlled documents, and the label is applied to distinguish how they should be handled.

Creating a label

Let's create a label for internal documents. Enter a name and description:

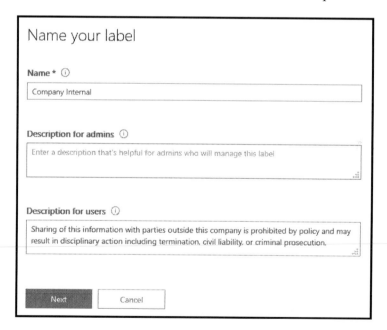

Create a label, name, and description

Once we have a name and description, we can choose retention settings.

Our label is mostly about preventing leaks and information theft, but we could also mark the document for retention to prevent it from being deleted. Suppose we created the employee file label. In such a case, enabling retention makes a lot of sense. However, in this case, that doesn't seem like the best idea, so we'll leave this turned off for now.

After reviewing our settings, we save the label.

Labels by themselves do very little. However, combined with other tools they are the basis for controlling documents and information across the organization.

Auto-applying labels

Next, we'll configure auto-apply for our label using the aptly named **Auto-apply a label** button:

Auto-apply a label button

The first step is to choose a label:

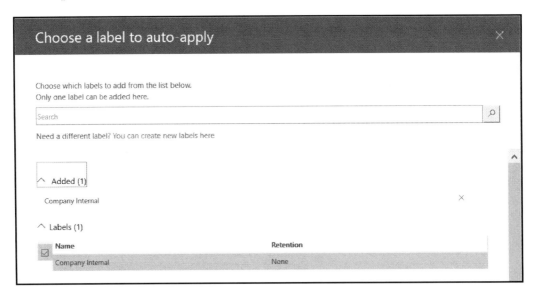

The choose a label dialog

As you can see, this dialog allows you to specify more than one label to apply, and it will let you search through labels. This strongly implies that Microsoft imagines that you may have several dozen labels or more.

Once you've picked your label, click on **Next** to continue.

The next screen gives you two choices for conditions:

- **Apply label to content that contains sensitive information**: Apply the label to content that contains sensitive information related to specific industries (such as financial). Or, hand pick the types of sensitive information you want it applied to (such as credit card and social security numbers).
- **Apply label to content that contains specific words or phrases**: Apply the label to content that contains the words or phrases you specify.

We could simply attach the label to any document that contains the phrase *company internal*, which would imply the latter choice.

First, let's have a look at the other option to see if that might fit our needs:

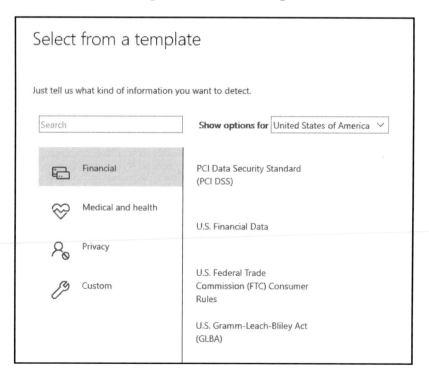

Select from label policy template

This brings up several options, including financial, medical, privacy, and custom policy templates. There's a lot to choose from, so it may be helpful to choose your region first, as we've done earlier.

Here's a rundown of the choices we have here in the USA:

- **Financial**:
    - **PCI Data Security Standard (PCI DSS)**: Credit/debit card numbers
    - **U.S. Financial Data**: Bank account and routing info, credit/debit card numbers
    - **U.S. Federal Trade Commission (FTC) Consumer Rules**: Bank account and routing info, credit/debit card numbers
    - **U.S. Gramm-Leach-Bliley Act (GLBA)**: Credit/debit card, bank account, SSN/TIN

- **Medical and health**:
    - **U.S. Health Insurance Act (HIPAA): Personal identification information (PII)** identifiers and medical terms (for example, diagnosis)

- **Privacy**:
    - **Patriot Act**: Credit card, bank account, TIN/SSN
    - **PII data**: TIN/SSN, US and UK passport numbers
    - **US State Breach Laws**: Credit card, bank account, driver's license number, SSN
    - **SSN Confidentiality**: Social security numbers

- **Custom**:
    - Choose your own type of content and how to protect it

None of the canned types earlier really apply to what we want to do, so let's try **Custom**.

On this screen, we need to add a sensitive information picker:

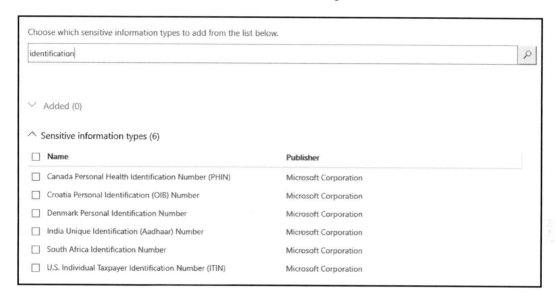

Examples of sensitive information pickers to choose

A few quick searches quickly demonstrate that we may be barking up the wrong tree. Unless you've already created an information picker of your own, you're unlikely to find anything here that can help identify documents meant for internal use only:

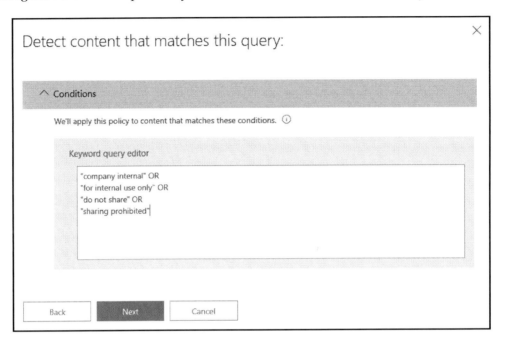

Custom label query condition

This is more our speed. The information box says that you can use Boolean logic and that searches for document properties are coming soon. It doesn't specify that you can use quotes or not, but let's assume we can for now:

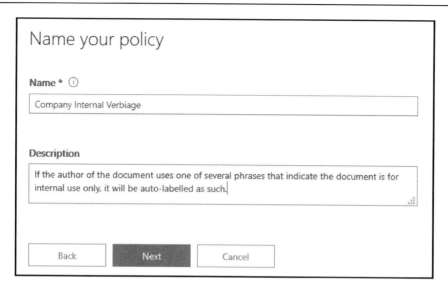

Create auto-apply label policy, name, and description

Next, we provide a name and description. This will be helpful later for those who want to know the conditions under which auto-labeling will take place, so be as descriptive as possible.

We could limit the scope of auto-labeling. For example, we could do this only in SharePoint documents, but not emails. Let's go ahead and leave the default for now.

Finally, we review our settings and save.

Microsoft warns **It will take up to 7 days to automatically apply the label to all items that match your conditions**. For now, we'll just have to rely on our users to mark their own documents for a few days.

Publishing labels

For our users to specify the `company internal` label on their documents while using applications such as Word, we need to publish the label. This is done from the main page of the **Labels** section using the **Publish labels** button at the top of the page:

Publish labels button

The first step is to pick a label you want to publish:

Choose labels to publish

This is fundamentally like the other menus, like the one we saw for auto-apply earlier. We'll select our `company internal` policy and click on **Next**:

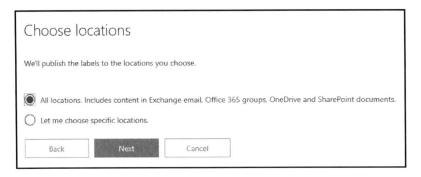

Publish labels, choose location(s)

Next, we can choose to publish to all applications or limit the label to any combination of Exchange, SharePoint, OneDrive, and/or Office 365 Groups. We'll leave the default for now:

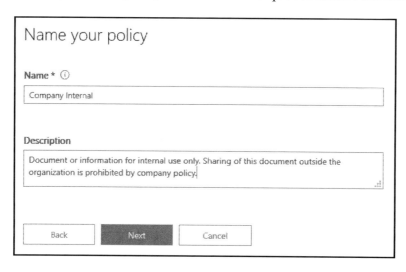

Publish labels, policy name, and description

Finally, we name our policy. This may seem a bit redundant, but it's the information entered here that the users will see when they choose a label, so be sure to enter a description.

Review your settings and confirm, and you're all set. Your label will appear in SharePoint, OneDrive, Groups, or Exchange. (Personally, we thought it was a bit inconvenient that there doesn't seem to be any mechanism to apply the label from within Word or Excel directly. However, the links mentioned later provide additional information about conveniences, such as how to apply a label to all documents in a library.)

Read more about labels at `https://support.office.com/en-us/article/overview-of-labels-af398293-c69d-465e-a249-d74561552d30` and `https://docs.microsoft.com/en-us/microsoft-365/enterprise/protect-files-with-o365-labels-dlp`.

Label policies

In the previous section, we created a label, set its auto-apply policy, and published it. We didn't realize it, but for two out of three of these steps, we were creating label policies and not the label itself:

Manage auto-apply and published label policies

Those policies will now be shown if we navigate to the **Classifications** | **Label policies** link in the left-hand navigation. From there, we can delete the policies or make any changes needed.

Sensitive information types

The last section of **Classifications** lists the available types, which we saw earlier when looking through labeling policy templates. This list is basically display-only, but it is possible to add your own types to the list.

The creation of custom-sensitive information types is a very advanced topic, so going into detail is beyond the scope of this book. If you choose to do so, you will need the following skills:

- Business knowledge of search criteria and document classification strategies
- XML
- **Regular expressions (RegEx)**
- PowerShell commands to upload the custom type to Office 365

 Read more about creating a custom sensitive information type at `https://support.office.com/en-us/article/create-a-custom-sensitive-information-type-82c382a5-b6db-44fd-995d-b333b3c7fc30`.

Data loss prevention

Data loss prevention, sometimes also known as **data leak prevention**, is an industry term for technologies and strategies designed to protect proprietary or sensitive information from a variety of threats both inside and outside your organization. This not only includes hackers, but also employees both past and present—whether their intentions are well-meaning or nefarious.

DLP policy

Policies are the core area of the DLP subsection, though others will appear if you have EMS plans. As such, there's a little dashboard here that will show you some reports about policies and policy matches:

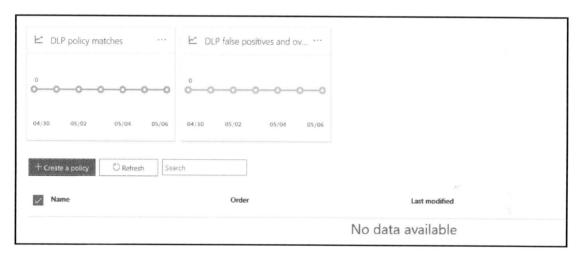

DLP policy page

Because we've only just created our first label in the previous topic, we don't yet have any DLP matches. However, we'd like to match for internal documents under certain circumstances and take appropriate action.

For example, we want to identify when internally labeled documents are shared externally, or when they are sent in email to someone outside the organization. In these cases, we don't just want to flag the behavior; we want to block the behavior and notify an administrator.

Let's start by clicking on **Create a policy**, as shown earlier.

Those who were paying attention during our discussion of labels earlier will notice that the DLP policy dialog looks very similar to the one for label policies.

Again, in our case, none of the policy templates will apply for our purpose, so choose **Custom**.

Next, we name the policy and provide a description:

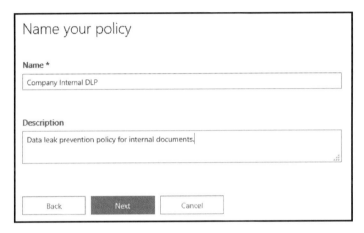

Create a DLP policy, name, and description

Again, like before, we choose a location. In our case, we want to monitor all the places where content may be shared inappropriately:

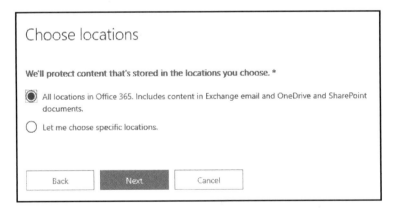

Create a DLP policy, choose location(s)

Up until now, you may have been wondering why our DLP policy looks very much like the label and label policies we created earlier:

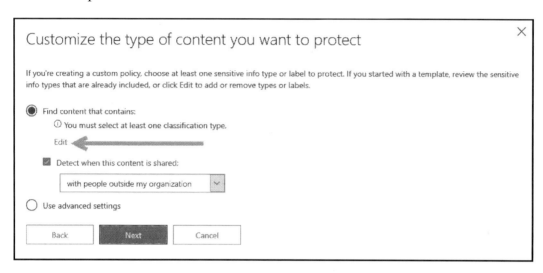

Create a DLP policy, link to label or sensitive information picker

The previous screen shows how these two connect to one another. Click on the **Edit** link to select a classification type (that is, label) for our DLP policy.

Here, you may choose an existing sensitive information type or you can choose a label:

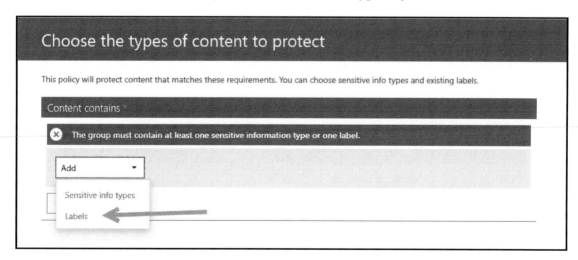

Create a DLP policy, add a content type

Once you have your first label added, you can optionally add more labels or SIT to the first group and choose between *any* or *all*. If you need complicated logic, you can create a second set of labels/SIT using the **Add group** button and specify **and** versus **or** logic to evaluate the match:

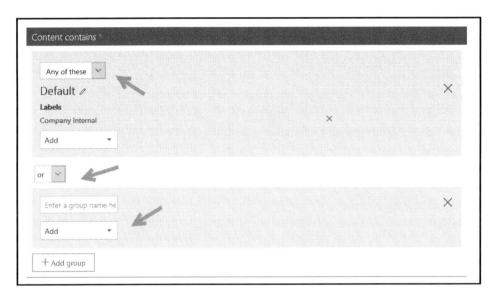

Create a DLP policy, define content criteria

For our purposes, one label is fine, so we'll delete the extra group we added and click on **Save**:

Create a DLP policy, can't use labels with Exchange emails

Here's a disappointing limitation. If we want to use labels, we can't protect content sent by email. We can choose to disable Exchange, but part of our goal was to keep people from forwarding internal emails. So, what do we do?

One option would be to go ahead and disable Exchange, then create a mail flow rule to do our searches and take action for emails. This is less than ideal because now our DLP strategy is no longer centrally managed. This could work as a fast and dirty solution.

The better choice would be to create our own custom sensitive information type using the advanced approach we described in the section on **Classifications**. This will keep everything managed under one roof, so to speak. However, it will take more time and resources to get the job done.

If you're working with a Microsoft Partner who specializes in cloud security, they may have done much of this work for you already. Certainly, for the partner company of this chapter's author, this is true. Such a benefit is among the many advantages of seeking out and relying upon a trusted Cloud Solution Provider to help support your efforts in Office 365:

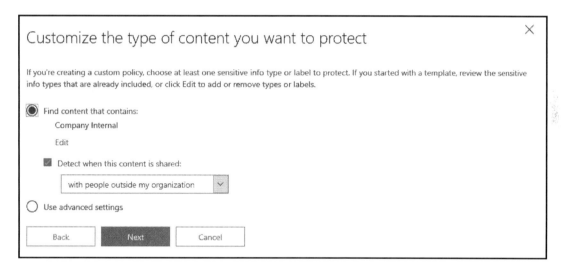

Create a DLP policy, settings with content type, and external sharing selected

For now, we'll do the workaround (without email protection), so we can finish our example.

We go back to Location and turn off Exchange. Note that only SharePoint and OneDrive are available in DLP policies; Groups isn't listed here. Upon returning to the **Policy settings** tab, we're now able to save our choice to use a label.

We choose the options to **Detect when this content is shared**: **with people outside my organization** and click on **Next**. This is exactly the type of sharing we want to prevent for internal documents:

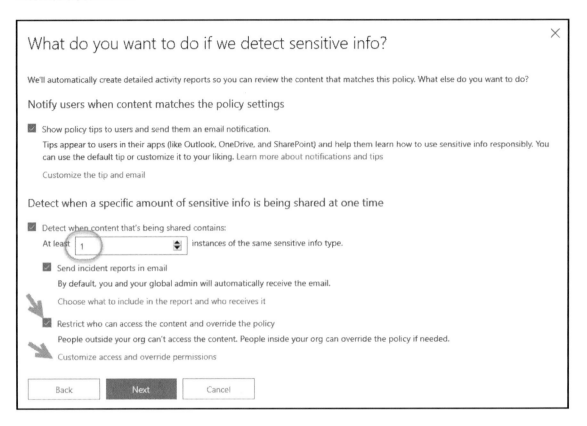

What do you want to do if we detect sensitive info?

We'll automatically create detailed activity reports so you can review the content that matches this policy. What else do you want to do?

Notify users when content matches the policy settings

☑ Show policy tips to users and send them an email notification.

Tips appear to users in their apps (like Outlook, OneDrive, and SharePoint) and help them learn how to use sensitive info responsibly. You can use the default tip or customize it to your liking. Learn more about notifications and tips

Customize the tip and email

Detect when a specific amount of sensitive info is being shared at one time

☑ Detect when content that's being shared contains:

At least [1 ⬍] instances of the same sensitive info type.

☑ Send incident reports in email

By default, you and your global admin will automatically receive the email.

Choose what to include in the report and who receives it

☑ Restrict who can access the content and override the policy

People outside your org can't access the content. People inside your org can override the policy if needed.

Customize access and override permissions

[Back] [Next] [Cancel]

Create a DLP policy, select policy actions

There are some important changes from the default for the next step in **Policy settings**. Reduce the **At least** field number from 10 to 1, since any document that contains the label should trigger the policy. Then, check the box for **Restrict who can access the content and override the policy**. This will prevent the content from being shared. Follow up by clicking on **Customize access and override permissions** and providing settings:

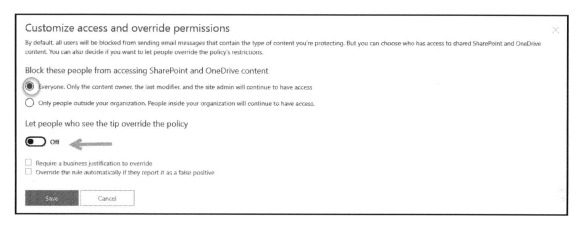

Customize access and override permissions ×

By default, all users will be blocked from sending email messages that contain the type of content you're protecting. But you can choose who has access to shared SharePoint and OneDrive content. You can also decide if you want to let people override the policy's restrictions.

Block these people from accessing SharePoint and OneDrive content

○ Everyone. Only the content owner, the last modifier, and the site admin will continue to have access

○ Only people outside your organization. People inside your organization will continue to have access.

Let people who see the tip override the policy

○ Off ←

☐ Require a business justification to override
☐ Override the rule automatically if they report it as a false positive

Save   Cancel

Create a DLP policy, set access, and override permissions

In our example, we have chosen an extremely restrictive policy. Upon violation, not only can the policy not be overridden for any reason, but the document in question will be locked out of the document. Thus, any subsequent attempt to circumvent policy (through copy and paste perhaps) will be thwarted.

Last, we can decide if we want to test our policy out or activate it later. Testing is generally a good idea, but with our settings, it isn't really an appropriate option, so we'll just go live with what we've got and hope for the best.

So now you've seen that DLP is all about creating policies. It has a great deal of power and some significant limitations. Building a consensus between IT, users, and management regarding what policy settings are appropriate will take time and effort. Feel free to experiment and find the right mix of settings that work in your organization.

App permissions and device management

These sections appear in Security & Compliance if you have Enterprise Mobility and Security plans. As such, they're outside the scope of a discussion of the core Office 365 offerings.

Data governance

Some components formerly found under **Threat management** and/or Office 365 Analytics now have their own section named **Data governance**.

Dashboard

Data governance | **Dashboard** has a lot of useful things on it, and (strictly speaking) not all of them are confined to functions within the **Data governance** section:

Data governance dashboard

Among other things, the dashboard will let you quickly jump to creating policies and labels (see previous topics). You can even enable self-service content classification from here. This screen will also show you how those are being applied to your content. You can see what plans are covering your content, which indicates the level of protection that content is receiving.

Explorer

This was previously known as threat explorer. Threat explorer is a jumping off point to Office 365 Analytics that promises to help you identify and understand anomalous behavior in your Office 365 tenant.

You can also configure alerts and respond as needed. Much of this is now also displayed in the **Alerts** section, as described earlier.

Once Office 365 Analytics is enabled, threat explorer gives you the ability to review activities that have been identified by the system as potentially dangerous, such as malware being sent by email.

Import

This section seems to be entirely for the purpose of uploading PST files into Office 365, specifically for organizations that require that the data needs to be shipped to Microsoft physically in order to be handled in a compliant fashion.

Threat management

In this section, we will cover threat management **Dashboard**, **Review**, and **Policy**.

Dashboard

Threat management | **Dashboard** shows trends in current cybersecurity threats, so you can educate yourself about the risks, who's vulnerable, and what actions you should take to protect yourself. This screen presents you with at a glance information regarding any recently identified malware or phishing attacks, security trends, targeted users in your organization, user email behaviors, and self-reported user incidents. (Because with E5 plans we didn't have any malware incidents, our screenshot was pretty boring.)

 Teach your users how to self-report when they receive a suspected phishing scam or malware. It's a lot more effective than relying on the system of using an `Is this a real email?` reply.

Review

This section is largely a rehash of the same tiles we saw in the dashboard, including links to incident reports—assuming you have had any.

Each of the tiles here are interesting in that there are reports within each that can give you more detail and allow you to report over longer periods of time. So, if you want to see malicious activity over the past 30, 90, or 365 days, this is where you'll want to visit.

One thing that's additional is the **Quarantine** report, which can be used to search for captured spam as well as phishing and malware emails. It will let you report going back up to 7 days—or even longer with a custom date range.

Choose the type of mail (**Spam**, **Transport rule**, **Bulk**, **Malware**, **Phish**), whether you want to see all email or just your own, and specify any other criteria using the dialog in the **Search** button:

Threat management | Review | Quarantine report

Policy

This section lets you manage policies for various components of Exchange Advanced Threat Protection. Specifically, there are jumping off points for anti-phishing, safe-attachments, safe-links, anti-spam (this is really part of EOP), DKIM settings, and anti-malware:

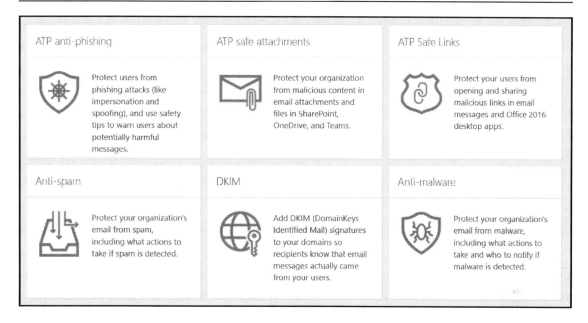

Threat management | Policy settings

Data privac

This is a new section Microsoft has created in response to privacy concerns such as those arising out of recent revelations regarding the misuse of users' Facebook information by Cambridge Analytica. Currently, it only has material concerning regulations in the EU, but more is expected over time.

If your organization has users who live and work in Europe, you'll need to familiarize yourself with these tools to stay compliant with international law. If you're entirely based in the US, they aren't so significant.

To stay GDPR compliant, also be sure to research and enable **Multi-Geo** in Office 365.

GDPR dashboard

The **GDPR dashboard** is your starting point for working with tools that will help you meet GDPR requirements.

Microsoft says:

> *"GDPR creates requirements around how personal data is collected, stored, processed, and deleted. To help lead you down the right path, we provide tools and guidance to facilitate ease in discovering, governing, protecting, and monitoring the personal data in your organization."*

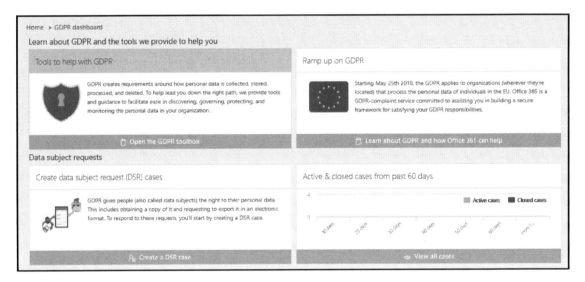

GDPR dashboard

DSR cases

According to Microsoft:

> *"GDPR gives people (also called data subjects) the right to their personal data. This includes obtaining a copy of it and requesting to export it in an electronic format. To respond to these requests, you'll start by creating a DSR case."*

If and when you start receiving requests from employees or other users from the EU who have access to Office 365, you'll need to open a case for them here.

Search & investigation

This section is all about finding certain types of content or behaviors. It can be useful for monitoring ongoing policy compliance and responding to incidents as needed. Subsections include **Content search**, **Audit log search**, **eDiscovery** (which is basically **Content search** by another name), and **Productivity app discovery**.

Content search

Content search replaces much of the functionality that was formerly only available through the **eDiscovery** center in SharePoint Online. With it, you can specify queries for specific keywords and other criteria, to help you identify potentially sensitive or inappropriate disclosure of information.

Over the years, we've used **Content search** and **eDiscovery** tools to help security officers (sometimes named FSOs) and their organizations with a variety of security-related matters. For example, some businesses subject to ITAR regulations (including foreign companies doing business with the US federal government) may be required to track emails between their US subsidiary and the foreign parent corporation. Other groups must conduct regular audits to ensure that sensitive information is being handled properly and need to report this information to their clients. Sometimes, a legal matter will arise that requires gathering all the available emails and documents regarding a specific project or topic.

We thought at one point that **Content search** and **eDiscovery** had disappeared from the left-hand navigation in **Security & Compliance**. As it turned out, we were just logged in as a user who didn't have the correct permissions via RBAC. If a section you think you should be seeing is missing, check there first, keeping in mind you will most likely need another admin to enable your access.

For our example, let's suppose that our organization has a special project code named `Master Shake`. Our business has nothing to do with fast food or cartoons, so it's unlikely that people will be chatting or sending emails that use this term unless they're doing work related to the project. As part of our quarterly security review, the FSO wants to make certain that discussion of this sensitive project stays within the team assigned to work on it.

We create a content search of **SharePoint** and **Exchange**. They will also include Skype messages that have been saved to people's mailboxes. We can safely leave out **Public Folders** because these aren't in use in our organization. You could also use **Custom location selection** to specify a search of only certain mailboxes, for example, if there are specific persons-of-interest in an ongoing investigation:

Content search, locations (old UI)

We'll do a keyword search on terms related to the project. In our case, we'll also include `Master Shake` and `MasterShake` (in case someone leaves out the space for some reason). We've also included `Frylock`, `Meatwad`, and `ATHF`, just in case we happen to sweep up some discussions-related ancillary projects—or maybe just the characters from Cartoon Network:

Content search, keywords, and conditions (old UI)

This is our first search, so we don't add any additional filters. To speed up our search activities, we could exclude certain date ranges or people known to be involved in our secret project. Many such scenarios are possible using **Add condition** to refine your query to a laser-sharp pinpoint.

Now, before you poke fun at our entertainment tastes, let us add that some other **Content search** examples haven't gone very well:

- For example, there were over 1,200 occurrences of terms specific to the nuclear industry (for example, *fission* and *deuterium*). Most likely these are all news articles arriving in people's mailboxes, and it dropped to only 86 items when we removed the word *nuclear* itself from the query.
- A search for items containing the word *confidential* turned up over 50,000 items! Too many people are using this term in their email footer. That's going to make life difficult!

For the `Master Shake` project, just 36 items appear, so we know already that there isn't much activity and it would be feasible to review each message or document to determine if it was communicated within appropriate boundaries. It's a silly name, with a very practical result.

> You'll want to craft your queries carefully. Coming up with a labeling scheme that makes searches practical is very important.

Manage content searches (old UI)

Clicking on **Preview search results** gets us a list that we can browse. Most entries have a preview of the email, conversation, or document. There are a few exceptions where the preview isn't supported. It was also a bit disappointing that the searched terms aren't highlighted and there's no find/find all in document capability. You'll end up having to paste these into Notepad or OneNote to search within an entry.

This content search query did produce some false positives, turning up some entries about chicken and burgers also. Maybe Microsoft is doing some smart matching of synonyms and thought those terms were close to `meatwad`?

 Food for thought: If you name your secret initiatives after lunch, you can expect to discover emails about the company picnic. Similar issues arise if you use players from your local football team.

Despite this, content search was very reliable overall when it comes to always bringing back results whenever someone mentioned `Master Shake`.

The system can discover mentions in email, various SharePoint document types, OneDrive for Business, Skype for Business, Yammer, and even discussions on Teams (shown later as **IM**). So, this is about as close as you can get to a digital dragnet.

As you can see from the list mentioned later, the highlighted entry was a company-wide announcement in 2012 regarding the policy toward code-named projects, and few people have used the specific term we're interested in. However, it recently came up in conversations again this year, so perhaps it's worth investigating why this topic has resurfaced lately:

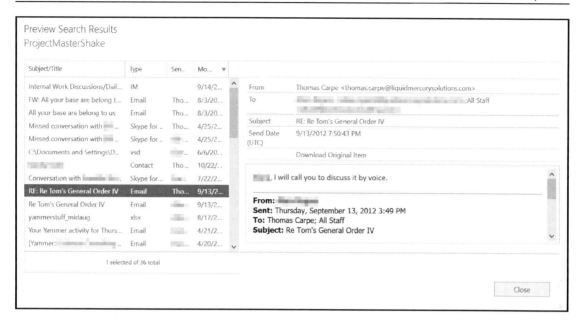

Content search, run, and preview (old UI)

If your investigations turn up something interesting, you can export the results (**Start export**) or just an Excel worksheet with the headers (**Generate a report**). In this way, its capabilities are very much like the eDiscovery tools that have been part of Office 365 for a long while now.

There are many applications for these tools: they can be used to meet all sorts of security and privacy requirements, including DFARS, ITAR, NIST in the US, GDPR in Europe, and other regulatory regimes. Truly, **Content search** is a security or compliance officer's dream come true.

Audit log search

If you happen to be a seasoned SharePoint administrator, you've probably had the experience of being frustrated by the complete inscrutability of SharePoint's audit logs. Fear not! Not only is **Security & Compliance | Audit log search** the answer to your SharePoint security woes, it also has visibility into other aspects of Office 365 outside of SharePoint.

Let's suppose that someone deleted an important document in SharePoint, or at least the CEO thinks somebody has. People are in the hallway waving torches and pitchforks, demanding to know who should be tarred, feathered, and terminated with prejudice! (Don't laugh: this *is* based on a true story.) They want answers, answers that could take you days of effort and will only bring sorrow down on everyone when you eventually discover it was the boss's kid who's the culprit. In the past, you may have put your effort into trying to talk down the angry mob—risking that they'll accept your head in a basket in lieu of someone else's.

Just to make sure that we know where things truly stand, let's do a quick audit check before we face the multitudes and their discontent.

To start, pick all the events related to deleting a document:

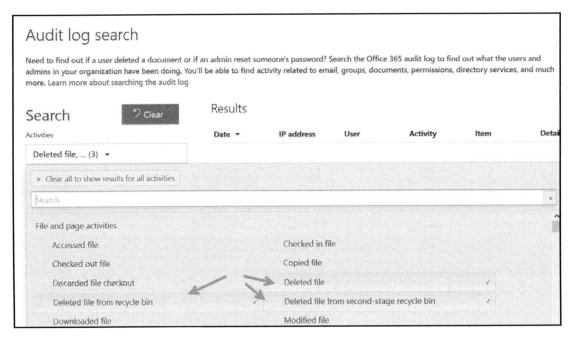

Audit log search, choose activity types

We give it a date range as we know the incident occurred sometime in the past week.

In a real-life case, maybe we know the location of the missing document. We'll cast a wider net here as we happen to know that management are not always perfectly precise when it comes to the technical details when they're working in SharePoint.

Results may take a while to appear, in which case you'll see the message **Results (loading)**. This search took less than a minute to appear:

Results	13 results found					
Date ▾	IP address	User	Activity	Item	Detail
2017-09-05 18:...	72.60.145.251	thomas.carpe@...	Deleted file	▓+LMS - Clo...	Deleted from "...
2017-09-05 18:...	72.60.145.251	thomas.carpe@...	Deleted file	▓+LMS - Clo...	Deleted from "...
2017-09-05 16:...	173.8.7.241	▓▓▓@li...	Deleted file	Case-Study---H...	Deleted from "s...
2017-09-05 16:...	173.8.7.241	▓▓▓@li...	Deleted file	Case-Study---H...	Deleted from "s...
2017-09-05 16:...	173.8.7.241	▓▓▓@li...	Deleted file	Case-Study---H...	Deleted from "s...
2017-09-05 15:...	173.8.7.241	▓▓▓@li...	Deleted file	Case-Study---H...	Deleted from "s...

Audit log, search results

This report event shows us documents that were deleted from Tom's OneDrive for Business folder and files from a public facing SharePoint website. What's more, it is 99.51% certain that we never enabled SharePoint audit logs in either of these locations.

Ultimately, it turns out that the document people are screaming about doesn't show up in this report. Further investigation reveals that the document was never deleted. Someone edited a page in SharePoint, so the link to the document no longer appeared and then everyone panicked. Thanks to Office 365 Security & Compliance audit logs, the admins quickly figured out what really happened, repaired the damage, and soothed everyone's frazzled nerves. The boss's kid got some much-needed training on SharePoint site and page development, and everyone kept their jobs and their heads.

eDiscovery

Up until recently, **eDiscovery** was basically just a wrapper around **Content search**. However, Microsoft recently made major changes to the UI. This new functionality drastically increases both the functionality and complexity of the eDiscovery tools.

This is fantastic if your entire job is focused around providing accountability for a large organization, but it can be daunting if you're just a run-of-the-mill sysadmin who needs only the basics. We'll do our best to stick to those aspects of eDiscovery, that might be useful to the average person:

eDiscovery, create case (new UI)

Creating a case

Click on **Create a case**, and you'll be taken to a screen with many of the same options you'll find in **Content search**:

eDiscovery, create case, name, and description (new UI)

Managing cases

Once you've created a case, it will appear in the eDiscovery list:

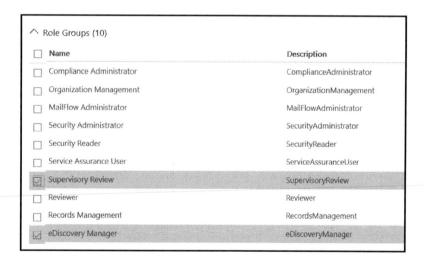

Case name	Status	Created	Last modified ∨	Modified by
Open Who Framed Roger Rabbit	Active	2017-09-17 21:34:25	2018-05-07 12:57:05	Thomas Carpe

eDiscovery, manage cases (new UI)

Although it's not immediately obvious to the naked eye, Microsoft expects you to click on the name of the case if you want to review details or add users. The **Open** button takes you into the case itself, which is where you perform search and hold activities.

If you have a team who need to work on the case, you would add them in the same place where you would update the name and description, by clicking on the case name. There's no option to do either of these once you **Open** the case.

You can also add **Role Groups** in the same way. These are groups that can contain multiple people, so in this way, for example, you can invite all the records managers to participate in the case:

∧ Role Groups (10)

Name	Description
Compliance Administrator	ComplianceAdministrator
Organization Management	OrganizationManagement
MailFlow Administrator	MailFlowAdministrator
Security Administrator	SecurityAdministrator
Security Reader	SecurityReader
Service Assurance User	ServiceAssuranceUser
☑ Supervisory Review	SupervisoryReview
Reviewer	Reviewer
Records Management	RecordsManagement
☑ eDiscovery Manager	eDiscoveryManager

eDiscovery, manage cases, details dialog, and add role groups (new UI)

Once you add a user or role group, you'll see an alert indicating that it was successful. If something went wrong, you may see a notification here indicating that there was a problem.

Although we didn't attempt to add them, we did see guest users in the list. It would be an interesting experiment to find out if users outside the organization can be invited to participate in an eDiscovery case. For example, perhaps this could be used to invite outside legal counsel to participate.

Core versus advanced

We've talked a bit about how **eDiscovery** is similar to **Content search**. Unlike **Content search**, once you create a case, **eDiscovery** will include both search and hold functions:

eDiscovery case home, core (new UI)

Under the new UI, the case will default to **Core ED**. You can switch to advanced eDiscovery and easily switch back:

eDiscovery case home, advanced (new UI)

As you can see, **AED** has three levels instead of two and includes a lot of additional features designed to structure complex eDiscovery cases.

Advanced eDiscovery functions could easily fill an entire chapter, plus we wouldn't want to confuse everyone. So, here we'll cover **Core ED**. (Perhaps this is something we can come back to for the online appendix.)

Search

In **eDisovery**, core search functionality is inherently similar to what's available in **Content search**. But, the screens have been updated. If you're more comfortable with the old UI, you have a chance to switch back into it, at least for the moment:

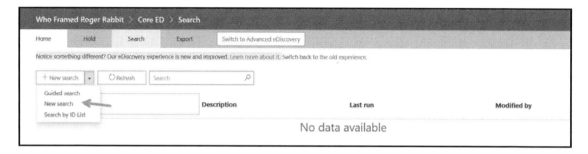

eDiscovery, new search (new UI)

New search is the default and will open on the left-hand side of the current screen. It is a streamlined search interface designed for more experienced eDiscovery users. **Search by ID list** is for uploading CSV documents that identify specific items of interest that were previously exported. New users will likely prefer **Guided search**, which offers just a bit more hand-holding.

Let's quickly walk through our `Master Shake` example again to show how the new UI works in eDiscovery. We'll select **Guided search**.

The first step is to give your search a name and description, as usual:

eDiscovery, new guided search, name, and description (new UI)

The list of locations subject to eDiscovery is much larger now. It now includes Exchange email, Office 365 Groups email, Skype for Business messages, Teams messages, To Do, My Analytics, other Office 365 Data, SharePoint sites, OneDrive accounts, Office 365 Groups sites, Teams sites, and Exchange public folders:

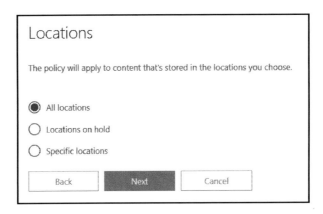

eDiscovery, new guided search, choose location(s) (new UI)

Note that if you choose **Specific locations**, you'll have to manually enable each subcategory. Let's select **All locations** for simplicity:

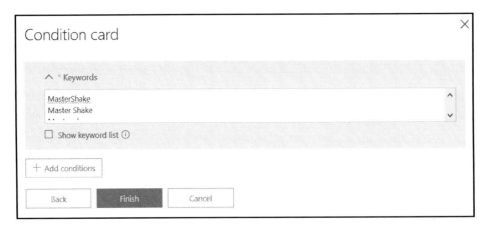

eDiscovery, new guided search, keywords, and conditions (new UI)

The UI here is still a bit glitchy, so be careful. We actually managed to crash Firefox with this window (several times!) by clicking around on all the controls.

Type keywords or phrases, one per line, in the provided textbox. As the description states, these will be searched using OR conditions. Use **Add conditions** if you want to add additional criteria, such as limiting the scope to specific users or a date range. Click on **Finish** to end the walkthrough:

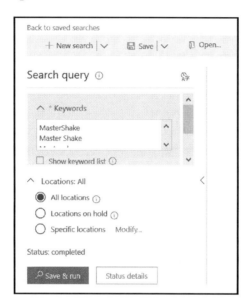

eDiscovery, new search (new UI)

At this point, the screen looks just as it would if you had used **New search** instead of **Guided search**. Click on **Save & run** to complete the search setup and run your query.

At this point, although we followed the instructions, we received a warning about illegal characters. Having double-checked what we have set up, we decide to choose **Keep query** and see how things turn out. Seems like Microsoft may still be working on some of the bugs in the new UI.

Searching may take quite a while to complete, depending on how complex your query is and how many locations you're searching.

In this case, our query returned no results, so we assume that there's something the matter with the way we provided the keywords. Unfortunately, every time we check the **Show keywords** checkbox, the browser freezes. Perhaps there's still some justification for keeping the old UI available.

Hold

As you'll see, the **Hold** functionality is very similar to **Search**. The main difference is that **Hold** will put retention policies into place for all content that matches the provided query. As such, there are fewer options currently in place (since there are fewer systems that support retention **Hold**):

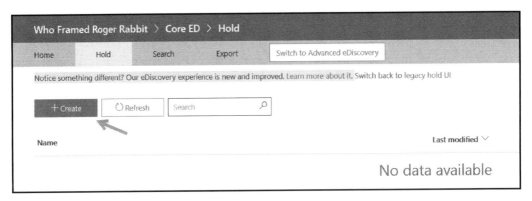

eDiscovery, hold (new UI)

Let's create a hold to capture email for a user we think might be terminated later this week.

As usual, the first step is to name the hold and provide a description:

eDiscovery, create hold, name, and description (new UI)

In a real-world case, maybe you would put the employee's name in the title—or maybe you wouldn't want to have that out there where everyone will see it.

Unlike other content searches, you will have to explicitly define locations here:

eDiscovery, create hold, location(s), Exchange details (new UI)

It didn't show on the main screen previously, but we selected the mailbox for **Cody Netstein**. We don't think he'll mind, since he's only a fictional company mascot and doesn't draw a paycheck anyway.

If we wanted to retain all the mail that mentions Cody, whether it was in his mailbox or not, we'd need to include more users in the earlier selection—possibly many more. Here, we're only concerned about protecting ourselves in places Cody has access to write (or delete) information:

eDiscovery, create hold, location(s), SharePoint details (new UI)

We enter two sites for SharePoint, one for the intranet and the other is a team site used by our Cloud Support team.

Leave keywords blank for a blanket capture in the Query conditions page.

We'll use **Add condition** to ensure that only documents Cody modified are put on hold. (Created would be used to only hold documents created within a given date range.)

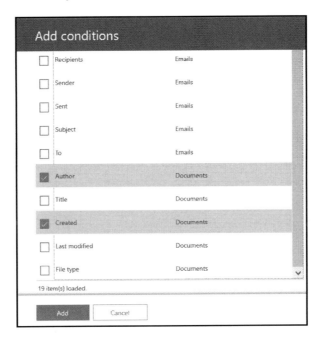

eDiscovery, create hold, add condition details (new UI)

Finally, review your settings and create your hold:

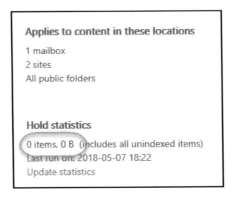

eDiscovery, hold settings, and statistics (new UI)

It didn't take very long for Office 365 to show us that actually as Cody isn't a real person, he doesn't have any items in his mailbox nor was he the author of any documents in SharePoint. Who knew?!

 Read more about the new eDiscovery UI at `https://support.office.com/en-us/article/ediscovery-cases-in-the-office-365-security-compliance-center-8dd335ab-29d0-41c3-8dd8-9f7c7481e60c`.

Productivity app discovery

Productivity app discovery is a springboard into Office 365 Cloud App Security, which is a component provided in Office 365 E5 plans. This service allows you to monitor and control how different cloud-based productivity applications are used in your organization and what Office 365 data they can access. It is provided outside the Office 365 admin center via the website: `https://portal.cloudappsecurity.com`. The checkbox and button that appear on this page will take you there:

Productivity app discovery link to Cloud App Security

Note that Microsoft Cloud App Security is a separate service provided in Enterprise Mobility and Security E3 and E5 plans. Some of the capabilities of this service are very similar to those in Office 365 Cloud App Security, but work through different methods. A full discussion of all the available features would be beyond the scope of this book.

To use Cloud App Discovery, you will need to either manually upload logs from a firewall or compatible device, or otherwise create a data source and log collection connector using FTP, FTPS, or Syslog. The list of compatible devices has many vendors including BlueCoat, Barracuda, CheckPoint, Cisco, Clavister, Digital Arts, Dell SonicWall, Fortinet, Jupiter, McAfee, Microsoft, Palo Alto, Sophos, Squid, WebSense, and ZScaler.

Security & Compliance reports

`Chapter 14`, *Usage Reporting* will talk about most common Office 365 reports, which are centered around driving user adoption and tracking activity. **Reports** in the **Security & Compliance** center focus on identifying threat activity and providing information on compliance-related features such as document labeling and DLP policies.

> Security & Compliance reports can now be bookmarked at `https://protection.office.com/#/insightdashboard`.

Reports dashboard

The top-line view of **Security & Compliance** | **Reports** offers a lot of information at a glance with very little depth. If you have yet to configure DLP or labels, the first two rows of tiles will be completely without any valuable information:

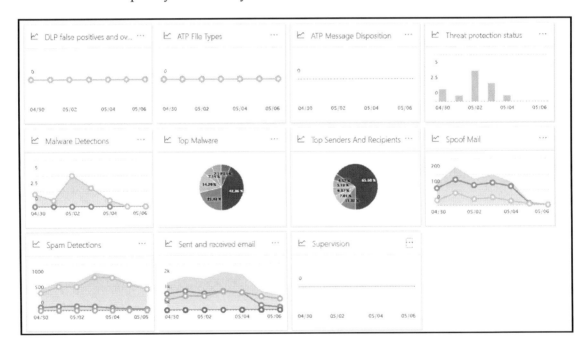

Excerpts from Security & Compliance | Reports | Dashboard

By default, the **Dashboard** only displays about 5 days' worth of data. This can make it exceedingly difficult to determine whether any apparent decline might just be a weekend phenomenon, as shown earlier where many metrics appear to show some improvement—until you consider that 5/5 was a Saturday and data for Monday 5/7 isn't available yet.

There are some things worth looking at, but we'll need to drill down into the underlying reports to get any true insight:

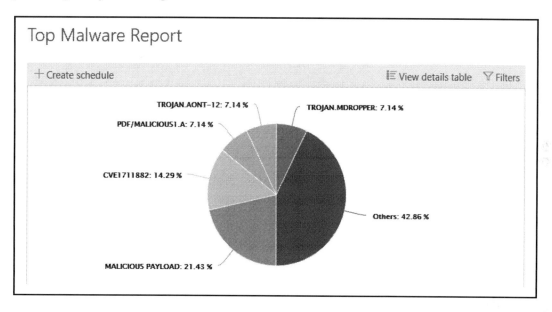

Top Malware Report

For example, the **Top Malware Report** will only show us what the threats are called when it had sufficient room to do so. From here, we can gain some insight into what threats are active and ensure that we have countermeasures in place on the desktop, which can provide an additional layer to protect users:

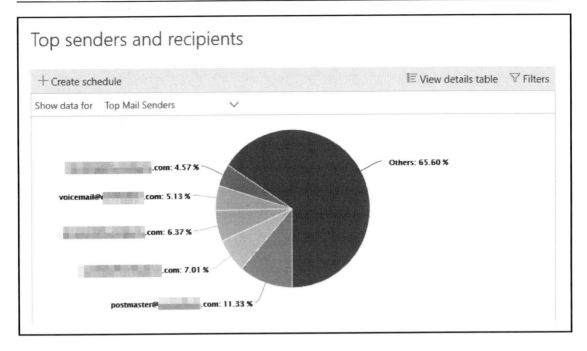

Top email senders and receivers report

This is also true for the top senders and receivers (of email) report. A quick check of the report details tells us that senior members of the company and the VoIP telephone voicemail system are among the most prolific email users, which isn't surprising at all.

We also see that Postmaster has a lot of traffic, presumably because people are emailing old accounts, or attempting to use brute force tactics to find legit email addresses they can spam. It might be worth spending some time to research whether some senders of email should be blacklisted in EOP:

Malware detections report and request report dialog

Here, we can see that the **Malware Detections Report** isn't much more useful in the detailed view than it is in the dashboard. It still only goes back a week.

If we want a longer date range, we can use a request report to receive one by email. However, even this will only go back 90 days. Also, you can only email it to people within your organization. It would seem you'll need to create Exchange contacts or mail flow rules if you also want to send it to your cloud security partner. When it is ready, your requested report will show up in the **Dashboard** under **Recent reports for download**:

.

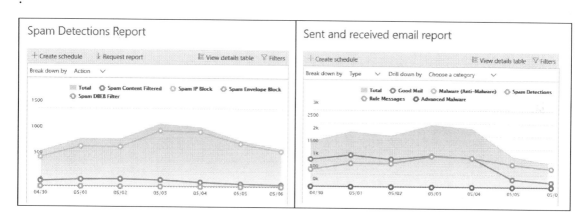

Spam detection and email send and receive report

Here, we see that the spam detection report tells us only part of the story. Once we view the total of emails sent and received, we're finally able to determine that it is a *drop in good emails* that is responsible for the apparent downward trend. Next time, we'll open that report first.

All these reports give you the opportunity to review the tabular data that drives the graphs, so if you see something abnormal, you may be able to learn more about the cause by looking there.

Read more about Office 365 Security & Compliance reports at `https://support.office.com/en-us/article/monitor-security-and-compliance-in-office-365-b62f1722-fd39-44eb-8361-da61d21509b6` under the Monitor Reports section, with additional information available at `https://support.office.com/en-us/article/reports-in-the-office-365-security-compliance-center-7acd33ce-1ec8-49fb-b625-43bac7b58c5a.`

Scheduled reports

To manage scheduled reports, you need to set up at least one report schedule. This is done using the **Create schedule** button from any of the available reports:

.

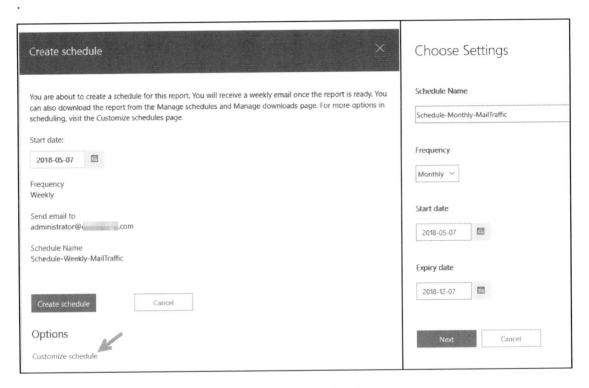

Schedule report and customize schedule options

Of course, the default options here may not be what you want. Use the **Custom schedule** link to specify different options, including frequency.

You have only the choice between weekly and monthly, and you must choose an expiration date. Be sure to mark your calendar if you want to keep these reports coming after they expire.

One useful feature is that you can schedule a report to filter on specific data, such as a specific sender or recipient. This can be useful if you are monitoring an ongoing situation or trying to diagnose a problem for a single user. Other reports also have different criteria that may apply to their unique data.

Like the downloadable custom reports, you may specify other users to receive the email notices. Just like before, we are constrained to users who are in our system and have a mailbox, so you will need to jump through hoops if you want to send the data to your support partner's email.

Unfortunately, there doesn't appear to be any means to consolidate multiple reports into a single scheduled email notification.

Once you have a scheduled report configured, you can come back to **Manage schedules** if you need to make changes:

	Schedule start date ...	Name	Report type	Frequency	Last sent
☐	May 7, 2018	Schedule-Monthly-MailTraffic	MailTraffic	Monthly	

Manage your report schedules here

Search

Manage scheduled reports

Since all scheduled reports expire, it might be a good idea to set a date on your calendar to return to the **Manage schedules** page and set the expiration date farther into the future.

Downloadable reports

The **Recent reports for download** tile on the dashboard includes a link to **View all downloads**, and this will take you to the same page as the **Recent reports for download** link in the left-hand navigation. From here, you can see all requested reports. Clicking on a report will pull its details. If the **Download** button is disabled, this means that your data is not ready yet. Come back later, or after you get the email notification.

Security score card

Perhaps one of Microsoft's best kept secrets in terms of security tools is the **Security score** application. Although it was originally announced via the **Security & Compliance** dashboard, this platform isn't even listed under the current iteration of the site.

 To access Security Score, visit `https://securescore.office.com/`.

Recent news indicates that Microsoft has renamed the Office 365 Security score to Microsoft SecurityScore, which is perhaps an indication that it will be rolled into Enterprise Mobility and Security (and thus Microsoft 365, formerly Secure Productive Enterprise). Therefore, we can't promise you that your E3 or E5 license will always guarantee access to it.

Regardless, we're going to highlight SecurityScore anyway. It is an extremely useful and visually compelling way to improve your Office 365 security practices, whether or not you have specific compliance requirements. Even if you only rarely use the other tools in the **Security & Compliance** section, SecurityScore can help you immediately from day one to implement best security practices. It will also help you generate tangible metrics to demonstrate that you're taking security seriously and seeking continual improvement over time.

As Microsoft emphasizes, having a good Security Score does not guarantee that you won't get hacked. No tool can do that. What it does indicate is whether you are doing those things that will help to reduce the likelihood of a breach. It will also recommend specific things that you can do to improve. Use the SecurityScore to guide continual improvement over time and to identify when efforts may be slipping:

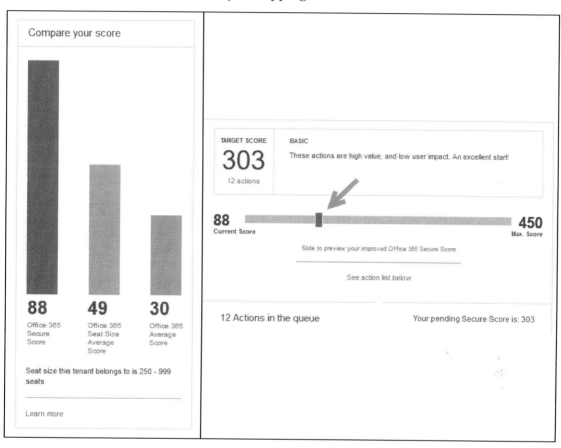

Excerpts from Secure Score Dashboard

Use the chart provided on the Dashboard to compare your score to other organizations of your size. Higher scores are better. While it's clear that at 88, we're doing much better than the average organization of our size, there's still a lot of room to improve.

Microsoft considers any action below about 305 to be **Basic**, meaning the bare minimum no-brainer actions that need to be taken. Target scores from 300 to 400 are considered **Balanced**, and anything over 400 is **Aggressive**.

You'll see language referring to `pending score`. This is your target score, or what you're aiming for. You can use the sliding control, as shown earlier, to adjust your ambitions. Then, click the **Actions** link or just scroll down to review actions you can take to improve your score.

In some cases, merely following the prompts within a recommended action will activate certain security features and give you benefits right away. We recommend you consider carefully if there will be implications for end users, communication requirements, or other ramifications. Pay attention to the indicated **User Impact** for the recommended action:

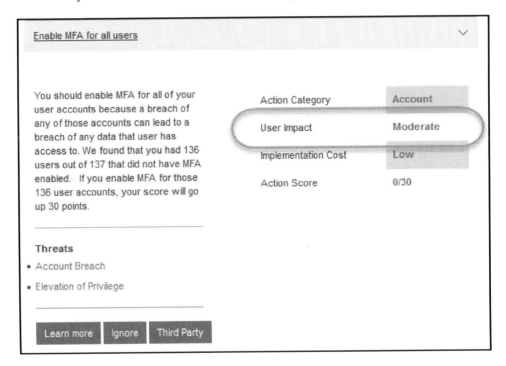

Recommended action list item details

Clicking the **Learn more** button will bring up a side panel with additional information about the recommended change. If it can be implemented automatically, there will be a **Launch** button at the bottom of this panel. Otherwise, the change must be done manually. In many cases, using the automated wizard may have a negative effect on usability. At the very least, be sure you fully understand if it is OK to make a change or if perhaps you should implement it manually.

If you see recommendations that you know do not apply in your environment, you may use the **Ignore** or **Third Party** buttons to suppress those messages and their impact on your security score.

Use **Third Party** in cases where you know the risk is being mitigated by tools or technology that is provided outside of Office 365 and Microsoft's ability to monitor it. For example, perhaps you have security monitoring software such as GFI LanGuard which is responsible for updating Windows machines or disabling inactive accounts in Active Directory, and Office 365 has no visibility into what you've implemented in your on-premises environment.

Keep in mind, you should only suppress recommended actions conservatively; you wouldn't want to lull yourself into a false sense of security. Be sure to leave a comment about why the item is ignored.

If you use the security tool regularly over time, you'll up your security game considerably. Just scheduling a few hours every so often to review tips and act on those you can will go a long way. If you have a security team meeting, you can bring its recommendations to your meeting and look like an expert. If you're an army of one, put a reminder on your calendar to set time aside once a month.

Summary

In this chapter, we reviewed all the varying capabilities of the **Security & Compliance** admin center (`https://protection.office.com`). We went over permissions, and how to set up the **Security & Compliance** center so your security team can get the best use from it by using **Service assurance** tools. We walked through **Alerts**, including what's provided out of the box, adding new ones, and how to manage them. We looked at labels and other tools for document classification, and we discussed how these inturn feed into and empower data leak prevention policies. We explored research tools such a **Content search**, **Audit logs**, and the new-and-improved **eDiscovery** center. We detailed some real-life use cases where these tools can be useful in day-to-day situations that come up in IT. Finally, we looked at reporting capabilities, including the SecurityScore card. With this information in hand, you should now have a well-rounded understanding of what's available and any additional work that may be required to maximize your tenant's security and meet compliance requirements, while also enabling user productivity.

In the next chapter, we will learn how to manage Skype for Business.

9
Administering Skype for Business

Skype for Business offers many exciting capabilities for the modern, distributed office. These go beyond simply being able to send instant messages to your coworkers or attend the weekly meeting. Skype for Business has evolved into a modern, robust telecommunications platform that includes digital voice services that can replace online meeting services, such as GoToMeeting or WebEx, and even your phone provider. As an Office 365 administrator, you'll need to be familiar with how to effectively leverage and manage these services.

In this chapter, we'll show you how to:

- Configure Skype for Business's global and user-specific settings
- Control audio/video conferences and online broadcasts
- Build complex systems for inter-department call routing
- Deploy Skype for Business as a PBX telephone system
- Plan for advanced aspects of deploying telephonic solutions, including caller ID, number portability, hybrid systems, phone hardware, and the needs of call centers

So, let's jump right in and start configuring Skype. This can be done via the admin portal through the link to the Skype for Business admin center.

Configuring organization-wide settings

Oddly enough, organization-wide settings are given a second billing, underneath the section for managing users, but this is probably the first place you'll want to go when you first set up your tenant.

Settings are organized into two tabs: **general** and **external communications**:

Skype general organization-wide settings

In the **general** tab, there are only three settings: **presence privacy mode**, **Microsoft Push Notification Service**, and **Apple Push Notification Service**.

Let's consider **presence privacy mode** for a moment. By default, anyone can access your presence information—whether they're in your Skype for Business contacts list or not. While we cannot confirm this, we interpret this to mean that those who are able to may be able to invade your privacy by coding against Skype's APIs and guessing your SIP address from your email address. Therefore, we recommend that you should set this to **Display presence information only to a user's contacts**.

According to Microsoft:

> "*On Android and Symbian (Nokia) phones, Skype for Business notifications pop up in real time. For Windows Phone, iPhone, and iPad devices, however, push notification is used to show the alerts whenever you're not actively using Skype for Business on your phone or tablet.*"

Thus, the checkboxes in the **general** tab only affect iOS and Windows mobile phones; it's likely you'll never need to uncheck these.

Now, let's move on to the **external communications** tab. The purpose of this tab is to control who can send messages to users in your tenant, and who your users can send messages to:

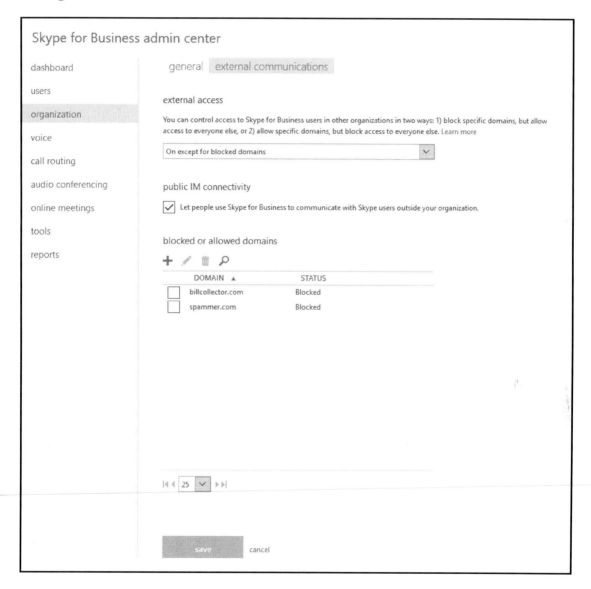

Skype organization-wide settings for external communications

These settings operate in one of two modes. Blacklisting allows all accounts specified, whether outside Skype for Business or Lync organizations, to be blocked. The preceding screenshot shows an example where a couple of (fictional) nuisance domains are blocked in this way. The whitelisting mode will block everyone except the domains you specify, which can be a good approach to preventing information leaks and ensuring that only authorized business partners can chat with your staff.

In the event your company has policies that disallow personal IM in the workplace, you may need to uncheck the box under **public IM connectivity**. Note that this could have an impact if you have users who need to communicate regarding business matters with outside parties who use personal Skype accounts.

Audio conferencing

The **audio conferencing** section has a global configuration for Skype for Business meetings. These settings can also be overridden on a per-user basis. It's also worth noting that many settings for **audio conferencing** can't be set globally using the website, and you will need to configure them for each user individually. We'll go into more detail on configuring **audio conferencing** user settings a bit later.

Microsoft bridge

Microsoft provides a couple dozen conference bridges worldwide. Depending on your tenant settings, you may also see several dedicated service numbers assigned to your company for use with conferencing, as shown in the following screenshot:

Skype for Business admin center

dashboard

users

organization

voice

call routing

audio conferencing

online meetings

tools

reports

Microsoft bridge   Microsoft bridge settings   users

These are the phone numbers used with this conference bridge. You can change languages for dedicated numbers or change the default toll number.

	Phone number	Type	Category	Location	Primary language	Default
✓	+1 872-212-	Toll	Dedicat	Chicago, United State	English (United S	
	+1 213-493-	Toll	Dedicat	Los Angeles, United S	English (United S	
	+1 469-480-	Toll	Dedicat	Dallas, United States	English (United S	
	+1 646-844-	Toll	Dedicat	New York City, Unite	English (United S	Default
	+31 20 258 8	Toll	Shared	Amsterdam, Netherla	Dutch (Netherla	
	+32 2 890 97	Toll	Shared	Bruxelles/Brussels, Be	Dutch (Netherla	
	+45 32 72 05	Toll	Shared	København, Denmarl	Danish (Denmarl	
	+1 469-480-	Toll	Shared	Dallas, United States	English (United S	
	+49 69 6677:	Toll	Shared	Frankfurt am Main, G	German (Germar	
	+1 773-917-	Toll	Shared	Chicago, United State	English (United S	
	+44 20 3321	Toll	Shared	London, United King	English (United F	
	+1 213-373-	Toll	Shared	Los Angeles, United S	English (United S	
	+34 910 38 8	Toll	Shared	Madrid, Spain	Spanish (Spain)	
	+39 02 0062	Toll	Shared	Milano, Italy	Italian (Italy)	
	+1 646-838-	Toll	Shared	New York City, Unite	English (United S	
	+33 1 70 99	Toll	Shared	Paris, France	French (France)	
	+46 8 505 21	Toll	Shared	Stockholm, Sweden	Swedish (Swede	
	+1 647-749-	Toll	Shared	Toronto, Canada	English (United S	
	+43 1 20563	Toll	Shared	Vienna, Austria	German (Germar	
	+41 43 210 5	Toll	Shared	Zurich/Zürich/Zurigc	German (Germar	
	+351 21 121	Toll	Shared	Lisbon, Portugal	Portuguese (Porl	
	+61 2 8318 (	Toll	Shared	Sydney, Australia	English (Australi	
	+81 3-4510-	Toll	Shared	Tokyo, Japan	Japanese (Japan)	
	+64 4-280 8	Toll	Shared	Wellington, New Zea	English (Australi	
	+63 2 231 31	Toll	Shared	Manila, Philippines	Filipino (Philippi	
	+7 495 118-(	Toll	Shared	Moscow, Russia	Russian (Russia)	
	+65 3157 60	Toll	Shared	Singapore, Singapore	English (United S	
	+66 2 104 0€	Toll	Shared	Bangkok, Thailand	Thai (Thailand)	
	+886 2 5592	Toll	Shared	Taipei, Taiwan	Chinese (Traditic	

+1 872-212-431 7

Chicago, United States

Unassign
Set as default
Set languages

Primary language

English (United States)

Secondary languages

Spanish (Mexico)

Audio-conferencing: Microsoft bridge

The table will identify **Dedicated** and **Shared** numbers, as well as **Toll** numbers versus **Toll-Free**. The assignment of **Dedicated** and **Toll-Free** numbers is handled in the **voice** section.

The only really useful thing you can do from this screen is to specify the default bridge, which is the number that will be displayed in calendar invites and emails when conference information is included. To change this, simply check a number and click **Set as default** in the right-hand margin.

You can also specify additional language options for **Dedicated** numbers. However, most numbers come with reasonable defaults for their region. The only useful scenario we could imagine here is if you needed to configure the French language with a number for Montreal, Quebec; for all we know, this might already be the default option.

Microsoft bridge settings

The **Microsoft bridge settings** tab has a few more options that will apply regardless of which bridge line a caller uses, as shown in the following screenshot:

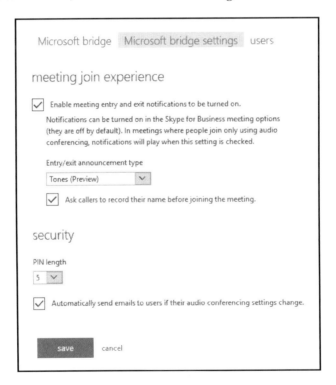

Microsoft bridge settings

You can enable or disable meeting entry and exit notifications and ask callers to provide a name before they join the call. There's even a new setting allowing you to choose between announcing a name or phone number or just playing the customary *ba-beep* tone when someone joins a call. In our experience, however, these announcements don't seem to play no matter what settings we choose. Maybe we're doing something wrong. Go figure.

You can also choose the number of digits used in audio-conference PINs. You may specify anything from **4** to **12** digits. In our opinion, **4** is probably reasonable for most applications and anything bigger than **5** or **6** digits would be very difficult to use. We recommend leaving the option to automatically notify users about changes enabled; however, there may be cases where you will want to turn it off, such as during initial configuration or testing.

Audio conferencing users

Settings shown under the **users** tab are just quick links that take you to the **audio conferencing** section of the edit user(s) screens. The functionality here is identical, so we'll talk about this in detail in the next section.

Managing Skype for Business users

Now that we've looked at global settings, let's return to the users under the first heading. The following screenshot shows the **users** section with a few items redacted for security:

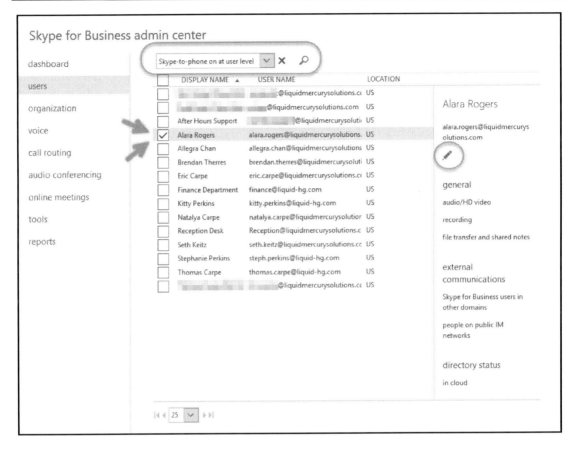

Managing Skype users

Looking at the top of the users list, you'll see the usual handy tools to filter and search. Filtering options include: all users, audio only, A/V on or off, high-def A/V, audio conferencing on or off, external access on or off, recording on or off, Skype-to-phone (POTS dialing) on or off, and in cloud or synced. The search box will find users based on either their username or display name.

Use the checkboxes on the left-hand side to select users. When selecting a user, their settings will appear in the margin along the right-hand side. You may select and edit multiple users; you can't do this across pages, so you may need to increase the page size in the lower-left corner. For this reason, larger organizations will find the web interface completely impractical for bulk edits and will need to use PowerShell instead.

In our example, let's select three users and click the edit icon, which is a small pencil shown in the upper-right corner. The following screenshots show the edit settings pages.

General user settings

The **general** section shows the basic settings available. Here, you can set audio-video options, enable or disable the ability to record meetings, and turn off features that don't work with message retention:

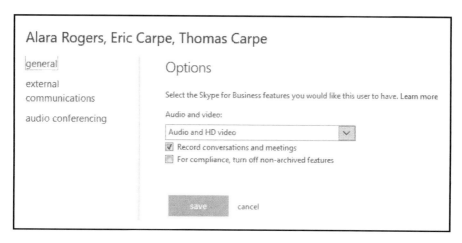

Editing Skype user(s), general settings

The **Audio and video** options include **None**, **Audio only**, regular **Audio and video**, and **Audio and HD video**. Turning off advanced video for certain users can help to control bandwidth or improve call quality.

User settings for external communications

The **external communications** section lets you specify instant messaging settings for people outside your organization on an individual user basis:

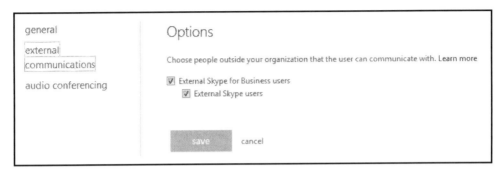

Editing Skype user(s), external communications

You may need to utilize this setting if you have a team doing sensitive work or some part-time college students that you need to keep from chatting in Skype. Note that disabling **External Skype for Business users** will also block personal Skype users.

User voice settings

If you're editing a single user, you'll see a **voice** section appear. You can view their assigned voice telephone number here but the web application doesn't allow you to modify it. Use the main **voice** section to configure voice services for users.

Audio conferencing user settings

The **audio conferencing** section has a lot of options. If you're bulk editing users, some of these will be missing and a warning will be displayed along the right-hand side of the page:

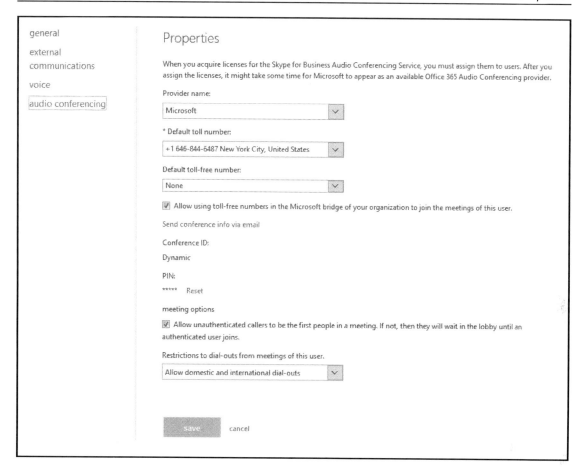

When you acquire licenses for the Skype for Business Audio Conferencing Service, you must assign them to users. After you assign the licenses, it might take some time for Microsoft to appear as an available Office 365 Audio Conferencing provider.

Edit Skype user(s), audio-conferencing

If you're using one, you can specify an external provider. (This was more useful back in the days when Microsoft didn't have dial-in conferencing of their own.) You can set the default dial-in number on a per user basis, which is helpful if your organization has folks in various parts of the world or spread across the US. If you have a toll-free dial-in service enabled, you can enable or disable it per-user, which can help control costs.

There's also a link to send the user information about their dial-in conference settings. There's not much to this email except to indicate the dial-in number and whether the user's PIN or other settings have changed. It can be a time saver when notifying multiple users. There's also a link to reset the user's dial-in PIN, which also sends an email, but doesn't let you choose the PIN.

> You can learn more about dynamic meeting IDs at the following address: `https://docs.microsoft.com/en-us/skypeforbusiness/audio-conferen cing-in-office-365/using-audio-conferencing-dynamic-ids-in-your- organization`.

There is a checkbox that controls how and if external parties can join meetings, as shown in the following screenshot. By default, these users can join the meeting before the organizer. This could allow folks in the same company to kibitz with each other, but it can also be awkward or even risky to let callers who may be from different businesses do this without a moderator. We recommend changing this setting to enable the lobby:

 ☐ Allow unauthenticated callers to be the first people in a meeting. If not, then they will wait in the lobby until an authenticated user joins.

The audio-conferencing lobby setting

The last setting controls how the user can place calls. The choices are to allow domestic and international calling, allow domestic calling only, or don't allow outside calls. For example, you may have people working in the help desk call center where placing outbound calls is prohibited, or you may a have rate-based international calling plan enabled but still need to prevent expensive calls from certain users.

Online meetings

There's not much to configuring online meetings. For example, we thought this would be the logical place to define settings for the lobby, but these are simply not available here.

Meeting invites

Here's what's shown under the **meeting invitation** tab:

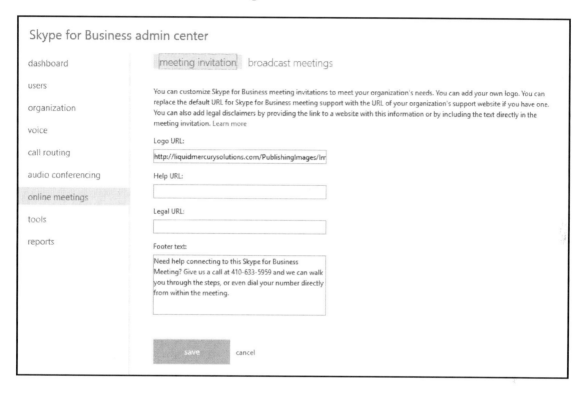

Online meeting invitations

Here, you can also specify a **Logo URL**. This is nice for branding purposes in your meeting invites. As you can see in the preceding screenshot, we provide a URL pointing to an image hosted on our public-facing SharePoint site, but you can use any website that doesn't require authentication.

Optionally, if you have a help page or a legal disclaimer, you can also provide those.

The **Footer text** is a helpful place for providing additional tips or instructions that will be included in the meeting invitation. You might also use this to add a disclaimer that doesn't require clicking a link. For example, we might add `All meetings may be recorded for management or training purposes`.

Broadcast meetings

If you plan to have very large company-wide meetings or if you're interested in hosting your own webinars, you may want to enable broadcast meetings. While most of the functionality for this service is located at `https://portal.broadcast.skype.com`, there are a few basic settings available in the Skype for Business admin center, as shown in the following screenshot:

meeting invitation | broadcast meetings

You can change your organization settings for Skype Meeting Broadcast, a service which allows thousands of attendees to join a single meeting. Learn more

Meeting Settings and Access Policies

☑ Enable Skype Meeting Broadcast.

☑ Enable Skype Meeting Broadcast Preview features for my organization. Learn more

☑ Allow organizers to schedule anonymous meetings.

☑ Allow broadcast meetings to be recorded.

Helpdesk support URL for attendees:

[💾 SAVE] [✕ CANCEL]

Settings for broadcast meetings

From the **broadcast meetings** tab, you can completely disable this part of the service. You can also turn on features that are still in preview mode. You can allow or disallow meetings with anonymous attendees, as well as the ability to record broadcast meetings. If you have a help desk page, you can also provide its URL so that users can access it during the broadcast.

Once the service is enabled, from the **broadcast meetings** portal users can schedule a meeting; pick meeting coordinators; make the meeting public, company-wide, or invitation only; and specify if the meeting will be automatically recorded and whether to provide video-on-demand to the audience.

Broadcast meetings do not appear to support event registration or invites for users who are not already members of your Azure AD. In fact, external or guest users in Azure AD did not show up when we tried to invite them. To handle these parts of the process, you may need to stick to anonymous meetings and develop a custom solution, or even integrate with a third-party service such as Eventbrite.

Managing voice services and calling plans

Now that we've mastered the basics of managing Skype for Business's global and user settings, we can finally dig into the topic that everyone's most excited about—using Skype for Business as a voice telephone service.

Like most VoIP services, Skype for Business offers the capability to use soft-phones (the Skype for Business client), headsets that connect to the computer, and dedicated handsets which can work independently of your PC and even stay on a call while you reboot. Accounts include features you'd expect, such as call forwarding, conference calls, and voicemail with email notification and transcription service. All of these features make Skype for Business well suited to replace other business-class cloud- and hardware-based VoIP phone services.

A word about licenses and costs

Skype for Business calling plans are an add-on to the Office 365 E5 plan. Although you could theoretically add a-la-carte conference calls and PBX services to the E3 plan, doing so adds $12/month to the cost. This is almost as much as the $15/month difference between E3 and E5, so it's not typically worth it—especially when you factor in other E5 features such as Power BI Pro or Exchange Advanced Threat Protection.

Combined with the $35/month cost of the E5, voice calling will add another $12/month for domestic calling or $24/month for unlimited international calls. So, all-in, you'll be spending $47 or $59/month per line. How does one justify such an expense?

For starters, when you factor out the cost for Office Pro Plus desktop and other features of Office 365, the cost of Skype for Business's domestic calling plan will amount to much less per month than a comparable plan from another provider. Even budget plans charge $20/month and above. Providers such as Vonage or 8x8 are charging as much as $40-50 for the same set of premium features that you can find in Skype for Business.

Some business VoIP plans do include services such as online meetings, but if you're also using a service such as GoToMeeting or WebEx, you should factor in those costs too. If you're able to reduce the number of different providers you use, your total costs could drop noticeably. Savings gained by eliminating on-premise hardware and bandwidth used by traditional VoIP solutions will be exponentially greater.

Keeping in mind that none of the services mentioned include any business collaboration tools or software, Office 365 plus a Skype for Business voice plan starts looking like very good value for money.

Obtaining and assigning phone numbers

The first tab under the **voice** section is **phone numbers**, as shown in the following screenshot. This is where the numbers assigned to you will be displayed:

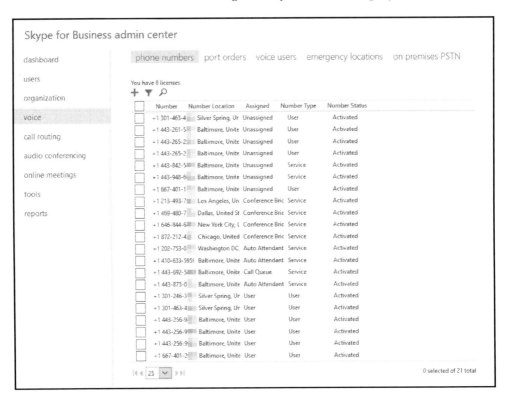

Voice phone numbers

The list shows all phone numbers, their location, whether they're available or assigned, if they are a user number or a service number, and the status (hopefully, activated).

You can filter the list by number range, number status, assignment status (user, conference, or unassigned), number type (user, service, and toll-free), and city. You can use the search function to look up a specific number, numbers starting with an area code and prefix, or just an area code—just remember to start it with the country code (for example: +1), otherwise no results will appear.

To get a new phone number, you'll want to use the plus sign in the upper-left. If you have an existing phone number with another provider, see the following section on number portability. In those cases, you may want to grab a temporary phone number for use in the short term:

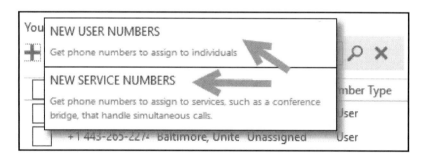

Creating user or service numbers

Be certain to pay careful attention to your choice of user number or service number, because switching from one to the other after-the-fact can be quite daunting. (More on that when we talk about number portability.) Choose a user number if you want to assign the numbers to actual users or stand-in accounts that will be used to forward to an outside service. Choose a service number if you plan to use the number for dial-in conferencing, auto-attendant, or call queues. For example, if you're setting up a main number for the company or department, you will want a service number.

In our example, shown as follows, we're opening an office in Connecticut, and we'll want to use the auto-attendant to let callers from our main line choose that office. We also want folks to be able to dial the new service number to get the CT branch office directly:

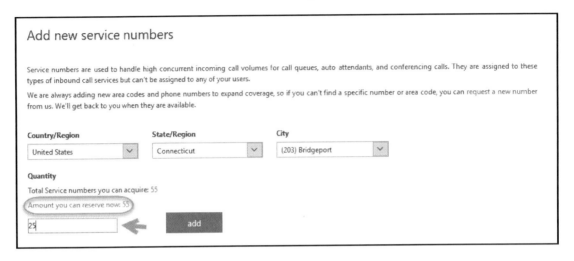

Adding new phone numbers

As you can see in the preceding screenshot, we have a lot of flexibility in terms of how many service numbers we're permitted to claim. With user numbers, we were only allowed as many as we have actual calling plans, so we're overextended.

Since the system will allow us to pick and choose the best numbers from the pool provided, we'll choose an amount on the larger side. By grabbing 25 numbers at once, chances are good that we'll see a few that appeal to us, and probably several with the same prefix:

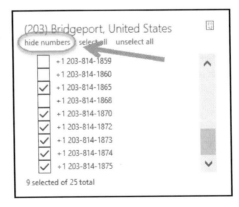

Showing and choosing new phone numbers

Immediately, you're going to want to click on **show numbers** (shown where **hide numbers** is displayed in the preceding screen). Scroll through the list and toss out any numbers you don't like. We ruled out any number where we couldn't get a contiguous block (such as **1831**, **1832**, **1833**, and so on), and we decided to keep **1865** in commemoration of the end of the United States' Civil War.

When you're sure you have the ones you want, click **acquire numbers**. Just be sure to do this before 5 minutes have passed. (We almost ran out of time while performing the preceding example.) If everything was successful, the numbers will appear in **voice | phone numbers** as **Unassigned**, and you can now start using them in services such as the **Auto Attendant**.

Providing emergency locations

If you plan to assign user numbers to users, you're going to need to provide an address to be used for emergency services (that is 911 in the US, 999 in UK, and so on). In most geographies, this will be required:

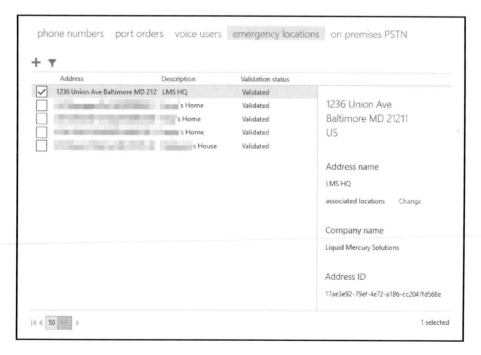

Managing emergency locations

Usually, you would specify the office address, but if you know that a user will be primarily (or frequently) working from home, it may be safer to provide their home address. You should consider the likelihood of calling the police or fire department from your Skype for Business client as opposed to your cell phone or a phone on your desk.

Be sure to schedule routine check-ups for your list of emergency locations. Our preceding example had at least one address of an employee who was no longer working with the company, and another for an employee who had moved to a completely different city and state.

While the web page doesn't provide a way to delete locations, you can change an address without creating extra clutter. It's not particularly obvious, but to do so, go to the existing location, click **Change**, add a second address, and then remove the first address. Maybe someday Microsoft will even give us a way to clean up addresses we don't need anymore.

For more information on how to change the emergency location for a user, visit the following address: `https://docs.microsoft.com/en-us/ SkypeForBusiness/what-are-calling-plans-in-office-365/change- the-emergency-location-for-a-user`.

To add a new location, use the plus sign on the upper-left side and fill out the form that appears along the right-hand margin, as shown in the following screenshot:

Adding a new emergency location address

The form will do its best to auto-validate the address based on Outlook contacts and other mysterious methods. Once entered, use the **validate** button to test that the address is legitimate. If the button does not light up, try entering a company name (or N/A for a home address). You may need to spell the city in capital letters. Once validated, you'll see a green alert box at the top of the form. Be sure to click **save** after this to officially add the location.

Configuring voice users

Now that we have phone numbers to use and emergency locations that we can assign, the final piece of the puzzle is to activate the user's voice account. This is done under the **voice users** tab, shown as follows:

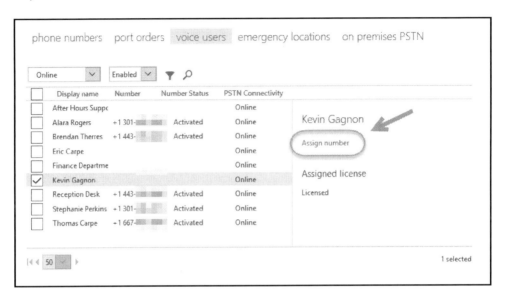

Managing voice users

Before a user appears here, there's a propagation delay of a few minutes after you assign voice licenses. You may see licenses for upcoming users by changing the filter to pending licenses. You can refresh the data by toggling back to active licenses.

Select a licensed user and click **Assign number** in the right-hand margin. You'll be given a list of available user numbers to choose from and be asked to specify an emergency location. Once you've chosen both, click **save** to confirm, as shown in the following screenshot:

Assigning a voice user's number and emergency location

As you can see, setting up a voice phone number isn't too difficult—provided you laid out the groundwork beforehand. Now let's look at Skype for Business's call routing features.

Call routing

Call routing covers two types of service: **auto attendants** and **call queues**. The **auto attendants** service is your basic automated message plus a calling tree. The **call queues** service provides a hold queue and a pool, so the user is asked to wait while somebody can be contacted. These two services can be chained together to create very professional and elaborate calling trees—even if your company is rather small.

The auto attendants service

The **auto attendants** service is an automated service that handles answering the phone and giving the user routing options. Basically, it's what everyone hates: calling a company and ending up in a list of options rather than being able to talk to a human. It's a lot more valuable when it's your company and it's saving your people time and money, however.

The general info section

The **general info** section will let you enter a name for the auto-attendant (for example, main line), assign a service [phone] number, pick the time zone and language, enable or disable speech recognition, and specify an operator (which can be a call queue or a specific user).

The hours of operation section

The **hours of operation** section is a weekly calendar view from Sunday to Saturday that allows you to designate half-hour blocks in which the system is open for business. You can specify different closing times for different days of the week, and you can even choose to close the auto-attendant for a lunch break. You can also choose 24/7, but we don't recommend it unless you're staffed accordingly. During business hours, the attendant follows the rules in **business hours call handling**; otherwise, it follows after hours call handling.

Business hours and after hours call handling

Call handling options are the same for business hours and after hours. The only difference is which set of rules will be applied based on the time the call was connected.

You must set an initial company greeting. This can be either an uploaded audio file or computer-generated text-to-speech. Audio files must be in either the MP3, WAV, or WMA format and less than 5 MB.

You can choose to disconnect the call, play a menu, or redirect it to a call queue, yet another auto-attendant, or a specific user. Disconnecting comes across as somewhat harsh, so use it with care.

If you choose **Play menu options prompt**, there's a second message that can be configured to play with options that are just like those for the initial greeting. This message should include your verbal instructions for the different available options. For example: *Press 1 for sales, 2 for directions and store hours, or 0 for the operator.*

You can choose to enable or disable **Dial by name**. There are buttons to enable or disable each of the phone keypad buttons, **0** to **9** plus star (*). The hash (#) is reserved, as shown in the following screenshot:

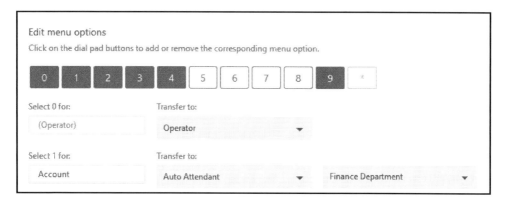

Auto-attendant menu options

For each available option you can specify a name and whether to transfer to an **Operator**, a **Call Queue**, an **Auto Attendant**, or a specific user. In complex trees, it is customary to use star (*) to transfer to the parent main menu. If enabled, **0** is always reserved for the **Operator**, but you can specify other behaviors for this function.

When picking the names for each choice, we recommend something clear, unique (compared to other menu choices), and short. This way, you can use the voice recognition feature and it will behave consistently and reliably.

Holidays

You may add certain days that are an exception to the normal schedule. During the specified times, the system can play a different message and follow alternate rules. The usual options for audio and call handling are present, except without the menu. For example, you might choose to forward calls to a different department's auto-attendant or simply disconnect.

It is possible to have multiple holidays and even assign multiple date ranges per holiday. One nice feature is that you can choose a specific time for the beginning and end of a holiday, so you can start the holiday message at 3 p.m. when closing early for Thanksgiving weekend.

There is one thing to watch out for—the button to save an individual holiday is at the bottom of the page. The **save** button at the top is to save all auto-attendant settings, and clicking here will result in your new holiday being lost. The button can take a long time and will save all your auto-attendant settings anyway, so it can be a bit annoying to work with if you have lots of holidays that you want to configure.

Dial scope

Dial scope controls who can participate in the auto-attendant, as well as which names appear for redirecting calls to a specific person. Thus, you can limit the scope of dial-by-name to a specific department or team. You can choose to include all users or a custom set. You can also exclude specific users, so your CEO knows that gate-crashers can't harass her while she's hard at work.

Call queues

The **call queues** option work a bit differently from **auto attendants**. They're designed to take many incoming calls and route them to a pool of available agents.

To start, you give the call queue a name and assign a service number. This is handled in the usual way.

One disappointing feature of a call queue is that you can't use the text-to-speech function to create a custom greeting the way you can elsewhere. Your only option is to upload an audio file. However, you can choose to upload your own hold music instead of using the default. The file still needs to be under 5 MB though, so it isn't like you can give callers a very long playlist.

Call distribution options include all-at-once and serial. The former is best for small teams and will ring everyone on the team simultaneously, routing the call to the first person to pick up. The latter option is better for large teams. It will use the user's Skype availability to route calls to individual agents as they are free to accept them.

For the pool of agents, you may choose any Office 365 group, security group, or distribution list.

You can specify whether agents are able to opt out of the pool. Agents can do this through the online settings (web page) of their Skype for Business client.

Learn more about **call queues** and the agent opt in/out feature at the following address:
`https://techcommunity.microsoft.com/t5/Skype-for-Business-Blog/C`
`all-Queues-Agent-Opt-In-Out-feature-has-been-rolled-out-to-`
`all/ba-p/145323`.

There are options available to specify the maximum number of calls and the maximum time that each call can remain on hold. In both cases, you can configure options for what action to take, including whether to disconnect the call or transfer it to another call queue, an auto-attendant, or a specific person. It would be nice to see *play a message then disconnect* but sadly this is not a choice. However, you can hack this behavior with an auto-attendant specifically designed for overflow calls.

Advanced topics for call routing

There are a few additional tricks, and some gotchas, we need to go over that are associated with call routing.

Text-to-speech

Microsoft's text-to-speech capability in Skype for Business isn't too shabby. The automated voice is reasonably good, though you can still tell it's a computer. Wouldn't it be just awesome if we could have Cortana answer our phones for us?

We were able to tweak minor issues (such as mispronounced words and cadence) simply by altering spelling and punctuation. Here are some annotated examples:

- **help@liquidmercurysolutions.com**: Help at liquid mercury solutions dot com (slow down!)
- **Windows Azure**: Windows as-ur (otherwise pronounced: *As you're*)
- **Chimera**: Chai-mera (otherwise pronounced: *She-mera*)
- **Kraken**: Crackin (otherwise pronounced: *Cray Ken*)

Routing calls to external phone services

Unfortunately, there's no capability to put an external phone number into the calling tree at this time. People keep recommending it on user voice, so maybe it will appear some day. Meanwhile, if you're willing to spring for an extra calling plan, you can create a fake user, sign into the Skype for Business client, and forward their calls to any phone number. This requires having a voice plan, but we didn't need to assign the fake user a real phone number; they can make and forward calls without it.

A brief word about offboarding users

One last caveat about call routing that needs to be mentioned. If you have any user who is in any call tree using **Transfer to**: **Person in your company**, you will need to make sure you change that setting before you remove the calling plan license and de-provision their account. If you forget to do this, it will become impossible to make changes to the auto-attendant settings. Woe to anyone who deletes a user completely before discovering this issue!

Advanced telephony services

If your company plans to use Skype for Business as an alternative or supplement to an on-site PBX, here are some additional things you'll need to know to get everything set up properly with minimal headaches.

Number portability

Okay, let's be honest here. Number portability sucks—at least in the United States. Some forum posts seem to indicate it can be quite bad in Europe too. Frankly, it's kind of a small miracle that we have it at all. Laws were passed to require phone companies to allow it, but the process is slow and often severely underfunded. In many cases, phone providers know that this is the last thing you'll do before you say goodbye, so they have no incentive to make the process of switching quick or painless.

So, as nice as it is that Microsoft provides an online form to port your numbers into Office 365, the reality is that you should proceed carefully, be well prepared, and understand the process fully. After all, failure to do so could lead to interruptions for incoming calls—a dreadful thing if it's just your own phone, and a far worse one if it's the company's main line.

So, what do you really need to be able to port phone numbers into Office 365?

Have a copy of your old phone bill

There are many details of the port request that will need to be copied exactly as they appear in your old provider's records. Failure to provide a request that exactly matches your existing account information will result in the phone company denying the port request, causing substantial delays and additional paperwork.

So, what will they ask for?

- **Account info**:
    - Account number (your old telco, not Microsoft's)
    - Billing telephone number in an international format (for example, +18005551212)
    - Security PIN, if you have one set up with your carrier
    - If it's a business account, the first 25 characters of the company's name
    - First 15 characters of the authorizing person's name
    - Service address as listed on your bill including city, state, and zip code
- **Phone numbers**:
    - List all the phone numbers you want to port over
    - Be sure to exclude the main service number if you're only porting partially
- **Transfer date**:
    - You will usually pick a date a few weeks into the future
- **Letter of authorization**:
    - Type the name exactly as provided in **Account Information | Authorizing person**

Learn more about how to create a port order and transfer your phone numbers to Skype for Business at the following address:
`https://docs.microsoft.com/en-us/skypeforbusiness/what-are-calli`
`ng-plans-in-office-365/transfer-phone-numbers-to-office-365.`

Know whether you need a manual port

The automated port request form is great if you're just moving a few desk phones from another provider to your Skype for Business accounts. However, it's not suitable for most other purposes, a fact that we find ironic because this is probably the least common scenario for businesses looking to port existing phone numbers.

Microsoft says:

> *Let us help you by opening a service request if you need to do one or more of these:*

- Transfer more than 999 user phone numbers
- Transfer service numbers such as for conference bridges, auto attendants, and call queues
- Transfer toll-free numbers in the U.S.
- Transfer any numbers in the U.K., Ireland, France, Spain, and the Netherlands
- If porting numbers isn't your thing

That last point basically means that, if you're the end-customer and not either a Microsoft partner or a seasoned admin who's read this book, you should probably be reaching out for help.

The most common use for number portability is probably moving the main company phone number into Skype for Business to configure an auto-attendant and calling tree. Because this is a service number and not a user number, this will require a manual port, which you would initiate by opening a service ticket and requesting it. Support will then send a manual authorization form that you'll have to fill out and sign and send back via email. Then, porting will likely take twice as long as it normally would because everything must be done by real human beings.

Be patient, very patient

Number porting can take a few or several weeks, depending on how the slow unwieldy process of your old phone company's mail room plays out. Eventually, you'll be given a date. Once you have that, things will generally happen as they are supposed to happen.

If this is a main number, be prepared to act quickly

On the date of the port, your phone(s) will no longer work. Plan ahead accordingly. You will need to assign it to a user or service. So that things will go smoothly on cutover day, you should test services in advance using a temporary number.

User numbers versus service numbers

User numbers are those that can be assigned to individual people on their Skype for Business client and/or compatible VoIP phones. Service numbers are those that can be assigned to a call tree (auto-attendant or call queue), dial-in conference, and the like. To many, this seems like a minor distinction, but trust us, it isn't.

For reasons we find difficult to understand, these two types of number seem to be run by completely different departments within Microsoft. Maybe someday they will fix that. So far, that hasn't been the case. Perhaps this book will help call attention to the problem. Based on the volume of complaints in public forums and suggestions in user voice, Microsoft probably already knows.

If you're simply pulling numbers from the public pool, this issue probably won't affect you too much. The worst case scenario is perhaps pulling a number you really like and later deciding you want to convert it to use for its counterpart purpose.

If you're porting a number from another phone provider, this could be disastrous. You cannot use a user number to host the company's main phone number. You have been warned.

What if you get a user number by mistake?

We have, on occasion, seen instances where an Office 365 customer initiated a port without realizing there was a distinction between user and service numbers. This is unfortunate, but even though the documentation is now more complete than it once was, there is still so much of it that we think such errors are probably inevitable.

In such a case, you will need to do a few things to minimize the damage done:

1. Set up a temporary service number to use with your auto-attendant.
2. Set up a voice calling plan with a fake user and assign the erroneous user number to it.
3. Forward its calls to the AA's service number using the settings of the Skype for Business client. (Sadly, there is no way to do this via the web or PowerShell, so you'll have to temporarily sign into Skype for Business or Office as that user.)
4. Initiate a manual port request within Microsoft to port the number from the user number pool to the service number pool.
5. Wait a long time for the situation to resolve itself.

These first three steps keep your house from burning down. Try not to complain about spending an extra 30-something bucks per month for this. After all, it's better than not receiving any phone calls for several weeks.

Step 4 may seem unfathomable, but it's true. Microsoft treats user numbers and service numbers almost as if they're two completely different phone providers. Why this is the case, we can't say. It is what it is.

So, now you know what to do if the worst case scenario happens to you. It would be best to take steps to avoid that misfortune entirely, if you can.

Caller ID

We all understand that caller ID is the technology that allows a caller's name and number to appear on our home telephone or smartphone, so we know right away whether we should take the call or let it go to voicemail. As such, how your business presents itself—and what kind of information you're giving away when you make a call—are often critical factors in running a successful business.

The problem with caller ID

Caller ID is a system that's been around quite a while now—since the days of long distance, Baby Bells, and the breakup of AT&T. As such, it was never really designed for the kind of hyper-integrated, hyper-competitive, global communication network that the modern phone service has become.

When caller ID was developed, control over how to present your information was left to the local phone company. At a time when most calls were local, and there was only one local phone provider, this made sense.

Fast forward to the present, where there are half a dozen or more mobile providers in any given geographic area and internet-based providers such as Mitel, Vonage, Vitelity, and Skype—and every local provider becomes a nationwide carrier. Next, pass laws to require phone number portability between carriers, but not enough regulation to ensure things will be handled promptly or that caller ID records will be updated when you switch providers, and suddenly the fact that each carrier controls its own database for caller ID is now a huge problem for which there's no easy answer.

Let us restate this. While your number belongs to another provider, keeping caller ID data is its responsibility. If you move that number to Microsoft's platform, you'll be able to get Microsoft to adjust your caller ID records only in certain cases, and the changes they make will have no effect at all on records kept by other providers.

Thus, if your phone number began its life in the hands of another person (as many do), or if perhaps it belonged to you or a family member but was a personal line, it may present in caller ID as something like BLAKE M when in fact it is now used as a business such as Blake's Cakes. Ironically, this phenomenon seems to occur most often for people in the local geographic area, which is exactly the area in which most businesses would prefer that it doesn't happen. (We're not actually sure if there's a Blake family who founded Blake's Cakes, but if so please accept our apologies for using you as an example.)

Potential solutions for inaccurate caller ID data

There are now services that promise to list or update your information in caller ID databases—both free and paid. There are companies that promise to crawl all the providers and do their best to *scrub* your information. Your mileage may vary, but we are weary of these services due to a substantial lack of accountability or provable results. Please don't take any links here to be an endorsement.

If you have a number that you've ported to Microsoft—and it's configured as a service number—then you may get some positive results by opening a support ticket and requesting that they erase whatever caller ID data exists in their database for the number, replacing it with your tenant's company name. We have gotten some good, but still imperfect, results for customers using this method.

You may also reach out to the provider that used to have control of your number and request that they remove the data from their database. Good luck with that. You're not their customer anymore, so why should they care? If you're planning to move to Office 365 for its phone service, this is something you may want to consider doing before you port your numbers over.

See who phone providers think your number belongs to at `https://www.twilio.com/lookup`.

You can try to get your CNAM (directory assistance or caller ID) listing changed for free using one or more of these services:

- `https://www.listyourself.net/ListYourself/listing.jsp`
- `https://www.truecnam.com`

Find services that claim to help with directory listings at `https://www.voip-info.org/wiki/view/CNAM`.

People see my desk number when I call them

Consider this scenario. You have a potential new customer, so you give them a call from your desk using Skype for Business. Convenient! Caller ID shows up on their mobile, so they quickly add you as a contact. That's great, right? You win the business, and everyone is happy.

Suppose that, as much as you enjoy talking to them and like their business, they have the habit of picking up the phone and dialing your desk whenever they have a question, regardless of the urgency. They call you preferentially, regardless of whether you're the correct person in your company to address their need. Sometimes they call you while you're in the middle of another call, meeting, or presentation. Sometimes they call you after business hours. Often, they call you during the 30 seconds when you've just stepped away to top up your coffee. (If only they'd called your mobile! How do they know?)

Now, suppose that, over time, you have two or three dozen customers with habits like these.

How will you get any work done?

Fortunately, there's something you can do about this kind of thing. You can choose to keep your Skype for Business phone number a secret.

"But how?" you ask, "Caller ID will give me up, and if I block it, people won't pick up when I call."

The solution here is to configure Skype for Business so that your caller ID information presents as the main company or department phone number. Thus, you can ensure that anyone who creates a contact from it will get the receptionist when they call on you, but the number should be familiar enough that they recognize who you are when you call on them.

This trick requires a service number with an auto-attendant or call queue, and can only be done in PowerShell. Here's how to make it work.

First, connect to the Skype for Business remote PowerShell session as we described in Chapter 2, *Using PowerShell to Connect to Office 365 Services*.

Once connected, you can review your current caller ID policies, shown as follows:

```
PS> Get-CsCallingLineIdentity | fl
  Identity                  : Global
  Description               :
  EnableUserOverride        : True
  ServiceNumber             :
  CallingIDSubstitute       : LineUri
  BlockIncomingPstnCallerID : False
```

In the default policy, note the settings for `ServiceNumber` and `CallingIDSubstitute`. These indicate that the caller ID will show the number attached to the user's Skype for Business calling plan.

Now, let's set a user's calling identity to change their caller ID so it will show the main line:

```
PS> New-CsCallingLineIdentity -Identity MainNumber -Description "Show the
main number" -CallingIDSubstitute Service -EnableUserOverride $false -
ServiceNumber 18005551212
  Identity                  : Tag:MainNumber
  Description               : Show the main number
  EnableUserOverride        : False
  ServiceNumber             : 18005551212
  CallingIDSubstitute       : Service
  BlockIncomingPstnCallerID : False
```

Notice that in the preceding example we are using the international format phone number, but that the leading plus sign should not be included in the `ServiceNumber` parameter.

Now that we've created a caller ID a policy, we assign it to users as follows:

```
Grant-CsCallingLineIdentity -Identity
"cody.netstein@liquidmercurysolutions.com" -PolicyName MainNumber
```

It may take a few minutes for things to fall into place. You can test this by making a few calls from the user's Skype to a cell or land line phone.

Remember to set the caller ID policy when you welcome new employees who use Skype for Business voice plans.

 Learn more about caller ID options in Skype for Business at: `https://docs.microsoft.com/en-us/skypeforbusiness/what-are-calling-plans-in-office-365/set-the-caller-id-for-a-user`.

Phones and other third-party products

While Skype for Business has a lot of powerful features, it is a relatively new platform and thus it can't be expected to do all things for all people.

Even if all you want is a phone or headset, you'll end up needing to shop around. (Microsoft may now be a phone company, but they don't make telephones.)

Fortunately, Microsoft has developed a thriving marketplace for third-party products and solutions that work with Office 365 and they're working closely with several manufacturers.

Microsoft's Partner Solutions catalog is a complete searchable and filterable collection of all the available devices built to work with Skype for Business. Every type of hardware can be found here, including desk phones, headsets, and conference room phones. Although it's not prominently displayed, you should also pay specific attention to the many apps that are available to extend Skype for Business's native capabilities. These can be found under **Applications**.

Visit Partner Solutions for Skype for Business at: `https://`
`partnersolutions.skypeforbusiness.com/solutionscatalog`.

Learn more about getting phones for Skype for Business Online at:

- `https://docs.microsoft.com/en-us/skypeforbusiness/what-`
  `is-phone-system-in-office-365/getting-phones-for-skype-`
  `for-business-online/getting-phones-for-skype-for-`
  `business-online`
- `https://technet.microsoft.com/en-us/office/dn947482.`
  `aspx`

Hybrid environments

Some larger organizations will have existing investments in Lync- or communicator-based solutions for unified communications. Likewise, if you have specific needs that can't be met by the capabilities of Skype for Business in the cloud, then you may need to deploy on-premise equipment. In both of these cases, it makes sense to configure hybrid configuration so that each system knows about the other and they can work together in harmony.

To set up a hybrid configuration, you'll need the following first:

- An Office 365 tenant with Skype for Business Online enabled
- Global administrator rights
- Access to DNS configuration
- Synchronized passwords via AD Connect
- On-premise Skype for Business Server 2015, Lync Server 2013, or 2010 (with the March 2013 update)

Hybrid configuration could easily become its own book, so we won't be going into details. If hybrid Skype for Business is something you need to be familiar with, the following are a few links that may get you started.

Plan and Deploy hybrid connectivity between Skype for Business Server and Skype for Business Online:

- `https://technet.microsoft.com/en-us/library/jj205403.aspx`
- `https://technet.microsoft.com/en-us/library/jj204669.aspx`

Step-By-Step: Skype for Business 2015 Hybrid Configuration: `https://blogs.technet.microsoft.com/canitpro/2015/12/23/step-by-step-skype-for-business-2015-hybrid-configuration/`.

Running a call center

Many folks ask about running their call center out of Skype for Business. The direction you go in will have a lot to do with whether you're running an inbound call center (people call you) or an outbound call center (your staff call people), as well as the number of calling stations.

If your inbound operation is small, you may be able to get by for a while on auto-attendant combined with call queues. Small outbound calling teams might be able to throw a solution together using Excel and Skype for Business alone.

If your call center is large, you'll need a third-party solution to manage it. Prepare to make a considerable investment in software and services, technical implementation, and possibly even hardware.

Most of the Skype for Business solutions we found were focused on inbound call centers, such as a help desk or billing department. There were a few which seemed promising for those who may want to work exclusively in the cloud. In some cases, it wasn't clear if a hybrid configuration would be needed.

If you're interested in running a sophisticated outbound call center, you'll probably need a hybrid solution to meet your needs. We found that Mitel's MiVoice platform has decent integration with Skype for Business and it also offers outbound call center management. It does have its own VoIP services that complete with Microsoft's, but they also stress that they offer solutions that will work in the cloud, on-premise, or hybrid. No other vendor we talked to offered outbound call management.

Learn more about third-party call center solutions from the following vendors:

- **Mitel**: `https://www.mitel.com/products/mitel-mivoice/mitel-mivoice-for-skype-for-business`
- **Enghouse Interactive**: `http://enghouseinteractive.co.uk/solutions/skype-for-business/`
- **Clarity Connect**: `http://connect.claritycon.com/`
- **ComputerTalk**: `http://www.computer-talk.com/en/solutions/contact-center-applications`
- **AVST**: `http://www.avst.com/blog/2013/informal-call-center-for-skype-for-business`

The marketplace will perhaps come up with more pure cloud-based solutions that address these needs in due course. Skype for Business features may also improve over time to provide more robust call center-like capabilities.

Summary

In this chapter, we demonstrated how to configure Skype for Business users in both standard and advanced scenarios. This included controlling the experience for audio-conferencing and online meetings. We also learned about the various aspects of voice services and calling plans, including calling trees and hold queues. We even explored some of the less rigorously traveled aspects of working with Skype for Business as a VoIP solution. You should now be ready to address virtually any conferencing or calling requirement that your users can imagine.

In the next chapter, we will be looking at administering Yammer.

Administering Yammer 10

Yammer is an enterprise social platform acquired by Microsoft in 2012 and integrated into the Office 365 platform. An enterprise social platform, unlike other social platforms, is a platform used by enterprises or businesses to share ideas and information and communicate, mainly internally. An enterprise social platform is very much like the Facebook social platform in feel and functionality, with @ mentions and the ability to like.

In this chapter, we will be looking at administering Yammer. We are going to explore:

- A general overview of Yammer
- Administering via the Yammer and Office 365 admin centers
- Administering via PowerShell

Overview

Yammer gives you a way to connect and collaborate across your company as well as with external team members, customers, vendors, and so on. It is a way to ask questions, discuss and share ideas and solutions, and share updates.

In Yammer, documents can be discussed, edited, and co-authored via Office Web Apps and content in Yammer can be discussed and shared directly from Office 365 services such as SharePoint, Delve, Skype Meeting Broadcast, and more:

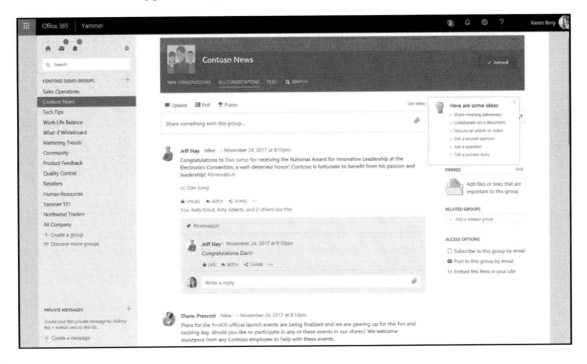

Yammer needs to be activated in Office 365. By default, Newsfeed is on instead of Yammer. Newsfeed is an enterprise social platform included in Office 365 and limited to Office 365 only, unlike Yammer, which can be used via Office 365 or can be signed up for outside of Office 365 as a separate service via `https://www.yammer.com`.

You can turn Yammer on via **settings** in the **SharePoint admin center**:

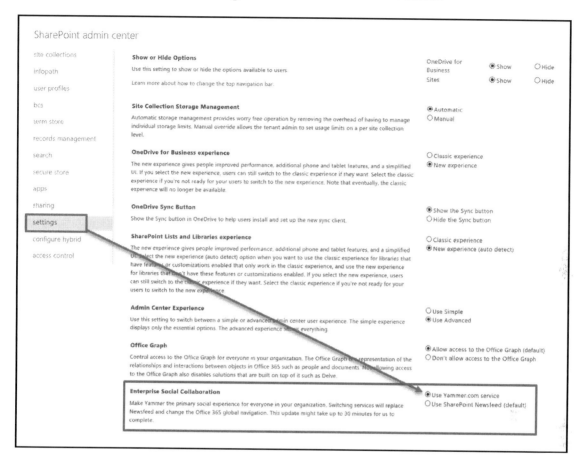

Administrating via Office 365

There are quite a few admin centers that you can reach via the Office 365 admin center.

Getting to the Yammer admin center

Most Yammer administration will not be done in Office 365 but in the Yammer admin center. To get to its admin center, from the Office 365 admin center expand the left navigation bar and click on **Yammer admin center** under **Admin centers**:

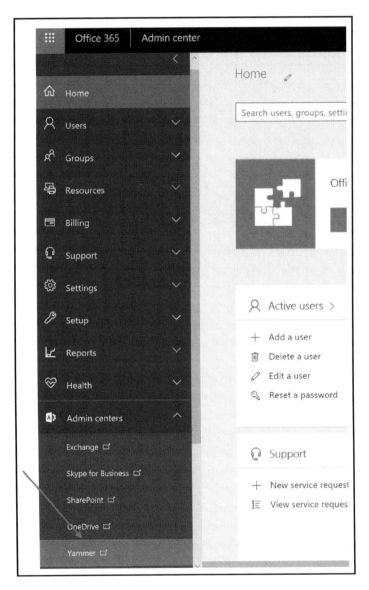

This will open the admin center in a new tab:

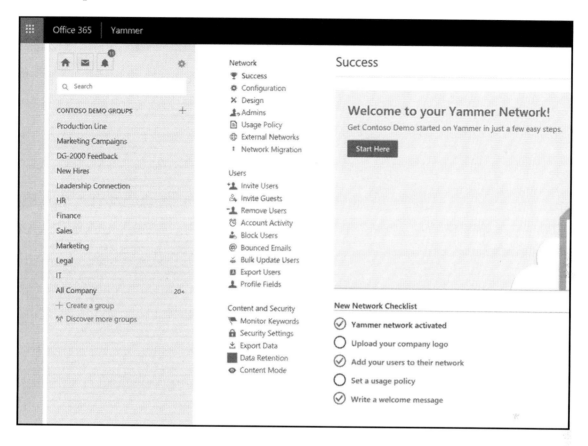

If you are already in Yammer, you can get to the admin center by clicking on the gear icon then on **Network Admin** from the drop-down menu:

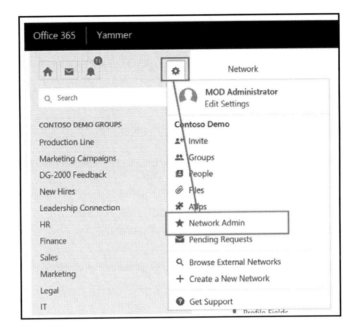

 You will need to be an Office 365 global admin in order to administer Yammer for the first time. Once you are in, you can set others as Yammer admins via the Yammer admin center.

Managing user licenses

There is one Yammer administration function that needs to be done from the Office 365 admin center—administrating user access. Yammer licensing is included in the following Office 365 subscriptions:

- Business Essentials
- Business Premium
- Enterprise E1
- Enterprise E3
- Enterprise E5

When managing your users via the Office 365 admin center, you can remove access to Yammer if/when needed:

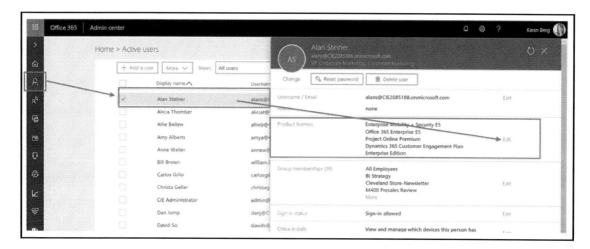

After clicking **Edit**, you will have the opportunity to turn access to Yammer **On** or **Off**:

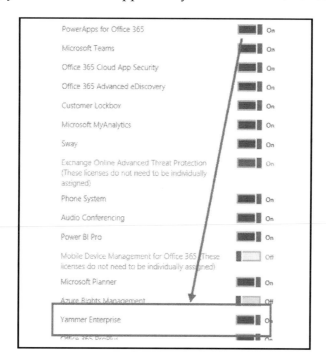

Getting started

When you first start to use Yammer, you may want to follow the steps in the **New Network Checklist** section of the admin page:

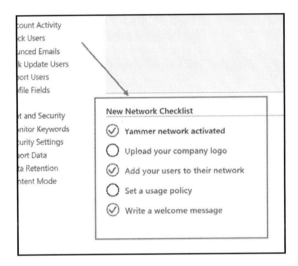

This checklist will help you set up the basics of Yammer before your users begin using it. The options in the screenshot are mostly obvious but let's take a moment to take a brief look at the last two items in the checklist.

Setting a usage policy

On this page, you can set a usage policy for Yammer usage, require users to accept it, and display a reminder:

 You can also get to this page by clicking on **Usage Policy** under **Network** in the left navigation bar.

If you already have an acceptable use policy online, you can click on **Set a custom browser policy URL within your company** and enter the URL which users will be redirected to.

Writing a welcome message

Clicking on the **Write a welcome message** link will take you to the Yammer page to write a post:

Network

Let's look at the functions available to you in the **Network** section:

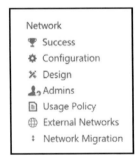

As seen in the preceding screenshot, the following functions are available:

- **Success**: This is the home page of the Yammer admin center.
- **Configuration**: On the **Configuration** page, you will have the ability to name your network, manage your network domain, enable user message confirmation, manage users' ability to upload files, and enable the org chart, language translation, and third-party apps:

Configuration

Basics

Network Name:

Contoso Demo

Email: m365x158077.onmicrosoft.com@yammer.com
URL: https://www.yammer.com/m365x158077.onmicrosoft.com

Message Prompt:

What are you working on?

Network Domains

Domains on this Yammer network: m365x158077.onmicrosoft.com (primary domain) . Click here to see all network domains.

Managing Your Networks Domains

You can manage Yammer domains across their lifecycle in Office 365.

When you add or remove domains in Office 365, they will be automatically added to or removed from this Yammer network. Also, the default verified domain in Office 365 will automatically become the primary domain in Yammer

Email Settings

☐ Require all users in your network to confirm their messages posted via email before posting.

File Upload Permissions

☑ Allow people to upload and attach files in any format

Enabled Features

☑ 3rd Party Applications
☑ Org Chart
☐ Message Translation (powered by Microsoft Translator)

Save

- **Design**: Through **Design**, you can set colors and logos:

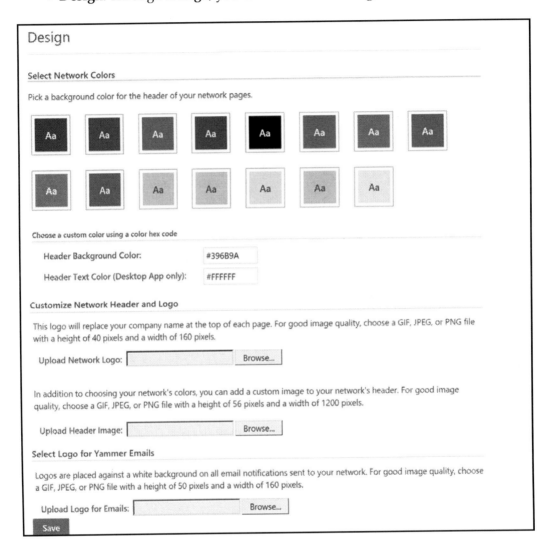

- **Admins**: In this section, you can manage the current admins and set new ones. Some admins may need to be managed in the Office 365 admin center and they will be flagged as such:

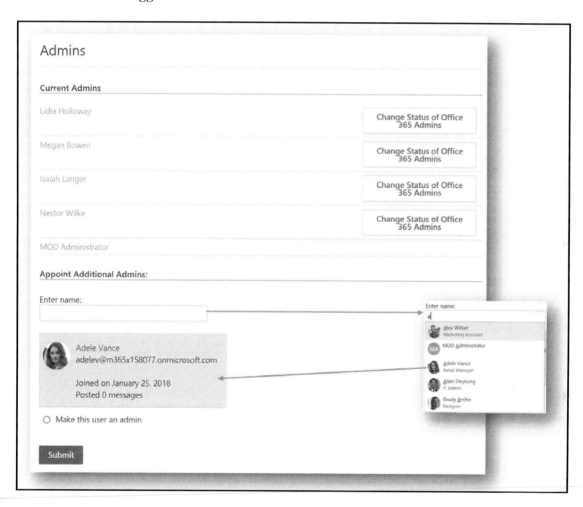

- **Usage Policy**: In this section, you can set the acceptable use policy for Yammer. See the previous *Setting a usage policy* section for more information.

- **External Networks**: External networks are networks that can be used to collaborate with people external to your organization. In this section, you can set who can create this type of network and whether admin approval of members will be required; you can also disable some settings for related external networks:

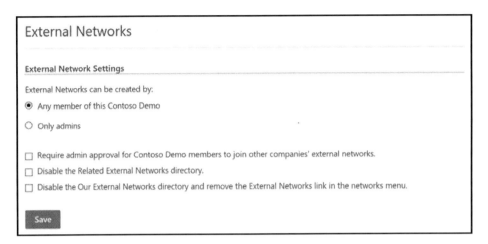

- **Network Migration**: If you have other Yammer networks you would like to add, you can walk through the steps in this section:

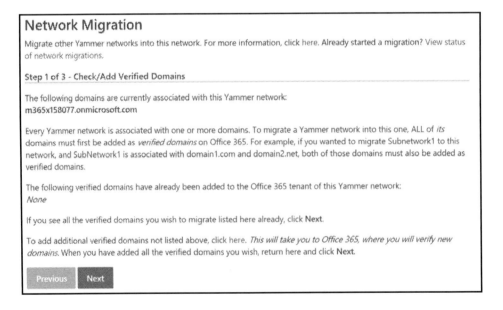

Users

Let's explore the next section, **Users**:

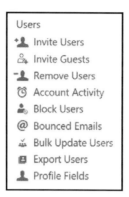

As seen in the preceding screenshot, the following subsections are available:

- **Invite Users**: Invite users to your network in this section:

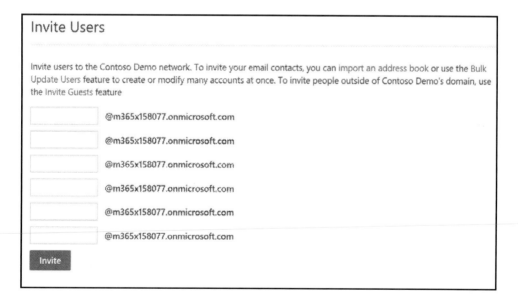

- **Invite Guests**: Invite guests to your network in this section:

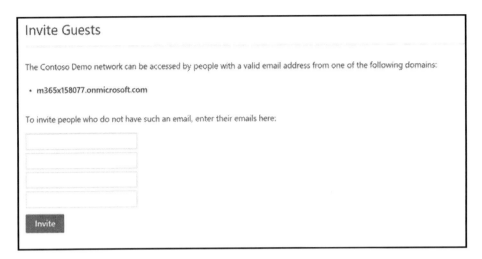

- **Remove Users**: Remove users from your network in this section:

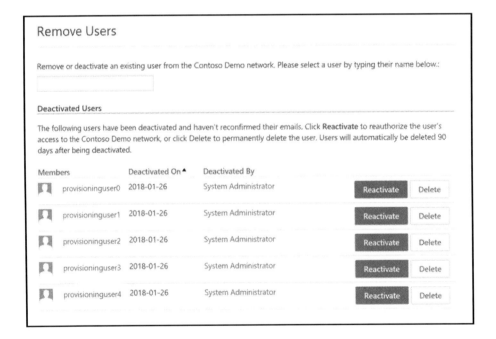

- **Account Activity**: View some user activity details in this section. You also have the ability to log them out:

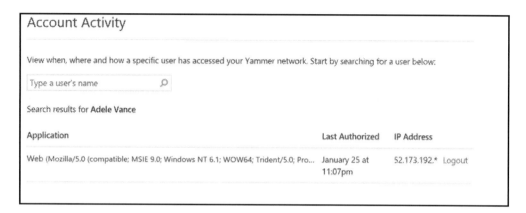

- **Block Users**: In this section, you can block users:

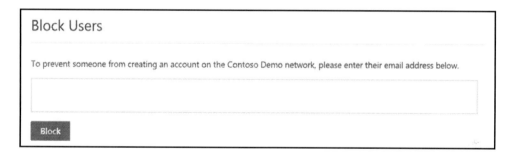

- **Bounced Emails**: If any emails bounced, you can see them in this section:

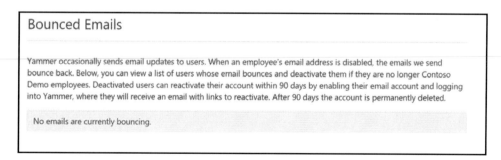

- **Bulk Update Users**: You can add users via a bulk upload in this section:

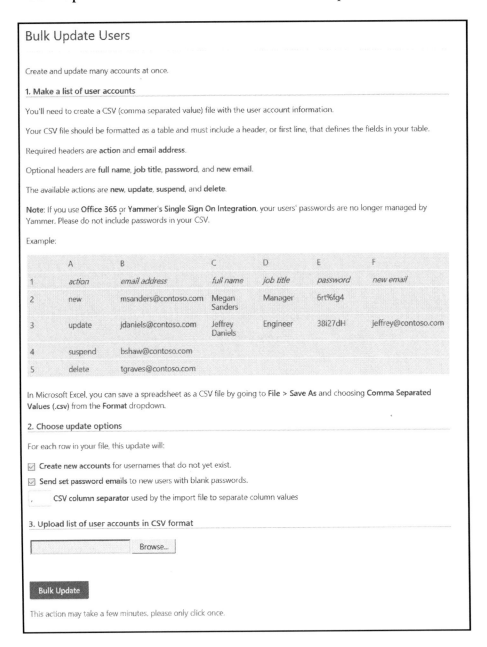

Bulk Update Users

Create and update many accounts at once.

1. Make a list of user accounts

You'll need to create a CSV (comma separated value) file with the user account information.

Your CSV file should be formatted as a table and must include a header, or first line, that defines the fields in your table.

Required headers are **action** and **email address**.

Optional headers are **full name**, **job title**, **password**, and **new email**.

The available actions are **new**, **update**, **suspend**, and **delete**.

Note: If you use **Office 365** or **Yammer's Single Sign On Integration**, your users' passwords are no longer managed by Yammer. Please do not include passwords in your CSV.

Example:

	A	B	C	D	E	F
1	action	email address	full name	job title	password	new email
2	new	msanders@contoso.com	Megan Sanders	Manager	6rt%fg4	
3	update	jdaniels@contoso.com	Jeffrey Daniels	Engineer	38i27dH	jeffrey@contoso.com
4	suspend	bshaw@contoso.com				
5	delete	tgraves@contoso.com				

In Microsoft Excel, you can save a spreadsheet as a CSV file by going to **File > Save As** and choosing **Comma Separated Values (.csv)** from the **Format** dropdown.

2. Choose update options

For each row in your file, this update will:

☑ **Create new accounts** for usernames that do not yet exist.

☑ **Send set password emails** to new users with blank passwords.

☐ **CSV column separator** used by the import file to separate column values

3. Upload list of user accounts in CSV format

[　　　　　　　　] Browse...

[Bulk Update]

This action may take a few minutes, please only click once.

- **Export Users**: In this section, you can export a list of users to a CSV file:

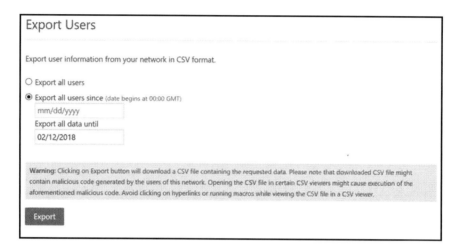

- **Profile Fields**: In this section, you can manage the fields that can show up in a member's profile:

Content and Security

Now we will look at the last section, **Content and Security**:

As seen in the preceding screenshot, the following subsections are available:

- **Monitor Keywords**: In this section, you can monitor single keywords and/or use regular expressions. If a keyword or pattern is used, such as a social security number, an email will be sent to the email in the **Email Address** box.
- **Security Settings**: In this section, you can set some security options for the IP range of access, external messaging, and connected groups:

Security Settings

IP Range

Set an IP range for your network to only allow it to be accessed from your office network or VPN.

IP Ranges

no range defined

Start: [_____]   End: [_____]   Name: [_____]

⊙ Add another IP range

What happens when someone tries to login to an application from outside this IP range?

◉ Allow login

○ Deny login (Warning: this will disable the iPhone, Android and Windows Phone applications for all users.)

External Messaging

☐ Enforce your Exchange Online Exchange Transport Rules (ETRs) in Yammer

Office 365 Identity Enforcement

Whenever enforcing Office 365 identity, be mindful that this setting replaces any existing Yammer SSO setup and ensures that users log in to Yammer with their Office 365 accounts. Learn More

☑ Enforce Office 365 identity

Status: Committed ❶

☐ Block Office 365 users without Yammer licenses

Office 365 Connected Yammer Groups

Once your organization has committed to enforcing Office 365 identity and has one Office 365 tenant associated with a single Yammer network, connected groups will be enabled for this network. Learn More

Status: Enabled   Connected Groups are turned on for this network.

[Save]

- **Export Data**: In this section, you can export Yammer data to a CSV file:

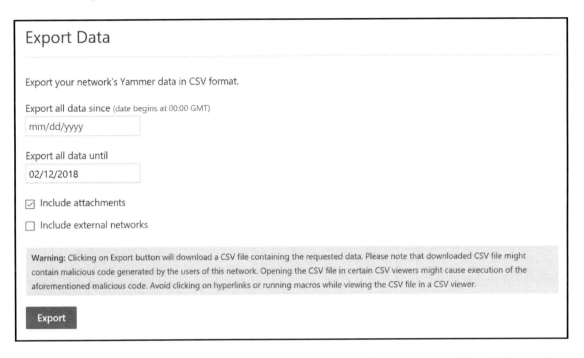

- **Data Retention**: In this section, you can set whether you want deleted data to be deleted permanently or not:

Data Retention Policy

This setting applies to your entire company network.

◉ **Hard Delete (Recommended)**
  Deleted data is permanently removed and not visible in data exports.

○ **Soft Delete**
  Data that is deleted remains on Yammer's servers unless specifically removed via the Developer API. Deleted data is not visible to users but can be accessed via data export.

Save

For details on how to export data, see the *Data Export API* section of the *Yammer Developer Center* page (`https://developer.yammer.com/docs/data-export-api`).

For more details on APIs, see the *Rest API* section (`https://developer.yammer.com/docs/rest-api-rate-limits`) and the *API Requests* section (`https://developer.yammer.com/docs/api-requests`) of the *Yammer Developer Center* page.

Audit reports can be run on Yammer to gather information on topics such as deleted groups and messages. You can find more details on the *Office 365 Security & Compliance center* at `https://support.office.com/en-us/article/Search-the-audit-log-in-the-Office-365-Security-Compliance-Center-0d4d0f35-390b-4518-800e-0c7ec95e946c`—look for **Yammer Activities** under the **Audit Activities** tab at the top of the page.

- **Content Mode**: If you need to see private messages for legal reasons, you can change to **Private Content Mode** in this section.

Administering via PowerShell

Yammer does not have as much PowerShell capability as other parts of Office 365. These snippets enable you to manage user Yammer licensing:

* The following example assigns a license from the litwareinc:YAMMER_ENTERPRISE_STANDALONE (Yammer Enterprise Standalone) licensing plan to the unlicensed user belindan@litwareinc.com.

```
Set-MsolUserLicense -UserPrincipalName "belindan@litwareinc.com" -AddLicenses
"litwareinc:YAMMER_ENTERPRISE_STANDALONE"
```

* The following example unassigns the Yammer Enterprise license from the litwareinc:ENTERPRISEPACK (Office 365 Enterprise E3) to the user belindan@litwareinc.com.

```
$UPN = "belindan@litwareinc.com"

$LicenseDetails = (Get-MsolUser -UserPrincipalName $UPN).Licenses

ForEach ($License in $LicenseDetails) {

  $DisabledOptions = @()

  $License.ServiceStatus | ForEach {

    If ($_.ProvisioningStatus -eq "Disabled" -or $_.ServicePlan.ServiceName -like
"*YAMMER*") { $DisabledOptions += "$($_.ServicePlan.ServiceName)" }

  }

  $LicenseOptions = New-MsolLicenseOptions -AccountSkuId $License.AccountSkuId -
DisabledPlans $DisabledOptions

    Set-MsolUserLicense -UserPrincipalName $UPN -LicenseOptions $LicenseOptions

}
```

* If you'd instead like to enable Yammer for a user without affecting anything else in their license, you can run the above script but change:

```
If ($_.ProvisioningStatus -eq "Disabled" -or $_.ServicePlan.ServiceName -like
"*YAMMER*") { $DisabledOptions += "$($_.ServicePlan.ServiceName)" }
```

to

```
If ($_.ProvisioningStatus -eq "Disabled" -and $_.ServicePlan.ServiceName -notlike
"*YAMMER*") { $DisabledOptions += "$($_.ServicePlan.ServiceName)" }
```

* The following example returns information about any users who are not currently licensed for Office 365.

```
Get-MsolUser -All -UnlicensedUsersOnly
```

Summary

In this chapter, we looked at Yammer. We went through a brief overview then delved into administering via the Yammer admin center. We looked at the other Yammer administrative functions completed via the Office 365 admin center. We also looked at how to manage user licenses via PowerShell.

In the next chapter, we will cover OneDrive for Business administration.

11
Administering OneDrive for Business

OneDrive for Business is fairly simple to administer for the most part. Most of what you'll need to do is accessible through the **OneDrive admin center**, with a few important functions relegated to the administration portal and the Security & Compliance Center.

As you might guess from the fact that any OneDrive for Business URL uses the format `https://yourtenantname-my.sharepoint.com/personal/your_name_yourtenantname.com`, OneDrive for Business is actually SharePoint underneath the hood. It's a highly specialized SharePoint that's less about sharing and more about keeping work under a user's personal control. But there's often a lot of confusion for users in figuring out when it's more appropriate to put a document in SharePoint or OneDrive, so there will most likely be plenty of sharing from OneDrive going on, and that can create headaches you'll need to resolve.

There aren't very many native PowerShell functions for OneDrive administration, but there also isn't a lot of need for them. We won't be covering PowerShell commands for OneDrive in this chapter; the ones that do exist are actually SharePoint cmdlets.

OneDrive dashboard

You don't have a OneDrive dashboard yet! The **OneDrive admin center** is brand new; Microsoft hasn't quite finished building it yet:

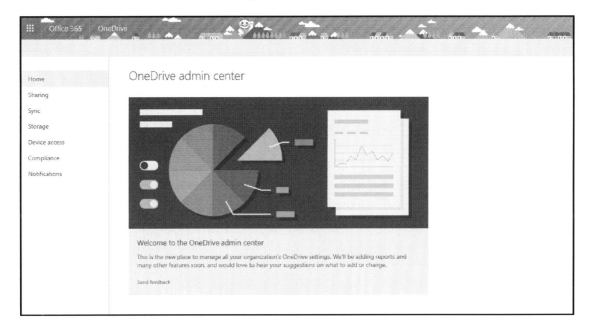

OneDrive admin center

Now, Microsoft moves very quickly sometimes; it might be that by the time you have this book in your hands, the reports and many other features they're promising will have been built, and you'll see something much more interesting than a stock picture of a pie chart.

What you *actually* need to pay attention to is the left-side navigation bar. The various functions you can perform in the **OneDrive admin center** are:

- **Sharing**
- **Sync**
- **Storage**

- **Device access**
- **Compliance**
- **Notifications**

Let's go through each one in turn and see what we can do here.

Sharing

One of the main purposes of OneDrive, aside from keeping all of a user's documents in a location where they can reach them no matter what machine they're accessing them from, is to share documents with other members of an organization or outside parties such as clients, vendors, and partners. Sometimes, however, an organization wants to lock this down and restrict who can share what and with who.

In the past, you'd have set these restrictions through SharePoint, but the new **OneDrive admin center** allows you to perform these tasks through a convenient specific interface:

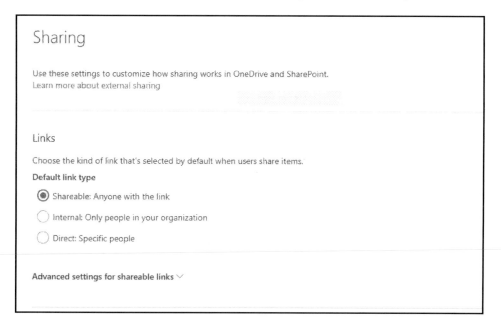

Sharing settings

The settings on this page actually apply to SharePoint as well, so make sure that anyone who may be impacted by the choices you make here understands what they imply.

Link types include anonymous guest links, which are listed here as **Shareable: Anyone with the link** (anyone who has the link can access the file); **Direct: Specific people** (often referred to as *share with external users*, meaning that, when you send a link to an external user, they must use a verifiable identity to log in and access the file); and **Internal: Only people in your organization**, which means that you can't share with people outside your organization, period:

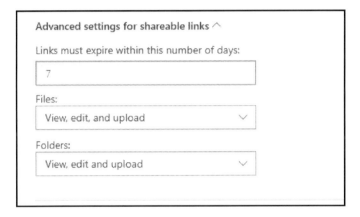

Advanced settings for shareable links

You can click on the carat beside **Advanced settings for shareable links** to open up additional options. Set a number of days for the link to expire—the default is 7. It's especially important to keep this tight if *shareable*, anonymous links are permitted, as you have no way of tracking whether or not the person who was sent such a link has sent it anywhere else.

You can set **Files** and/or **Folders** to **View** only or to the default, **View, edit and upload**:

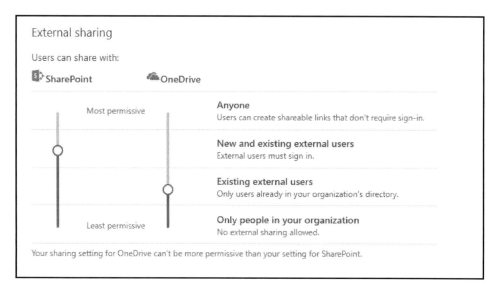

External sharing settings for SharePoint and OneDrive

You can use the external sharing sliders to adjust sharing rights. **New and existing external users** can create a new external user, who will have never received a sharing link before, as a mail contact or guest user in your tenant (we went over these in `Chapter 1`, *The Office 365 Administration Portal* and `Chapter 4`, *Administering Exchange Online – Essentials*). **Existing external users** won't permit the creation of new guest users; you'll have to have the user who's supposed to receive the link already set as a mail contact or guest user.

Settings can be stricter for OneDrive than for SharePoint—remember which one has *share* in the name—or the same, but cannot be more relaxed. So if there are separate SharePoint administrators in your organization who've already determined that SharePoint needs to be set to a certain sharing level, you can't set OneDrive to be more permissive than that level.

However, keep in mind that, in SharePoint, sharing levels can be set differently for each individual site. A good strategy, if OneDrive needs a more permissive policy than the sites in SharePoint currently allow, *might* be to relax SharePoint at the tenant level—which is what this setting applies to—and then tighten up the specific site collections (this may not be appropriate if there are a lot of site collections, though):

Advanced external sharing settings for SharePoint and OneDrive

Expand the carat at the bottom to get to the **Advanced settings for external sharing**.

You can add domains and allow or block sharing from them. Click the **Allow or block sharing with people on specific domains** box and you'll get a button that says **Add domains**. When you click that, you'll have the opportunity to create a list of domains and set them as either allow or block. What you can't do is mix them—so you can't get a whitelist and a blacklist. Under most circumstances, you wouldn't need one, though, because if you have external sharing of any type enabled then all domains are allowed unless you block them, and if you don't all domains are blocked unless you allow them.

Setting the **External users must accept sharing invitations using the same account that the invitations were sent to** option ensures that the person who received the invitation is the only person who can use it, but you deny the user a certain degree of flexibility that way. The user will be asked to sign-in with a Microsoft account or Office 365 account, and if the email you sent the link to is not one of those, they might not want to create a second Microsoft account if they already have one. If you set this, make sure users understand the implications.

Let external users share items they don't own allows external users to re-share what has already been shared with them. If your settings permit anonymous sharing, this could quickly get out of hand. It's a more acceptable option if your settings allow external sharing with named users only, as anyone who receives a share link from one of your guest users themselves becomes one of your guest users, so you can keep track to a certain extent.

The final setting shows owners who shared their files. While some of the data might be less useful if you have anonymous sharing turned on, overall this is valuable information for most content owners.

Sync

If you've read Chapter 6, *Administering SharePoint Online*, you will have at least touched on the **Sync** functionality. If not, you're probably familiar with it from your own use of it. But just in case you're getting your first job on earth in Office 365 after having come straight off the mothership of a distant planet, **Sync** is a function in SharePoint and OneDrive that makes a copy of a OneDrive site, or a SharePoint library, on the user's hard drive.

There's a button in the user's console for OneDrive or SharePoint that lets them create a sync relationship. Once the user presses that button, they will be taken through a series of prompts to set up **Sync** on their machine. After that, the user will have a local copy of the OneDrive site or SharePoint library on that machine, and it will sync whenever changes are made to one side or the other:

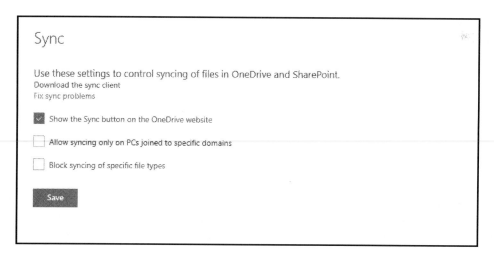

Sync settings

If you don't have the latest **Sync** client, or more likely the user you're troubleshooting for doesn't, you can download it from this page, as shown in the preceding screenshot, but it's unnecessary to go specifically into OneDrive administration to do this—OneDrive itself will prompt the user to get the latest **Sync** client if theirs is out of date (and, often, if they're not—it has a bad habit of prompting to update when in fact the user has the latest version).

The link **Fix sync problems** simply takes you to a *Microsoft Knowledge Base* article on common sync problems and how to resolve them; it's not a troubleshooting wizard.

There are only three settings here, so controlling **Sync** is straightforward:

- **Show the Sync button on the OneDrive website**: It's *possible* to sync without the button, but it's a pain to do it. We've seen users who have indeed requested that their employees should not be able to sync OneDrive and asked for the button to be removed, but most of the time OneDrive is a lot more useful with its ability to easily create a sync relationship, so you'll usually want to leave this one in the default position of *on*.
- **Allow syncing only on PCs joined to specific domains**: For security reasons, you may not want to allow users to sync their OneDrive to personal machines or machines that are used at home. Requiring that the PC be joined to one of your organization's domains is a simple way to prevent that behavior.
- **Block syncing of specific file types**: Certain file types, such as Microsoft Access `*.mdb` or `*.accdb` database files, or programs and their associated libraries, may be considered too sensitive to risk letting them sync. Other file types, such as video files, might be too large to allow them to passively sync; in such cases users might be required to specifically download the file if they need it on their PC, but it won't tie up bandwidth and space on their hard drive if they don't need it. If you choose this, you'll be given the opportunity to enter a list of extensions to block.

Storage

The default amount of storage each user gets is 1 TB. This can be increased to 5 TB if the user has an E3 or E5 license, a OneDrive for Business Plan 2, or a SharePoint Online Plan 2. You can also decrease this if there's some reason to do so:

Storage

Use these settings to specify storage limits for all users and retention for deleted users.

Default storage in GB

| 1024 |

What's the maximum for my Office 365 plan?

Days to retain files in OneDrive
after a user account is marked
for deletion

| 30 |

Save

Storage settings

Set the default storage for all users in gigabytes and the number of days to retain files in OneDrive after a user account has been deleted. The maximum number of days you can pick is 3650, or ten years (minus a couple of leap days).

Note that the deletion process for an account in OneDrive is kicked off only by the *deletion* of a user account. Simply removing the user's license, blocking their sign-in, or both does not delete their OneDrive files. It's often a good practice to disable and remove licenses on user accounts without actually deleting them, and this is one of the reasons why.

We'll discuss how to access the files in a terminated user's OneDrive later in the chapter.

The Device access page

The **Device access** page has two parts—**Device access** itself, which determines the properties of devices that are allowed to access OneDrive, and **Mobile application management**, which regulates access to features in the OneDrive and SharePoint mobile apps.

Device access

Device access is about controlling access from certain network locations and types of authentication:

Device access settings

Your options are:

- **Allow access only from specific IP address locations**: If you choose this, you'll enter a list of authorized IPs, and those will be the only ones allowed access to OneDrive.
- **Allow access from apps that don't use modern authentication**: If an application is too old to be able to use one of the modern authentication methods, do you want to prevent it from connecting to OneDrive?

The defaults here are to allow access from any IP and to allow access from older apps.

Mobile application management

These settings affect SharePoint and OneDrive applications on Android and iOS mobile devices, and can only be applied to users who are licensed for Intune or Enterprise Mobility + Security:

Mobile application management

Use these settings to control access to features in the OneDrive and SharePoint mobile apps. If you created other policies in Intune, they will take precedence for the selected users. The settings do not apply to personal accounts that users may have added to the apps.

These settings apply to the apps for Android and iOS.
Learn more about access policies

Deploy this policy 🔘

☐ Block downloading files in the apps

☐ Block taking screenshots in the apps (Android only)

☐ Block copying files and content within files

☐ Block printing files in the apps

☐ Block backing up app data

☐ Require app passcode

☐ Block opening OneDrive and SharePoint files in other apps

☐ Encrypt app data when device is locked

☑ Require Office 365 sign-in every 7 days

When a device is offline

Minutes to verify user access after

| 90 |

Days to wipe app data after

| 720 |

Save

Mobile application management

You can set the following restrictions in terms of the capabilities of the mobile app:

- Block downloading
- Block taking screenshots (currently on Android only)
- Block the copying of files and/or content inside files
- Block printing
- Block backing up the app's data
- Require an app passcode
- Block the opening of OneDrive and SharePoint files from other mobile apps

- Encrypt app data when device is locked
- Require Office 365 sign-in every 7 days
- Verify user access after x number of minutes of offline time (x by default is 90)
- Wipe app data after y number of days of offline time (y by default is 720)

Don't forget that once you've set the policy, you still need to deploy it. The toggle at the top activates policy deployment.

By default, the policy is not deployed and the only value set within it is the requirement for sign-in every 7 days.

Compliance

The **Compliance** center consists of a number of quick links to the Security & Compliance Center:

Compliance

If your organization has legal, regulatory, or technical standards that you need to meet, or if you want to help identify and protect sensitive information in OneDrive, use the Security and Compliance Center to perform the following tasks.

Auditing

View user activities related to OneDrive, such as who recently accessed, deleted, or shared files.
Search the audit log

Data loss prevention (DLP)

Protect your organization's sensitive information so it doesn't get into the wrong hands. You can also view reports to see which files match your policies.
Create a DLP policy
View DLP policy match reports

Retention

Preserve OneDrive files as long as you need.
Create a preservation policy

Compliance settings

You can quickly jump to **Auditing, Data loss prevention (DLP)**, **Retention, eDiscovery**, or **Alerts** from here.

For details on how to use any of these features, see `Chapter 8`, *Understanding Security and Compliance.*

Notifications

There's a fine line between keeping users informed when important events are occurring and nagging them to death. The notifications available for OneDrive are usually fairly unobtrusive, but if your organization makes very heavy use of OneDrive, balance the user's need to stay informed with their need to avoid information overload:

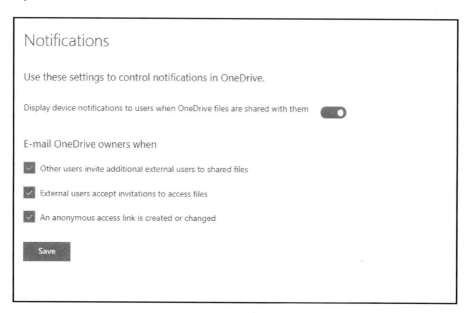

Notifications settings

The settings here are fairly simple. You can turn on notifications for devices so that, when a OneDrive document is shared with a user, if that user has the OneDrive app on their device, they will receive a device notification. You can also send out emails to alert users to the following circumstances:

- **Other users invite additional external users to shared files**
- **External users accept invitations to access files**
- **An anonymous access link is created or changed**

None of these notifications apply if the file is being shared with an *internal* user. Users will receive emails when a file is shared with them, and the administrator doesn't have the ability to turn these notifications off here. What we have available here pertains entirely to device notifications in addition to emails for receiving a share link, and emails regarding the behavior of external users and anonymous users.

Accessing the files of terminated employees

When an employee leaves, you can disable their account and block their sign-in, and you can alter your retention policy so that their files are kept practically forever even if you do delete them. But how do you access them? OneDrive generally keeps a given user's username or password, so unless they were thoughtful enough to share literally everything in their OneDrive with another user before they left the company, don't you need to log in with their username and password in order to be able to access their OneDrive?

Nope. That's not necessary. If you don't already have the rights to access their files, you can give them to yourself by quickly hopping over to the Office 365 administration portal center.

Manager access

Firstly, a well-maintained set of metadata about employees can prevent this from ever becoming a necessity in the first place, because, by default, if an employee has a manager defined in their Office 365 profile, their manager will be given rights to their OneDrive once they are deleted. On the other hand, even if your organization is careful about maintaining such metadata, you may not want to delete the employee's record at all—simply disable and block it—and if not, then the automated process that will transfer control to the employee's manager won't ever happen. So you may need to take control manually anyway.

Administrator access

In the old days, we used to have to go into the SharePoint admin center and grant ourselves site collection owner rights to the user's OneDrive, but fortunately Microsoft has greatly simplified the process:

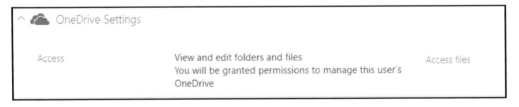

Per-user OneDrive settings in administration portal

Go to the administration portal and select the user. Underneath their contact information, there will be expandable carats with the headings **Mail settings** and **OneDrive settings**. Expand **OneDrive settings**.

Click **Access files** next to the text with the text **View and edit folders and files** and **You will be granted permissions to manage this user's OneDrive**. It'll churn for a moment and then present you with a direct link to the user's OneDrive. You can do this even if the user has not been blocked, disabled, or deleted; perhaps they're on vacation and someone needs to access a file they have.

Microsoft has recently improved their capabilities for handling folders. Generally speaking, you have two means of capturing files from anyone's OneDrive—direct download and **Sync**. In the past, you couldn't download folders, but you can now: select a folder, click **Download**, and it'll download as a ZIP file.

If you don't need it this instant, but you'd like the convenience of having the full structure of the user's OneDrive built out on your PC—where you could perhaps simply copy and paste it into your own OneDrive or someone else's—you can use **Sync** and sync the user's files to your own PC. To transfer the whole kit and caboodle to someone else's OneDrive, sync that person's OneDrive, sync the terminated user's OneDrive, and when both are complete, just copy the terminated user's files and structure directly to the other person's synched OneDrive folder.

Summary

In this chapter, we covered how to use the **OneDrive admin center** to manage OneDrive for your organization. We saw how to manage functions such as **Storage**, **Sync**, and **Device access**, to name just a few. For some relevant tasks, we learned the SharePoint Online cmdlets that allow us to perform them in PowerShell. We saw that one administration function has been left out of the admin center because it pertains more directly to a user rather than to OneDrive settings for your organization in general, so we went back to the administration portal and saw how to get access to a user's OneDrive files that way.

In the next chapter, we will be looking at administering Power BI.

Power BI Administration 12

Power BI is a way to bring in data from many different data sources, then analyze, mash up, and crunch that data and share it using easily consumable dashboards and reports that you can drill down into. Power BI comes with templates for representing data from Google Analytics, MailChimp, Azure Services, Salesforce, Dynamics, Oracle, and many more. These templates were created by Microsoft and other third parties to create beautiful, insightful, and dynamic reports and dashboards easily. Although they are preconfigured, users can edit and configure them further. Users can also choose to create their own templates and/or create dashboards and reports from scratch.

In this chapter, we will be looking at administering Power BI. We are going to explore:

- Administering via Office 365
- Administering via PowerShell
- Where to get more information

Administering via Office 365

The title of this section is a bit misleading. In order to administer Power BI, you have to go to Power BI. There is no admin center in Office 365 admin centers for Power BI:

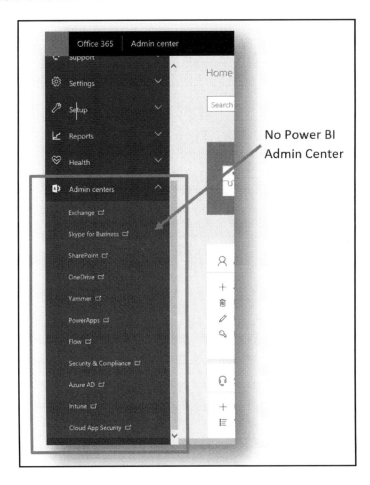

Once you go to Power BI, you can click on the gear icon and choose **Admin portal** from the drop-down menu:

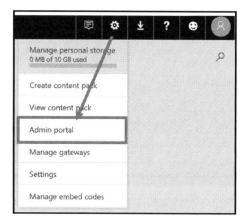

The following is the home page for the Power BI **Admin portal**, which shows usage metrics for Power BI. There are also a few additional sections in the portal. Let's go through them one by one:

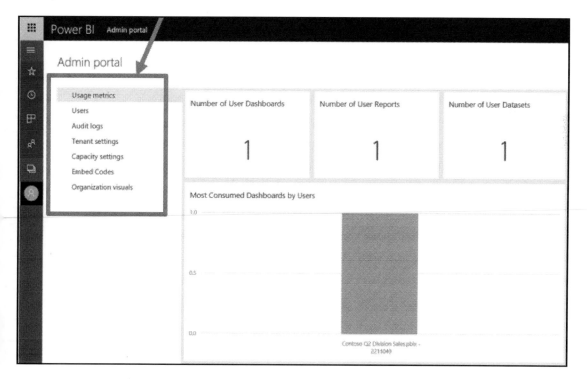

Usage metrics

This is the home page for the Power BI **Admin portal**. This page is a dashboard that shows you metrics on how your Power BI's user adoption is going. The following are the sections of the dashboard that you will see:

- **Number of User Dashboards**
- **Number of User Reports**
- **Number of User Datasets**
- **Top Users with Most Dashboards**
- **Most Consumed Dashboards by Users**
- **Most Consumed Packages by Users**
- **Top Users with Most Reports**
- **Number of Group Dashboards**
- **Number of Group Reports**
- **Number of Group Datasets**
- **Top Groups with Most Dashboards**
- **Most Consumed Dashboards by Groups**
- **Most Consumed Packages by Groups**
- **Top Groups with Most Reports**

 When you first log in, or if you haven't logged in for a while, the dashboard may load a little slowly.

Users

This tab will give you the ability to manage users, but you will have to do so by going back to the Office 365 admin center:

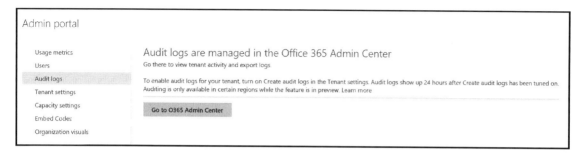

Click on the **Go to O365 Admin Center** button. Now, on the new tab, click on **Active users**:

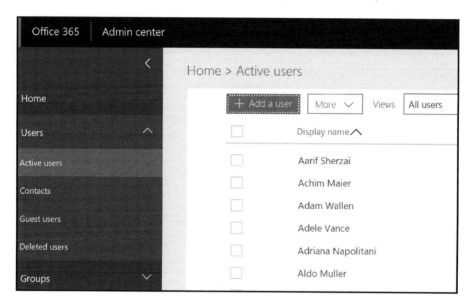

Audit logs

Through this tab, you are able to go to the audit logs which live in **Security & Compliance**:

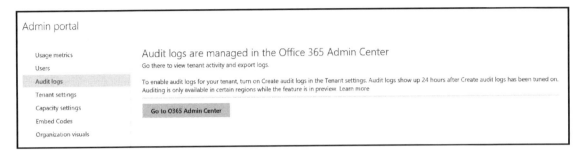

Click on the **Go to O365 Admin Center** button and the **Audit log search** screen in **Security & Compliance** will open in a new tab:

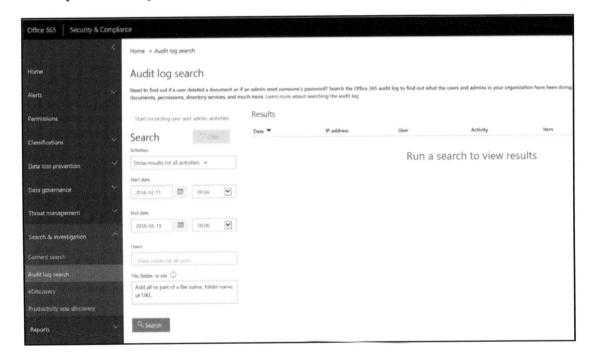

From there, you will want to filter the audit log activity options. There are a lot of audit log activity options available to choose from and you can choose more than one:

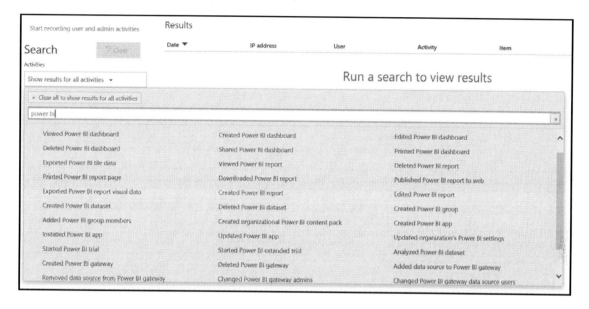

Here is a screenshot of the available activities:

Activity	Description	Additional details
CreateDashboard	This activity is logged every time a new dashboard is created.	- Dashboard name.
EditDashboard	This activity is logged every time a dashboard is renamed.	- Dashboard name.
DeleteDashboard	This activity is logged every time a dashboard is deleted.	- Dashboard name.
PrintDashboard	This event is logged every time that a dashboard is printed.	- Dashboard name. - Dataset name
ShareDashboard	This activity is logged every time a dashboard is shared.	- Dashboard name. -Recipient Email. - Dataset name. - Reshare permissions.
ViewDashboard	This activity is logged every time a dashboard is viewed.	- Dashboard name.
ExportTile	This event is logged every time data is exported from a dashboard tile.	- Tile name. - Dataset name.
DeleteReport	This activity is logged every time a report is deleted.	- Report name.
ExportReport	This event is logged every time data is exported from a report tile.	- Report name. - Dataset name.
PrintReport	This event is logged every time that a report is printed.	- Report name. - Dataset name.
PublishToWebReport	This event is logged every time that a report is Published To Web.	- Report Name. - Dataset name.
ViewReport	This activity is logged every time a report is viewed.	- Report name.
ExploreDataset	This event is logged every time you explore a dataset by selected it.	- Dataset name
DeleteDataset	This event is logged every time a dataset is deleted.	- Dataset name.
CreateOrgApp	This activity is logged every time an organizational content pack is created.	- Organizational Content Pack name. - Dashboard names. - Report names. - Dataset names.
CreateGroup	This activity is fired every time a group is created.	- Group name.
AddGroupMembers	This activity is logged every time a member is added to a Power BI group workspace.	- Group name. - Email addresses.

After making your activity choices, you will need to specify a date range. You could also specify certain users as well as a file, folder, or site URL if needed:

Once audit log search is turned on, it may take a couple of hours before you start seeing results. The search will return up to 1,000 results. If there are more, then you will see the latest 1,000.

Once you get your results, you will have the option to export them.

Tenant settings

This tab provides options for setting Power BI tenant-wide settings:

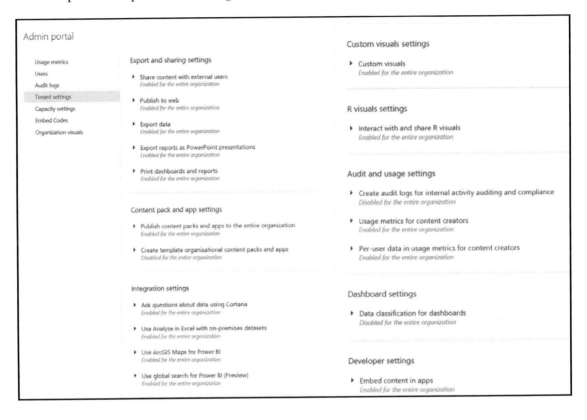

Once changes are made, it could take ten minutes before they take effect for your entire organization.

You will be able to enable or disable settings for the entire organization. You will also be able to enable and/or disable some settings for certain subsets of your organization:

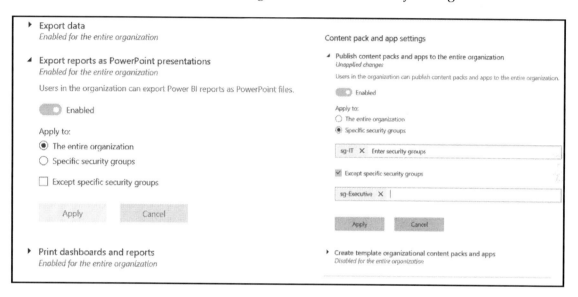

 You will need to specify your subset via security groups.

Capacity settings

In this tab, you can purchase extra capacity via **Power BI Premium**:

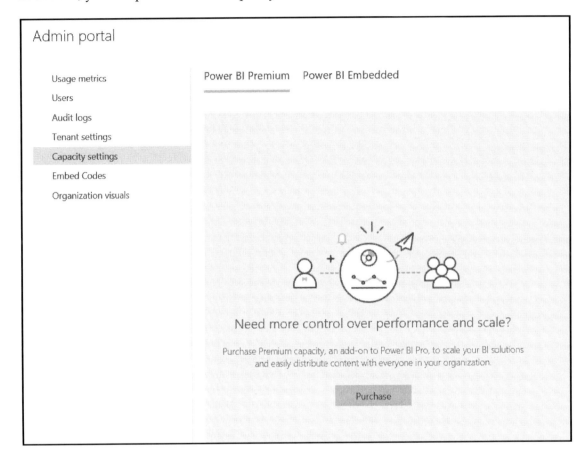

You can also learn more about **Power BI Embedded** and get access to the API for developing applications:

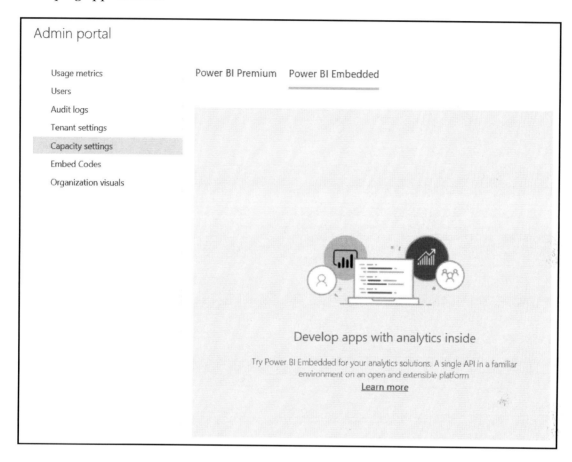

Embed Codes

In this tab, you can view any embed codes created in your organization. You will also be able to delete any codes:

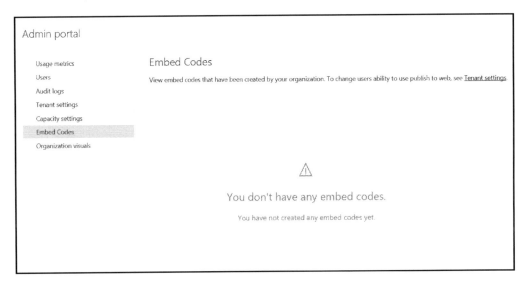

  You may need to enable some users to be able to create these codes under **Tenant settings**.

Organization visuals

In the final tab, you will be able to add any custom visuals that your organization may have created or acquired:

In order to upload a new visual, click on the **Add a custom visual** link and a side window will open:

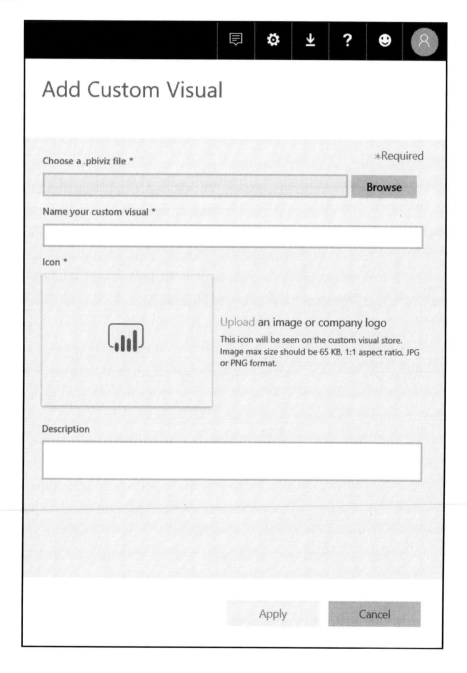

You need to ensure that the author of the visual is a trusted source. The visual could easily contain privacy or security risks. The file you upload must be a versioned API custom visual.

Once you have visuals available, you will be able to delete them.

 Deleting a visual is irreversible.

You can also upload a new version of the visual.

 You will have to upload a visual with the version number in the name (that is, `Visual 2.0`) since the original file cannot be overwritten with the new version. Keep the visual ID the same as the previous version so that users are prompted to use the updated version.

Administering using PowerShell

There are some scripts in GitHub that you can use for Power BI: `https://github.com/DevScope/powerbi-powershell-modules`. In GitHub, you will find modules for REST APIs and for connecting Power BI Desktop to SQL Server.

Another script that you will probably use is this script taken from `https://docs.microsoft.com/en-us/power-bi/service-admin-auditing`. This script allows you to access and search audit logs:

```
Set-ExecutionPolicy RemoteSigned

$UserCredential = Get-Credential

$Session = New-PSSession -ConfigurationName Microsoft.Exchange -ConnectionUri
https://outlook.office365.com/powershell-liveid/ -Credential $UserCredential -
Authentication Basic -AllowRedirection

Import-PSSession $Session

Search-UnifiedAuditLog -StartDate 9/11/2016 -EndDate 9/15/2016 -RecordType PowerBI -
ResultSize 1000 | Format-Table | More
```

You will need to connect to Exchange Online PowerShell to run the script.

Where to get more information

Microsoft maintains a site, dedicated to Power BI. Visit https://powerbi.microsoft.com/ for blogs, product information, walkthroughs, videos, and more.

Summary

In this chapter, we looked at Power BI. We went through a brief overview then delved into administering it via the Power BI **Admin portal** as well as via PowerShell.

In the next chapter, we will cover administering PowerApps, Flow, Stream, and Forms.

13
Administering PowerApps, Flow, Stream, and Forms

Every day, Microsoft adds more small products to Office 365, and frequently adds new ways to administer those products. It's impossible for a printed book to cover all of these in real time; by the time we hand this to our editors and it comes off the press and into your hands, it's likely there will be new administration centers we never touched on, and possibly entirely new products as well. Even now, there are a number of products related to Office 365 with administration centers accessible from the portal: Dynamics 365, Intune, and others—these are outside the scope of this book.

We will cover administration for four small products, PowerApps, Flow, Stream, and Forms, because they follow similar patterns that we expect Microsoft may adopt with other smaller, specialized additions to Office 365. To be specific, two of these products have admin centers in the Office 365 portal, and two of them do not and must be administered in other ways. None of them involve any kind of heavy administration burden.

Defining PowerApps, Flow, Stream, and Forms

Firstly, because they're so new, let's briefly address what these products are and what they do, how to tell if you have them, and what you can do to get them if you don't.

PowerApps

PowerApps is a product that can be obtained as part of Office 365, as part of Dynamics 365, or as a standalone product. It allows users to quickly and easily create business applications that link multiple products together—including Microsoft products and products from outside providers such as Twitter, Facebook, Slack, and so forth—and then publish those apps to the web and to mobile.

The licensing is somewhat arcane, as one might expect, given how many different ways there are to get the product. There's an impact on the capabilities of the users and the administrators that are affected by licensing considerations. Many of the connectors that allow the user to work with outside providers require the more expensive PowerApps Plan 1 or Plan 2. For instance, you can only establish multiple environments and company policies regarding the uses of different connections and apps if you have the PowerApps Plan 2.

Every version of Office 365 that includes an email address comes with some version of PowerApps, though the F1 frontline plans get a heavily stripped down version that doesn't allow them to create applications, only use them.

Flow

Any plan that includes PowerApps, aside from a standalone license, also includes Flow. Flow is not a replacement for SharePoint workflow, or any other workflow product; it's a means of automating simple tasks, usually with short two- or three-step algorithms that connect products to each other, using the same products you can access via PowerApps. (It's possible to build more robust and lengthier Flows, but it doesn't appear to be the primary use for people using the product.) As with PowerApps, if you want the premium connectors—Salesforce, Oracle, JotForm, Stripe—or the expanded administration capabilities, you pay extra.

Stream

Stream is a replacement for Office 365 Video, although currently the two coexist. Since Stream is being built from the ground up and doesn't rely on SharePoint as Office 365 Video does, it doesn't yet have all the same capabilities as Office 365 Video, as of writing this book. Microsoft's plan is to allow users to migrate, if they wish, in quarters one and two of 2018, then opt out of migration if they don't want to move, and eventually, everyone will be migrated once Stream is feature-complete.

Stream comes with enterprise versions of Office 365. If a business premium plan is the highest anyone in your organization has, you won't see it.

Forms

When Microsoft announced that they were retiring InfoPath, their venerable forms creation tool, in 2013, most of the SharePoint-using world was thrown into a bit of a panic. There was no formal substitute for InfoPath, only a handful of third-party products, none of which were necessarily compatible with SharePoint workflows and few of which weren't even compatible with SharePoint.

Today, there's a large number of good third-party applications that utilize SharePoint native forms and give them more robust features, without being nearly as time-consuming or requiring as much training to create as with InfoPath.

One would think a product called Forms would be a planned replacement for InfoPath. One would be wrong. PowerApps is actually Microsoft's replacement plan for InfoPath; Microsoft Forms is much more lightweight. It's a tool for creating surveys, quizzes, and polls, and capturing the data thus generated.

Initially, Forms was only available for Office 365 Education customers, but it should now be widely available to any commercial subscribers as well (which means business and enterprise plans).

Administering PowerApps and Flow

As of writing this book, there isn't much to do to administer PowerApps or Flow. The screens are identical for administering both products, although they are separate admin centers, so we will cover both at the same time. Screenshots are all taken from PowerApps unless otherwise specified, but they look the same in Flow administration:

PowerApps administration

There are four basic areas you can work with: **Environments**, **Data policies**, **Data integration**, and **Tenant** settings. You might not have access to all of these areas; **Environments**, for example, come with PowerApps Plan 2 only.

Environments

The concept of multiple environments is simple. You may want to segregate certain PowerApps to stop them from interacting with others, for example, in a production versus development scenario. Being able to create multiple environments allows us to do that.

Not all PowerApps licenses come with the ability to work with more than one environment. Most Office 365 and Dynamics 365 plans don't. According to Microsoft's documentation, you need to have a PowerApps Plan 2 to be able to create additional environments:

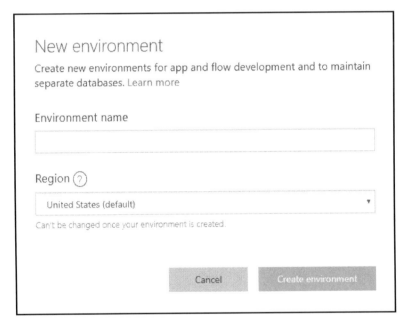

New environment creation

All you have to do to create an environment is click the plus sign next to **New environment**, fill out a name, and set the region.

You may be prompted to create a database once you've created your environment. Then, you will have access to the **Common Data Service**, available only with Plan 2. You can also add a database to the default environment:

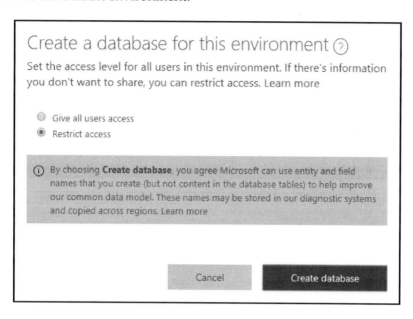

Creating a database—control access

You can't actually design the database in the admin center for PowerApps; you need to be in PowerApps itself to do that.

The **Common Data Service** that PowerApps databases are built on is generated from Dynamics 365 options, but even if your organization is licensed for Dynamics 365, you'll need a PowerApps Plan 2 license to use the **Common Data Service**. It'd be helpful, but not necessary, to understand Dynamics 365 before setting out to build the database. Since both Dynamics 365 and working with PowerApps as a user are outside the scope of this book, that's all we're able to say about that.

Once you've got an environment and a database, you have a few more options in terms of what you can do with them. When you click on an environment, you'll see four tabs: **Details**, **Security**, **Resources**, and **Database**.

The Security tab

On the **Security** tab, you can work with admin roles and, if there is a database or there are resources to control, user roles and permissions:

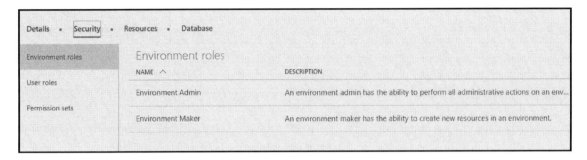

Security tab

There are two types of admin. An environment admin has the ability to perform all the administrative tasks that can be performed within an environment; an environment maker can create resources in that environment. In an environment you created, you'll be in both groups by default. You can add other users to either group:

User roles

Initially, you'll have two user roles as well: the **Organization User** (the default role, which has access to public data) and the **Database Owner** (who has full access to all database and resource schema). You can create a new user role as well by clicking the plus sign with the label **New role**, but all you'll be creating is a shell with a **Name** and **Description**. Adding the actual permissions comes later:

Creating a user role

When you edit the new user role, you'll have the opportunity to add **Permission sets** to the role. Type the name of the permission set into the box:

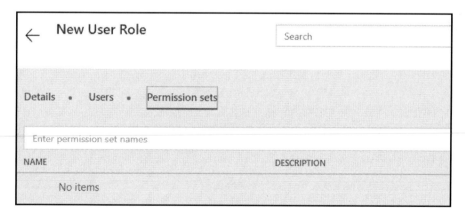

Adding a permission set to a user role

If you don't see any to your liking, if you need more information about what they are, or if you want to edit one, you'd go to the **Permission sets** tab under **Security**:

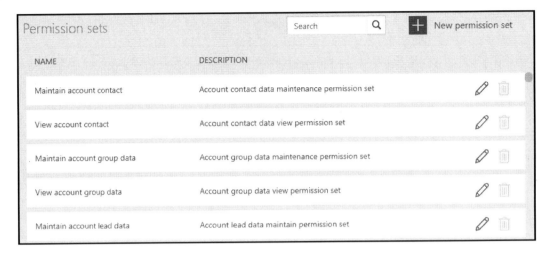

Permission sets

You can edit an existing permission set or create a new one, but as with creating a new user role, it's going to come down to editing it anyway because all creation does is assign it a name:

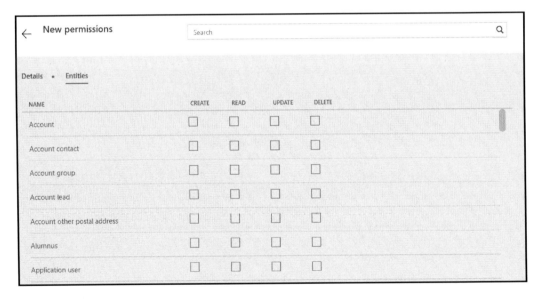

Setting permissions in a permission set

Click on the permissions you want to assign the permission set and then save.

The Resources tab

In the **Resources** tab, you can see **Apps** and **Flows**:

Resources and Apps screen

You can view the details of an app if you click on it, on the initial **Details** tab. When you want to set permissions, you go to the secondary tab, **Share**:

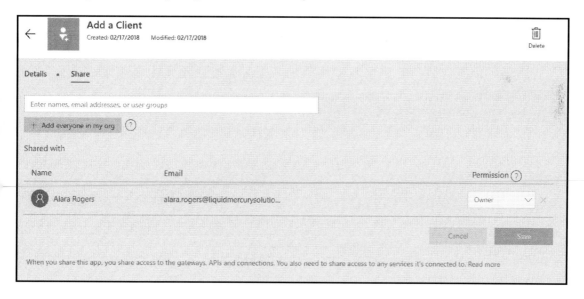

Sharing an app

The Database tab

Administering a database in PowerApps involves creating it and setting its security; as mentioned previously, you can't design it here:

Database tab

If you create a database that's available to everyone in your organization, and that's how you want it to stay, there's nothing else to do here. However, it's more common that access to a database would be restricted within an organization.

Click on **Restrict access** to control who has what rights to your database. It'll warn you that you'll need to create user roles:

Warning on restricting access to database

So head on over to the **Security** tab again, create a user role, and assign it **Permission sets** appropriate for working with the data the way you want:

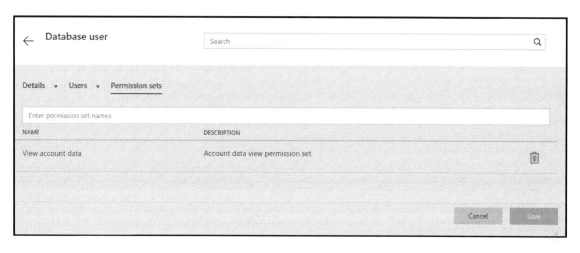

Example of a permission set for viewing account data, added to a new user role

Data policies

Data policies in this context really means *DLP policies*. You'd think that this would mean there would be overlap with security and compliance, but in fact, the DLP policies you can create there cover Exchange, SharePoint, and OneDrive—not PowerApps or Flow. At some point, Microsoft may integrate them, but as of writing this book, you'll need to come here to protect data in PowerApps:

Example of a permission set for viewing account data, added to a new user role

DLP policies in PowerApps revolve around segregating connectors from each other. First, you choose what **Environments** this policy will apply to:

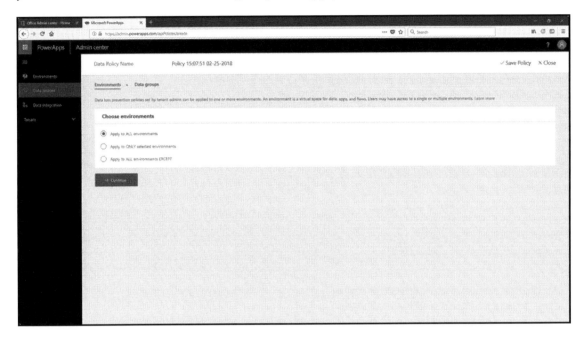

Choosing environments for the data loss prevention policy

Then, you'll add connectors to the **Business data only** group. The two groups—**Business data only** and **No business data allowed**—cannot be connected to each other in any environment that your data policy applies to:

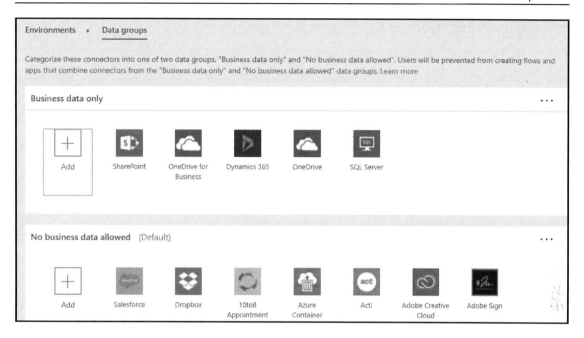

Choosing data groups

Data integration

This feature only works if your tenant has Dynamics 365 Enterprise for Finance and Operations, and as such is outside the scope of this book.

Tenant

On the **Tenant** tab, you can download user license information, and you can check out and download information about how many **Flow runs** have gone through your tenant in comparison to your quota:

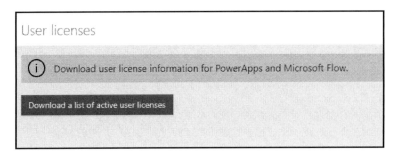

User license information

Because there are multiple licenses that can grant access to PowerApps and Flow, you might find duplications in your CSV:

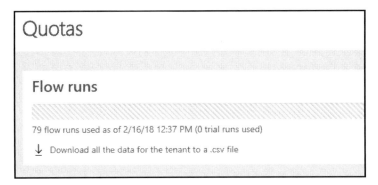

Flow runs

The CSV that you can get here shows which Flows have run, who owns them, and what the number of runs is, as well as what environment they're running in, but it won't tell you the date or time of the runs.

Stream

Administering Stream is unusual. You don't do it through the administration portal; you do it by clicking on your own profile in the Stream portal.

Go to **Stream** in your list of Office 365 apps:

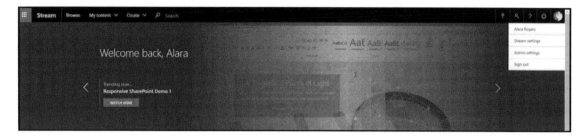

The Stream portal

Click on the top-right corner, where your own name is, and you'll get a drop-down menu consisting of your name, **Stream settings**, **Admin settings**, and **Sign out**. You will need to be a global administrator on your tenant to have the rights to do this, unless someone else has made you a Stream administrator.

There are two sections to Stream administration: **Manage streams** and **Manage users**.

Manage streams

This is where most of your capabilities as an administrator are.

Administrators

On the first screen, you can assign administrators. Any user on this list, and any user who is a global administrator of the tenant, has the right to enter the administration portal for Stream:

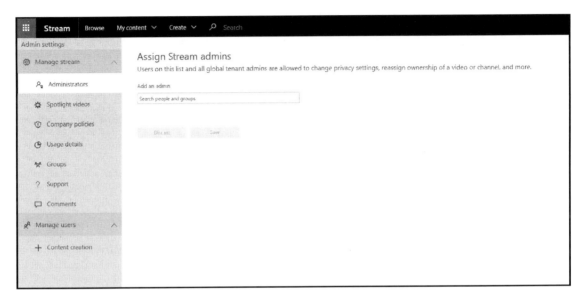

Stream admin settings: Administrators

Spotlight videos

Spotlight videos will appear in the Stream portal for your company in the four-page carousel at top. You can add up to four videos to be spotlighted here. If you don't add any videos, the carousel will populate itself with the most popular trending videos at your company:

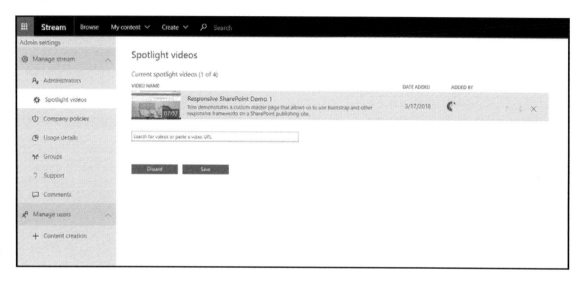

Stream admin settings: Spotlight videos

Company policies

Here, you can add a link to your company's video policy and require policy acceptance before users can upload a video. You might want to do this to avoid being flooded with funny cat videos, home movies, and copyrighted material:

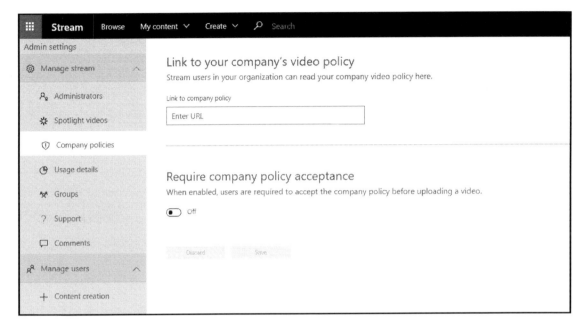

Stream admin settings: Company policies

Usage details

The **Usage details** screen is where you can see how much of your company's video quota you're using up. Most of the kinds of videos uploaded by most companies—how-to videos, training, meetings, and maybe some office videos from the company picnic—are not that large, so the space you get (500 GB, plus 0.5 GB per licensed user, where F1 plans do not count toward the quota of licensed users) should be sufficient.

However, if you have a user who likes to upload raw footage taken with an iPhone, you might want to advise them it'd be better to process those videos and convert them to a smaller format first:

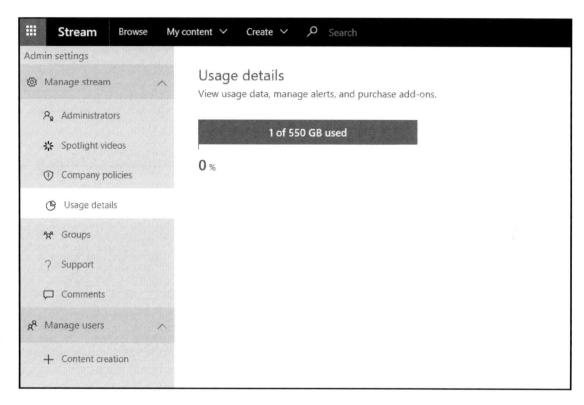

Usage details

Groups

You can't actually administrate Stream groups through the Stream portal, because they are Office 365 groups. Manage Office 365 groups through the Office 365 administration portal.

Support

Here's where you can open a support ticket with Microsoft if you're having problems with Stream:

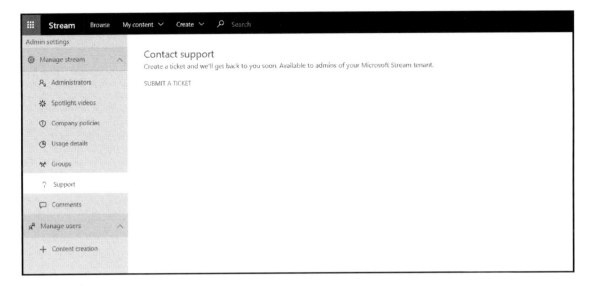

Support

Comments

You can decide to **Restrict comments on videos** here. At the moment, there's limited means for moderating comments—you can view a video in admin mode, and that gives you the ability to edit or delete comments, but there's no way to pre-emptively grant some users the right to comment while restricting others, or to hold comments in a queue to inspect them before release.

Your options here are to allow all comments or prevent all comments:

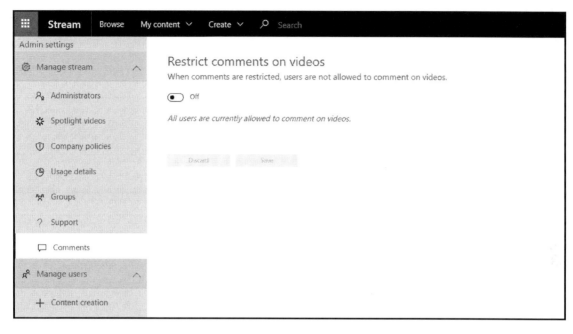

Manage users

At the moment, the only thing you can do in **Manage Users** is manage the rights to content creation.

Content creation

You can restrict who is allowed to upload videos to a specific list of users, and you can restrict who may create a channel for your company to a specific list of users.

Note that if you turn on these buttons but you don't provide a list of users, no one will be able to use these functions:

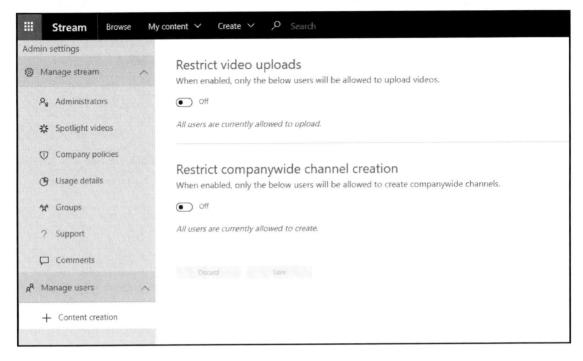

Content creation

Outside the Stream admin portal

As mentioned earlier, some administrative functions are only available within the pages for the individual videos.

View in admin mode

To perform administrative functions on a specific video, you go to that video's page and click on **View settings** and then **View in admin mode**.

This will allow you to edit the auto-generated transcript, hide or unhide people associated with the video (useful if there was stock footage in your video and the people feature identified a person who wasn't actually associated with your company at all), and edit or delete comments that you didn't make. You always have the ability to edit and delete comments that are yours:

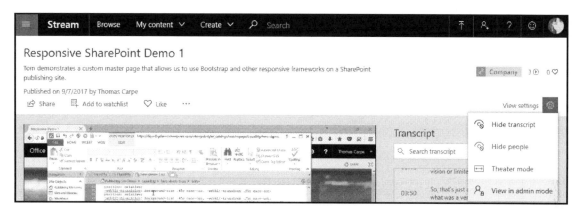

Viewing a video page in admin mode

While you're in admin mode, this banner will appear at the top of the page. To exit admin mode, click the button shown on the banner that says **Exit admin mode**:

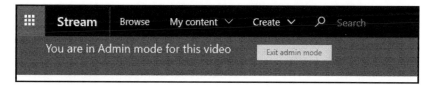

Exiting admin mode

Forms

There is actually very, very little you can do to administrate Forms. You can turn Forms on or off for individual users in the Office 365 administration portal, but there's no central place you can visit to see the Forms users have created or to change any information about them. For this reason, it's a good idea to centralize who's allowed to create Forms.

Users can only create Forms if Microsoft Forms is turned on for them, but they can use Forms that others have created, so you can limit who is permitted to create them without limiting who can use them. Letting everyone in your company create Forms can cause an administrative nightmare since there's so little ability to manage them centrally.

If a user creates Forms that are important to your company and then leaves, you will have to maintain that user's license indefinitely. It might be best to create specialized accounts for the purpose of creating Forms and then share the login information with whoever needs access.

Summary

In this chapter, we reviewed how to administer some of the smaller Office 365 products: PowerApps, Flow, Stream, and Forms.

PowerApps and Flow have separate administration centers, but those administration centers operate identically. PowerApps and Flow work together tightly and are much more useful with each other, so while it's possible to have a license for one and not the other, we expect that in the future Microsoft might integrate the products to a greater degree and allow them to be administrated as a single product.

Stream's administration center is not accessible via the Office 365 administration portal and doesn't include all administrative activities. The latter isn't necessarily unusual for a Microsoft product—SharePoint, for example, has many administrative tasks that can't be performed in the SharePoint admin center—but the former is definitely unusual for an Office 365 product. We expect that in the future perhaps the Stream admin center will be moved out of the Stream portal and into the Office 365 admin portal with the rest of the admin centers.

Forms cannot be centrally administrated at all, although you can control which users can create a new Form. Unless you're an Office 365 Education user, Forms is currently in preview as this book is being written, which suggests it may change substantially in the future. We can only hope that Microsoft will make it more friendly to administrators in the future.

In the next chapter, we will check out all the usage reports that are available in Office 365.

14
Usage Reporting

Office 365 offers a broad array of usage reports that are designed primarily to help you track and improve the adoption of the product.

In this chapter, we'll discuss the available reports for Office 365 in general, Exchange, OneDrive for Business, SharePoint, Skype for Business, Teams, and Yammer. We'll finish up with a brief conversation about advanced topics such as anonymizing your report data, using Power BI, and Security & Compliance reports.

We'll also do our best to avoid reciting a litany of dull sequential descriptions about data and graphs. Instead, we'll seek to explore how this information may be useful to you as an Office 365 administrator or consultant whose goals include ensuring that your users will make effective use of the platform and spotting trends that might create issues or affect long-term costs.

Although you could safely skip this entire chapter without endangering your job, we encourage you to check out all the reports that are available and use your imagination to find ways to incorporate them into your plans for Office 365.

How useful are usage reports?

Going beyond the abstract, let's consider the practicality, utility, and features provided by these reports.

Although some of the bar charts are pretty, we were disappointed to find that they do not use responsive web design. They neither scale at all with the size of the browser, nor do the detailed data tables scale to fit the space available.

If you're curious about why a metric has a particular value, you may feel left a bit short. Many of the charts don't allow you to drill down into the underlying datasets like pivot tables would. Changing the filters on tabular data does not update the chart display, and you can't dynamically check or uncheck specific values like you might be used to doing in Excel tables.

In short, while Office 365 Reporting may offer some useful insights, it should not be considered a business intelligence tool. Further, because these tools are limited, it's difficult to imagine Office 365 usage reports being very manageable for larger organizations.

If you need this kind of functionality, you may export the data from a tool of your choice (via Excel), write PowerShell to get the data that you need, or we strongly recommend checking out the Power BI content pack described later in this chapter.

Overall, although we wish that reporting could do more than it does, there are some useful insights to be gained and even some hidden gems if you take the time to look for them. To answer questions about whether these reports serve any practical purpose, let's look at each one in more depth.

What reports are included?

As mentioned, the **Reporting** section includes charts and tables with data describing how all the core Office 365 products are used. In addition, many in-depth reports have also been added to the **Security & Compliance** section, which deliver detailed audits and accountability for organizations with regulatory compliance needs. There are very few products that are not covered, specifically—Bookings, Forms, Planner, StaffHub, Streams, and Sway.

For a more-or-less complete list of all the reports included in Office 365 Admin Center, plus some helpful tips, visit `https://support.office.com/en-us/article/activity-reports-in-the-office-365-admin-center-0d6dfb17-8582-4172-a9a9-aed798150263`.

The dashboard

The dashboard shows tiles that highlight each of the more detailed reports. It's a useful place to get a bird's eye view of everything that goes on in your tenant.

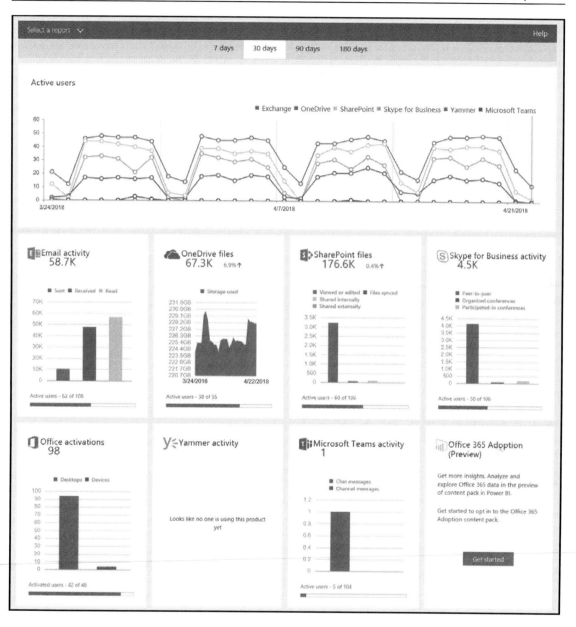

Office 365 Usage Reporting Dashboard

In the previous screenshot, we see a tenant with very good adoption metrics across Exchange, SharePoint, OneDrive, and Skype for Business. Employees are using nearly every aspect of Office 365. This is the kind of story Microsoft loves and one you want to be able to share with your boss. There's some room for improvement, but the overall trend is that adoption is not only healthy but growing. This year, maybe we'll see about rolling out Teams or introducing Yammer as ways to improve communication both internally and with customers.

While the dashboard shows the past 30 days by default, practically every chart in Usage Reports can be set to show 7, 30, 90, or 180 days.

Office 365

The **Office 365** section is the general-purpose catch-all section. It covers both product activation and the use of specific features. It includes the activations report, as well as the Active Users and Office 365 Groups reports. Since these, together, help to paint a picture of how users are making use of the various parts of the platform, it could just as easily have been called the Adoption section.

Activations

This report will show you product activation for all licensed users.

Somewhat surprisingly, it is not a report against a time range. Instead, the report shows all licensed users and the last date/time they were activated for each product. Unlicensed users are not shown, and each product gets its own detail line. Likewise, products that do not require separate activation (for example, Skype for Business, OneDrive for Business, or Planner) do not appear in this report.

The top-line chart will show activations by product, stacked by operating system. Desktop and mobile OS are shown as side-by-side bars. You can choose to show users instead of activations. However, to be completely honest, we didn't see any difference at first between the two in terms of the data being displayed. Only by clicking on these links repeatedly, we eventually convince the report to display the alternative graph. Your mileage may vary.

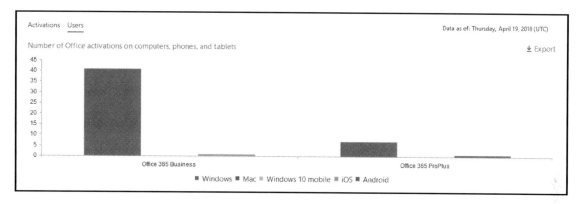

Office 365 Activations by Users Chart

The following **Details** table shows activations by operating system: Windows, Mac, iOS, Android, and Windows 10 mobile.

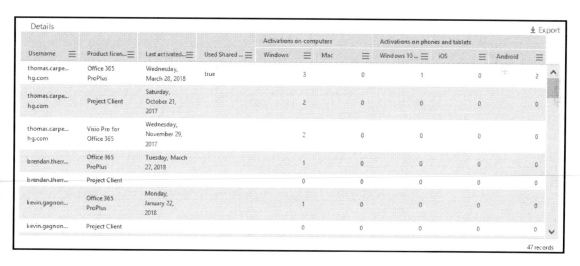

Office 365 Activations Details Table

One caveat is that the activation dates shown do not necessarily include reactivation or subsequent devices. We observed several cases of users whose activation date was significantly farther in the past than when we knew in reality they had last installed office on a device.

The table also shows which users are activated using *Shared Computer Activations*, which could be helpful if you're trying to test a VDI or Remote Desktop Services configuration. However, if a user activated on both a regular Office 365 installation and SCA, only the most recent entry appears in the report. You may want to keep this in mind when trying to troubleshoot such activations, as there are definitely other ways to test this on the local computer.

One interesting observation was that the Activations report does not always accurately distinguish between Windows 10 workstations and Windows 10 mobile devices, so some of our fleet of computers ended up being shown in-line with our Android phones. While the reasons for this are not clear, it seems to be a matter of the specific hardware and possibly whether the machine was using Office 365 Mobile Device Management versus Intune management. Our tests showed that 2-in-1 tablets such as the Dell Inspiron 1300 or 1500 series will always show up under mobile devices, even when they're functionally being used as PC replacements.

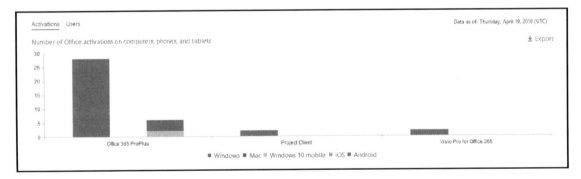

Office 365 Activations by Number Chart

Because the different operating systems are shown in separate columns and the data generated wasn't consistent with our expectations, it would be quite difficult to use the **Activations** report in some useful ways we thought should be obvious. There's no way to filter the report, for example, to show only those products that were licensed but never activated at all, perhaps with the goal in mind of reclaiming unused licenses.

Nevertheless, you can accomplish this goal easily enough through the clever use of sorting and filtering. Simply sort by product and then filter **Last Activation Date** against some arbitrary date in the distant past. Those products that were never activated will still appear in the list. If you wish, you can reach out to each user directly and enquire about why the report says they haven't activated Office in several years.

Read More about the Activations report at `https://support.office.com/en-us/article/office-365-reports-in-the-admin-center-microsoft-office-activations-87c24ae2-82e0-4d1e-be01-c3bcc3f18c60`.

Active users

This report will show you active users by service (product) over time. The primary purpose of this report is to drive end user adoption, which helps you get the most value from Office 365 services you've purchased. (Of course, this benefits Microsoft too, so it's a win-win.)

The following chart shows a pretty typical adoption pattern, where use of Office and email begin fairly quickly as users are migrated onto the platform. Once folks are comfortable in Outlook and any installation and activation issues are addressed, then training on platforms like Skype for Business and Exchange starts having a positive impact on adoption for those services too. We can see that trend beginning in the right-hand side of the chart.

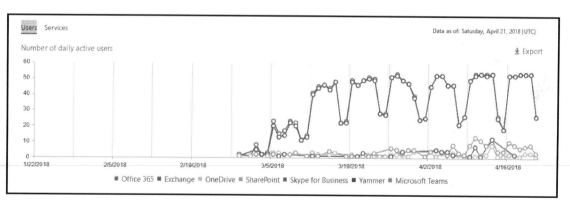

Office 365 Active Users by User and Date Chart

You can also view active versus inactive users for each service. Here, we see that nearly half the business has become active in using SharePoint, which is actually quite a bit better than average—though we'd always like to see these numbers get as high as possible.

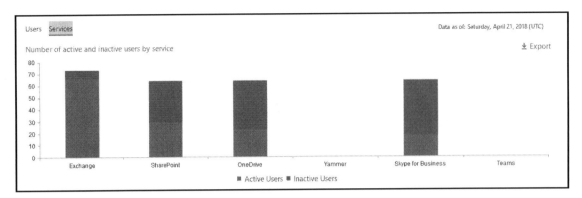

Office 365 Active Users by Service Chart

The data from the two charts earlier suggests that while the core business users are making good use of enhanced services in SharePoint, OneDrive, and Skype, many employees are still living mostly in email. To drive adoption, we'll need to come up with strategies to bring them into using other aspects of Office 365.

One possible opportunity that presents itself will be to discuss Teams and Yammer, including how they compare to using Skype and the difference between these two platforms.

If you're interested in zeroing in on specific groups of users, the detail table will allow you to do this:

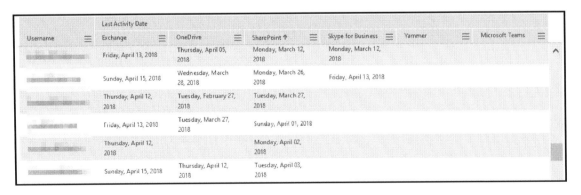

Office 365 Active Users Details Table

For example, by sorting any service in ascending order, it's not difficult to get a list of those users who have never broken the shrink wrap on that part of Office 365 (as well as those who may have fallen off the wagon). From this, you can spot trends such as whether a certain department or geographic region may be struggling more than others. Perhaps some more SharePoint training will help them with that.

Read more about the active users report at `https://support.office.com/en-us/article/office-365-reports-in-the-admin-center-active-users-fc1cf1d0-cd84-43fd-adb7-a4c4dfa8112d`.

Office 365 Groups activity

This report is useful to show adoption of features specific to Office 365 Groups. Note that use of Groups does appear as a service in the **Active users** report, so you'll need to review both reports to get a complete picture of end user adoption in your organization.

There are several aspects to the Groups report, and the charts don't make these perfectly clear. So, let us take a moment to review each one.

The **Groups** panel shows you how many groups have been created and how many were active. Because Office 365 Groups can be used for security and synced with a local Active Directory, it is not unusual to have many more groups in existence than are actively in use.

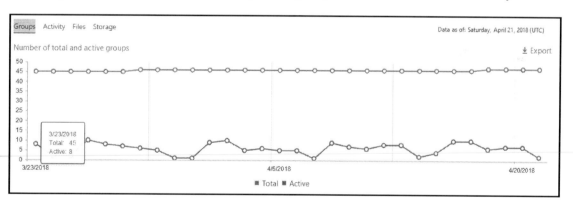

Office 365 Groups Activity by Amount and Date Chart

The **Activity** panel will show messages sent to the group in email. It will also show various statistics for Yammer, but only if the group is active there. Later, we see data that indicates that users are primarily using Groups as a kind of enhanced Distribution List, and that Yammer hasn't yet been adopted. It would be nice if similar statistics existed for Teams, but at the time of writing, these were not available. Likewise, even though Planner is built on Groups, activity in that tool does not show up.

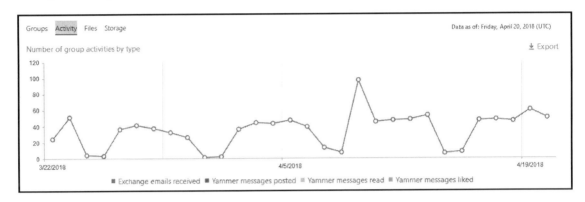

Office 365 Groups Activity by Activity and Date Chart

The **Files** panel will show the number of total and active files that are stored in the Document Library for the Group's embedded SharePoint site. Note that how you use SharePoint will greatly affect whether these metrics will be useful. That's because Groups is a comparatively new feature, total files may completely dwarf active files, and many organizations will choose to keep their essential files in a SharePoint intranet that will be managed separately from the sites created automatically by Groups:

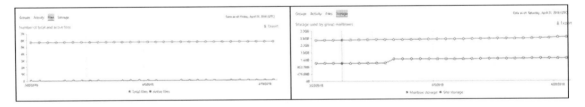

Office 365 Groups Activity by Files and Storage Charts

The **Storage** panel will show the same files as presented in the **Files** chart, but they will be presented by how much storage space they consume, rather than how many there are. It also shows storage consumed by the Group Mailbox, which will include attachments sent to the group. This provides a useful counterpoint when the emphasis inevitably shifts from user adoption to staying under storage limits and controlling costs.

There's also the **Details** table, which can be useful in its own right. Later, we've hidden some of the columns that weren't very informative and chosen instead to show the **Group owner**, and number of (Internal) **Members** and [Guest] **External members**.

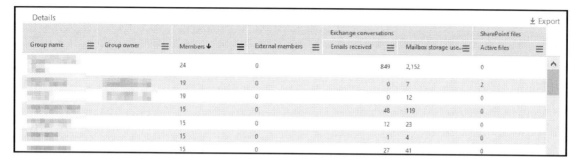

Group name	Group owner	Members ↓	External members	Exchange conversations		Mailbox storage use..	SharePoint files Active files
				Emails received			
		24	0	849	2,152		0
		19	0	0	7		2
		19	0	0	12		0
		15	0	48	119		0
		15	0	12	23		0
		15	0	1	4		0
		15	0	27	41		0

Office 365 Groups Activity Details Table

Learn more about this report at `https://support.office.com/en-us/article/office-365-reports-in-the-admin-center-office-365-groups-a27f1a99-3557-4f85-9560-a28e3d822a40`.

Exchange

Because email is the first thing most organizations adopt in Office 365, one of the report sets that you'll most likely use first will be the Exchange reports.

Email activity

This report will show you trends in emails sent and received. Here, you see the **Activity** chart, which shows a fairly typical pattern where email traffic drops noticeably over weekends:

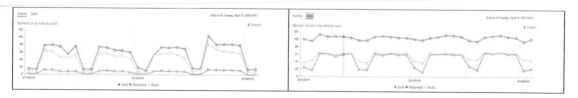

Exchange Email Activity Charts

Some things to watch out for here would be a noticeable change in the ratio between emails received and read, or a dramatic or atypical increase in the number of emails being sent. Any of these could indicate problems with spammers, mail bots, viruses, or malware. (The spike in data later can most likely be explained by that Monday 4/16 being US Tax Day although it's possible that this was just a coincidence.)

The **Users** panel shows the same categories by the number of users who performed each task (send, receive, and read) at least once. The data mentioned earlier is interesting because it indicates that while everyone in the organization is receiving emails, only about half the users who have mailboxes were confirmed as reading their email, and fewer still actually sent any mail on the same day. Because we happen to know this organization's business cycle, we can say with some confidence that this fact is not too strange. However, it is atypical. Unless you can explain this due to large numbers of unmonitored Shared Mailboxes or inactive accounts, you should be somewhat concerned to see this pattern in most businesses.

Digging into the tabular data may help us explain some of these mysteries.

 Read more about the Email Activity report at `https://support.office.com/en-us/article/office-365-reports-in-the-admin-center-email-activity-1cbe2c00-ca65-4fb9-9663-1bbfa58ebe44`.

Email app usage

This report will show users, apps, and versions for the Outlook email applications. Although you're entitled to your own opinion, we find the Apps panel to be more comprehensible, as the **Users** panel tends to overwhelm with data for which we were hard pressed to find a use case. Whichever you prefer, these charts give us a sense of which methods of checking email are most popular, and they can also highlight excessive use of some of the less savory methods such as POP3 and SMTP we may wish to discourage, except when absolutely necessary of course:

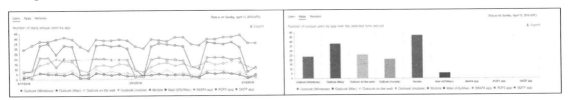

Exchange Email App Usage Charts

Finally, the **Version** panel will give you a sense of whether your users have all upgraded to the latest version of Office. Of course, literally all our users were on Outlook 2016, so we didn't bother to show this chart. It will be useful to you during periods where upgrades are being deployed.

 Read more about the Email App Usage report at `https://support.` `office.com/en-us/article/office-365-reports-in-the-admin-center-` `email-apps-usage-c2ce12a2-934f-4dd4-ba65-49b02be4703d.`

Mailbox usage

These reports primarily tell the story of how users are consuming mailbox storage.

The **Mailbox** panel really tells us the same story that we should already know from the Email Activity report, albeit just a bit more explicitly. It shows the number of mailboxes, and how many of those were active on a given day. One assumes that the number of mailboxes corresponds to users plus other mailboxes, such as group, shared, and resource mailboxes—and that a mailbox is active whenever users read or send email with it.

The **Storage and Quota** panels are marginally more informative.

Since **Storage** only provides the total for all users, this top-line number is only truly useful in identifying trends over time or perhaps for calculating the cost of archival and backup solutions:

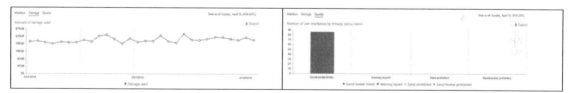

Exchange Mailbox Usage Charts

The **Quota** panel will give you a better sense of how many users might be exceeding their limits, which could require archiving some mail or upgrading their email plan. Since Microsoft is so generous with email storage, more than likely most times your chart will look just about as dull as the one above.

As can see, these charts are basically ignorable for the most part. For the **Mailbox Usage** report, where the real meat and potatoes lies is in the tabular data because it provides you a convenient way to view the top-ranked mailboxes in terms of storage use, lets you quickly see which users you need to contact about going overlimit, and even shows you how useful (or not) a particular mailbox may be, by way of how recently it was last used.

Exchange Mailbox Usage Details Table

 Read more about the Mailbox Usage report at `https://support.office.com/en-us/article/office-365-reports-in-the-admin-center-mailbox-usage-beffbe01-ce2d-4614-9ae5-7898868e2729`.

OneDrive and SharePoint

The reports for OneDrive and SharePoint are virtually identical, so we'll only show the SharePoint charts later. This should be no surprise as OneDrive for Business' backend is a series of SharePoint site collections, formerly known as "My Sites". For each category, there is an Activity report and a Usage report.

OneDrive and SharePoint activity

The **Files** panel will show you metrics on files read or edited in SharePoint, and how Sync (to OneDrive for Business) and Share (both internal and external) are being used:

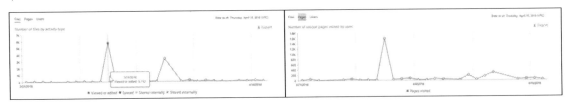

SharePoint Activity by Files and Pages Charts

Any dramatic increase in reads, syncs, or external sharing is likely to attract the attention of security conscious system admins. The previous charts are interesting because they show unusual spikes in the number of SharePoint documents being viewed or edited.

The earlier chart prompted a call from the Office 365 Admin to the SharePoint Admin, who was able to explain that the first spike was a planned migration to reorganize content from one site collection to another. The coinciding spike in page edits happened because the migration included replicating content in Publishing Pages. The second spike was SkyKick Backup for SharePoint reading all the files that were moved, so they could be backed up. Thus, the second spike is about half the size of the first, which included access at both the source and destination.

The **Users** panel goes deeper into user behavior than the Active Users chart under the Office 365 section which presented OneDrive and SharePoint among other services. Here, users' views/edits, syncs, and shares are shown. Page visits are also displayed for SharePoint but are omitted in the OneDrive report. Note that sharing data may be displayed with discontinuities, as invitations are made and later expire.

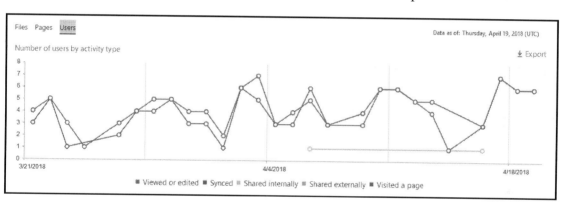

SharePoint Activity by Users Chart

Read more about SharePoint Activity report at
https://support.office.com/en-us/article/office-365-reports-in-t
he-admin-center-sharepoint-activity-
a91c958f-1279-499d-9959-12f0de08dc8f.

Read more about OneDrive for Business Activity report at https://
support.office.com/en-us/article/office-365-reports-in-the-
admin-center-onedrive-for-business-activity-8bbe4bf8-221b-46d6-
99a5-2fb3c8ef9353.

OneDrive and SharePoint usage

These usage reports show the number of files and size of files, and for SharePoint, the number of sites and pages is also included:

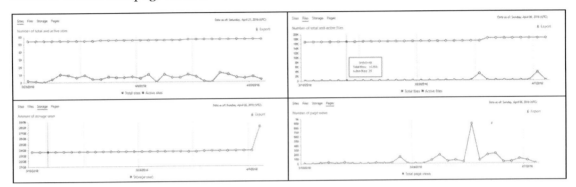

SharePoint Usage by Sites, Files, Storage, and Pages Charts

In our charts, we see similar indications that there was a file migration that took place on March 31 and about a week later.

At first, a look at the **Storage** panel seems to indicate a drastic increase in the use of storage space. However, a closer look will show that the chart is misleading because it baselines at 21 GB and not 0 GB and therefore not actually representing the 150% increase it appears to be.

Another interesting point to note is that where we see a noticeable increase in the number of files, we do not see a corresponding increase in the amount of storage space. As long as these files are identical copies of the originals, Microsoft's file optimization platform ensures that only one instance of the data is stored, regardless of how many copies you make. (Also, most of these files happened to be web pages, so the actual number of files was more noticeable than the size.) Thus, only a very small increase in storage consumption occurred. How cool is that?

All our usage data is telling a consistent story, and it lines up with the activity data too. Thus, the initial concerns of the global admin have been more than satisfied.

But this is not the end of our user story.

On the OneDrive side of usage reporting, a new panel named Accounts is also available. Nothing much surprising here, but we obviously have a lot of OneDrive accounts that aren't being used.

OneDrive Usage by Account, Files, and Storage Charts

But what's this? We have a dramatic increase in OneDrive storage around the same time we saw this happening in SharePoint on the previous reports. Well, it's not actually as big as it looks, for the same reason mentioned earlier (the chart starts at 25 GB). But, it is still large enough to make us a bit curious.

Like other reports we've seen before, the value of the SharePoint and OneDrive usage reports is often buried in the tabular data. For example, it might be helpful to know the top 10 most visited sites, a list of sites that haven't been accessed in a long time, or the top five consumers of storage space – whether they are SharePoint sites or OneDrive users.

Let's see if we can explain the storage increased from April 7. We start by clicking the date on the chart, then we wait for the tabular data to refresh.

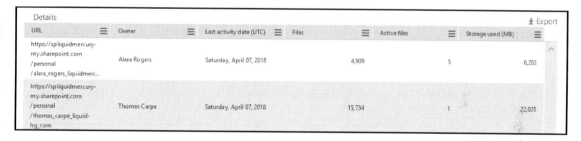

URL	Owner	Last activity date (UTC)	Files	Active files	Storage used (MB)
https://spliquidmercury-my.sharepoint.com /personal /alara_rogers_liquidmerc...	Alara Rogers	Saturday, April 07, 2018	4,909	5	6,203
https://spliquidmercury-my.sharepoint.com /personal /thomas_carpe_liquid-hg_com	Thomas Carpe	Saturday, April 07, 2018	15,734	1	22,038

OneDrive Usage Details Table

The data shows Alara's OneDrive is about 6 GB. This is close to the amount of our increase. A quick jump to the day before (after several repeat-clicks on the stubborn chart control) confirms that she has moved a large amount of content into her OneDrive over the weekend.

Seems Alara was backing up documents on her laptop. She's preparing to have the IT send it out for repairs, which involves wiping the hard drive for privacy. This is exactly the kind of usage we like to see for OneDrive for Business, so all is well.

However, SharePoint storage (shown earlier) also increased on the 8th, which was the following day. Why? Using the data table in SharePoint usage and selecting that date gives us the answer.

Details							
Site URL		Site owner	Last activity date (U...	Files	Active files	Storage used (MB) ↓	Page views
https://spliquidmercury.sharepoint.com/		Company Administrator	Saturday, April 07, 2018	7,410	0	18,452	0
https://spliquidmercury.sharepoint.com/sites/alarasite		Alara Rogers	Saturday, April 07, 2018	167	0	4,299	0

SharePoint Usage Details Table

Here, we see that Alara has not only uploaded several GB to her OneDrive, she's also put another 4 GB onto a site collection named just for her.

When we asked Alara why she did things this way, she told us she wanted greater control over which files would sync to her PC using OneDrive and so she broke things out into multiple document libraries. Perhaps we should have mentioned to her sooner that the latest version of OneDrive for Business lets you perform selective sync on specific folders. Oh, well! No harm done.

Read more about SharePoint Site Usage report at
`https://support.office.com/en-us/article/office-365-reports-in-t`
`he-admin-center-sharepoint-site-usage-4ecfb843-`
`e5d5-464d-8bf6-7ed512a9b213.`
Read more about OneDrive for Business Usage report at `https://`
`support.office.com/en-us/article/office-365-reports-in-the-`
`admin-center-onedrive-for-business-usage-0de3b312-c4e8-4e4b-`
`a02d-32b2f726a680.`

Skype for Business

Most of the reports in the Skype for Business section will apply whether you have phone service or not, but many of these will only apply if you're using Skype for Business to conduct online meetings with audio conferencing. Wherever you are in the process of driving Skype adoption, these reports can give you insights that can help boost communication and productivity.

Skype for Business activity

This report drills into Skype for Business usage in more detail than the data expressed in the Office 365 activity report. The **Activity** panel shows the number of sessions by type, and the **Users** panel shows unique users by activity type. Types include **Peer-to-peer** (for example, IM/chat) session, **Organized** (meeting host), and **Participant** (meeting attendee):

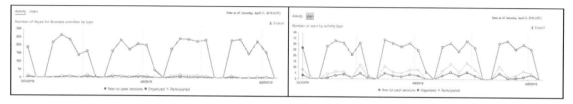

Skype for Business Activity by Amount and Users Charts

A normal pattern of adoption will show more peer-to-peer activity than meetings and (somewhat obviously) more attendees than meeting organizers. In certain cases, you may find that some organizations do not use instant messaging and tend to focus on structured meetings. This may be an indication of workplace culture that relies on email, or they may have moved ad hoc conversations to Yammer or Teams. Once you review other reports to get a sense of what's going on, you can decide if training or promotion is needed to get more people using Skype for Business messages.

The **Details** pane can give you specifics about who your primary Skype adopters are. Sorting by the last activity date will give you a sense of people who might have stopped using Skype, possibly because they switched computers and are no longer loading it when Windows starts. When sorting by the number of peer-to-peer sessions, you can see who is getting the most use from it. Just keep in mind that it isn't really possible to tell if folks are chatting about work or just trading links to cat GIFs. (In fact, in Teams that sort of thing is actively encouraged.)

Read more about the Skype for Business Activity report at `https://docs.` `microsoft.com/en-us/SkypeForBusiness/skype-for-business-online-` `reporting/activity-report`.

Peer-to-peer activity, conference organized, and participant activity

The next three reports are essentially drill-downs of the Skype for Business **Activity** report. They are fundamentally alike, so we'll summarize the three of them together:

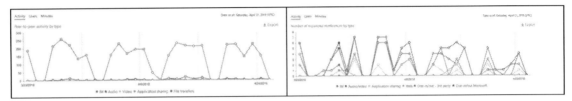

Skype for Business Peer-to-Peer and Organized Conference Activity Charts

The **Activity** panel shows these by number of calls/conversations; the Users panel will show this by number of users instead of number of conversations. Activities are subdivided into IM, Audio, Video, App (desktop) sharing—with File transfers added for Peer-to-peer charts, and Web client plus Dial-in metrics shown for both organized and participated in online meetings.

A typical organization will show significantly higher use of IM in peer-to-peer conversations, with a more evenly distributed proportion of services being used during online meetings. Participant report data will generally be similar to the organizer reports, with higher numbers for both meetings and users:

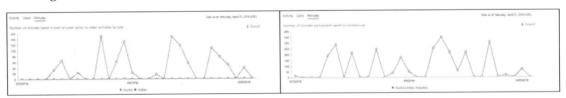

Skype for Business Peer-to-Peer and Attended Conference by Minutes Charts

In all cases, the **Minutes** panel only tracks time for audio/video calls, since IM are typically conducted asynchronously over extended periods of time. The organizer chart will show whether video (or screen sharing) was presented during the call, whereas the presenter chart only indicates A/V as a combined total.

There aren't many practical uses for all this data, but tangible evidence of teleconferencing adoption might help you justify the expense of upgrading from E3 to E5 plans or lobby to get more people upgraded to better plans. Plus, the graphs sure do look pretty, don't they?

If you're having bandwidth issues in your office, the **Details** table will be useful for determining who could be impacted by the issue because A/V quality will tend to suffer more from such problems than other applications. Sort or filter based on the number and type of meetings to identify who you should be reaching out to.

It's important to keep in mind that even though audio conferencing can suffer from network interruptions and latency, it doesn't consume a great deal of bandwidth itself. Even video presentations will be no more bandwidth intense than a typical Remote Desktop connection. So, there's not much use in running around the office asking people to curtail the number of meetings they attend.

Read more about these Skype for Business activity reports using these links:

Participant: `https://docs.microsoft.com/en-us/SkypeForBusiness/skype-for-business-online-reporting/conference-participant-activity-report`

Organizer: `https://docs.microsoft.com/en-us/SkypeForBusiness/skype-for-business-online-reporting/conference-organizer-activity-report`

Peer-to-peer: `https://docs.microsoft.com/en-us/SkypeForBusiness/skype-for-business-online-reporting/peer-to-peer-activity-report`

Device usage

This report will show you what device types are being used to access Skype for Business. Available choices include Windows, Windows Phone, Android, iPhone, and iPad. The Users panel shows trends over time, and the Distribution panel gives you a more concise average across the selected period. Neither chart appears to track Skype Web Access or Mac (OSX) clients currently:

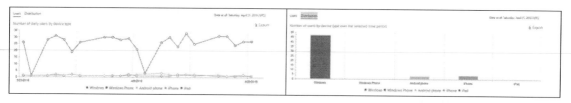

Skype for Business Device Usage by Users and Distribution Charts

The earlier-mentioned charts is a typical use case. In that, most users are accessing the desktop client, whereas a smaller handful of folks are leveraging the mobile client. Android and iPhone users at this company are roughly equal.

These figures are useful because they give admins a sense of where support resources should be allocated and can give management a sense of how the workforce leverages mobile technology to communicate. Although a lower percentage of mobile clients is normal, it can indicate an opportunity to encourage users to make the most of tools they can use while on the go.

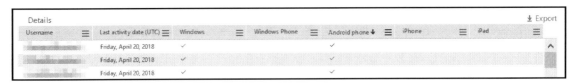

Skype for Business Device Usage Details Table

The **Details** table can tell you who your mobile adopters are. Note, however, that there's not enough information presented here to tell when people may be taking the use of mobiles too far. If you suspect that a remote employee may be literally *phoning it in*, you're going to need to bring data together from several different reports in order to know for sure.

 Read more about the Skype for Business Device Usage report at `https://docs.microsoft.com/en-us/skypeforbusiness/skype-for-business-online-reporting/device-usage-report`.

PSTN (Telephone) usage

If you have calling plans that allow you to make phone calls using Skype for Business, this report will be added to the standard list. Choosing it will take you to the Skype for Business Admin Center, where you can see the phone history for every Skype for Business user in your organization, including service numbers like dial-in meetings or the auto-attendant.

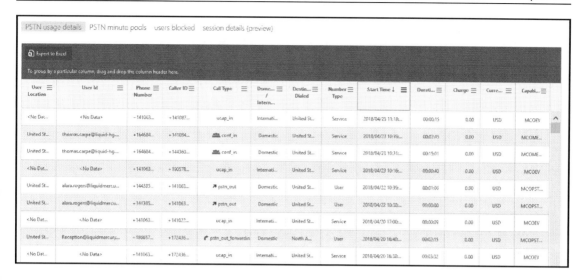

Skype PSTN Usage Details Report

Data is presented starting with most recent calls first, but you can easily use the menu at the top of each column to filter the data for a specific period or by other criteria.

There's a wealth of information presented here. Interesting data includes the Caller ID of each incoming call, whether the call was answered directly using the Skype client or forwarded to an outside number, and the duration of each call. The report will also show you the user's country and if there were costs associated with the call.

Users blocked

This report also takes you to the Skype for Business Admin Center. Though the name would imply that perhaps this report shows you users who were blocked from communicating with those in your organization, instead it shows users in your organization who are blocked from making PSTN (telephone) calls. It isn't entirely clear if this report will tell you if another organization or user has requested to have one of your users blocked. Microsoft's documentation on the purpose of this report is pretty thin.

Since Skype for Business calling plans are not free, none of the authors have ever encountered a case where a customer wanted to pay for PSTN plans but not allow users to place calls as they wish. If you know of a use case for this feature, please reach out to us and let us know, and we'll do our best to update this in a future edition or the online version.

Read more about the Users Blocked report at `https://docs.microsoft.com/en-us/SkypeForBusiness/skype-for-business-online-reporting/users-blocked-report`.

Session details

This report was in preview at the time of writing, and it is not shown in the Office 365 Usage Reports list. Use one of the other reports to navigate to the Skype for Business Admin Center, and you can view this report from there.

Unlike some other reports we've seen, this one uses a date range and targets a specific user. You must provide at least a user and a "from date". You can optionally specify a "to date". When you hit **Submit**, be prepared to wait a while to see results.

There's a wealth of data in this report that could potentially be very useful if you're trying to diagnose system issues with online meetings or audit a user's activity. However, the data is not presented in the most intuitive or easily understandable fashion. One thing to be aware of is that the report can show multiple lines for a single online meeting.

Skype PSTN Session Details Report

Note the chevron on the left-hand side of the report. If your meeting included files or audio, you can expand this to see those details.

 Read more about the Session Details report at `https://docs.microsoft.com/en-us/SkypeForBusiness/skype-for-business-online-reporting/session-details-report`.

Teams and Yammer

Yammer and Teams are both platforms for social communication. They each do things a bit differently, and they overlap in functionality with other aspects of Office 365. As a result, driving adoption of one or more of these will require a concentrated effort on your part. Usage reporting will be a key to determining how receptive your users are to give Teams or Yammer a try, and whether the information, training, and encouragement you provide are having the desired impact.

Microsoft Teams User activity

This report displays activities that can be performed in Teams, specifically channel and chat messages, as well as (Skype) calls and meetings. There are panels showing the number of activities performed and the number of users participating:

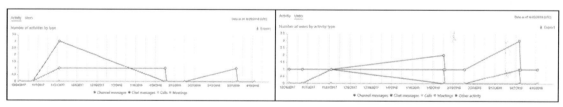

Teams Activity by Amount and User Charts

The previously mentioned data indicates one of a few people, probably in IT, trying out different Teams features in a very lonesome fashion. However, if it weren't for this report, we might not even realize that this was happening at all. It should probably not surprise anyone that a chart like the one shown earlier is not uncommon. That is mostly because Teams is so new, but also because users don't understand what Teams is for, how it can benefit them, and how to use it.

It's hard to have a Team with only one member. Why not get in there with a few people and just have fun, get messy, and figure it out together?

Further investigation in the details table shows that this pilot was being done by the IT manager, the administrative officer, and one other employee. Perhaps with some more volunteers and a little training, they'll be able to put Teams to work building... well, teams.

 Read more about Teams User Activity report at `https://support.office.com/en-us/article/office-365-reports-in-the-admin-center-microsoft-teams-user-activity-07f67fc4-c0a4-4d3f-ad20-f40c7f6db524`.

Microsoft Teams Device Usage

This report focuses on how users are accessing Teams rather than what they are doing with it:

Teams Device Usage by User and Distribution Charts

In our scenario, we can see the pilot group are mostly using their web browser, with one person who installed the Teams app for iOS. They aren't using the Teams App for Windows, so it is no wonder that adoption is so low. Perhaps it's time to bring this up at the next weekly IT meeting and see if there's anything that we can do to help improve the current situation.

Like other reports, the details table is useful in helping you determine who's making good use of Teams, and who may have used it once but stopped a while ago for whatever reason.

 Read more about the Teams Device Usage report at `https://support.` `office.com/en-us/article/office-365-reports-in-the-admin-center-` `microsoft-teams-device-usage-917b3e1d-203e-4439-8539-` `634e80196687.`

What the heck happened to Yammer?

Disclaimer: The opinions expressed in this section are the author's alone. Microsoft certainly hasn't given us any information or made any statements to support them.

Though there may be many organizations out there still using Yammer, it's getting more and more difficult to find real-life examples. Let us take just a moment to say a few words in fond remembrance for the once mighty collaboration platform that billed itself as Twitter for the Enterprise.

We first became aware of Yammer through work at the IMF back in 2008. Being such a large organization, and always looking for ways to innovate, the IMF made Yammer a core part of its internal communication strategy. Even though our consulting practice was small, we made good use of Yammer for quite a few years. We even developed the first ever web part to display a Yammer feed in a SharePoint page and an API to connect Yammer with other systems.

Then Microsoft bought Yammer saying they hoped to learn from Yammer's agile development practices and promising to make it a key part of their collaboration platform. Large parts of SharePoint's enterprise social platform were entirely replaced with Yammer. Around this time Microsoft had also bought Skype, and the future seemed bright. Yammer became part of Office 365 (as did Skype), it became a part of the E3 plan, and it seemed like adoption would continue to rise.

But something happened along the way.

Along came Slack with their IRC-like chat interface, promising to change the world by changing the way teams talk to each other at work. One thing Microsoft has never been able to tolerate is somebody else coming up with an idea that's even cooler than theirs. Eventually, Microsoft announced Teams as a direct alternative to Slack, with functionality that strongly competes with many of their own products—especially Yammer. Then Microsoft bought LinkedIn, putting them into a position somewhat competitive to Twitter and Facebook.

Before we knew it, Yammer had been relegated to the IT equivalent of the holiday kids' table, along with SharePoint and Access—looking nervously out the window for signs it might be the next ForeFront, Site Server, or (*shudder*) Microsoft Money.

Customers already using Yammer started to wonder if they were missing out. Those who had never adopted it were confused about which of several similar Microsoft solutions they should bank on. All the while, Yammer customers' usage reports were, across the board, showing smaller and smaller numbers. Even Microsoft's support page (link below) shows Yammer usage dropping over 6%!

Today, in a survey of 50+ businesses—many of which once used this platform—all show the same result.

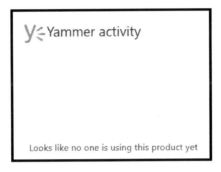

Yammer Activity Tile
"Looks like no one is using this product"

R.I.P. Yammer; we hardly knew you.

So it goes, we suppose. But, let's say you have a client truly committed to Yammer. Heck, it even integrates into Dynamics 365 and Teams can't do that! Let's talk about how to tell if Yammer will pull a turnaround (like "zombie InfoPath"), or if there may be subtle signs that it's time to try something else.

In May 2018, Microsoft made some changes to SharePoint Online that indicate maybe they're not quite ready to give up on Yammer just yet, beginning to remove the News Feed feature and instructing administrators to use Yammer instead. Don't call it a comeback, 'cause Yammer's always been here!

Yammer activity

Like the Teams Usage Activity report, this report will show you how many users are taking advantage of Yammer. The **Activity** panel will show you actions taken by users, and the Users panel will show you unique users over time:

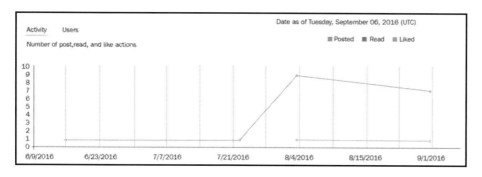

Yammer activity chart
"Our screenshot may be old, but our Yammer users have hearts of gold!"

Both the **Activity** and **Users** panel will show you trends for up to the past 180 days. If you have a thriving community in Yammer today, now might be the time to start scheduling regular check-ins every 30 to 90 days to see if anything's happening which could put that in jeopardy. A little timely maintenance will go a long way toward getting the most out of the communities you've worked so hard to build.

If you're fortunate enough to have a few die-hard users in Yammer, the details table will help you identify who they are. Perhaps it might be time to get them out in front of the rest of the organization to extol the virtues of Yammer to the incoming generation.

Read more about the Yammer Activity report at `https://support.office.com/en-us/article/office-365-reports-in-the-admin-center-yammer-activity-report-c7c9f938-5b8e-4d52-b1a2-c7c32cb2312a`.

Yammer device usage

This report will show you which Yammer apps are being used. Specifically, this includes the web browser as well as apps for Windows mobile, iOS, or Android. There's even a category for "something else" though we're not sure what that might be. (Note the Yammer desktop application isn't even listed.)

The **Users** panel will show you trends over time. Like other reports, the **Distribution** panel is a more concise bar chart that's easier to follow:

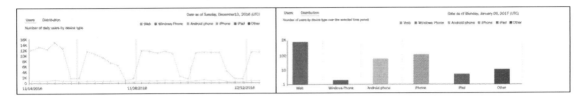

Yammer Device Usage by Users and Distribution Charts
"Hey, don't leave! Oh, wait. It's just Friday. Never mind."

If you're concerned about losing Yammer users, keep an eye on the mobile clients. While its true that most people use the Yammer web client almost exclusively, those who are using the mobile apps are the true believers who hold the community together. If those metrics start to fall, it's a sign of serious trouble ahead. (Can you even imagine the Twitteratti without smart phones?)

Read more about the Yammer Device Usage report at `https://support.office.com/en-us/article/office-365-reports-in-the-admin-center-yammer-device-usage-report-b793ffdd-effa-43d0-849a-b1ca2e899f38`.

Yammer groups activity report

This report conveys Yammer activity according to the number of Yammer groups. The **Activity** panel will show messages posted, read, and liked. The **Groups** panel shows the number of existing Yammer groups and how many are active:

Yammer Group Activity by Groups and Activities Charts
"Actually, I'm not quite dead yet, sir!"

Having lots of groups with a dwindling number of active groups is a bad sign. Note that if you have Yammer Groups populated by Office 365 Groups, you may have created a lot of groups that aren't active, and you won't be able to avoid that.

Suppose that your graphs look just as pathetic as ours. Can you bring Yammer back from the brink? Absolutely! Since it has strong integration to other Office 365 components like SharePoint and Dynamics 365, it's an excellent tool to use either as a bully pulpit or to collect feedback from others. It's important to understand that Yammer cannot do everything that Teams can, and it shouldn't want to. If you let Yammer play to its strengths, it can become a lasting part of your community building strategy. Reporting will help ensure that it doesn't slip out from under you.

 Read more about the Yammer Groups Activity Report at `https://support.office.com/en-us/article/office-365-reports-in-the-admin-center-yammer-groups-activity-report-94dd92ec-ea73-43c6-b51f-2a11fd78aa31`.

Advanced reporting topics

So, you've reviewed the available usage reports, considered some hypothetical use cases, and internalized some of the limits and shortcomings of the tools you get out of the box. It's time to talk about what's coming down the pipe and how to take things to the next level.

Anonymizing user data

By default, Office 365 reports show usernames in the details. In some organizations, this may not be desired or even allowed. You can mask usernames so that the people responsible for reviewing reports will not have access to information about who exactly is doing what. Of course, if you need to reach out to an impacted audience or service champions, that's going to make finding people's identities difficult.

But rules are rules. To mask user data, go to **Office 365 Admin Center | Settings | Services and Add-ins | Reporting**.

 Reports
Show anonymous IDs instead of names in all reports or enable the Power BI content pack

Office 365 Reports Settings

From here, you'll be presented with a dialog in which one of the options is to mask username data.

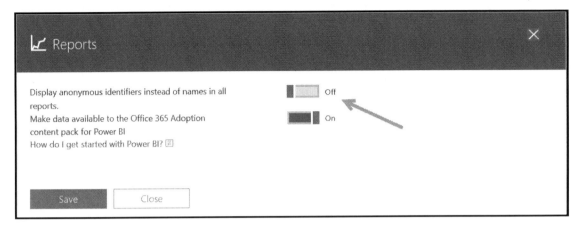

Office 365 Reports Settings Dialog

Flip the switch and hit **Save**. From this point on, anyplace you would normally see a user's name will show an anonymized GUID instead.

The change will take a few minutes to go into effect. Once it does, your detail tables will look something like this.

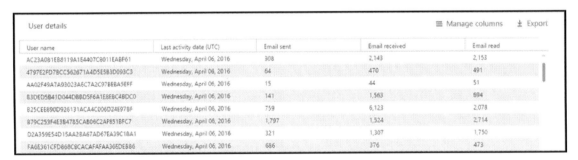

Anonymized User Identifiers in Office 365 Usage Reports

Note that changing this setting also affects reporting APIs, so any third-party reporting tools you use will be similarly masked.

Power BI Content Pack

The Power BI Content Pack for Office 365 Usage Reports promises to deliver all the cool BI capabilities that we spent the first section of this chapter griping about because they are missing from Usage Reporting.

If you find the Power BI Content Pack tile in the Usage Reporting Dashboard and click on the **Get Started** button, the very first thing you'll see is a dialog box asking for permission to share data between Office 365 and Power BI that looks suspiciously like the **Usage Reporting Settings** dialog with other options hidden.

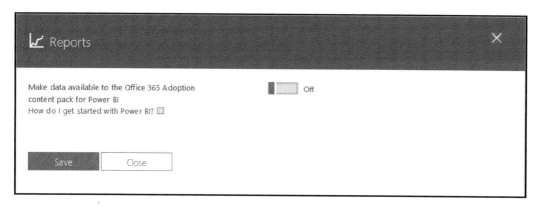

Report Settings for Power BI Content Pack

We didn't see any harm in turning this on, so we flipped the switch and hit **Save**.

Read on because it turns out we were [nearly] very wrong about that first part.

From there, the tile shows a message indicating that it is setting up. Microsoft says this *normally takes between 2 and 48 hours depending on the size of the tenant.*

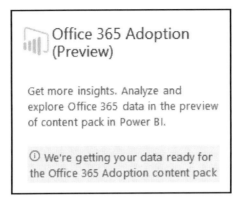

Power BI Content Pack During Installation

Microsoft also says:

> *"User-level details will only become available after the 1st or 15th day of the calendar month after opting in."*

That'll teach us for not reading the docs before clicking on the shiny button! Now, because we did this just after the 15th, several reports that display user-level data won't appear for as at least 2 weeks. Our boss is gonna be so angry.

Relax. Fortunately, this warning is only expectation-setting that applies to the Power BI dashboards and reports and doesn't seem to affect the existing Office 365 Usage Reporting in any way. Of course, it would be several days before we'd realize that. Guess it's a good thing we took all our screenshots for this chapter before trying this out, huh?

So, after about 2 days (!) of waiting patiently for the process to complete, we finally see the tile has changed to reflect access to our newly available tools.

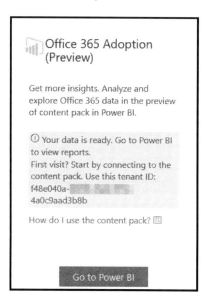

Power BI Content Pack Tile After Installation

Note the tenant ID shown earlier. You'll want to copy this to the clipboard, since you will be asked to enter it in a moment.

There's also a helpful link with info about how to use the content pack. Learning our lesson from rushing in blind earlier, we decided to give it a quick read. A few highlights from this article are listed later, for the benefit of the truly reckless or lazy.

Once that's out of the way, click on the **Go to Power BI** button.

1. From the main Power BI screen, go to **Get Data** (link in lower left corner or just scroll down).
2. Under the **Discover Content** section, find the **Services** tile, then click on the **Get** button. (Microsoft changed the name of this section between the time that their own help file for the content pack was written and the time we installed it, so stay sharp!)
3. You'll see the **Office 365 Adoption Preview** at the top of the list.
4. Click on the **Get it Now** button to install it.
5. Enter the tenant ID you copied earlier.
6. Wait for install, then open the App.

If that all sounds a bit convoluted, you're not alone. Microsoft didn't make it easy. We had to grope around a bit ourselves to find where this was waiting for us. The Content Pack is an App; you'll need to install it from the same screen you'd install other Apps like those for Google Analytics or Dynamics CRM.

Get the Office 365 Adoption Preview Power BI App

At the point where you clicked **Get it now** you'll see the screen where you can paste your tenant ID. We assume that if you have delegated access to somebody else's tenant, you could also enter their tenant ID here instead to see data for that organization. (We have not tried to install the content pack twice in the same tenant using different IDs, but that sounds like a fun experiment.)

Another moment and you'll be taken to the **Apps** screen. You'll see a new tile for Office 365 Adoption Preview. Click the tile to open the dashboard.

At this point, it took quite a while to refresh the data. A few minutes passed, so you might want to grab a cup of coffee or take a little break to stretch your legs.

Here's a peek at the main dashboard. As you can see, there's just a ton of cool stuff to explore!

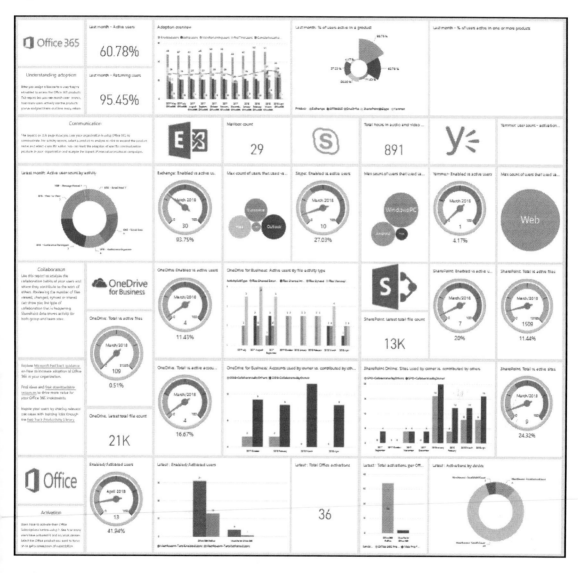

Office 365 Main Dashboard

Office 365 Adoption Preview Dashboard

The content pack includes the following report sets:

- Adoption
- Storage use
- Communication
- Collaboration
- Access from anywhere

Here are a few tips:

- To use the content pack, you need to be a Global Admin or Service Admin for Exchange, Skype for Business, or SharePoint.
- Only the user who created the Power BI App can customize it, so if you care about this, be careful what account you create it with.
- The content pack is free, but you (and anyone you share dashboards with) will need a Power BI Pro license to use it, so either obtain that license individually or as part of the E5 plan.
- User-specific data can take as much as a couple weeks to populate. It can be anonymized just like other Office 365 usage reports.
- You will get the best results if your Azure AD profiles are populated with details, such as Department, Job Title, and Office (location). (There are good reasons besides this to also assign each user a Manager.)

There's so much content in this expansion, we could easily write an entire chapter on this alone. We encourage you to explore and keep in mind that this is still in preview. It will most likely change (and hopefully improve) significantly by the time of final release.

Read about the Power BI Content Pack at `https://support.office.com/en-us/article/Office-365-Adoption-Content-Pack-77ff780d-ab19-4553-adea-09cb65ad0f1f`.

Learn more about how to enable the Power BI Content Pack Preview, including the implications of activating it on your tenant) at `https://support.office.com/en-us/article/Enable-the-Power-BI-adoption-content-pack-for-Office-365-9db96e9f-a622-4d5d-b134-09dcace55b6a`.

User count by Geo

Currently, there is very little information available regarding the Usage Reporting tile named **User count by Geo**. Only the cryptic message **There is no information available for user count by geo** appears in the preview tile. So, what is this exactly?

In March 2018, the European Union passed something called the GDPR. In a nutshell, this says that for privacy and law enforcement reasons, users in Europe must have their data stored in Europe. To help globally distributed companies comply with the requirements of GDPR, Microsoft added a capability named "Multi-Geo" to Office 365 and Azure.

Since both Multi-Geo and GDPR are very new, we have not yet seen any instances of customers seeking to enable this feature although we expect we will quite soon because GDPR is being phased in and will be the law of the land by the time you read this.

If the Multi-Geo feature is enabled, does this tile suddenly light up with data about how many users are in each global region? We'd like to imagine so, but only time will tell. If you know something about this, drop us a line and tell us about it, so we can update the book.

Security & Compliance

We covered Security & Compliance reports in detail during the chapter on Security & Compliance.

Most reports related to system protection can be found in the reporting dashboard of the **Security & Compliance** center. These fall into a few categories:

- Labeling, data loss prevention reports
- Compliance reports
- Advanced threat protection reports

- Email and spam reports
- Supervisory review report
- Note that audit reports described in some older Microsoft documentation are now found in the Exchange admin center

Security & Compliance reports can now be bookmarked at `https://protection.office.com/#/insightdashboard`.

For more details about reports available in the Security & Compliance admin center, see our chapter on Security & Compliance or visit `https://support.office.com/en-us/article/reports-in-the-office-365-security-compliance-center-7acd33ce-1ec8-49fb-b625-43bac7b58c5a` with additional information also at `https://support.office.com/en-us/article/monitor-security-and-compliance-in-office-365-b62f1722-fd39-44eb-8361-da61d21509b6` under the *Monitor Reports* section.

Summary

As you can see, Microsoft provides a lot of information about how Office 365 products are being leveraged within your tenant. It's up to you as the administrator of your tenant to interpret this information and use it to further your organization's goals.

The first barrier to overcome is knowing what options are available to you. The next steps are keeping an open mind, using your creativity, and remembering to consistently set aside time to check in at regular intervals, all while striving to understand the kind of questions to which your users or managers will seek answers.

Congratulations on having come this far. With knowledge about what Office 365 Usage Reporting can and cannot tell you and other options available to gain insights, you should be well prepared for what lies ahead.

Other Books You May Enjoy

If you enjoyed this book, you may be interested in these other books by Packt:

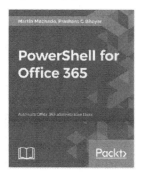

PowerShell for Office 365
Martin Machado, Prashant G Bhoyar

ISBN: 978-1-78712-799-9

- Understand the benefits of scripting and automation and get started using Powershell with Office 365
- Explore various PowerShell packages and permissions required to manage Office 365 through PowerShell
- Create, manage, and remove Office 365 accounts and licenses using PowerShell and the Azure AD
- Learn about using powershell on other platforms and how to use Office 365 APIs through remoting
- Work with Exchange Online and SharePoint Online using PowerShell
- Automate your tasks and build easy-to-read reports using PowerShell

Microsoft Office 365 – Exchange Online Implementation and Migration - Second Edition

David Greve, Ian Waters, Loryan Strant

ISBN: 978-1-78439-552-0

- Sign up for an Office 365 account and configure your e-mail domains
- Migrate mailboxes from Exchange server, Google, and any other POP3 or IMAP based system in to Office 365
- Configure a hybrid configuration by using Azure AD Connect to synchronize your on-premises Active Directory with Office 365
- Deploy Active Directory Federation Services (AD FS) to enable Single sign on and streamline the login process for your users
- Set up a hybrid Exchange configuration and host mailboxes locally or in the cloud and move mailboxes between the two with ease
- Configure a public folder hybrid and share existing on-premises public folders with users hosted in Exchange online
- Setup a hybrid Skype for Business (SFB) configuration and move users into SFB online
- Configure a SharePoint configuration, allowing users to create and search content hosted on an existing SharePoint server as well as in SharePoint online

Leave a review - let other readers know what you think

Please share your thoughts on this book with others by leaving a review on the site that you bought it from. If you purchased the book from Amazon, please leave us an honest review on this book's Amazon page. This is vital so that other potential readers can see and use your unbiased opinion to make purchasing decisions, we can understand what our customers think about our products, and our authors can see your feedback on the title that they have worked with Packt to create. It will only take a few minutes of your time, but is valuable to other potential customers, our authors, and Packt. Thank you!

Index

passwords, resetting 98
photo, uploading 94
user login name, changing 95, 96
user
converting, to shared mailbox 105
deleting, alternative strategies usage 104
DLP 110
login, disabling 104
mailbox retention, using 108
mailbox, downloading to PST 106
safeguarding 110
switching, to archive license 107
third-party backup solution, acquiring 107
users blocked report
reference link 483
users offboarding, Office 365 users
user recycle bin 103
user, deleting alternative strategies usage 104
user, deleting in portal 103
users, left sidebar navigation menu
about 13
active users 14
contacts 22

V

voice services
managing 351

Y

Yammer activity
reference link 489
Yammer device usage
reference link 490
Yammer groups activity
reference link 491
Yammer
about 384, 485, 487, 488
activity 489
admin center 380, 382
administrating, via Office 365 379
content 396, 398
device usage 489
groups activity report 490
network 386, 389, 390
overview 377, 378
security 396, 398
URL 378
usage policy, setting 384
user licenses, managing 382
users 391, 392, 393, 395
welcome message, writing 386

Printed in Great Britain
by Amazon